# The Essential Civil Society Reader

# The Essential Civil Society Reader

## *Classic Essays in the American Civil Society Debate*

DON E. EBERLY, EDITOR

ROWMAN & LITTLEFIELD PUBLISHERS, INC.
*Lanham • Boulder • New York • Oxford*

ROWMAN & LITTLEFIELD PUBLISHERS, INC.

Published in the United States of America
by Rowman & Littlefield Publishers, Inc.
4720 Boston Way, Lanham, Maryland 20706
http://www.rowmanlittlefield.com

12 Hid's Copse Road
Cumnor Hill, Oxford OX2 9JJ, England



British Library Cataloguing in Publication Information Available

**Library of Congress Cataloging-in-Publication Data**

The essential civil society reader : classic essays in the American civil society debate / edited by Don E. Eberly
p. cm.
Includes bibliographical references and index.
ISBN 0-8476-9718-5 (cloth : alk. paper)—ISBN 0-8476-9719-3 (pbk. : alk. paper)
1. Civil society. 2. Civil society—United States. I. Eberly, Don E.

JC337.E77 2000
306′.0973—dc21 00-029086

Printed in the United States of America

⊗ ™The paper used in this publication meets the minimum requirements of American National Standard for Information Sciences—Permanence of Paper for Printed Library Materials, ANSI/NISO Z39.48-1992.

# Contents

# Part One

# Introduction and Overview

# 1

# The Meaning, Origins, and Applications of Civil Society

*Don E. Eberly*

The most important development at the dawn of the twenty-first century may be the rediscovery of the nongovernmental sector of civil society, or as some call it the voluntary or social sector. If the twentieth century was about the steady erosion of civil society through neglect or conscious abandonment, the twenty-first century may represent the era of its restoration.

The term civil society has made a sudden and dramatic reappearance after near complete disappearance in the public discourse. After decades of neglect, Americans are rediscovering that the social sector—consisting of families, neighborhoods, voluntary associations, and an endless variety of civic enterprises—is an essential and irreplaceable part of the American democratic experiment. Within the realm of civil society, thousands of essential community functions are performed every day, from compassionate neighborly care to maintaining public order to mentoring youth and providing charity to the poor and the frail.

Few things are more important to America's social order than the dynamic role voluntary associations have played in creating a stronger society. This social sector represents the most dynamic and unique force within the American sociopolitical system. It stands out as a peculiarly American mechanism for social action and moral renewal. Many of the great social reform movements in history, whether centering on moral uplift, justice for women and children, or the eradication of poverty and suffering, were orchestrated by voluntary associations.

Still more important than the practical functions of civil society is the role this sector plays in cultivating citizenship and generating democratic values. Contained within civil society are the most vital and intimate institutions that socialize infants into adults and transform private individuals into public-spirited citizens. Public in nature, though not governmental, the social sector of civil society provides public "space" where people learn through practice such essential democratic habits as trust, collaboration, and compromise.

The story of America's wide network of voluntary associations and activities has long been considered a principal source of America's distinctiveness and strength. Few fully appreciate just how inseparable this civic vitality is from other American distinctions, such as the tradition of limited government and the separation of church and state. Historically in America, if civic work was to be done, it was to be done largely by individuals—not exclusively or even predominantly by government—and by an empowered religious laity, not merely by the ordained clergy of an official church, as was common throughout Europe.

In other words, civil society is part and parcel of what America is. It may be the most indispensable characteristic of American society and of the American state. And it has played a central role in periodically bringing about renewal. Much of the most consequential social change in America was produced by the stirrings of concerned individuals joining together in association with others. At various periods in its history, America witnessed an explosion in new civic initiative, a renaissance that may be repeating itself today.

Many signs indicate the social sector is coming alive again. There is a fresh outpouring of social entrepreneurship and a public debate suddenly focused on civil society and community-based remedies. Also a renaissance of theoretical interest in civil society appears to be sweeping across numerous social science fields.

## THE PURPOSE OF THIS BOOK

The purpose of this anthology is to give students of civil society an overview, in one reading, of some of the foremost theoretical contributors to civil society over the past several decades, men and women who largely account for the concept's rescue from analytical obscurity. In this volume, the leading scholars and authors from the past several decades present their most consequential and enduring contributions to the understanding of civil society.

The renewal of civil society is also the object of a growing popular movement. Though diverse in its makeup, this movement is commonly described as having several related objectives: it reflects a search for a new citizenship that is less self-interested, more civil, and more civically engaged. Civil society is the framework that is guiding attempts to restore community institutions, to recover the spirit of volunteerism and responsible citizenship, and to draw Americans together at a time of social isolation and fragmentation.[1]

As such, this popular movement is only responding to the hopes and expectations the people themselves have for a renewed civil society. According to numerous surveys, the American people sense that social institutions have become weakened, public debate and conduct has too frequently been toxic, and both personal and social responsibility have eroded.

In poll after poll, overwhelming majorities of Americans express the belief that the United States has lost its moral and cultural center, that responsibility and accountability have become rare commodities, and that public institutions no longer hold the respect they once commanded. Political debate continues to search for ways to connect with the basic hopes and aspirations of the people and to draw citizens into a common vision that transcends social divisions and private interests.[2]

All of these concerns and more fall within the scope of discussion that takes place under the rubric of civil society. This book will focus predominantly on the social and political theory that guide today's inquiry into civil society, focusing heavily on the role civil society plays in sustaining a viable democratic order. This anthology will offer extensive discussion of what are understood as by-products of civil society such as trust, civility, social authority, democratic skills and habits, along with a focus on the substantive problems of modern democracy.

It is impossible in this introductory chapter to do justice to the leading theorists, the overarching themes, and the intellectual history of civil society. What is presented is a general survey that provides explanatory and descriptive background on the recent resurgence of interest in civil society and examines some of the key ideas emanating from it.

## DEFINING THE TERM

Formulating a definition of civil society that is precise and that enjoys wide acceptance is not easy. The shape and definition of civil society is often affected by the purposes to which a given group directs it.

For some, civil society is synonymous with a search for civility. For conservatives, it embodies a vision for a larger role for community-based charities, especially faith-based ones, which can be substituted for flawed governmental programs. Libertarians have recently embraced the term civil society and frequently use it as a synonym for privatization, implying that the term's major attraction may be its usefulness in expanding the marketplace and limiting the state.

Alternatively, many liberals see civil society as a means to deepen community participation in public projects, thereby improving both the performance of government and the public's acceptance of it. Some advocate civil society as a means of improving democratic deliberation, creating more "public space," and curbing public distrust and cynicism. For most, civil society contains variations on the above ingredients.

Some are prone to ask, in the face of these diverse and even competing conceptions, whether the recent interest in civil society represents anything new at all. The skeptic will ask whether civil society even represents a publicly useful concept or whether it merely serves as a useful rhetorical cover for essentially the same ideological debate that has been taking place for decades. Some wonder whether the civil society movement has any real capacity to influence the shape of public debate.

Civil society is dismissed by some as a trendy public idea which will surface and just as quickly recede from public notice. Others, like E. J. Dionne, a journalistic observer and frequent contributor to the civil society debate, disagree. Civil society's emergence, he argues, is explained by real inadequacies in the current ideological frameworks of Left and Right. The civil society debate "is not a flash in the pan," he says, because it responds to "problems inherent in other ideas" that have been competing for the attention of Americans. Its rise and continued popularity, says Dionne, is a function in part at least of the willingness of leaders on the political left and right to "reflect on the failures of their respective sides and face evidence that is inconvenient to their arguments."[3]

As Dionne's reflections suggest, civil society represents a search for a greater degree of harmony, balance, and cohesion—within scholarship, public policy, and the wider public alike. There are different interpretations and even more divergent applications, but nevertheless the embrace of civil society can be seen as a desire to transcend social division and political chaos.

Those who doubt the validity of civil society, or are tempted to view it as a fad, need only consider its role in the long sweep of American and Western history. Civil society cannot be defined merely by those purposes to which it is presently being applied. As various contributors to this volume explain, it has played a unique role in shaping western political and social theory for centuries; indeed, if one includes the classical and biblical traditions, for millennia. As Daniel Bell (chapter 18) argues, civil society is a central feature of the American sociopolitical system; indeed it is the basis of American "exceptionalism."[4]

Just as relevant is the question of what the term is generally understood to mean within informed circles today. Chris Beem, a political theorist and civil society scholar, points out that civil society is "an inherently lax and expansive concept, incorporating every phenomenon that is not the state." Throughout history, argues Beem, "one's understanding of civil society has been narrowed analytically by one's normative objectives; in a phrase, civil society is what you want it to do."[5]

In other words, civil society often takes its definition from the things—namely, the tasks—one has in mind seeing performed by civil society. Still, as Beem points out, there is a near universal affirmation of civil society that centers largely on what he calls "social capital institutions," and that these institutions can and should play a pivotal role in social and cultural renewal.

Although civil society is often used as an adjective to describe many things people want, it is best understood as a noun—as a real flesh and blood "thing"—a social realm, consisting of a range of actual institutions with moral substance and function. Above all, civil society denotes that sector of society in which nonpolitical institutions operate—families, houses of worship, neighborhoods, civic groups, and just about every form of voluntary association imaginable.

Always implied in the term are activities and associations that are voluntary and free. Michael Walzer describes civil society as "the space of uncoerced human association" and "the set of relational networks—formed for the sake of family, faith, interest, and ideology—that fill this space."[6]

Alexis de Tocqueville, in many ways the theoretical godfather of civil society on the American scene, described civil society as civic association: It consisted of legions of charities, lodges, fraternal orders, civic leagues, and religious associations. According to the French political theorist, Americans were founders and joiners of civic associations. They formed associations "of a thousand kinds: religious, moral, serious, futile, general or restricted, enormous or diminutive." Nothing, he said, was more deserving of attention, than these associations that dotted the United States' unique civic landscape. They were indispensable to the functioning of American democratic society, for they were the "necessary" foundation upon which "the progress of all the rest depends."[7]

Just as in Tocqueville's time, Americans are still forming—and reforming—civic associations. Some are large, some small and not so serious—all serving a myriad of purposes. However, the central point is that these associations are voluntary and serve larger social purposes. While many voluntary associations are formed to meet the private needs of individuals, they too serve important social purposes, even if unconsciously.

The civic networks that fascinated Tocqueville arose spontaneously from the aspirations and desires of free people. They take form as the people themselves desire to join together voluntarily, work toward common purposes, and in the process learns the essential habits of collaboration and trust.

It is the social and democratic purpose served by voluntary associations that is of direct interest to most scholars. As we will see later, a healthy civil society yields by-products necessary for sustaining democracy. In addition to performing many practical tasks, the institutions of civil society do three things: mediate between the individual and the large mega-structures of the market and the state, tempering the negative social tendencies associated with each; create important social capital; and impart democratic values and habits.

Civil society builds social ties and a sense of mutual obligation by weaving together isolated individuals into the fabric of the larger group, tying separate individuals to purposes beyond their private interests. The reciprocal ties nourished in civil society are the wellspring of democratic life, as Tocqueville said. Through civic participation, he said, "feelings and opinions are recruited, the heart is enlarged, and the human mind is developed."[8]

## DETERMINING ANALYTICAL BOUNDARIES

It is hard to establish boundaries around civil society to everyone's satisfaction. Some argue that civil society must include the economic market within its conceptual boundaries. The economic realm of society is, after all, a voluntary and spontaneous order. Much like civil society, it is a sphere of human exchange that enjoys considerable freedom from government control. The market also overlaps with civil society in its function as a transmitter of ideas and intellectual goods.

Tocqueville included "commercial and industrial associations" in his description of civil society, although most will quickly acknowledge that this was before the modern, national, and multinational corporation. The more important point, though, is that while civil society is similar in some ways to the market, it runs on a different set of impulses. It operates, not like government, on the basis of compulsion, nor like the market, on the basis of competition or the profit motive. Though in many ways private, civil society serves public purposes as it calls people beyond the minimalist obligations of the law and the narrow self-interest of the market's bottom line to a higher plane of social cooperation and generosity.

Some analysts, like Alan Wolfe (chapter 3), make the argument that the economic realm should be part of the civil society debate, not on the grounds that the economic sphere is part of civil society, but for the reason that free markets, by reducing all decisions to the calculation of self-interest, weaken the bonds of loyalty, friendship, and trust upon which civil society depends. Thus in understanding the forces that have disrupted or displaced the institutions of civil society, the dynamic effects of the economic market must be included.

As used by Tocqueville, civil society appears to possess boundaries of scale as well as scope. The term civil society frequently connotes the idea of localism, both in reference to community and small-scale local associations. Freedom for the individual is accompanied by attachment to the interests of others as mediated through local associations.

It is through this bond of personal attachment and significance that the individual is rendered more willing to act on behalf of his fellows, to "sacrifice some of his private interests to save the rest." Untrammeled self-interest becomes self-interest "rightly understood" when it is moderated by human cooperation and tethered by virtue. By reason of their being imbedded in the local community, possessing local civic loyalties, it could be argued that civil society includes the local grocer, dentist, or shopkeeper, but probably not the international corporate conglomerate.

If the term civil society does not apply predominantly to economic interests, neither does it encompass the totality of political interests and action. This area may be even more difficult to sort out. While the civil society debate frequently includes discussion of such problems as declining voter participation, flawed public debate, rights-based individualism, and more, the institutions and functions of civil society are usually not understood primarily in relationship to the political realm.

That an entire section of this volume is dedicated to political theory and its significance to civil society suggests an important relationship. Perhaps the concept that best builds the bridge between civil society and the political realm is the idea of citizenship. Properly understood, the citizen is an active member of civic community, which entails nonpolitical activity and also participation in democratic life, which at a minimum involves voting.

In many ways, civil society entails activity that is prepolitical or that transcends politics, even though it supplies political society with essential democratic qualities. Political action is regarded as only one form of civic responsibility, and is often seen as a by-product of civic health. According to Jean Bethke Elshtain, while some may reject the notion that associations are not political, "theorists of civil society would insist, in response, that this network and the many ways we are nested within it, lie outside the formal structure of state power."[9]

Tocqueville distinguished, rather than confused, civil society and political society. Social movements in American history have often had political goals as part of their purpose, but civil society does not generally consider modern political action organizations as synonymous with civic community. These mass membership organizations serve important and legitimate political as well as civic roles, but they do not directly or primarily serve civic purposes. Harvard professor and civil society expert Robert Putnam places such groups in a "tertiary" category of associations because for most members, the only act of participation consists of signing up as a member and sending in a check.

Based upon his study of regional governments in Italy, Putnam argues that civic institutions shape politics and are the origins of effective government. What is widely acknowledged is that a healthy political system is more dependent upon a strong civil society than it is capable of creating it, or recovering it once it has eroded, for the simple reason that civil society is not a subsidiary of the state.

## THE SCOPE OF THE CIVIL SOCIETY DEBATE

Just as civil society has again become the subject of serious scholarly inquiry, it is at the center of an unfolding public debate, a debate that is raising many important topics for inquiry and discussion. These include calls for a new public philosophy emphasizing the need to elevate the common good over private self-interest, renewing social values and institutions, encouraging wider civic participation, and encouraging citizen involvement in community problem solving.

## Public Philosophy: Liberal Individualism versus Civic Republicanism

Civil society theorists generally do not separate their interest in social institutions from concerns relating to the democratic state, but rather see the latter as dependent upon the former for health and vitality. Most civil society scholars do not take a sanguine view of the present health of democracy. They see the democratic process reflecting the many maladies they find in civic community.

Many observers from the civil society school make the claim that public debate in recent years has been impoverished. If democracy was hoisted upon the examination table and its contents subjected to clinical inspection, the examination would reveal a body riddled with disabling viruses. Typically cited by civil society analysts are declining rates of voter participation, civic illiteracy, weak public deliberation, the rise of narrow and polarizing interest group politics, and the domination of public policymaking by money.

More directly relevant to the analytical domain of civil society is the matter of political theory, most particularly the loss of a public philosophy grounded in a civic vision. Much of the analytical interest in civil society arose over the past several decades out of a concern over the pervasive influence in political theory and practice of liberal individualism. This is the belief that the self is sovereign and essentially unbound by any constraints or obligations that exists independent of the individual.

Robert Bellah (chapter 4) describes this notion as a "radically unencumbered and improvisational self," cut off from community, history, tradition, or civic duty.[10] Bellah sees this hyperindividualism as linked to the replacement of the idea of freedom as ordered and constrained by a "natural freedom" which views freedom as an end in itself. This boundless freedom centers on the rights of the person to be "left alone by others, not having other people's values, or styles of life forced upon one, being free of arbitrary authority in work, family and political life."[11]

It is this radical vision of individual autonomy, which has been embraced by modern political ideologies, that is regarded by civil society thinkers as the chief means by which many of the social and political maladies which Alexis de Tocqueville foretold with such remarkable prescience in *Democracy in America* have been brought to American society. The ideas of boundless "natural freedom" and individual autonomy have produced far-reaching consequences for American law and social order.

Liberal individualism has gained strong adherents on both the Left and

Right of the political spectrum in America. Neither of today's competing political philosophies of liberal egalitarianism or conservative libertarianism presents a framework for human progress outside of the human person as an autonomous, rights-bearing consumer. In fact, they draw from the same liberal individualism and thus have common tendencies.

Liberal individualists of all stripes have largely sidestepped the importance of personal responsibilities and social boundaries in their search for an ever-wider vision of personal freedom. One ideology envisions the person as the bearer of ever multiplying legal rights; the other pictures the human as mostly a consumer in an unfettered marketplace.

Politically Left liberals embrace individualism to advance expressive rights and lifestyle freedoms, without regard to the legitimate prerogatives of the social group or the need for social order and restraint. Politically Right liberals (or libertarians) advocate economic freedoms as the sole and sufficient basis for the good society. To suggest to either liberal individualist faction that intervention by means of applying either public policy or social restraints on an activity, whether moral or economic, might occasionally be appropriate is frequently regarded by them as an intolerable blow to private autonomy.

In neither framework is the individual encumbered with a duty to serve something one would call society. American society has invented more rights and provided more consumers choices than any in human history. But neither wider legal rights nor expanded opportunities for consumption are sufficient by themselves to hold society together. In fact, it can be argued that modern political ideologies draw resources from the institutions of civil society that they do little to replenish. Some refer to scavenging tendencies of modern liberalism in drawing heavily on the social capital of a more traditional past.

## Thinning Civil Society; Thickening State

The drive to emancipate the individual from social restraints has left democratic society with a host of deficiencies, including the loss of community, declining social trust, a preoccupation with rights and entitlements, and an increased assertion of individual will without regard for the common good. These are topics frequently addressed by civil society theorists.

When government becomes the ally of an unbalanced rights-based individualism, cut off from any connection to higher forms of morality, it is forced to accommodate continued demands for greater individual gains, which often come at the expense of community. This restless search for human progress through legal reforms is the very root of the politicized society.

The American legal and political system has responded to the rise of liberal individualism by developing the tendency to translate every dispute into the language of untrammeled individual entitlement, or what Harvard Law

Professor Mary Ann Glendon (chapter 15) termed "rights talk." When only the law and politics arbitrate human affairs, everything becomes political—even the most basic human relations. What emerges is a state that expands even while its competence and legitimacy ebb.

The result is the replacement of substantive constitutional principles with what political scientist Michael Sandel (chapter 14) calls "a procedural republic" in which individuals are endowed with rights and entitlements but have little civic consciousness. The struggle within democracy focuses entirely on adjusting the process to accommodate the demands of individuals and groups, not on serving the substantive purposes of democracy.

When it is concluded that all matters should be decided on the basis of democratic majorities, people are subjected to the whims of whoever controls the law-making process. The law degenerates into an arbitrary tool of the politically organized. A right conferred on one group becomes an obligation imposed on another. The legal system is forced to find ever more perfect balances and boundaries between conflicting parties and claims.

When civil society thins out, what emerges is a picture of the law and the state thickening. The law is simultaneously expected to confer the right to sexual freedom as well as freedom from sexual assault; to guarantee gender and racial advantage for some and the protection of reverse discrimination for others; to protect the rights of criminal offenders and the rights of the offended; to guard the rights of free speech but initiate new rights against the insult of hateful speech; to defend both the rights of individuals and communities, and so on.

The law has always been expected to strike careful balances in these areas, but never before has it been called on to split conflicting demands with such exasperating precision. This degree of legal harmony and balance is, of course, beyond the capacity of the law and state agencies to achieve. The law begins to resemble a harried referee who has the impossible task of policing a sport that is both choked by rules and overwhelmed by rule infractions. The pursuit of a just and good society is reduced to fighting over the rules.

Jean Bethke Elshtain (chapter 6) observes another consequence for law and democracy when civic institutions weaken—the confusion of public and private. When civic space declines, she says, a politics of displacement emerges to fill the gap. Elshtain describes the "complete collapse of a distinction between public and private," which she says is anathema to democratic thinking. "In the first," she says, "everything private—from one's sexual practice to blaming one's parents for one's lack of self-esteem—becomes grist for the public mill. In the second, everything public—from the grounds on which politicians are judged, to health politics, to gun regulations—is privatized and played out in a psychodrama on a grand scale."[12]

An alternative to rights-based individualism is what is described in chapter 14 by Michael Sandel as the "classical republican tradition," which recognizes the role of private interests but seeks to temper self-interest by calling upon individuals to serve "the public good" in the hope that "community life takes precedence over individual pursuits."[13] The classical republican tradition offers a vision for the individual operating, not just in competition with others or in conflict with the state in a struggle for greater rights, but in relationship to community.

Sandel criticizes the dominant liberal paradigm for viewing citizens merely as "freely choosing, independent selves, unencumbered by moral or civic ties antecedent to choice."[14] Under the liberal vision of society that Sandel critiques, it is assumed that "government should not affirm, through its policies or laws, any particular concept of the good life; instead it should provide a neutral framework of rights within which people can choose their own values and ends."[15]

Civil society advocates seek above all to restore balance where it has been lost, not erode basic freedoms. None of the contributors to this volume doubt the need to find greater social cohesion by working firmly inside American philosophical traditions and core constitutional principles. If the search for a deeper, more substantive public philosophy is centered on any one objective, it is in elevating the common good or public good, terms often used by civil society theorists.

Once again the difficulty of defining a term presents itself. The common good consists of specific moral and social goods—such as justice, compassion, and consideration for all—that are desired and deserved by all human beings by virtue of their being human. The means by which the common good is pursued is just as important. The common good cannot be achieved by simply imposing one's way by means of will or force of personality.

The common good is not an equivalent term for the greatest good for the greatest number, or the outgrowth of the popular will as reflected in whatever majority happens to be in charge at any given time. The common good is grounded in a substantive and universal set of ethical principles which exist independent of our choosing them as citizens and which therefore place a claim on all of us.

Rediscovering a fuller and richer American public philosophy will aid in elevating the common good without eroding elementary freedoms and without collapsing individual identity into group identity, or eroding the private sphere. What a public philosophy centering on the common good will attempt to do is find greater balance between rights and responsibilities, and between the individual and community.

Adam Seligman, a noted civil society scholar, puts it this way: "Despite the differing theoretical perspectives and political agendas, what nevertheless makes the idea of civil society so attractive to so many social thinkers is its assumed synthesis of private and public 'good' and of individual and social desiderata. The idea of civil society thus embodies for many an ethical ideal of the social order, one that, if not overcomes, at least harmonizes, the conflicting demands of individual interest and social good."[16]

Not surprisingly, those who see the old paradigms of Left and Right as increasingly less useful and more internally incoherent have especially embraced civil society. Frequently, civil society theorists are associated with approaches to politics that emphasis a "third way," which tends to reject a heavy reliance on either the market or the state for the ordering of society, and less emphasis on either rights or self-interest and more interest in the ethic of cooperating.

Little about politics today seeks to fortify public-spirited citizenship. Politics reinforces a vision of society inhabited by unencumbered private individuals, pampered with promises, fortified with multiplying legal rights and awash in consumer choices, yet paradoxically, more subject than citizen. Political debates which once entertained public reflection on the higher ends of life in a just and good society have been replaced by a politics that is little more than what author Jonathan Rauch has termed "governmentalism." In such a society every social argument is turned into "an argument about government, politics, and law." Says Rauch, "Liberterians, anti-government conservatives and left-liberals disagree on many things, but they are all governmentalists."[17]

The civil society debate reflects a deep frustration over the preoccupation with the state to the exclusion of society. Political ideology has become little more than arguing for more or less of the state, or its sole alternative, the market. Lawrence Chickering makes the point that liberalism and conservatism alike are preoccupied with the central state, although with different objectives. One is for more; the other for less, but in both cases the political ideology seems to be directed, almost deterministically, toward issues of the central state.

Viewed this way, the good society is a function of the size, shape, and scope of the state. Almost no one, says Chickering, "is concerned with building positive forms of individual and community self-governance."[18] To the extent that this is now changing, credit can generally be given to the theorists and spokesmen of the civil society movement.

Finally, civil society thinkers and writers frequently address the toxic nature of public debate. In no area are society's extremes of individualism more evident than in its public debate. Rarely is the faintest reference to any concept of the common good made. *Washington Post* columnist William Raspberry describes a process that has moved beyond the normal give and take among various competing sectors and ideologies into "a near-total breakdown of the American society into warring component parts."[19] Raspberry questions whether anyone speaks the language of a national interest or public interest that transcends the cacophonous parts.

Civil society is offered, in part at least, as an antidote to this social division.

The realm of civil society serves, among other things, as a place for the exchange of ideas—even vigorous arguments over competing ideas and values. But the very premise of civil society suggests that public discussion be "civilized and civilizing," grounded in a minimal consensus where at least some things are held in common and not everything is in disagreement.

Many civil society advocates believe that public discourse must search for grounding in universal principles, having respect for what Vaclav Havel (chapter 19) calls "a basic code of mutual coexistence, a kind of common minimum we can all share, one that will enable us to go on living side by side." Havel describes that "minimal code" as something that transcends us, a universal principle "that comes to us from heaven, or from nature, or from our own hearts; a belief that our deeds will live after us; respect for our neighbors, for our families, for certain natural authorities; respect for human dignity and for nature; a sense of solidarity and benevolence towards guests that come with good intentions."[20]

## SOCIAL THEORY, SOCIAL INSTITUTIONS: THE SEEDBEDS OF CIVIC VIRTUE

Studies in civil society combine the best of political and social theory, borrowing heavily from the social sciences, especially sociology. Civil society theory takes as its starting point a substantially different philosophical outlook than liberal individualism regarding the needs of the human person in relationship to society. It regards the human person as a social creature by nature, bearing distinct social needs and tendencies, which relies upon society and its institutions to flourish.

Much of the focus of inquiry within civil society centers on the kinds of questions that are commonly addressed by sociologists, such as: how do people come by their capacity for self-mastery and citizenship; By what means does the human person proceed from infancy to become a caring, conscientious adult; By what process does the individual acquire democratic habits, skills, and values; and How is moral conscience, so vital for a civil and humane society, formed?

Many of the major contributors to the civil society debate have drawn in part at least from the sociological tradition represented by such figures as Emile Durkheim, Robert Nisbet, and Ferdinand Tönnies, to name only a few. A volume such as this would not be complete without paying tribute to the contribution that communitarian thought has played in the revival of civil society.

As the proliferating literature of communitarianism points out, the movement to fortify social institutions is a movement in search of new social equilibrium built on a greater balance between rights and responsibilities, one which checks the deepening impulse toward moral license, and one which seeks to apply brakes to an excessive individualism.

Guided by such leading sociologists as Amitai Etzioni (chapter 7) and Robert Bellah (chapter 4), a growing number of social scientists operating under the banner of communitarianism are attempting to build a sociopolitical framework that takes direct aim at the excesses of individualism, one which would be, in Bellah's words, "less trapped in the clichés of rugged individualism" and "more open to an invigorating, fulfilling sense of social responsibility."

While civil society theorists focus more generally on the vast nongovernmental sector consisting predominantly of voluntary associations and such social institutions as the family and neighborhood, the communitarians are interested in the idea of community in its various forms. Community has much in common with civil society, but it is more likely to be geographically grounded and tied together by ethnicity, religion, or simply residency. As Etzioni has stated: "it is best to think about communities as nested, each within a more comprehensive one."[21]

A priority of communitarians is to encourage greater social cohesion as a corrective to the rapid and often reckless social change, but without permitting such a search to degenerate into nostalgic and reactionary yearning for a lost golden age, one that was perhaps more harmonious and virtuous, but also more stratified by race, gender, and class. Communitarians remind us that achieving greater balance must not be offered without returning to the 1950s, or at the expense of progress. The need for shared identity and belonging that most Americans now sense will have to be achieved by accommodating, not reversing, the social advances of recent decades, especially for certain categories of Americans such as women and minorities.

### "Mediating Institutions"

The most frequent target of concern by civil society scholars and writers is the health of that realm of society that is voluntary and consensual—associational life. Much analysis within the civil society movement has centered on the weakening of social institutions and civic associations in the face of such modernizing influences as bureaucracy, commercialization, and technology.

A well-functioning society is made up of vital subunits, often small and local: what Edmund Burke called "little platoons" and "subdivisions," Tocqueville called "associations," and Emile Durkheim called "the little aggregations," which are thought of as the building blocks of the larger social order.

Much as Tocqueville observed, civic associations of a thousand different kinds are formed, and for as many reasons. Associations are the context in which most citizens live out a large portion of their lives in community. These associations serve many purposes, some intentional, some unintentional. They set out to accomplish a particular task, but become laboratories of democracy—what Tocqueville called "little schools of citizenship"—in the process.

For one, they mediate on behalf of the individual before the larger structures of the state. This "mediating" aspect of civil society was developed most effectively in our own generation by Peter Berger and Richard John Neuhaus in their classic *To Empower People,* which entered the term "mediating structures" into the vernacular.

By mediating structures they meant, above all, the institutions such as families, churches, synagogues, voluntary associations, and neighborhoods, that stand between the individual and the large megastructures of both the market and the state. Mediating structures, they argued, "are essential for a vital democratic society" because they help otherwise isolated individuals navigate through a complex, competitive society. In a sense, individuals who are imbedded in associations find protection and representation to the outside world they would otherwise not have.

This emphasis on the mediating role of local civic associations is offered as the antidote to a problem widely understood as the atomization of the individual. Civil society represents a search for life on a more humane scale. Daniel Bell touches upon this theme (chapter 18) when he states that "the demand for a return to civil society is the demand for a return to a manageable scale of social life," one which "emphasizes voluntary association, churches and communities, arguing that decisions should be made locally and should not be controlled by the state and its bureaucracies."[22]

## Seedbeds of Virtue

Civil society not only mediates on behalf of the individual, and works to curb atomization; it inculcates core democratic values. By developing positive sentiments toward others and ultimately the larger society, local institutions of civil society are frequently portrayed as the seedbeds of civic virtue. They cultivate social empathy. To be attached to the "subdivision," said Burke, is "the first link in the series by which we proceed toward a love of our country and to mankind."

When civic institutions decline, civic virtue declines with them. No one has popularized this view quite like Robert Putnam, the Harvard professor made famous by his essay called "Bowling Alone" which warned of civic decline and its consequences. Putnam described citizens who were connected to civic community as "helpful, respectful and trustful toward one another."

These democratic habits are derived, he said, from the thick layer of "horizontal relations" in which citizens are bound to relations which cultivate a spirit of reciprocity and cooperation. Putnam adds that in civic community, citizens are "bound together by horizontal relations of reciprocity and cooperation, not vertical relations of authority and dependency."[23] This argument by Putnam echoes the work of Robert Nisbet (chapter 2) in the *Quest for Community,* in which Nisbet argues essentially that the weaker our local horizontal ties are in civic community, the stronger our vertical relationship of dependency will be on the central state.

## Generators of Trust

Another important by-product of civil society is social trust. Few topics have generated more interest in the civil society debate than the subject of trust. Strong communities are rooted in relationships that are voluntary, consensual, and mutually trustful. Francis Fukuyama (chapter 13) has examined the role that trust and collaboration play in enabling individuals to compete in a rapidly changing and interconnected global marketplace. Economic life, he says, is maintained by "moral bonds of social trust, an unspoken, unwritten bond between fellow citizens that facilitates transactions, empowers individual creativity, and justifies collective action."[24]

Fukuyama concludes that societies with strong bonds of social trust and collaboration will gain important advantages over those characterized by individual isolation and social fragmentation. Putnam and Fukuyama both emphasize the importance of trust as a form of social lubricant that smoothes human transactions, whether civic or commercial, and a glue that secures bonds of human association.

In other words, both government and the market need the nutrients of civil society to function well. As discussed earlier, much of the civil society discussion focuses on the limits of a market-state dualism, which neglects the social sector, and this is especially true on the topic of trust. Markets, says Alan Wolfe (chapter 3), "flourish in a moral order defined by non-economic ties of trust and solidarity; markets are necessary for modernity, but they tend to destroy what makes them work." Similarly, he says, "the liberal theory of the state was neither purely liberal, for its originators relied on the preexisting moral ties to temper the bleakness of the social contract, nor purely statist, because it assumed a strong society."[25]

The reasons cited for declining trust are varied, among them political corruption, crime, economic dislocation, racial discrimination, and a lack of roots for a large segment of the American people. It appears that distrust can contribute to civic withdrawal, but it is also caused by withdrawal from civic life. Wendy Rahn, a political science professor at the University of Minnesota who has pioneered research into the causes and consequences of personal distrust, contends that a lack of participation breeds suspicions and distrust, which in turn decreases people's sociability and community involvement. She states "this 'vicious cycle' results in communities being less well off and their inhabitants less satisfied both with their personal and public lives."[26]

Another factor often cited in the decline of trust is in the erosion of such core institutions as the family. The late sociologist James Coleman used the term "social capital"—a term now widely used in the civil society debate to mean many things—to describe a range of personal strengths cultivated in the family, especially the capacity to cooperate in pursuit of common goals.[27] For Coleman, the term applied to qualities that were generated mostly by the family.

No human bond is more intimate or perceived by children to be more naturally durable than the parent-child relationship. Unlike more fragile social ties, the bonds of family are rooted in nature. An adult will be less trusting and cooperative if, as a child, he or she experienced a painful loss of trust in his own parent—the one person in whom he believed he could surely place his trust.

Certainly not all civil society scholars pay the same importance on stable families. Some see the family unit as private and beyond the scope of public scrutiny and debate. But most acknowledge that the prerequisites of democracy—the habits of the heart—as Tocqueville put it, are nourished and transmitted from generation to generation by the family. Mediating associations are important, but even they draw important resources from the family. Human socialization occurs mostly through patterns of trust and interdependency that are developed within the family structure. Healthy families cultivate a capacity for self-restraint, empathy toward others, and compromise.

Civil society theorists tend to view democratic society as fragile, and see democracy depending for its success on those institutions which socialize infant individuals into adult citizens, including and especially the family. If this is true, the central task of democracy is for older generations to devote themselves to socializing the young by not only passing along character and democratic habits, but also preserving the character-shaping institutions that play this role in the community.

## Social Authority

Closely related to the topic of social trust is social authority. Social authority is not the first topic to surface in connection with civil society, although it is beginning to be the subject of significant debate.

The collapse of legitimate social authority is often identified with the rise of an ideology of individual autonomy and the preeminence of individual choice. No society on earth has made a greater range of personal choices available to individuals than America, making choice probably the most dominant and popular impulse operating in the culture today. One searches in vain for examples of employers, educators, or politicians who have gained broad favor by seeking to limit the range of personal choice.

Perhaps no one has better captured the social consequences of this phenomenon better than Allan Ehrenhalt (chapter 12), author of *The Lost City*. In a widely discussed study, Ehrenhalt attempted to determine what the core factor might have been in the demise of the Chicago neighborhood in which he was raised in the 1950s. Ehrenhalt concluded that while many factors explained the economic and social disintegration of his urban neighborhood, it was the driving desire to be "emancipated from social authority" that was at the root of the problem.

According to Ehrenhalt, to worship both choice and community "is to misunderstand what community is about." Says Ehrenhalt, "The worship of choice has brought us a world in which nothing we choose seems good enough to be permanent, and we are unable to resist the endless pursuit of new selections—in work, in marriage, in front of the television set." "The suspicion of authority," he adds, has meant "the erosion of standards of conduct and civility, visible mostly in the schools."[28]

It is impossible, says Ehrenhalt, to have an orderly world without someone making the rules by which order is sustained. "Every dream we have about creating community in the absence of authority will turn out to be a pipe dream in the end."[29]

## Citizenship

A related theme that frequently surfaces in civil society literature is the need to recover the idea of the individual as a citizen, not merely as a private consumer. A central feature of the American experiment is the core principle of self-government. The people in the American system are considered sovereigns, not subjects, because they were expected to be capable of self-governance. When Chesterton spoke of the creed that animated American life, he described its core component as the pure classic notion that "no man must aspire to be anything more than a citizen, and that no man shall endure to be anything less."[30]

The American framers saw that maintaining a capacity for self-government required an ample supply of individual character, knowledge, and commitment to democratic participation. Anything less than an informed and active citizenry could lead to the abuse of government power. The call to civic action issued then and periodically since, has also been presented as a direct challenge to the American tendency toward egoism, individualism, and privatism.

A number of leading civil society theorists can be frequently heard recommending the development of an older, larger, and richer tradition of citizenship, one that involves more than the minimal duties of political participation, such as getting out to vote, but which embraces the more encompassing duties of neighbor, volunteer, and a willingness to bear greater responsibility for the quality of public life.

A society that is strong on citizenship is one in which rank and file members of society take it upon themselves to nourish the character-shaping institutions and democratic character upon which a humane public order rests. The duties of citizenship, understood in this larger sense, include meeting human need directly and voluntarily, not merely relying on the larger caregiving institutions of the state.

Several contributors to this volume have attempted in their contribution to the civil society debate to enlarge our understanding of citizenship. For example, Bill Schambra (chapter 16) and his colleague Michael Joyce have issued the challenge to recover a richer and more encompassing concept of the American citizen as an alternative to the pervasive role of the "helping" and "caring" professionals, which have in too many cases supplanted the direct involvement of citizens. Rather than expand the reach of social service providers throughout society, Joyce recommends that social policy instead turn to the "rich, vital web of civic life" that encompasses the work of individual citizens.[31]

Schambra maintains that local civic community was consciously undermined by the twentieth-century Progressive movement that saw in local citizen networks inefficiencies and retrogrades attitudes that stood directly in the path of their campaign to build national community. Twentieth-century Progressives, he argues, have viewed local civic community organized by citizens as a vast "chaotic jumble of divergent civic institutions and local loyalties" that the state in the twentieth century was tasked "ruthlessly to extirpate or absorb."[32]

According to this view, the work of community was seen as too important to be left to untrained local caregivers; it required organizing and sending into neighborhoods a cadre of professionals trained with the most advanced theories from elite policy schools. In other words, citizenship has been shrunken in large part due to the expansionist ambitions of twentieth-century scientific professionalism and their policy management models.

Also sounding this theme has been John McKnight (chapter 9). McKnight laments the fact that vast resources in both the public and private sectors are now under the control of professional caregivers. The concept of the individual, not as citizen, but as client is now pervasive, he says. The provision of public assistance to tens of millions of Americans is often accompanied by the subtle message that recipients are hopelessly trapped in conditions that require the permanent help of advocates, interest groups, and government workers.

Such a "paternalistic" approach is thought to produce a mindset that dwarfs citizenship for poor and nonpoor alike. It leaves the poor feeling justified in doing little to reclaim control of their lives and the nonpoor feeling like they have discharged their duties while bearing no obligation to personally intervene with neighborly aid. The language of social action today is not the common language of a caring citizenry, but rather the technical jargon of a professionalized therapeutic state. It is the language of programs, policies, and healing through clinically certified experts.

Many advocates of a more complete view of citizenship argue that the assumptions of social service providers regarding the nature and needs of the human person are simply wrong and must be replaced with more holistic approaches, which can only be done through functioning communities and genuine citizenship. The real objective then of a renewed citizenship would be to reclaim the individual by refusing to delegate the business of public life and public aid entirely to government professionals.

Public policy would attempt to strengthen mediating institutions and would view citizens as the very lifeblood of society. Robert Nisbet described as the chief aim of policy "protecting, reinforcing, nurturing where necessary, the varied groups and associations," which he said, "are the true building blocks of our social order." This argument was captured in Berger and Neuhaus (chapter 8) as well, who said that whenever possible, the state should protect and foster mediating structures and turn to them for "the realization of social purposes."

Policy would join the poor and nonpoor together as neighbors, volunteers, and partners in community renewal.

This facet of civil society has recently gained fresh momentum through public policy measures to encourage wider support of local civic initiatives and charities. Community-based solutions, including local faith-based organizations, have very recently become the subject of growing scholarly interest. For example, John DiIulio (chapter 11) is in the process of evaluating the effectiveness of numerous local faith-based charities in improving outcomes for children and families.

## THE ORIGINS OF CIVIL SOCIETY IN WESTERN POLITICAL THOUGHT

That the idea of civil society has played a key role in the development of Western political thought is widely acknowledged. According to Adam Seligman, "the very idea of civil society touches on and embraces the major themes of the Western political tradition."[33]

Less clear are the origins of the idea of civil society itself. There are different interpretations and articulations, but most observers acknowledge roots in several major, as well as minor, sources. Among the major sources are classical philosophy, reformation religion as articulated in the Scottish Enlightenment and early American Protestantism, Catholic social thought and Alexis de Tocqueville. One also finds civil society in the thought of John Locke, Immanuel Kant, G.W.F. Hegel, and Karl Marx.

Only the major sources of influence prior to the twentieth century can be addressed here, and only briefly. Entire volumes on the theory and origins of civil society are available for the more serious students of social and political theory. It should also be noted that several of the leading civil society theoreticians from the twentieth century, including Robert Nisbet, Daniel Bell, Robert Bellah, Peter Berger, and Richard John Neuhaus, are included in this volume.

For many students and analysts, a question of equal importance to *where* civil society came from, is perhaps *why* civil society? Much like the practical applications of civil society discussed earlier, the theoretical interest in civil society appears to have emerged periodically as a result of convulsions in the public order, a pattern being repeated again today. The breakdown of existing social structures tends to generate renewed theoretical as well as practical interest in the inner workings of society.

During times of upheaval, people have a greater desire to understand, explain and cope with developments by articulating an alternative vision for a better society, a vision usually bearing the characteristics of civil society. As noted earlier, civil society presents itself again and again as part of this search for fresh balance and harmony in the midst of the many conflicts and disintegrating impulses of modern society: in the rise of autonomy and the loss of social authority, for example.

Christopher Beem, who has comprehensively examined the theoretical wellsprings of civil society, finds that the major intellectual contributors to civil society in history were responding to concerns "dramatically similar to our own, as was their use of the concept of civil society to control and ameliorate those concerns." Beem sees the movement as unified in its commitment to moral and civic renewal with collective eyes set on the revival of social institutions as the "single most important means" by which this renewal can be achieved.[34]

Echoing Beem, Adam Seligman notes that the burst of interest in civil society in the seventeenth and eighteenth centuries was due to a concern about the need to restore public order and social ethics in the midst of huge social and economic change.

According to Seligman: "although the concept of civil society was defined differently by the different theorists of the French, Scottish, and German Enlightenments, what was common to all attempts to articulate a notion of civil society was the problematic relation between the private and the public, the individual and the social, public ethics and individual interests, individual passions and public concerns."[35] This description of earlier times certainly rings true to the contemporary debate.

According to Christopher Beem, eighteenth-century thinkers associated with the Scottish Enlightenment, such as Francis Hutcheson, Adam Ferguson, Adam Smith, and David Hume, "present for the first time the modern social problem." He states, "They saw that the community life that characterized a feudal and aristocratic order was dying, and an emergent modern world—the world of the Enlightenment and capitalism and democracy—was coming."[36]

Their task, he says, "was to help society respond to this new social reality: either by embracing it and finding new and more appropriate forms of civic virtue, or by finding ways to preserve the best elements of the older forms of social order." In broad terms, their task was "to find a way for modern society to preserve the felicitous changes of political freedom and economic growth while either maintaining former sources of civic virtue and cohesion or finding new ways to do so."[37]

Civil society, then and now, has received strong support from several sources, including the Christian religion, both Protestant and Catholic. According to Seligman, the revival of interest in civil society in the late sixteenth and seventeenth centuries was accompanied by a renewal of interest in natural law reasoning, which at the time was being directed against monarchical political power. For John Locke, civil society represented the realm of political association which enabled men to leave "state of nature" and enter a commonwealth.[38] Of interest to Locke and other theorists was how to fashion a social contract that enabled free men, with shackles of aristocracy thrown off, to build and maintain both liberty and order. This project would require an embrace of both natural and divine law.

Although civil society and political society was closely linked at the time, civil society would later take on even greater differentiation from the state. The drift during and following the Scottish Enlightenment was to move further in the direction of separating society and state, and thus differentiating more clearly between civil society—those institutions which are mostly social—and political society.

Important elements of civil society can also be found in the Calvinist vision for individuals dwelling together in community under the dominion of God. Common to this vision was an articulation of an ultimate good as defined by a transcendent source of morality. Scottish Enlightenment thinkers such as Adam Ferguson were especially inclined to treat civil society, not merely as an arena of civic association and free exchange, but as a moral sphere.

Ferguson described man as, by nature, a "member of a community; and when considered in this capacity . . . no longer made for himself." Civil society was a space for mutual service, grounded in clearly defined moral principles. Ferguson further argues that for this vision of society to materialize, individuals must yield a portion of their own happiness when it conflicts with "the good of society."[39]

Mention was made in earlier sections of the role "mediating institutions" within civil society to serve as a buffer between the individual and the state. This understanding of civil society as a realm of mediating institutions was heavily informed by a core principle of Catholic social thought, namely the concept of "subsidiarity." According to Catholic teaching "it is an injustice, a grave evil and a disturbance of right order for a larger and higher organization to arrogate to itself functions which can be performed efficiently by smaller and lower bodies."[40]

Subsidiarity is grounded in a vision of man as intelligent, free, and social by nature, and a vision of society in which free persons organize to advance common goals within an ethical framework.[41] Closely linked to subsidiarity is the notion of the common good, a concept which also receives strong support from Catholic moral teachings.

## The Legacy of Tocqueville

Perhaps no one has left a more influential or enduring legacy on the American understanding of civil society than Alexis de Tocqueville, the Frenchman who traveled the United States in 1833. Tocqueville is broadly regarded as one of the most astute observers of America's unique social and political culture. Many of the essays in this volume are a direct tribute to his enduring impact. In many ways his keen analysis of American problems of democracy is being tapped again to address the very imbalances he predicted would come.

Tocqueville, the Frenchman, was clearly the theorist who influenced, more than any other observer, America's own self-understanding, and who has defined the terms of analysis and shaped the perceptions of theorists up until the very present. Thus it is only fitting that this introductory chapter be concluded with a summation of his penetrating analysis.

Tocqueville noted the creative tension in American society that exists between the power of self-interest and the pull of the public interest, much like the tension noted above between today's liberal individualism and competing public philosophies. He said Americans tended to explain almost all of the actions of their lives by "the principle of self-interest rightly understood." An enlightened regard for themselves prompted them, according to Tocqueville, "to assist one another" and to be willing "to sacrifice a portion of their time and property to the welfare of the state." This was American self-interest, enlightened and pragmatic, in full and unique display.

Notice that Tocqueville did not wish self-interest away. Self-interest exists and can be harnessed to develop continents and to supply the energy for industrial and technological innovation. But the need to rise above the narrow pursuit of private interest is equally important to preserve a well-ordered society in which the fruits of one's labors are enjoyed.

It was Tocqueville who described our tendency to build and join voluntary associations. American proclivities to form and join associations are captured in his famous and widely quoted description: "Americans of all ages, all stations in life, and all types of dispositions are forever forming associations. There are not only commercial and industrial associations in which all take part, but others of a thousand different types—religious, moral, serious, futile, very general and very limited, immensely large and very minute. Americans combine to give fetes, found seminaries, build churches, distribute books, and send missionaries to the antipodes. Hospitals, prisons and schools take shape in that way. Finally, if they want to proclaim a truth or propagate some feeling by the encouragement of a great example, they form an association. In every case, at the head of any new undertaking, where in France you would find the government or in England some territorial magnate, in the United States you are sure to find an association."[42]

Tocqueville was amazed at the almost limitless sweep of this activity. Civil society captured nearly all forms of human endeavors—intellectual, moral, social, religious, and as some insist, economic. Civic functions overlapped sometimes with political, and even those purely civic activities served to cultivate democratic habits and skills. In the truest sense, they were laboratories of democracy. Local civic associations put democracy within people's reach, inculcating the customs and many uses of democratic process, tempering self-interest and isolation.

Associations represented an independent source of political power and as such exercised a powerful check against either powerful private interests or tyranny by political majorities. Without associations, Tocqueville said, "I see no other direct way to hold back tyranny of any sort."[43] Americans were free and equal and enjoyed a sovereignty that their European cousins would have considered unimaginable.

Tocqueville was determined to understand why American democracy thrived whereas so many European societies stagnated, and he hoped that in presenting his observations, America's long-term prospects would be improved. For one, Tocqueville observed America to possess strong egalitarian tendencies that resulted in a restless search for human betterment. The American state and civil society were put to the task for human equality, he said.

The American taste for equality, said Tocqueville, is "ardent, insatiable, eternal, and invincible."[44] American democracy was not merely about better political arrangements; it was tied inexplicably to a vision for a better society. He noted that "no novelty in the United States struck me more vividly during my stay here than the equality of conditions."[45]

Yet this drive for equality carried corresponding risks. Tocqueville worried that Americans, in their drive for equality, might become impatient with distinctions that naturally evolve among individuals of different talent, and turn to the state for correction. Attitudes against aristocracy extended to tastes and manners could in time produce a love for leveling.

Absent an aristocratic system to hold the bonds of society together, this driving freedom, always seeking to expand, would loosen social cohesion by nursing the ills that were the target of Tocqueville's concern—materialism, individualism and egoism. These maladies, if unchecked, were capable of placing freedom itself at risk.

Tocqueville worried about a "separateness," which has manifested itself in the twentieth century by a phenomenon that has been dubbed "bowling alone." He detected the early signs of civic stagnation when he observed "a calm and considered feeling which disposes each citizen to isolate himself from the mass of his fellows and withdraw into the circle of family and friends; with this little society formed to his taste, he gladly leaves the greater society to look after itself."[46]

The individualism which Tocqueville observed could easily and quickly evolve, he believed, into a more extreme form of egoistic self-interest, characterized by an indulgent search for "paltry pleasures," in which the individual becomes oblivious to the demands of public duty. The effect would be a damming up of the "the spring of public virtues." Closely linked to individualism was "an inordinate love of material pleasure."[47]

In Tocqueville, we find an uncanny foretelling of the American cultural and social debate at the turn of the twenty-first century. Without a vibrant and functioning civic realm, he held that the state would emerge to fill the vacuum, producing an "immense, protective" if gentle despotism. Such a state would take on the paternalistic characteristics of a parent, keeping the people in "perpetual childhood" and robbing them of their dignity.

It was associational life, according to Tocqueville, that would elevate citizens above narrow self-interest and cure a host of social ills. This face-to-face interaction in local community would produce the important social by-product of fellow feeling and social responsibility. That was the proposition that Tocqueville presented to America, and one which is being evaluated and debated like perhaps never before again today.

## NOTES

1. Deb Reichman, "Let's Be Civil," *Associated Press,* 5 February 1997.
2. For more analysis of current data of public attitudes, see Don Eberly, *America's Promise: Civil Society and the Renewal of American Culture* (Lanham, Md.: Rowman & Littlefield, 1998), 6.
3. E.J. Dionne, "Why Civil Society? Why Now?" *The Brookings Review,* Fall 1997, 6.
4. Daniel Bell, "American Exceptionalism Revisited: The Role of Civil Society," *The Public Interest,* no. 95 (1989), 38–56.
5. Christopher Beem, *The Necessity of Politics: Reclaiming American Public Life,* (Chicago: University of Chicago Press, 1999), 4.
6. Michael Walzer, "The Idea of Civil Society," *Kettering Review,* Winter 1997, 8.
7. Alexis de Tocqueville, *Democracy in America,* trans. by George Lawrence, ed. by J.P. Mayer (Garden City, N.Y.: Anchor Books, 1969), 513.
8. Tocqueville, *Democracy in America,* 515.
9. Jean Bethke Elshtain, "Catholic Social Thought, The City, and Liberal Amer-

ica," in K.L. Grasso, G.V. Bradley, and Robert P. Hunt, ed., *Catholicism, Liberalism, and Communitarianism* (Lanham, Md.: Rowman & Littlefield, 1995), 97.

10. Robert Bellah, et al., *Habits of the Heart: Individualism and Commitment in American Life* (New York: Harper and Row, 1985), 83.

11. Bellah, *Habits of the Heart,* 23.

12. Jean Bethke Elshtain, quoted by Don E. Eberly in *America's Promise: Civil Society and the Renewal of American Culture* (Lanham, Md.: Rowman & Littlefield, 1998), 142.

13. Michael J. Sandel, quoted from John O' Sullivan, *The Loss of Virtue: Moral Confusion and Social Disorder in Britain and America* (New York: National Review, 1992), 86.

14. Michael J. Sandel, "America's Search for a New Public Philosophy," *The Atlantic Monthly,* March 1996, 70.

15. Sandel, "America's Search," 58.

16. Adam Seligman, *The Idea of Civil Society* (New York: Free Press, 1992), 16.

17. Jonathan Rauch, "Caesar's Ghost," *Reason Magazine,* May 1993, 55.

18. A. Lawrence Chickering, *Beyond Left and Right: Breaking the Political Stalemate* (San Francisco: ICS Press, 1993), 159.

19. Don Eberly, ed., *Building a Community of Citizens: Civil Society in the 21st Century* (Lanham, Md.: Univestity Press of America, 1994), xxxviii.

20. Address by Vaclav Havel, Harvard University, Cambridge, 8 June 1995.

21. Amitai Etzioni, *The Essential Communitarian Reader* (Lanham, Md.: Rowman & Littlefield, 1998), xiv.

22. Bell, "American Exceptionalism Revisited," 56.

23. Robert D. Putnam, *Making Democracy Work: Civic Traditions in Modern Italy* (Princeton: Princeton University Press, 1993), 15.

24. Francis Fukuyama, *Trust* (New York: Free Press, 1995), 10.

25. Alan Wolfe, *Whose Keeper? Social Science and Moral Obligation* (Berkeley: University of California Press, 1989), 19.

26. Wendy Rahn, "An Individual-Level Analysis of the Decline of Social Trust in American Youth," unpublished paper presented to the First Plenary Session of the National Commission on Civic Renewal, Washington, D.C., 25 January 1997.

27. James S. Coleman, "Social Capital in the Creation of Human Capital," *American Journal of Sociology* 94 (1998), 95–120.

28. Alan Ehrenhalt, "Learning from the Fifties," *Wilson Quarterly,* Summer 1995, 8.

29. Ehrenhalt, "Learning from the Fifties," 21.

30. G. K. Chesterton, *What I Saw in America* (New York: Dodd Mead, 1922), 8.

31. See Michael Joyce, "Americans are Ready for a 'New Citizenship,'" adapted from a speech to the Milwaukee Bar Association (23 June 1993), and Joyce, "The Bradley Project on the 90s: An Overview," from a speech to the Thiensville-Mequon Rotary Club (12 October 1993).

32. William A. Schambra, "Toward a Conservative Populism? Some Questions for the Wilderness," prepared for "Populism in the 1990s" (Washington D.C.: Hubert Humphrey Institute for Public Affairs, University of Minnesota, and The Empowerment Network, 3 March 1994), 5.

33. Seligman, *The Idea of Civil Society,* 3.

34. Beem, *The Necessity of Politics,* 4.

35. Seligman, *The Idea of Civil Society*, 5.
36. Beem, *The Necessity of Politics*, 4.
37. Beem, *The Necessity of Politics*, 4.
38. Seligman, *The Idea of Civil Society*, 22.
39. Adam Ferguson, *An Essay on the History of Civil Society*, 5th ed. (London: 1782), 52.
40. Grasso, Bradley and Hunt, *Catholicism, Liberalism and Communitarianism*, 24
41. Quandragesimo Anno, 40.
42. Tocqueville, *Democracy in America*, 513.
43. Tocqueville, *Democracy in America*, 192.
44. Tocqueville, *Democracy in America*, 506.
45. Tocqueville, *Democracy in America*, 9.
46. Tocqueville, *Democracy in America*, 506.
47. Tocqueville, *Democracy in America*, 444.

# Part Two

# Civil Society Theory

# 2

# "The Quest for Community": A Study in the Ethics of Order and Freedom

*Robert Nisbet*

This is an age of economic interdependence and welfare States, but it is also an age of spiritual insecurity and preoccupation with moral certainty. Why is this? Why has the quest for community become the dominant social tendency of the twentieth century? What are the forces that have conspired, at the very peak of three centuries of economic and political advancement, to make the problem of community more urgent in the minds of men than it has been since the last days of the Roman Empire?

The answer is of course complex. Any effort to resolve the conflicting imperatives of an age into a simple set of institutional dislocations is both vapid and illusory. The conflicts of any age are compounded of immediate cultural frustrations and of timeless spiritual cravings. Attempts to reduce the latter to facile sociological and psychological categories are absurd and pathetic. Whatever else the brilliant literature of political disillusionment of our day has demonstrated, it has made clear that efforts to translate all spiritual problems into secular terms are fraught with stultification as well as tyranny.

The problem before us is in one sense moral. It is moral in that it is closely connected with the values and ends that have traditionally guided and united men but that have in so many instances become remote and inaccessible. We do not have to read deeply in the philosophy and literature of today to sense the degree to which our age has come to seem a period of moral spiritual chaos, of certainties abandoned, of creeds outworn, and of values devalued. The disenchantment of the world, foreseen by certain nineteenth-century conservatives as the end result of social and spiritual tendencies then becoming dominant, is very much with us. The human skepticism of the early twentieth century has already been succeeded in many quarters by a new Pyrrhonism that strikes at the very roots of thought itself. Present disenchantment would be no misfortune were it set in an atmosphere of confident attack upon the old and search for the new. But it is not confident, only melancholy and guilty. Along with it are to be seen the drives to absolute skepticism and absolute certainty that are the invariable conditions of rigid despotism.

The problem is also intellectual. It cannot be separated from tendencies in Western thought that are as old as civilization itself, tendencies luminously revealed in the writings of Plato, Seneca, Augustine, and all their intellectual children. These are profound tendencies. We cannot avoid, any of us, seeing the world in ways determined by the very words we have inherited from other ages. Not a little of the terminology of alienation and community in our day comes directly from the writings of the philosophical and religious conservatives of other centuries. The problem constituted by the present quest for community is composed of elements as old as mankind, elements of faith and agonizing search which are vivid in all the great prophetic literatures. In large degree, the quest for community is timeless and universal.

Nevertheless, the shape and intensity of the quest for community varies from age to age. For generations, even centuries, it may lie mute, covered over and given gratification by the securities found in such institutions as family, village, class, or some other type of association. In other ages, ages of sudden change and dislocation, the quest for community becomes conscious and even clamant. It is this in our own age. To dismiss the present quest for community with vague references to the revival of tribalism, to man's still incomplete emancipation from conditions supposedly "primitive," is to employ substitutes for genuine analysis, substitutes drawn from the nineteenth-century philosophy of unilinear progress. Moral imperatives, our own included, always hold a significant relation to *present* institutional conditions. They cannot be relegated to the past.

It is the argument of this essay that the ominous preoccupation with community revealed by modern thought and mass behavior is a manifestation of certain profound dislocations in the primary associative areas of society, dislocations that have been created to a great extent by the structure of the Western political State. As it is treated here, the problem is social—social in that it pertains to the statuses and social memberships which men hold, or seek to hold. But the problem is also political—political in that it is a reflection of the present location and distribution of power in society.

The two aspects, the social and the political, are inseparable. For, the allegiances and memberships of men, even the least significant, cannot be isolated from the larger systems of authority that prevail in a society or in any of its large social structures. Whether the dominant system of power is primarily religious, economic, or political in the usual sense is of less importance sociologically than the way in which the power reveals itself in practical operation and determines the smaller contexts of culture and association. Here we have reference to the degree of centralization, the remoteness, the impersonality of power, and to the concrete ways in which it becomes involved in human life.

We must begin with the role of the social group in present-day Western society, for it is in the basic associations of men that the real consequences of political power reveal themselves. But the present treatment of the group cannot really be divorced from political considerations, which will be dealt with later.

It has become commonplace, as we have seen, to refer to social disorganization and moral isolation in the present age. These terms are usually made to cover a diversity of conditions. But in a society as complex as ours it is unlikely that all aspects are undergoing a similar change. Thus it can scarcely be said that the State, as a distinguishable relationship among men, is today undergoing disorganization, for in most countries, including the United States, it is the political relationship that has been and is being enhanced above all other forms of connection among individuals. The contemporary State, with all its apparatus of bureaucracy, has become more powerful, more cohesive, and is endowed with more functions than at any time in its history.

Nor can the great impersonal relationships of the many private and semipublic organizations—educational, charitable, economic—be said to be experiencing any noticeable decline or disintegration. Large-scale labor organizations, political parties, welfare organizations, and corporate associations based upon property and exchange show a continued and even increasing prosperity, at least when measured in terms of institutional significance. It may be true that these organizations do not offer the degree of individual identification that makes for a deep sense of social cohesion, but disorganization is hardly the word for these immense and influential associations which govern the lives of tens of millions of people.

We must be no less wary of such terms as the "lost," "isolated," or "unattached" individual. However widespread the contemporary ideology of alienation may be, it would be blindness to miss the fact that it flourishes amid an extraordinary variety of custodial and redemptive agencies. Probably never in all history have so many organizations, public and private, made the individual the center of bureaucratic and institutionalized regard. Quite apart from the innumerable agencies of private welfare, the whole tendency of modern political development has been to enhance the role of the political State as a direct relationship among individuals, and to bring both its powers and its services ever more intimately into the lives of human beings.

Where, then, are the dislocations and the deprivations that have driven so many men, in this age of economic abundance and political welfare, to the quest for community, to narcotic relief from the sense of isolation and anxiety? They lie in the realm of the small, primary, personal relationships of society—the relationships that mediate directly between man and his larger world of economic, moral, and political and religious values. Our problem may be ultimately concerned with all of these values and their greater or lesser accessibility to man, but it is, I think, primarily social: social in the exact sense of pertaining to the small areas of membership and association in which these values are ordinarily made meaningful and directive to men.

Behind the growing sense of isolation in society, behind the whole quest for community which infuses so many theoretical and practical areas of contemporary life and thought, lies the growing realization that the traditional primary relationships of men have become functionally irrelevant to our State and economy and meaningless to the moral aspirations of individuals. We are forced to the conclusion that a great deal of the peculiar character of contemporary social action comes from the efforts of men to find in large-scale organizations the values of status and security which were formerly gained in the primary associations of family, neighborhood, and church. This is the fact, I believe, that is as revealing of the source of many of our contemporary discontents as it is ominous when the related problems of political freedom and order are considered.

The problem, as I shall emphasize later in this chapter, is by no means restricted to the position of the traditional groups, nor is its solution in any way compatible with antiquarian revivals of groups and values no longer in accord with the requirements of the industrial and democratic age in which we live and to which we are unalterably committed. But the dislocation of the traditional groups must form our point of departure.

Historically, our problem must be seen in terms of the decline in functional and psychological significance of such groups as the family, the small local community, and the various other traditional relationships that have immemorially mediated between the individual and his society. These are the groups that have been morally decisive in the concrete lives of individuals. Other and more powerful forms of association have existed, but the major moral and psychological influences on the individual's life have emanated from the family and local community and the church. Within such groups have been engendered the primary types of identification: affection, friendship, prestige, recognition. And within them also have been engendered or intensified the principal incentives of work, love, prayer, and devotion to freedom and order.

This is the area of association from which the individual commonly gains his concept of the outer world and his sense of position in it. His concrete feelings of status and role, of protection and freedom, his differentiation between good and bad, between order and disorder and guilt and innocence, arise and are shaped largely by his relations within this realm of primary association. What was once called instinct or the social nature of man is but the product of this sphere of interpersonal relationships. It contains and cherishes not only the formal moral precept but what Whitehead has called "our vast system of inherited symbolism."

It can be seen that most contemporary themes of alienation have as their referents disruptions of attachment and states of mind which derive from this area of interpersonal relations. Feelings of moral estrangement, of the hostility of the world, the fear of freedom, of irrational aggressiveness, and of helplessness before the simplest of problems have to do commonly—as both the novelist and the psychiatrist testify—with the individual's sense of the inaccessibility of this area of relationship. In the child, or in the adult, the roots of a coherent, logical sense of the outer world are sunk deeply in the soil of close, meaningful interpersonal relations.

It is to this area of relations that the adjective "disorganized" is most often flung by contemporary social scientists and moralists, and it is unquestionably in this area that most contemporary sensations of cultural dissolution arise. Yet the term disorganization is not an appropriate one and tends to divert attention from the basic problem of the social group in our culture. It has done much to fix attention on those largely irrelevant manifestations of delinquent behavior which are fairly constant in all ages and have little to do with our real problem.

The conception of social disorganization arose with the conservatives in France, who applied it empirically enough to the destruction of the gilds, the aristocracy, and the monasteries. But to Bonald and Comte the most fundamental sense of the term was moral. The Revolution signified to them the destruction of a vast moral order, and in their eyes the common manifestations of individual delinquency became suddenly invested with a new significance, the significance of social disorganization, itself the product of the Revolution. The term disorganization has been a persistent one in social science, and there is even now a deplorable tendency to use such terms as disintegration and disorganization where there is no demonstrable breakdown of a structure and no clear norm from which to calculate supposed deviations of conduct. The family and the community have been treated as disintegrating entities with no clear insight into what relationships are actually disintegrating. A vast amount of attention has been given to such phenomena as marital unhappiness, prostitution, juvenile misbehavior, and the sexual life of the unmarried, on the curious assumption that these are "pathological" and derive clearly from the breakdown of the family.[1]

But in any intelligible sense of the word it is not disorganization that is crucial to the problem of the family or of any other significant social group in our society. The most fundamental problem has to do with the *organized* associations of men. It has to do with the role of the primary social group in an economy and political order whose principal ends have come to be structured in such a way that the primary social relationships are increasingly functionless, almost irrelevant, with respect to these ends. What is involved most deeply in our problem is the diminishing capacity of organized, traditional relationships for holding a position of moral and psychological centrality in the individual's life.

Interpersonal relationships doubtless exist as abundantly in our age as in any other. But it is becoming apparent that for more and more people such relationships are morally empty and psychologically baffling. It is not simply that old relationships have waned in psychological influence; it is that new forms of primary relationships show, with rare exceptions, little evidence of offering even as much psychological and moral meaning for the individual as do the old ones. For more and more individuals the primary social relationships have lost much of their historic function of mediation between man and the larger ends of our civilization.

But the decline of effective meaning is itself a part of a more fundamental change in the role of such groups as the family and local community. At bottom social organization is a pattern of institutional functions into which are woven numerous psychological threads of meaning, loyalty, and interdependence. The contemporary sense of alienation is most directly perhaps a problem in symbols and meanings, but it is also a problem in the institutional functions of the relationships that ordinarily communicate integration and purpose to individuals.

In any society the concrete loyalties and devotions of individuals tend to become directed toward the associations and patterns of leadership that in the long run have the greatest perceptible significance in the maintenance of life. It is never a crude relationship; intervening strata of ritual and other forms of crystallized meaning will exert a distinguishable influence on human thought. But, at bottom, there is a close and vital connection between the effectiveness of the symbols that provide meaning in the individual's life and the institutional value of the social structures that are the immediate source of the symbols. The immediacy of the integrative meaning of the basic values contained in and communicated by the kinship or religious group will vary with the greater or less institutional value of the group to the individual *and to the other institutions in society.*

In earlier times, and even today in diminishing localities, there was an intimate relation between the local, kinship, and religious groups within which individuals consciously lived and the major economic, charitable, and protective functions which are indispensable to human existence. There was an intimate conjunction of larger institutional goals and the social groups small enough to infuse the individual's life with a sense of membership in society and the meaning of the basic moral values. For the overwhelming majority of people, until quite recently the structure of economic and political life rested upon, and even presupposed, the existence of the small social and local groups within which the cravings for psychological security and identification could be satisfied.

Family, church, and local community drew and held the allegiances of individuals in earlier times not because of any superior impulses to love and protect, or because of any greater natural harmony of intellectual and spiritual values, or even because of any superior internal organization, but because these groups possessed a virtually indispensable relation to the economic and political order. The social problems of birth and death, courtship and marriage, employment and unemployment, infirmity and old age were met, however inadequately at times, through the associative means of these social groups. In consequence, a whole ideology, reflected in popular literature, custom, and morality, testified to the centrality of kinship and localism.

Our present crisis lies in the fact that whereas the small traditional associations, founded upon kinship, faith, or locality, are still expected to communicate to individuals the principal moral ends and psychological gratifications of society, they have manifestly become detached from positions of functional relevance to the larger economic and political decisions of our society. Family, local community, church, and the whole network of informal interpersonal relationships have ceased to play a determining role in our institutional systems of mutual aid, welfare, education, recreation, and economic production and distribution. Yet despite the loss of these manifest institutional functions, and the failure of most of these groups to develop any new institutional functions, we continue to expect them to perform adequately the implicit psychological or symbolic functions in the life of the individual.

The general condition I am describing in Western society can be compared usefully with social changes taking place in many of the native cultures that have come under the impact of Western civilization. A large volume of anthropological work testifies to the incidence, in such areas as East Africa, India, China, and Burma, of processes of social dislocation and moral insecurity. A conflict of moral values is apparent. More particularly, it is a conflict, as J.S. Furnivall has said, "between the eastern system resting on religion, personal authority, and customary obligation, and the western system resting on reason, impersonal law, and individual rights."[2]

This conflict of principles and moral values is not an abstract thing, existing only in philosophical contemplation. It may indeed be a crisis of symbolism, of patterns of moral meaning, but more fundamentally it is a crisis of allegiances. It is a result, in very large part, of the increasing separation of traditional groups from the crucial ends and decisions in economic and political spheres. The wresting of economic significance from native clans, villages, and castes by new systems of industry, and the weakening of their effective social control through the establishment of new systems of administrative authority has had demonstrable moral effects. The revolutionary intellectual and moral ferment of the modern East is closely connected with the dislocation of traditional centers of authority and responsibility from the lives of the people.

When the major institutional functions have disappeared from a local village government or from a subcaste, the conditions are laid for the decline of the individual's allegiance to the older forms of organization. Failing to find any institutional substance in the old unities of social life, he is prone to withdraw, consciously or unconsciously, his loyalty to them. They no longer represent the prime moral experiences of his life. He finds himself, mentally, looking in new directions.

Some of the most extreme instances of insecurity and conflict of values in native cultures have resulted not from the nakedly ruthless forces of economic exploitation but from most commendable (by Western standards) acts of humanitarian reform. Thus the introduction of so physically salutary a measure as an irrigation district or medical service may be attended by all the promised gains in abundance and health, but such innovations can also bring about the most complex disruptions of social relationships and allegiances. Why? Because such systems, by the very *humaneness* of their functions, assume values that no purely exploitative agency can, and having become values they more easily serve to alienate the native from his devotion to the meanings associated with obsolete functional structures. The new technology means the creation of new centers of administrative authority which not infrequently nullify the prestige of village or caste groups, leading in time to a growing conflict between the moral meaning of the old areas of authority and the values associated with the new.

What is to be observed so vividly in many areas of the East is also, and has been, for some time, a notable characteristic of Western society. The process is less striking, less dramatic, for we are directly involved in it. But it is nonetheless a profoundly significant aspect of modern Western history and it arises from some of the same elements in Western culture which, when exported, have caused such dislocation and ferment in foreign areas. We too have suffered a decline in the institutional function of groups and associations upon which we have long depended for moral and psychological stability. We too are in a state that can, most optimistically, be called transition—of change from associative contexts that have become in so many places irrelevant and anachronistic to newer associative contexts that are still psychologically and morally dim to the perception of individuals. As a result of the sharp reduction in meaning formerly inherent in membership, the problems of status, adjustment, and moral direction have assumed tremendous importance in the East as well as the West.

Nowhere is the concern with the problem of community in Western society more intense than with respect to the family.[3] The contemporary family, as countless books, articles, college courses, and marital clinics make plain, has become an obsessive problem. The family inspires a curious dualism of thought. We tend to regard it uneasily as a final manifestation of tribal society, somehow inappropriate to a democratic, industrial age, but, at the same time, we have become ever more aware of its possibilities as an instrument of social reconstruction.

The intensity of theoretical interest in the family has curiously enough risen in direct proportion to the decline of the family's basic institutional importance to our culture. The present "problem" of the family is dramatized by the fact that its abstract importance to the moralist or psychologist has grown all the while that its tangible institutional significance to the layman and its functional importance to economy and State have diminished.

It is doubtless one more manifestation of the contemporary quest for security that students of the family increasingly see its main "function" to be that of conferring "adjustment" upon the individual, and, for the most part, they find no difficulty at all in supposing that this psychological function can be carried on by the family in what is otherwise a functional vacuum. Contemporary social psychology has become so single-mindedly aware of the psychological gratification provided by the group for individual needs of security and recognition that there is an increasing tendency to suppose that such a function is primary and can maintain itself autonomously, impervious to changes in *institutional* functions which normally give a group importance in culture. For many reasons the contemporary family is made to carry a conscious symbolic importance that is greater than ever, but it must do this with a structure much smaller in size and of manifestly diminishing relevance to the larger economic, religious, and political ends of contemporary society.

Historically the family's importance has come from the fact of intimate social cohesion united with institutional significance in society, not from its sex or blood relationships. In earlier ages, kinship was inextricably involved in the processes of getting a living, providing education, supporting the infirm, caring for the aged, and maintaining religious values. In vast rural areas, until quite recently, the family was the actual agency of economic production, distribution, and consumption. Even in towns and cities, the family long retained its close relation to these obviously crucial activities. Organized living was simply inconceivable, for the most part, outside of the context provided by kinship. Few individuals were either too young or too old to find a place of importance within the group, a fact which enhanced immeasurably the family's capacity for winning allegiance and providing symbolic integration for the individual.

The interpersonal and psychological aspects of kinship were never made to rest upon personal romance alone or even upon pure standards of individual rectitude. Doubtless, deviations from the moral code and disillusionment with romance were as common then as now. But they did not interfere with the cultural significance of the family simply because the family was far more than an interpersonal relationship based upon affection and moral probity. It was an indispensable institution.

But in ever enlarging areas of population in modern times, the economic, legal, educational, religious, and recreational functions of the family have declined or diminished. Politically, membership in the family is superfluous; economically, it is regarded by many as an outright hindrance to success. The family, as someone has put it, is now the accident of the worker rather than his essence. His competitive position may be more favorable without it. Our systems of law and education and all the manifold recreational activities of individuals engaged in their pursuit of happiness have come to rest upon, and to be directed to, the individual, not the family. On all sides we continue to celebrate from pulpit and rostrum the indispensability to economy and the State of the family. But, in plain fact, the family is indispensable to neither of these at the present time. The major processes of economy and political administration have become increasingly independent of the symbolism and integrative activities of kinship.

There is an optimistic apologetics that sees in this waning of the family's institutional importance only the beneficent hand of Progress. We are told by certain psychologists and sociologists that, with its loss of economic and legal functions, the family has been freed of all that is basically irrelevant to its "real" nature; that the true function of the family—the cultivation of affection, the shaping of personality, above all, the manufacture of "adjustment"—is now in a position to flourish illimitably, to the greater glory of man and society. In a highly popular statement, we are told that the family has progressed from institution to companionship.

But, as Ortega y Gasset has written, "people do not live together merely to be together. They live together to do something together." To suppose that the present family, or any other group, can perpetually vitalize itself though some indwelling affectional tie, in the absence of concrete, perceived functions, is like supposing that the comradely ties of mutual aid which grow up incidentally in a military unit will long outlast a condition in which war is plainly and irrevocably banished. Applied to the family, the argument suggests that affection and personality cultivation can somehow exist in a social vacuum, unsupported by the determining goals and ideals of economic and political society. But in hard fact no social group will long survive the disappearance of its chief reasons for being, and these reasons are not, primarily, biological but institutional. Unless new institutional functions are performed by a group—family, trade union, or church—its psychological influence will become minimal.

No amount of veneration for the psychological functions of a social group, for the capacity of the group to gratify cravings for security and recognition, will offset the fact that, however important these functions may be in any given individual's life, he does not join the group essentially for them. He joins the group if and when its larger institutional or intellectual functions have relevance both to his own life organization and to what he can see of the group's relation to the larger society. The individual may indeed derive vast psychic support and integration from the pure fact of group membership, but he will not long derive this when he becomes in some way aware of the gulf between the moral claims of a group and its actual institutional importance in the social order.

All of this has special relevance to the family, with its major function now generally reduced by psychologists to that of conferring adjustment upon individuals. Yet in any objective view the family is probably now less effective in this regard than it has ever been. It is plain that the family is no longer the main object of personal loyalty in ever larger sections of our population, and it is an overstrain on the imagination to suppose that it will regain a position of psychological importance through pamphlets, clinics, and high-school courses on courtship and marriage. How quaint now seems that whole literature on sexual adjustment in marriage with its implicit argument that sexual incompatibility is the basic cause of the reduced significance of marriage. Some of the solemn preoccupations with "family tensions" which now hold the field of clinical practice will one day no doubt seem equally quaint.

The current problem of the family, like the problem of any social group, cannot be reduced to simple sets of psychological complexes which exist universally in man's nature, or to an ignorance of sexual techniques, or to a lack of Christian morality. The family is a major problem in our culture simply because we are attempting to make it perform psychological and symbolic functions with a structure that has become fragile and an institutional importance that is almost totally unrelated to the economic and political realities of our society. Moreover, the growing impersonality and the accumulating demands of ever larger sections of our world of business and government tend to throw an extraordinary psychological strain upon the family. In this now small and fragile group we seek the security and affection denied everywhere else. It is hardly strange that timeless incompatibilities and emotional strains should, in the present age, assume an unwanted importance—their meaning has changed with respect to the larger context of men's lives. We thus find ourselves increasingly in the position of attempting to correct, through psychiatric or spiritual techniques, problems which, although assuredly emotional, derive basically from a set of historically given institutional circumstances.

Personal crises, underlying emotional dissatisfactions, individual deviations from strict rectitude—these have presumably been constant in all ages of history. Only our own age tends to blow up these tensions into reasons for a clinical approach to happiness. Such tensions appear more critical and painful, more intolerable to contemporary man, simply because the containing social structures of such tensions have become less vital to his existence. The social structures are expendable so far as the broad economic and political processes of our society are concerned and, consequently, they offer less support for particular emotional states. Not a few of the problems that give special concern to our present society—sex role, courtship and marriage, old age, the position of the child—do so because of the modified functional and psychological position of the family in our culture.

The social roles of adolescence, old age, and affection have been profoundly altered by changes in the functional positions of the members of the family. Such states are *perceived* differently, both by the individuals immediately concerned and by others around them. So are the recurrent "crises" of personal life—birth, marriage, and death—regarded differently as a consequence of changes in the structure and functions of the family. Except from the point of view of the biologist, death, for example, is not the same phenomenon from one society to another, from one age to another. Death also has its social role, and this role is inseparable from the organization of values and relationships within which the physical fact of death takes place. Death almost everywhere is ritualized, ritualized for the sake of the deceased, if we like, but far more importantly for the sake of those who are left behind. Such ritualization has immensely important psychological functions in the direction of emotional release for the individuals most closely related to the dead person and in the direction, too, of the whole social group. But these death rites are not disembodied acts of obeisance or succor; they are manifestations of group life and function. They are closely related, that is, to other aspects of the family which have no immediate connection with the fact of death.

In our society we find ourselves increasingly baffled and psychologically unprepared for the incidence of death among loved ones. It is not that grief is greater or that the incomprehensibility of death is increased. It is in considerable part perhaps because the smaller structure of the family gives inevitably a greater emotional value to each of the members. But, more than this, it is the result, I believe, of the decline in significance of the traditional means of ritual *completion* of the fact of death. Death leaves a kind of moral suspense that is terminated psychologically only with greater and greater difficulty. The social *meaning* of death has changed with the social *position* of death.

The problems arising from the diminished institutional and psychological importance of the family in our society also extend into wider areas of social and economic behavior. We find ourselves dealing increasingly with difficulties that seem to resolve themselves into matters of human motivation and incentives. An older economics and politics and educational theory took it for granted that all the root impulses to buying and selling and saving, to voting, and to learning lay, in prepotent form, in the individual himself. The relation between crucial economic motivations and the social groups in which individuals actually lived was seldom if ever heeded by the classical economists.

The late Harvard economist Joseph Schumpeter wrote tellingly on this point.

> In order to realize what all this means for the efficiency of the capitalist engine of production we need only recall that the family and the family home used to be the mainspring of the typically bourgeois kind of profit motive. Economists have not always given due weight to this fact. When we look more closely at their idea of the self-interest of entrepreneurs and capitalists we cannot fail to discover that the results it was supposed to produce are really not at all what one would expect from the rational self-interest of the detached individual or the childless couple who no longer look at the world through the windows of a family home. Consciously or unconsciously, they analyzed the behavior of the man whose motives

> are shaped by such a home and who means to work and save primarily for wife and children. As soon as these fade out from the moral vision of the business man, we have a different kind of *homo economics* before us who cares for different things and acts in different ways.[4]

Much of the predictability of human response, which the classical economists made the basis of their faith in the automatic workings of the free market, came not from fixed instincts but from the vast conservatism and stability of a society that remained deeply rooted in kinship long after the advent of the capitalist age. Had it not been for the profound incentives supplied by the family and, equally important, the capacity of the extended family to supply a degree, however minimal, of mutual aid in time of distress, it is a fair guess that capitalism would have failed before it was well underway. The extraordinary rate of capital accumulation in the nineteenth century was dependent, to some extent at least, on a low-wage structure that was in turn dependent on the continuation of the ethic of family aid, even when this involved child labor in the factories.[5]

The same point may be made with respect to the relation of kinship symbolism and population increase. What Malthus and his followers regarded as embedded in the biological nature of man, the almost limitless urge to procreate, has turned out to be inseparable from the cultural fact of kinship, with its inherited incentives and values. As long as the family had institutional importance in society, it tended to maintain moral and psychological devotions which resulted in high birth rates—rates that invited the alarm of a good many sociologists. But with the decline in both the functional and psychological importance of kinship, and with the emergence of a culture based increasingly on the abstract individual rather than the family, there has resulted a quite different birth rate and a quite different set of population problems.

To be sure we are dealing here, in this matter of motivations and incentives, not merely with the effects of the changed significance of the family but with those of the changed significance of other social cohesions upon which our economy and political order depended for a long period of time. What has happened to the family has happened also to neighborhood and local community. As Robert S. Lynd has written: "Neighborhood and community ties are not only optional but generally growing less strong; and along with them is disappearing the important network of intimate, informal, social controls traditionally associated with living closely with others."[6] Within all of these lay not merely controls but the incentives that supplied the motive force for such pursuits as education and religion and recreation.

The point is that with the decline in the significance of kinship and locality, and the failure of new social relationships to assume influences of equivalent evocative intensity, a profound change has occurred in the very psychological structure of society. And this is a change that has produced a great deal of the present problem of incentives in so many areas of our society. Most of our ideas and practices in the major institutional areas of society developed during an age when the residual psychological elements of social organization seemed imperishable. No less imperishable seemed the structure of personality itself. Educational goals and political objectives were fashioned accordingly, as were theories of economic behavior and population increase.

But we are learning that many of the motivations and incentives which an older generation of rationalists believe were inherent in the individual are actually supplied by social groups—social groups with both functional and moral relevance to the lives of individuals.

Modern planners thus frequently find themselves dealing, not simply with the upper stratum of decisions, which their forebears assumed would be the sole demand of a planned society, but with often baffling problems which reach down into the very recesses of human personality.[7]

Basically, however, it is not the position of the family or of any other single group, old or new, that is crucial to the welfare of a social order. Associations may come and go under the impact of historical changes and cultural needs. There is no single type of family, anymore than there is a single type of religion, that is essential to personal security and collective prosperity. It would be wrong to assume that the present problem of community in Western society arises inexorably from the modifications which have taken place in old groups, however cherished these may be. But irrespective of particular groups, there must be in any stable culture, in any civilization that prizes its integrity, functionally significant and psychologically meaningful groups and associations lying intermediate to the individual and the larger values and purposes of his society. For these are the small areas of association within which alone such values and purposes can take on clear meaning in personal life and become the vital roots of the large culture. It is, I believe, the problem of intermediate association that is fundamental at the present time.

Under the lulling influence of the idea of progress we have generally assumed until recently that history automatically provides its own solution to the basic problems of organization in society. We have further assumed that man is ineradicably gregarious and that from this gregariousness must come ever new and relevant forms of intermediate association.

It is tempting to believe this as we survey the innumerable formal organizations of modern life, the proliferation of which has been one of the signal facts in American history, or as we observe the incredible number of personal contacts which take place daily in the congested areas of modern urban life.

But there is a profound difference between the casual, informal relationships which abound in such areas and the kind of social groups which create a sense of belonging, which supply incentive, and which confer upon the individual a sense of status. Moreover, from some highly suggestive evidence supplied by such sociologists as Warner, Lazarsfeld, and especially Mirra Komarovsky, we can justly doubt that all sections of modern populations are as rich in identifiable social groups and associations as we have heretofore taken for granted.

The common assumption that, as the older associations of kinship and neighborhood have become weakened, they are replaced by new voluntary associations filling the same role is not above the sharp question. That traditional groups have weakened in significance is apparently true enough but, on the evidence, their place has not been taken to any appreciable extent by new forms of association. Despite the appeal of the older sociological stereotype of the urban dweller who belongs to various voluntary associations, all of which have progressively replaced the older social unities, the facts so far gathered suggest the contrary: that a rising number of individuals belong to no organized association at all, and that, in the large cities, the unaffiliated persons may even constitute a majority of the population.[8]

As for the psychological functions of the great formal associations in modern life—industrial corporations, governmental agencies, large-scale labor and charitable organizations—it is plain that not many of these answer adequately the contemporary quest for community. Such organizations, as Max Weber pointed out, are generally organized not around personal loyalties but around loyalty to an office or machine. The administration of charity, hospitalization, unemployment assistance, like the administration of the huge manufacturing corporation, may be more efficient and less given to material inequities, but the possible gains in technical efficiency do not minimize their underlying impersonality in the life of the individual.

Much of the contemporary sense of the impersonality of society comes from the rational impersonality of these great organizations. The widespread reaction against technology, the city, and political freedom, not to mention the nostalgia that pervades so many of the discussions of rural-urban differences, comes from the diminished functional relationship between existent social groups in industry or the community and the remote efficiency of the larger organizations created by modern planners. The derivative loss of meaning for the individual frequently becomes the moral background of vague and impotent reactions against technology and science, and of aggressive states of mind against the culture as a whole. In spatial terms the individual is obviously less isolated from his fellows in the large-scale housing project or in the factory than was his grandfather. What he has become isolated from is the sense of meaningful proximity to the major ends and purposes of his culture. With the relatively complete satisfaction of needs concerned with food, employment, and housing, a different order of needs begins to assert itself imperiously; and these have to do with spiritual belief and social status.

C. Wright Mills writes:

> The uneasiness, the malaise of our times is due to this root fact: in our politics and economy, in family life and religion—in practically every sphere of our existence—the certainties of the eighteenth and nineteenth centuries have disintegrated or been destroyed and, at the same time, no new sanctions or justifications for the new routines we live, and must live, have taken hold. Among white-collar people, the malaise is deep-rooted; for the absence of any order of belief has left them morally defenseless as individuals and politically impotent as a group. Newly created in a harsh time of creation, white-collar man has no culture to lean upon except the contents of a mass society that has shaped him and seeks to manipulate him to its alien ends. For security's sake he must attach himself somewhere, but no communities or organizations seem to be thoroughly his.[9]

The quest for community will not be denied, for it springs from some of the powerful needs of human nature—needs for a clear sense of cultural purpose, membership, status, and continuity. Without these, no amount of mere material welfare will serve to arrest the developing sense of alienation in our society, and the mounting preoccupation with the imperatives of community. To appeal to technological progress is futile. For what we discover is that rising standards of living, together with increases in leisure, actually intensify the disquietude and frustration that arise when cherished and proffered goals are without available means of fulfillment. "Secular improvement that is taken for granted," wrote Joseph Schumpeter, "and coupled with individual insecurity that is acutely resented is of course the best recipe for breeding social unrest."[10]

The loss of old moral certainties and accustomed statuses is, however, only the setting of our problem. For, despite the enormous influence of nostalgia in human thinking, it is never the recovery of the institutionally old that is desired by most people. In any event, the quest for the past is as futile as that of the future.

The real problem is not, then, the loss of old contexts but rather the failure of our present democratic and industrial scene to create new contexts of association and moral cohesion within which smaller allegiances of men will assume both functional and psychological significance. It is almost as if the forces that weakened the old have remained to obstruct the new channels of association.

What is the source of this failure? The blame is usually laid to technology, science, and the city. These, it is said, have left a vacuum. But the attack on these elements of modern culture is ill-founded, for no one of these is either logically or psychologically essential to the problem at hand. Neither science, nor technology, nor the city is inherently incompatible with the existence of moral values and social relationships which will do for modern man what the extended family, the parish, and the village did for earlier man.

Here, our problem becomes inevitably historical. For the present position of the social group in political and industrial society cannot be understood apart from certain historical tendencies concerned with the location of authority and function in society and with certain momentous conflicts of authority and function which have been fundamental in the development of the modern State.

## NOTES

1. This approach is, happily, less common now than a generation ago. The writings of such men as R.M. MacIver, Talcott Parsons, Kingsley Davis, and Howard Becker, among others, have done much to place the study of the family in a more coherent perspective.

2. J. S. Furnivall, *Colonial Policy and Practice* (Cambridge University Press, 1948), 3.

3. There is a kind of historical awareness implicit in this focusing upon the family, for the overwhelming majority of communal or sacred areas of society reflect the transfer, historically, of kinship symbols and nomenclature to nonkinship spheres. We see this in the histories of religion, gilds, village communities, and labor unions. Kinship has ever been the archetype of man's communal aspirations.

4. Joseph Schumpeter, *Capitalism, Socialism, and Democracy* (New York, 1942), 160.

5. E. H. Norman, in his *Japan's Emergence as a Modern State* (Institute of Pacific Relations, 1940), 153, has pointed out the value of the extended family in Japan in making possible a relatively low-wage structure and, derivatively, greater profits and capital expansion.

6. Robert S. Lynd, *Knowledge For What?* (Princeton University Press, 1939), 83.

7. Throughout modern economic society the problem of incentives has become explicit. Both business and governmental planners find themselves with difficulties which, although economic in nature, begin in a structure of motivations that is noneconomic. The almost total absence in earlier economic thought, socialist as well as orthodox, of concern for the problem of incentives is some indication of the changes that have taken place in the institutional framework and psychological substructure of capitalism.

8. This paragraph is a paraphrase of Mirra Komarovsky's penetrating study, "The Voluntary Associations of Urban Dwellers," *American Sociological Review* (December 1946).

9. C. Wright Mills, *White Collar: The American Middle Classes* (New York, 1951), xvi.

10. Joseph Schumpeter, 145.

# 3

# Whose Keeper? Social Science and Moral Obligation

*Alan Wolfe*

## MODERNITY'S PARADOX

Capitalist economics and liberal democratic politics have given many citizens of Western societies two unique gifts: freedom from economics and liberation from politics. Raised by economic growth from the consciousness of scarcity, they can forget the nitty-gritty of survival and contemplate the building of culture. Released by politics from politics, they can, unlike those who lived before them, lead their lives unaware of the struggles for power taking place around them. The middle classes of Western societies, unconstrained by a real or imagined state of nature, are in a position to make for themselves the kind of social world they desire.

Yet for all its success, modernity is an ambivalent condition. There is, not far beneath the surface, a sense that something is missing: economic growth and political freedom do not seem enough. Max Weber's image of a society without a soul has become something of a popular lament. People are not always articulate about their discontents, but numerous signs—unstable voting patterns, a return to religious orthodoxy, increases in antisocial behavior, opposition to scientific and technological advance, a withdrawal from public issues into private worlds, and the rise of irrationality—indicate, for reasons both sound and unsound, a feeling of discontent with progress. Capitalist economics and liberal democratic politics have prepared the basis for the good life, but its actual attainment seems just beyond the possible.

The discontents of modernity may have to do with the difficulty facing liberal democratic citizens whenever they make their daily decisions. Severed from traditions and ties of place, they are free to make choices about how to lead their lives irrespective of the actions of others, yet, because they live in complex societies organized by large states and even larger economies, they are dependent on everyone around them to make their societies work. The essence of the liberal condition is freedom, yet a people who are completely free are a people unencumbered by obligations, whereas economic growth, democratic government, and therefore freedom itself are produced through extensive, and quite encumbered, dependence on others. Unlike Rousseau's natural man, who was born free but was everywhere in chains, modern social individuals are born into chains of interdependence but yearn, most of the time, to be free.

The citizens of capitalist liberal democracies understand the freedom they possess, appreciate its value, defend its prerogatives. But they are confused when it comes to recognizing the social obligations that make their freedom possible in the first place. They are, in a word, unclear about the moral codes by which they ought to live. A moral code is a set of rules that defines people's obligations to one another. Neither the liberal market nor the democratic state is comfortable with explicit discussions of the obligations such codes ought to impose. Both view social obligation as a by-product of individual action. Both prefer present benefits to sacrifices for future generations. Both emphasize rights rather than obligations. Both value procedures over purpose. When capitalism and liberal democracy combine, people are given the potential to determine for themselves what their obligations to others ought to be, but are then given few satisfactory guidelines on how to fulfill them.

Despite their discomfort in discussing moral obligation, modern liberal democrats have a greater need to do so than any people who came before. While the distinction between traditional and modern societies can be overdone, there is little doubt that smaller-scale societies characterized by handed-down authority present the problem of moral obligation in a different light than do those that value individual mobility and economic and political rights. In the former kind of society, moral obligations tend to be both tightly inscribed and limited in scope. On the one hand, rules are expected to be strictly followed; on the other, the number of others to whom the rules are expected to apply are limited—by blood, geography, ethnicity, or political boundaries. Moral obligation is "easy" in a double sense: individuals themselves are not called on to act as moral agents, since authority structures formulate rules of social interaction for them, and the others to whom they are tied by those rules are known to them or share with them certain known characteristics.

Both the scope and the specificity of moral obligations change as societies become more modern. The sheer complexity of modern forms of social organization creates an ever-widening circle of newer obligations beyond those of family and locality. Modern liberal democrats, for one, have obligations to perfect strangers, to those passing others who populate the bureaucracies and urban living arrangements of all Western societies. They have further obligations, at yet another remove from the traditional milieu, to what has been called the "generalized other," a term that might include, for example, those who will live in the future and will therefore be dependent on decisions made by the present generation. To be modern is to face the consequences of decisions made by complete strangers while making decisions that will affect the lives of people one will never know. The scope of moral obligation—especially at a time when issues of possible nuclear war, limitations on economic growth, and ecological destruction are public concerns—seems to be without limits.

Yet if modernity expands the scope of moral obligations, it also thins their specificity. Rather than following narrowly inscribed rules that are expected to be applied strictly and with little tolerance for ambiguity, modern liberal democrats find themselves facing unprecedented moral dilemmas without firm agreement, not merely about what their moral rules *are,* but even about where they can be *found.* Religion, to take the most prominent example, is certainly no longer the source of moral authority it once was. Even when one can pronounce the modern age a bit less secular owing to an upsurge in religious affiliation and belief, authoritative moral codes based on God's commands no longer guide much conduct in the modern world. Neither in Italy nor in the United States can the Catholic Church assume that its positions on moral issues will be followed by the bulk of its membership; splits between Orthodox and non-Orthodox Jews have made it clear that agreement within that religion on morality is nonexistent; and Protestant theology has become either highly secular or too strict to be obeyed even by its own preachers.

Nor is philosophy an adequate source of ideas about moral behavior. Moral philosophy, especially in Great Britain and the United States, has developed into an effort to establish the rule of reason, to search for universal standards of justice. (One looks for procedure, rules that regulate not only what we do but also how we do it, ironically making morality morally neutral.) The result, William Sullivan has written, is "a mistrust of the moral meanings embodied in tradition and contingent, historical experience."[1] Relying on logic, argumentative ability, and abstract formulations of universal criteria of justice, contemporary moral philosophy, for all its brilliance, tends toward obfuscation or restatements of the obvious. Thus a recent exploration into the thickets of moral obligation by Robert E. Goodin called *Protecting the Vulnerable,* wishing to make a case that protection of the vulnerable demands a special responsibility, relies on logic and on argument against competing moral philosophers—not content to argue instead that we have a special responsibility to the vulnerable simply because it is right.

Literature, furthermore, can no longer be counted on to serve as a guide to moral understandings. "For our time," Lionel Trilling once wrote, "the most effective agent of the moral imagination has been the novel of the last two hundred years."[2] Yet the novel of manners and morals, the tradition from Jane

Austen to E. M. Forster that explored so deeply questions of social obligation, has become an anachronism, replaced, as John Gardner noted, by introspective, if not narcissistic, explorations or inner worlds. In one of his political essays, E. M. Forster said that modern people needed to "combine the new economy and the old morality." That is precisely what no one today seems to know how to do. The question of personal responsibility that Forster explored in such microscopic detail in his great moral novel *Howard's End* seems old-fashioned to contemporary readers, who, like that novel's antagonist Henry Wilcox, believe that "as civilization moves forward, the shoe is bound to pinch in places, and it's absurd to pretend that anyone is responsible personally."[3]

Finally, modern politics, like modern literature, has also lost much of its moral sensibility. The left, which once prided itself on its ethical awareness, no longer speaks a resonant language of moral obligation. Its great objective, the welfare state, gave material benefits to modern people and created an important presumption in favor of equality, but the ethical energy that inspired its early years has for some time been on the wane. Where the welfare state has achieved its greatest success—in Scandinavia—is also where the welfare state has difficulty expressing a compelling moral vision. Social democracy there and elsewhere has become defensive, holding on to the gains of the past, unwilling to stake out a terrain for the future. It often represents quite well the interests of its major constituency, the labor movement, but it has difficulty speaking of solidarity within the classes, let alone solidarity between them.

The moral exhaustion of the left should be good news to the right, but such does not appear to be the case. The libertarian right, which believes that the market will solve all problems, is, of all political ideologies in the modern world, the most amoral, unwilling even to allow the possibility that people have any obligations other than to themselves. This moral nihilism is in contrast to the position of the fundamentalist right, for if market theories are all choice and no values, groups like the Moral Majority are all values and no choice. The religious right does have a moral vision, but it is one so confining in its calls for blind obedience to a handed-down moral code that it would negate all the gains of freedom that modern people have acquired. Nor, finally, do those known as "neoconservative" possess an appropriate moral language for modern politics. They ought to, for as former socialists they understand the need for binding ties in society (unlike the libertarian right), while as conservatives they insist on tradition and the importance of morality (unlike the relativistic left). Although there are neoconservatives who have ventured into moral-issue thickets, most have preferred to turn their attention from moral questions of how society *should* work to practical ones of how it actually does.

When uncertainty about how to treat others is compounded by a greater number of others to treat, moral obligation under modern conditions becomes ever more complicated. Because they are free but at the same time unsure what it means to be obligated, modern liberal democrats need one another more but trust one another less. At a time when they have difficulty appreciating the past, the are called on to respect the needs of future generations. When they seem not to know how to preserve small families, they must strengthen large societies. As local communities disintegrate, a world community becomes more necessary than ever. Modern people need to care about the fates of strangers, yet do not even know how to treat their loved ones. Moral rules seem to evaporate the more they are needed. The paradox of modernity is that the more people depend on one another owing to an ever-widening circle of obligations, the fewer are the agreed-upon guidelines for organizing moral rules that can account for those obligations.

## THREE THEORIES OF MORAL REGULATION

The decline of traditional notions about moral obligation (rooted in notions of Christian charity or faith in the virtue of an upper class) is often, especially by those of conservative disposition, seen as the cause of modernity's unease. The distance between the need for a moral code and the inability of modern societies to find one becomes a problem so incapable of solution that the forces of modernity which produced it ought to be distrusted, if not condemned. From such a perspective, the things that make modern liberal democracies rich and stable will always lack meaning, while things that give people meaning will have no effect on what makes their societies rich and stable. It is a short step from such a conclusion to a premodern nostalgia for some kind of organic moral community that is alleged to have been destroyed by the forces of modernity (or to a postmodern "deconstructive" consciousness that is distrustful of the binding power of any moral rules, indeed of any rational and intellectual understanding of modernity and its dilemmas).

Traditional morality, however, is not the only morality. Precisely because the moral codes of yesterday constrained the potential of an individual's self-development, they cannot be effective guides for the social ties that make contemporary Western societies work. Economic growth and political democracy are, presumably, here to stay, and so long as they are, moral ideas that protect the few against the many or call on large numbers to stultify their human potential are neither likely to be effective nor justifiable. The problem is not that modernity undermines morality but that modernity displaces moral discourse into new—one is tempted to say modern—forms.

In looking to religion, philosophy, literature, or politics to find the rules of moral obligation, we look in the wrong place. There is an arena in which modern liberal democrats discuss problems of moral obligation, and often with surprising vigor. Liberal democracies have done away neither with moral codes nor with institutions and practices that embody them. The gap between the need for codes of moral obligation and the reality of societies that are confused about where these codes can be found is filled, however uncomfortably, by the contemporary social sciences. Even those social sciences that pride themselves on rigorous value neutrality, insisting that they are only describing how people do act, not advocating how they should, contain implicit (and often explicit) statements of what people's obligations to one another should be. (The reliance on numbers, statistical techniques, and algebraic reasoning so common in modern social science journals is not, in my opinion, an alternative to moral philosophy but its continuation, an extension of an effort that began with Hobbes and Hume to systematize moral reasoning, greatly aided, these days, by a host of new technologies.) Adam Smith, the founder of modern economics, was by trade a professor of moral philosophy. His followers, though themselves often unwilling to admit it, have the same calling.

For all their tendency toward jargon and abstraction, the ideas of social scientists remain the most common guideposts for moral obligation in a secular, nonliterary age. (Witness the popularity of Milton Friedman's ideas on television or on the best-seller lists, let alone the constant attempts of mass media to find academic experts to comment on one social trend after another.) Moreover, the social sciences contain not only a moral theory of how people should act toward one another, but also a large body of empirical information about how they actually do. As the Kinsey Reports first illustrated, and as every survey since demonstrates again, when all are interested in how others behave but few are secure that they are behaving correctly, social scientists are the closest we have to savants. The contemporary social sciences, despite occasional claims to the contrary, have not done especially well as predictive sciences. One reason they nonetheless continue to flourish is because they are a particularly modern form of secular religion, involving, in their own idiosyncratic language, fundamental questions of what kind of people we who are modern are.

If the social sciences are taken as the theater of moral debate in modern society, the problem facing modern liberal democrats is not a lack of moral guidelines, but a plentitude. Instead of having one source for their moral codes, they have at least three: economics, political science, and sociology. (I have not included anthropology in this list, not out of lack of respect—quite the contrary, actually—but because its focus on modern societies tends to be indirect.) Corresponding to each are three sets of institutions or practices charged with the maintenance of moral responsibility: those of the market, the state, and what was once called civil society. When the theory of each social science is linked to the practices it favors, quite distinct approaches to the problem of how to structure obligations to the self and others emerge.

Society works best, says the economic approach, when there exists a mechanism for enabling people to maximize rationally their self-interest. Yet it is an extremely rare economist who stops at the point of simply asserting the ethical benefits of self-interest; most continue on to make a point about obligations to others as well: because the pursuit of my self-interest contributes to some collective good—economic growth or some form of welfare optimality—my obligation to you is to do what is best for me. That way of thinking about obligations, responds the political approach, is naive. People are not, as James Madison once told us, angels, and given the chance to escape their obligations to others, they will. Therefore, some restraint on their desires is necessary; if obligations to the community as a whole are not regulated by government, they will not exist at all. Both your ideas are too pessimistic, answers the sociological approach. People have a remarkable capacity, given them by the societies they create, to develop their own rules of cooperation and solidarity. The trick is to find a way to trust them so that they will do it. (It ought to be clear that not all economists share the economic approach, not all political scientists the political, and so on; if the disciplinary names are used from time to time in what follows, then, it is for stylistic, not intellectual, reasons.)

In comparing these three approaches to moral obligation, one is tempted to judge them on the basis of whether individual rights of collective needs are given the highest priority. By that standard, the economic approach would be valued by those placing an ethical primacy on freedom above any other value, and structuralist sociology or conservative political theory would be valued by those who emphasize obligations to the group before individual rights. Yet this debate, which goes on endlessly in social theory, tends to obscure an important point: all three approaches, because they seek to address the condition of modern liberal democrats, are theories of regulation as well as theories of freedom. It is certainly true that modern people have obtained, and value highly, individual freedom. But they also have obtained, even if they find them more frustrating and often seem to value them less, complex societies and large-scale institutions that provide them with jobs, wealth, and goods. Modernity would be just as thoroughly destroyed by complete freedom as it would be by complete regimentation. Because the fear of anarchy is at least as strong as the fear of authority in the development of the social sciences, rationalizing the art of saying no is as important to their development as justifying the desire to say yes.

To be relevant to modern conditions of social complexity, any theory of moral obligation needs to develop an adequate explanation of why people must take into account the effects of their actions on one another. The economic approach, although emphasizing self-interest, does not deny such interdependence. Individual action is generally viewed as purposive, directed toward some goal (such as the creation of wealth) that is beyond the capacity of any one individual to produce independently. Milton Friedman, for example, points out that "specialization of function and division of labor" could not advance if productive units were households and if we relied only on barter. "In a modern society," he notes, "we have gone much farther." Modern economies force us to rely on cooperation, Friedman argues. "fundamentally, there are only two ways of co-ordinating the economic activities of millions. One is central direction involving the use of coercion—the technique of the army and of the modern totalitarian state. The other is voluntary cooperation of individual—the technique of the market place."[4]

Economists with a somewhat more complex theoretical approach, however, recognize that the market is anything but a voluntary mechanism for organizing obligations to others. As two other defenders of the market, Geoffrey Brennan and James Buchanan, put it, "Only the romantic anarchist thinks there is a 'natural harmony' among persons that will eliminate all conflict in the absence of rules. . . . rules define the private spaces within which each of us can carry on our own activities." One of the enormous advantages of relying on the market to structure obligations to others is that it is an extremely efficient mechanism for ensuring obedience to such rules. Gary Becker has expressed the point as follows: "Prices and other market instruments allocate the scarce resources within a society and thereby constrain the desires of participants and coordinate their actions. In the economic approach, these market instruments perform most, if not all, of the functions assigned to 'structure' in sociological theory."[5]

The traditional critique of structural theories in sociology—that they have an overdeveloped conception of man so constrained by society that he has little autonomy and discretion—would seem, from Becker's remarks, to apply as well to economic theories stressing individual choice. It actually applies more. Economic approaches to moral regulation, indeed most sets of moral assumptions based on the premises of rational choice or methodological individualism, tell me that I am free to find the best way to satisfy my obligations to others. If I fail to do so, however, there are always back-up mechanisms—prices in economics, constitutions in public-choice theory, mass society in the theories of sociologists' influences by economics—to ensure that I eventually will. There is one major difference between these back-up mechanisms and the emphasis on social structure and norms found in sociology: it becomes enormously difficult for me to negotiate between my individual needs and the constraints placed on them when the latter are hazy at best, hidden at worst. I am forced, so long as I operate by individualistic moral codes, to organize my obligations to others by having a conversation with an authority I cannot see. The invisible hand is clenched into an invisible fist.

The opposite problem exists with those theories of moral regulation that emphasize collective obligation over individual freedom. In some contemporary political science, as well as in the Durkheimian reification of society or various forms of structuralism, obligations to groups tend to weaken the moral character of individuals. When, for example, government collects my taxes and distributes the money to others, it not only assumes responsibilities that would otherwise be mine, but it also decides to whom my obligations ought to extend. I am, therefore, not obligated to real people living real lives around me; instead my obligation is to follow rules, the moral purpose of which is often lost to me. Because my obligations are abstract and impersonal, I am tempted to avoid them if I can, and the collective rule-making authority, knowing full well of my temptation, will rely on its coercive powers to prevent me from doing so. Little of this would matter if modern states were simply administrative substitutes for society. The suspicion that they are not lies at the heart of the difficulty facing the political approach to moral regulation. When I rely on the state to organize my obligations for me I can be sure that my fate will be likened to others', but I lose a good deal of control over deciding how. Because modern states, even liberal democratic ones, are not, as Benjamin Barber has emphasized, very good on talk, to the degree that I rely on government to structure my obligations to others I can see an authority with which I cannot converse.

Liberal democracies face discontents because they tend to rely on either individualistic moral codes associated with the market or collective moral codes associated with the state, yet neither set of codes can successfully address all the issues that confront society. Should older people support bond projects that will build schools that benefit younger couples? Should younger couples oppose increases in social security benefits that help older people? How do mothers best satisfy their obligations to their children—by staying home and nurturing them or by enhancing their own self-esteem in a career? Do we best serve the interests of those who come after us by saving parkland or by enhancing economic growth? Ought we to give to charity if the decisions of many others to give to charity might be used as an excuse to cut back government programs that have a charitable intent? Should the land of farmers be saved, even if one result would be to preserve inefficient farms? If we do not save inefficient farms, who should pay the costs, including suicides and mental illness, of farmers whose market inefficiencies stand in the way of economic progress? Should individuals maximize the collective good by paying a fair tax share or seek to maximize self-interest by cheating? Should government take responsibility for unemployment, even if the risk might be permanent dependence on the state? Will a firm contribute more to society by closing a branch in an area of high unemployment, thereby causing considerable suffering, and then opening another branch that creates new jobs somewhere else? Ought culture—ranging from opera and ballet to sports and rock music—to be produced and preserved based on the market principle of sufficient demand, thus risking the neglect of at-first unpopular works, or should we rely instead on government funding, thus risking bureaucratization and possible censorship? Should we, to improve the quality of our air and water, stop relying on what the economist Charles Schultze calls "indignant tirades about social responsibility" and instead charge firms for the right to pollute, thereby "harnessing the 'base' motive of material self-interest to promote the common good"?[6] Is the best solution to the drug crisis to legalize drugs or to try and enforce laws against their use? Some societies rely more on the market to answer these questions, while others rely on the state. Yet both kinds of answers, because they tend to remove from the process of moral decision-making a sense of the individual's personal stake in the fate of others, often have consequences that are surprisingly similar.

To illustrate, consider just one question: how should a society ensure that its members feel an obligation to work for their collective defense against external enemies? During the 1960s, Americans relied on government to ensure their national defense; a compulsory system of conscription, complete with stiff penalties for avoiding obligation, was used to raise the army that fought in Vietnam. Americans were never asked their opinion about whether the war in Vietnam was necessary for their survival as a nation. Political leaders, whose power lay in their command over the resources of government, simply drafted young men, often against their will, and asked them to die for goals that the leaders themselves were incapable of publicly articulating. No wonder avoidance of obligation, as a presidential commission later established, was the rule, not the exception, and the drafting of people created resentment and inefficiency within the armed services. Reliance on the coercive powers inherent in government for the defense of the society, premised on a distrust of people's own sense of mutual loyalty and obligation, simply encouraged large numbers of people to forget about obligation entirely.

In the aftermath of Vietnam, public thinking about military obligations swung full circle. "The significant fact of the past decade," Charles Moskos wrote in 1984, "has been the almost complete triumph of economic man over citizen soldier in military manpower policy."[7] The military began to follow the advice of Milton Friedman, Walter Oi, and other economists who had argued that creating a system of monetary incentives would ensure an efficient match between personnel and needs. Yet it turned out that rewarding self-interest also created problems of obligation to society. Those who were better off, and presumably therefore more obligated to everyone else, avoided obligation entirely, leaving the armed forces to those for whom service was the only available job. The market was, like the state, viewed as one of only two realistic methods of recruiting people to defend their society. Exactly like reliance on the state, however, use of the market, by creating a separate sphere of military life divorced from civilian life, also weakened the concept of obligation to one's country. Americans, in short, were expected to believe in the survival of their society, but the two methods used to strengthen that belief (no modern society would ever rely on a purely volunteer army) seemed to have the exact opposite effect.

Neither individualistic nor collectivist accounts of moral obligation, as this example shows, are without substantial problems. As Amy Gutmann has put it, using only slightly different terms, "Most conservative moralists set their moral sights too low, inviting blind obedience to authority; most liberal moralists set them too high, inviting disillusionment with morality." The limitations of both the market and the state as codes of moral obligation may help explain why political sentiment in modern society is characterized, as Albert Hirschman has argued, by "shifting involvements."[8] When obsessed with efficiency and cost, modern liberal democrats look for market solutions to their problems; when precisely those concerns with efficiency and cost lead to problems of inequality and injustice, they turn to the state. One course offers a solution to the problems the other creates, yet simultaneously creates problems that the other offers to solve.

Although there are obvious and important differences between the market and the state, they also share similar logics, which is why, as in the case of military recruitment, they often have similar results. Neither speaks well of obligations to other people simply as people, treating them instead as citizens or as opportunities. Neither puts its emphasis on the bonds that tie people together because they want to be tied together without regard for their immediate self-interest or for some external authority having the power to enforce those ties. Finally, neither wishes to recognize one of the very things that make liberal democrats modern: that people are capable of participating in the making of their own moral rules. Modern liberal democracies face so many frustrations because their economic and political accomplishments create potentials that the operating logic of their moral codes denies.

In the face of approaches to moral regulation that no longer seem as promising as they once were, it makes sense to try to find a way of thinking about obligations to others that puts into better balance individual needs and collective restraints. Such an approach—to the degree that it calls on individuals to rely on self-restraint, ties of solidarity with others, community norms, and voluntary altruism—finds its roots in a historic concern with civil society. What was once a three-sided debate has become, as markets and states have both expanded, two-sided. Sociology itself has contributed to this narrowing of options, because it has found in markets and states seeming solutions to its own moral ambivalence. A third way to think about moral obligation cannot overcome the discontents of modernity, but it can give to people a moral code that, unlike those stressing either individualism or collective obligations, enriches a decision-making process that too often leaves modern people feeling incomplete. To revive notions of moral agency associated with civil society is to begin the development of a language appropriate to addressing the paradox of modernity and to move us away from techniques that seek to displace moral obligations by treating them purely as questions of economic efficiency or public policy.

## THE WITHERING AWAY OF CIVIL SOCIETY

Learning how to behave in modern society is not only difficult, but there are also few trusted signposts to guide the way. No one can ever be sure in advance how behavior in one part of society will affect behavior in any other. So great is the potential for unanticipated consequences and perverse outcomes that any effort to regulate society directly seems cumbersome, if not utopian. The uncertainty of the moral choices we must make every day enhances the attraction of the market and the state. (Simultaneously, this uncertainty makes economics and political science seem far more realistic and in greater accord with modern people's understanding of human nature than sociology.)

The market responds to the sense that consequences are best managed when left unanticipated, while the state offers to take choice out of individual hands and give it to the experts. Thus, if housing and other costs are allowed to rise because there are no controls on the market, women must go to work to earn extra income, and the question of how they should treat their obligations to the next generation is decided, without anyone really seeming to decide it. Similarly, if fiduciary experts tell us we need to raise the social security tax to keep the fund from going bankrupt, our obligation to the previous generation is resolved for us, and we need neither praise nor blame ourselves for whatever results. To the degree that the market and the state offer relief to the complexity of social coordination, they promise the possibility of reconciling the paradox of modernity behind the scenes. Both make the whole business of moral regulation seem easier than, in fact, it is.

Because they are conspicuously less demanding, the state and the market eventually come to be viewed as the only forms of regulation that modern people have at their disposal, especially in the economic organization of their society. As the sociologist Peter Berger puts it, "Under modern conditions . . . , the options are sharply reduced. Specifically, the basic option is whether economic processes are to be governed by market mechanisms or by mechanisms of political allocation. In social-scientific parlance, this is the option between market economies and command economies."[9] Yet there did exist, at the very start of the modern period, an alternative to both the market and the state. That alternative was called "civil society," a term with so many different meanings and used in so many different contexts that, before it can be used again, some clarification is in order.

In the eighteenth century, thinkers who unleashed modern bourgeois consciousness, such as Adam Smith, Adam Ferguson, and David Hume, believed that civil society was the realm that protected the individual against the (monarchical or feudal) state. Society was, in their view, a precious—and precarious—creation. "It is here that a man is made to forget his weakness, his cares of safety, and his subsistence, and to act from those passions which make him discover his force," wrote Adam Ferguson. Modern people, taking advantage of what Ferguson called "the gift of society to man," were no longer at the mercy of nature.[10] All progress, not only in commercial affairs but also in the possibility of curbing the passions and creating mutual sympathy, hinged on the mutual interdependence that men could obtain by leaving a state of nature. When Durkheim wrote of society as a secular god, he was reiterating a notion that found its first expression in the Scottish Enlightenment.

Like any god, society could be demanding. In return for the benefits it offers, it imposes obligations. "The general obligation," Hume wrote, "which binds us to government, is the interest and necessities of society; and this obligation is very strong." Therefore, in addition to our "natural" obligations, such as loving children, Hume wrote of justice and morality, obligations undertaken "from a sense of obligation when we consider the necessities of human society."[11] But how, if we are to be as secular as Hume was on his death bed, do we come to appreciate these necessities? The hopes of the theorists of civil society lay in a rational understanding of what made society work—what today we would call social science. In the writings of Montesquieu, for example, who has been called "the first moralist with a sociological perspective," we witness the idea that a science of society can help use modern intelligence to organize our obligations to others. The thinkers of the Scottish Enlightenment, who were deeply influenced by Montesquieu, were confident that "constant and universal principles of human nature," as Hume called them, would make possible a modern moral order:

> The mutual dependence of men is so great in all societies that scarce any human action is entirely complete in itself, or is performed without some reference to the actions of others, which are requisite to make it answer fully the intention of the agent. . . . In proportion as men extend their dealings and render their intercourse with others more complicated, they always comprehend in their schemes of life a greater variety of voluntary actions which they expect from the proper motives to cooperate with their own.[12]

For the thinkers of the Scottish Enlightenment, civil society was coterminous with what today we call "the private sector," a realm of personal autonomy in which people could be free to develop their own methods of moral accounting. The ethical superiority of what would come to be called capitalism was due to the moral energy unleashed by the idea that people are responsible for their own actions. Yet it was also clear to these thinkers that to the degree that capitalism encouraged pure selfishness, it ran the risk of destroying this very moral potential. The new economic order being created during the late eighteenth and early nineteenth centuries strengthened individual freedom, but it also made obvious the degree to which people in civil society were interdependent. Hegel, for example, like Ferguson and Hume, argued that the selfish energies unleashed by the market create "a system of complete interdependence, wherein the livelihood, happiness, and legal status of one man is interwoven with the livelihood, happiness, and rights of all."[13] Freedom, from this point of view, did not exist in opposition to society; rather, civil society, by forcing people to recognize the reality of their interdependence, made freedom possible. Freedom was a social, not a natural, phenomenon, something that existed only through the recognition, rather than the denial, of obligations to others.

Given this understanding of the relationship between civil society and moral potential, the development of capitalism through the nineteenth century—although seen by most theorists, including Marx, as a progressive force—also contained the potential to destroy the very civil society it helped create. In the eighteenth century the greatest threat to civil society was the old order symbolized by the state, against which both liberalism and the market were allied. By the mid-nineteenth century the old order was passing, and the moral autonomy of civil society began to be threatened from a new direction. Because the market, capitalism's greatest achievement, placed a monetary value on all things, it increasingly came to be viewed as undermining the ability of people to find and protect an authenticity that was uniquely their own. If an eighteenth-century theorist of civil society were to have appeared in the middle of the nineteenth century looking for a place where individuals could create their own moral rules, he would have found it neither in the private sector nor in the public.

In the nineteenth century, as a result of these developments, the meaning of civil society began to change. No longer a dualistic conception, it became tripartite, standing between the market and the state, embodying neither the self-interest of the one nor the coercive authority of the other. This idea was already implicit, if in somewhat different form, in Hegel, who viewed civil society as a place of transition from the realm of particularism to that of the universal. Other thinkers found in civil society an alternative to both markets and states. Alexis de Tocqueville, for example, anxious to guard against the centralizing power of the state, did not look to "industrial callings" (which, he felt, might reproduce the aristocracy of old) but instead paid attention to ideas of voluntarism and localism. Late-nineteenth-century liberals, wanting to reject laissez-faire but suspicious of governmental collectivism, discovered in pluralism a modified notion of civil society. Certain Marxists, especially Antonio Gramsci, were attracted to the idea of civil society as an alternative to Leninism. And the classical thinkers in the sociological tradition all used civil society as the focal point of their critique of modernity. Emile Durkheim and Max Weber were both strongly influenced by Hegel, and the notion of civil society lay also at the heart of Tönnies's notion of *Gemeinschaft,* Simmel's fear of the influence of large numbers, Cooley's conception of the primary group, the emphasis on local communities in the Chicago school sociology of Robert A. Park, and the concept of a lifeworld developed by Jürgen Habermas. If there is one underlying theme that unifies the themes in sociology that never developed the resiliency of concepts such as the market or the state—such as organic solidarity, the collective conscience, the generalized other, sociability, and the gift relationship—it would be the idea of civil society.

Although civil society seems to have all but disappeared from the modern political imagination, it has in recent years begun once again to attract attention. No doubt the reason for this appeal is an increasing feeling that modernity's two greatest social instruments, the market and the state, have become more problematic. Under extreme conditions of state oppression there can be no question of the power of the ideal of civil society. In Eastern Europe especially, where, in the words of Claude Lefort, "the new society is thought to make the formation of classes or groups with antagonistic interests impossible,"[14] the pluralistic vision associated with civil society seeks to protect an autonomous social realm against political authority. Georg Konrad suggests that "civil society is the antitheses of military society" and that "antipolitics"—his name for morality—"is the ethos of civil society." Adam Michnik writes of solidarity in Poland:

> The essence of the spontaneously growing Independent and Self-governing Labor Union Solidarity lay in the restoration of social ties, self-organization aimed at guaranteeing the defense of labor, civil, and national rights. For the first time in the history of communist rule in Poland "civil society" was being restored, and it was reaching a compromise with the state.[15]

One need not equate the oppression that exists in Eastern Europe with the imperfections of capitalism in the West to argue that the tripartite theory of civil society can serve as an alternative both to the market under capitalism and to the state under socialism. Contemporary capitalist societies bear little resemblance to the moral world of the Scottish Enlightenment. Composed more of bureaucratic firms than self-motivated individuals, these societies rationalize away personal responsibility rather than extend its realm. Instead of broadening the recognition of mutual interdependence, they deny it, arguing that capitalism is not the product of society but the result of a natural order determined by animalistic instincts. Rather than understanding that economic self-interest is made possible only because obligations are part of a preexisting moral order, they increasingly organize the moral order by the same principles that organize the economy. The more extensively capitalism develops, the more the social world that makes capitalism possible comes to be taken for granted rather than viewed as a gift toward which the utmost care ought to be given. Societies organized by the market need a theory of civil society as much as societies organized by the state, or else their social ecologies will become as damaged as their natural ecologies.

But given the confused meanings associated with the term, how ought civil society be understood? There is certainly a temptation, when faced with the limits of the market and the state as moral codes, to reject both in favor of some preexisting moral community that may never have existed or, if it did exist, was so oppressive that its members thought only of escape. That meaning of civil society is emphatically not the one discussed here. Not only is it unrealistic to expect that modern liberal democracies will somehow stop relying on the market and the state, but it is also unfair to ask modern liberal democrats to do without these organizing structures. The market, for all its problems, does promote individual choice, thereby enabling people to act as the creators of their own moral rules. The state, no matter how critical one may be of its authority, not only creates a certain level of security without which modern life would be impossible but, at the Scandinavian societies show, also promotes equality and generally creates a better life for most. Markets and states are here to stay, and it is not my intention to say otherwise.

Moreover, it is anything but axiomatic that the morality of civil society is more "moral" than that of the market or the state. For Hegel, the family was a crucial component of civil society, yet when husbands beat wives and parents abuse children, state intervention ought to take precedence over the sanctity of the family. Theorists of civil society have often put their faith in community, yet when communities practice racial segregation or close their borders, it would be difficult to deny that the market's emphasis on openness is preferable. Even when relations in civil society are based on reciprocity and altruism, they can satisfy obligations to immediate group members to the exclusion of obligations to strangers and hypothetical others. We became modern, in short, for a reason.

There is, however, another meaning to civil society that, instead of embodying some nostalgic hope for a passing order, is more relevant than ever to modern liberal democrats. The themes so important to Ferguson, Hume, and Smith, which later came to be embodied in some of the sociologists influenced by American pragmatism (especially George Herbert Mead), were those of autonomy and responsibility. We learn how to act toward others because civil society brings us into contact with people in such a way that we are forced to recognize our dependence on them. We ourselves have to take responsibility for our moral obligations, and we do so through this gift called society that we make for ourselves. What makes us modern, in short, is that we are capable of acting as our own moral agents. If modernity means a withering away of such institutions as the tight-knit family and the local community that once taught the moral rules of interdependence, modern people must simply work harder to find such rules for themselves. If we do not, then we sacrifice what is modern about us—often, and ironically, in the name of modernity itself.

Modernity's paradox is a paradox indeed. It cannot be resolved either by welcoming markets and states enthusiastically or by rejecting them completely. The question facing modern liberal democrats is whether they can live in societies organized by states and markets yet also recognize (more than they have) that reliance on states and markets does not absolve them of responsibility for their obligations to others—on the contrary, this responsibility becomes all the more necessary. Such a recognition can come, as it did in the days of Ferguson and Hume, only when those whose business is the understanding of society remind liberal democrats of their obligation to protect the social order that makes their freedom possible.

## NOTES

1. William Sullivan, *Reconstructing Public Philosophy* (Berkeley: University of California Press, 1982), 95.
2. Lionel Trilling, *The Liberal Imagination* (New York: Viking Press, 1950), 222.
3. E. M. Forster, *Howard's End* (London: Penguin Books, 1971), 179.
4. Milton Friedman, *Capitalism and Freedom* (Chicago: University of Chicago Press, 1962), 13.
5. Gary Becker, *The Economic Approach to Human Behavior* (Chicago: University of Chicago Press, 1976), 5.
6. Charles Schultze, *The Public Use of Private Interest* (Washington, D.C.: Brookings Institution, 1977), 18.
7. Charles C. Moskos, "Citizen Soldier Versus Economic Man," in *The Social Fabric,* ed. James F. Short Jr. (Beverly Hills, Calif.: Sage, 1986), 245.
8. Albert O. Hirschman, *Shifing Involvements: Private Interest and Public Action* (Princeton, N.J.: Princeton University Press, 1982).
9. Peter L. Berger, *The Capitalist Revolution: Fifty Propositions about Prosperity, Equality, and Liberty* (New York: Basic Books, 1986), 20.
10. Adam Ferguson, *An Essay on the History of Civil Society* (Philadelphia: Wm. Fry, 1819), 32.
11. Quoted in Michael Ignatieff, *The Needs of Strangers: An Essay on Privacy, Solidarity, and the Politics of Being Human* (New York: Penguin Books, 1985), 92.
12. David Hume, "An Inquiry Concerning Human Understanding" in *Essays: Moral Political and Literary,* ed. T. H. Greene and T. H. Grose (London: Longmans, Green, 1875), 2:72–73.
13. T. M. Knox, *Hegel's Philosophy of Right* (New York: Oxford University Press, 1967), 123.
14. Claude Lefort, *The Political Forms of Modern Society* (Cambridge, Mass.: MIT Press, 1986), 285.
15. Adam Michnik, *Letters from Prison and Other Essays* (Berkeley: University of California Press, 1985), 124.

# 4

# The Good Society: We Live through Our Institutions

*Robert N. Bellah*

In the last few years, the world democratic revolution that began in the seventeenth and eighteenth centuries in Europe and America, having suffered severe setbacks earlier in the twentieth century, entered a new stage of intensity in many parts of the world: in Eastern Europe, the Soviet Union, South Africa, and elsewhere. This new stage of political development will have significant repercussions in the United States, even though Americans' initial reaction was more or less to stay home and watch what was happening on television. In ways we could not have imagined when we began this work, it has turned out to be concerned with the shape of a new democratic transformation in the United States as part of the world democratic revolution. But if such a transformation is to be successful here, we must understand the peculiar obstacles we face—apparently less daunting than the obstacles faced, for example, in the Soviet Union, yet in their own way quite daunting enough.

Democracy requires a degree of trust that we often take for granted. In a democratic society citizens must be able to trust if they are defeated by opponents in a political struggle, for example, they will not be killed, and that if they win an election, their opponents will let them take power peacefully.[1] Building that kind of trust in the nations of Central and Eastern Europe will not be easy: it is much harder to build trust than to lose it. But that is our problem in the United States: we have begun to lose trust in our institutions—not yet, fortunately, in the electoral transfer of political power, though cynicism about elections is growing. The heritage of trust that has been the basis of our stable democracy is eroding.[2] This trust is not a nonrenewable resource, but it is much easier to destroy than to renew. That is why our problems are ominous in their implications for our future.

## INSTITUTIONS AS PATTERNED WAYS OF LIVING TOGETHER

Walking in any American city today, one participates in a ritual that perfectly expresses the difficulty of being a good person in the absence of a good society. In the midst of affluence, perhaps with a guilty sense of the absurd wastefulness of the expensive meal, new blouse, or electronic gadget that has brought us to town, we pass homeless men or, often, women with children asking money for food and shelter. Whether we give or withhold our spare change, we know that neither personal choice is the right one. We may experience the difficulty of helping the plight of the homeless people as a painful individual moral dilemma, but the difficulty actually comes from failures of the larger institutions on which our common life depends.

The problem of homelessness, like many of our problems, was created by social choices. The market-driven conversion of single-room-occupancy hotels into upscale tourist accommodations, government urban-renewal projects that revitalized downtowns while driving up rents and reducing housing for the poor, economic changes that "deinstitutionalization" of the mentally ill and reduced funding of local community health programs, have together created the crisis of homelessness. But with this issue, as with many others, we tend to feel helpless to shape the institutional order that made these choices meaningful—or meaningless.[3]

In *Habits of the Heart* we asked, "How ought we to live? How do we think about how to live?" and we focused on cultural and personal resources for thinking about our common life.[4] In *The Good Society* we are concerned with the same questions, but we are now focusing on the patterned ways Americans have developed for living together, what sociologists call institutions.[5] In a world undergoing enormous technological, economic, and political change, many of the established ways we have of living together are not working well. Some of them are not working as they were intended to. Others are having alarming and unintended consequences that affect not only people but the natural environment.

It is hardly surprising that institutions established at different times and under different conditions might need to be reformed from time to time. Some of our institutions date from the eighteenth century, when the United States was a small country with a largely agricultural economy, far from, and well insulated against, the major centers of world power. Other American institutions date from the postwar years when the United States was embarking on a gigantic militant effort to save the "free world" from Communist oppression—and indeed some of the institutions established then are serving us less well than some of those that date from the eighteenth century.

It is tempting to think that the problems that we face today, from the homeless in our streets and poverty in the Third World to ozone depletion and the greenhouse effect, can be solved by technology or technical expertise alone.

But even to begin to solve these daunting problems, let alone problems of emptiness and meaninglessness in our personal lives, requires that we greatly improve our capacity to think about our institutions. We need to understand how much of our lives is lived in and through institutions, and how better institutions are essential if we are to lead better lives. In surveying our present institutions we need to discern what is healthy in them and what needs to be altered, particularly where we have begun to destroy the nonrenewable natural and nearly nonrenewable human resources upon which all our institutions depend.

Our present situation requires an unprecedented increase in the ability to attend to new possibilities, moral as well as technical, and to put the new technical possibilities in a moral context. The challenges often seem overwhelming, but there are possibilities for an immense enhancement of our lives, individual and collective, an enhancement based on a significant moral advance. One of the greatest challenges, especially for individualistic Americans, is to understand what institutions are—how we form them and how they in turn form us—and to imagine that we can actually alter them for the better.

*Habits of the Heart* offered a portrait of middle-class Americans and of the cultural resources they have for making sense of their society and their lives. We described a language of individualistic achievement and self-fulfillment that often seems to make it difficult for people to sustain their commitments to others, either in intimate relationships or in the public sphere. We held up other traditions, biblical and civic republican, that had a better grasp on the truth that the individual is realized only in and through community; but we showed that contemporary Americans have difficulty understanding those traditions today or seeing how they apply to their lives. We called for a deeper understanding of the moral ecology that sustains the lives of all of us, even when we think we are making it on our own. "Moral ecology" is only another way of speaking of healthy institutions, yet the culture of individualism makes the very idea of institutions inaccessible to many of us. We Americans tend to think that all we need are energetic individuals and a few impersonal rules to guarantee fairness; anything more is not only superfluous but dangerous—corrupt, oppressive, or both. As we showed in *Habits of the Heart*, Americans often think of individuals pitted against institutions.[6] It is hard for us to think of institutions as affording the necessary context within which we become individuals; of institutions as not just restraining but enabling us; of institutions not as an arena of hostility within which our character is formed. This is in part because some of our institutions have indeed grown out of control and beyond our comprehension. But the answer is to change them, for it is illusory to imagine that we can escape them.

The problems with which *Habits of the Heart* and *The Good Society* are concerned are rooted in changes that began a long while ago. These changes have been preoccupying not only social theorists but religious and political leaders for several centuries, ever since the emergence of modern science and the modern economy made it clear that a radically new and rapidly changing kind of society was coming into existence. Recently one way of posing the argument about how to deal with the problems emerging in this new form of society has been to pit philosophical liberals against communitarians; *Habits of the Heart* was often termed communitarian.[7]

If philosophical liberals are those who believe that all our problems can be solved by autonomous individuals, a market, economy, and a procedural state, whereas communitarians believe that more substantive ethical identities and a more active participation in a democratic polity are necessary for the functioning of any decent society, then we are indeed communitarians. But we feel that the word "communitarian" runs the risk of being misunderstood if one imagines that only face-to-face groups—families, congregations, neighborhoods—are communities and that communitarians are opposed to the state, the economy, and all the larger structures that so largely dominate our life today. Indeed, it is our sense that only greater citizen participation in the large structures of the economy and the state will enable us to surmount the deepening problems of contemporary social life.[8] In order not to be misunderstood, we are reaching back into earlier twentieth century for terminology that will put the issues in terms that are helpful.

## IS THE GREAT SOCIETY A GOOD SOCIETY?

In 1915 Graham Wallas published a book entitled *The Great Society*,[9] which had an enormous influence, notably on two major American public philosophers, John Dewey and Walter Lippmann. By "the Great Society" Wallas meant the "invisible environment" of communication and commerce that was linking the whole modern world in ever more coercive ways but was almost beyond human capacity to understand, much less to manage. For Wallas the great society was a neutral, indeed rather frightening, term for modernity. In 1927 John Dewey, in *The Public and Its Problems,* posed the central problem of modernity as he saw it as follows: "Our concern at this time is to state how it is that the machine age in developing the Great Society has invaded and partially disintegrated the small communities of former times without generating a Great Community."[10] Dewey had no nostalgia for the old small communities, too enthralled by custom as they were to release the energies of individual and social growth. "The Great Community," a term Dewey probably derived from Josiah Royce, who published a book by that title in 1916,[11] was not to be a mere revival of the old small communities, what the Germans call *Gemeinschaft,* but something new that would infuse public spirit and public consciousness into those now largely invisible structures characterized by the Great Society. For Dewey, hope lay in the enlargement and enhancement of democracy throughout our institutional life.

It was that great twentieth-century advocate of political realism Walter Lippmann who used another contrast term to "the Great Society," namely "the Good Society," which was the title of a book he published in 1937.[12] Because "community" can be misunderstood if interpreted too narrowly, we have adopted Lippmann's term and his title for our own book. Lippmann kept reminding Americans of his day that they were living through a vast period of global transformation, the greatest since the coming of settled agriculture. For several centuries now the great society, particularly in the form of the division of labor and the exchange economy, but even, ironically, through the increased level of international violence, has been pushing more and more of human society toward an interconnected planetary whole. The process has been anything but smooth, causing repeated crises of moral meaning and solidarity, as well as breakdowns into extraordinary violence and anger, as the units and conditions of life develop unevenly.

The same process has given rise to possibilities unique to human history thus far. As Lippmann put it in *The Good Society:* "Until the division of labor had begun to make men dependent upon the free collaboration of other men, the worldly policy was to be predatory. The claims of the spirit were otherworldly." The news, according to Lippmann, is that with the coming of interdependence and technological abundance "the vista was opened at the end of which men could see the possibility of the Good Society on this earth. At long last," he continued, "the ancient schism between the world and the spirit, between self-interest and disinterestedness, was potentially closed, and a wholly new orientation of the human race became theoretically conceivable and, in fact, necessary."[13]

The necessity of the new orientation became clearest, Lippmann thought, in modern wars. These are more and more not battles between aliens but "internecine" struggles "within one closely related, intricately interdependent community." According to Lippmann, "Modern war tears apart huge populations which have become dependent upon one another for the maintenance of their standard of life—in some degree for the maintenance of life itself."[14] Certainly the development of nuclear weaponry has only strengthened Lippmann's argument.

Lippmann proposed that the reason war-mongering now elicits such strong moral sanction is that war makes less and less rational, practical sense as an instrument of long-term national self-interest. The great moral aspiration toward a global order of security based on equity increasingly seemed to him, a strategic realist, to be demanded by any sober calculation of interests. The good society emerges not only as an idealistic project but as the long-term practical necessity of the new era.

We shall draw from a number of observers and analysts of the modern world besides John Dewey and Walter Lippmann, but it is their spirit that we wish to emulate. Both were critical of much they saw around them. Neither was nostalgic for a vanished past. Both were moderately hopeful that Americans could meet the enormous challenges facing them, the challenge of transforming the great society into the good society. But as we look at the reality of our society today we can see that though we can learn from their suggestions about reforming our institutions, they provide only the beginnings for the constructive task that lies ahead. We shall build on the work of these and other predecessors, but we shall inevitably push beyond them into areas that they did not explore.

At this point, the reader may wish to know exactly what we mean by "the good society," how we would define it, how we would recognize it if we saw it. Some readers may also well ask, "A good society for whom?" or "A good society in whose opinion?" Even though we try to sketch out some of its features, our ultimate answer is that there is no pattern of a good society that we or anyone else can simply discern and then expect people to conform to. It is central to our very notion of a good society that it is an open quest, actively involving all its members. As Dennis McCann has put it, the common good is the pursuit of the good in common.[15]

As we understand it, pluralism does not contradict the idea of a good society, for the latter would be one that would allow a wide scope for diversity and would draw on resources from its pluralistic communities in discerning those things that are necessarily matters of the good of all. Some of the ideas we have just found in Dewey and Lippmann are part of our definition: a widening of democratic participation and the accountability of institutions; an interdependent prosperity that counteracts predatory relations among individuals and groups and enables everyone to participate in the goods of society; a peaceful world, without which the search for a good society is surely illusory.

Freedom, for most Americans, is an essential ingredient in a definition of a good society, and one we affirm. But, as with all the great moral terms, we need to probe more deeply to find out what "freedom" really means. For many of us, "freedom" still has the old meaning of the right to be left alone. In an older America, where one could spend most of one's life on one's own homestead, that kind of notion had a certain plausibility. But in the great society of today, freedom cannot mean simply getting away from other people. Freedom must exist within and be guaranteed by institutions, and must include the right to participate in the economic and political decisions that affect our lives. Indeed, the great classic criteria of a good society—peace, prosperity, freedom, justice—all depend today on a new experiment in democracy, a newly extended and enhanced set of democratic institutions, within which we citizens can better discern what we really want and what we ought to want to sustain a good life on this planet for ourselves and the generations to come.

## WHY AMERICANS HAVE TROUBLE UNDERSTANDING INSTITUTIONS

We need to understand why the very idea of institutions is so intimidating to Americans and why it is so important to overcome this anxiety and think creatively about institutions. In its formal sociological definition, an institution is a pattern of expected action of individuals or groups enforced by social sanctions, both positive and negative. For example, institutions may be such simple customs as the confirming handshake in a social situation,[16] where the refusal to respond to an outstretched hand might cause embarrassment and some need for an explanation; or they may be highly formal institutions such as taxation upon which social services depend, where refusal to pay may be punished by fines and imprisonment. Institutions always have a moral element. A handshake is a sign of social solidarity, at least a minimal recognition of the personhood of the other. Taxation, especially in a democracy, is for the purpose of attaining agreed-upon common aims and is supposed to be fair in its assessment.

Individualistic Americans fear that institutions impinge on their freedom. In the case of the handshake this impingement may give rise only to a very occasional qualm. More powerful institutions seem more directly to threaten our freedom. For just this reason, the classical liberal view held that institutions ought to be as far as possible neutral mechanisms for individuals to use to attain their separate ends—a view so persuasive that most Americans take it for granted, sharing with liberalism the fear that institutions that are not properly limited and neutral may be oppressive. This belief leads us to think of institutions as efficient or inefficient mechanisms, like the Department of Motor Vehicles, that we learn to use for our own purposes, or as malevolent "bureaucracies" that may crush us under their impersonal wheels. It is not that either of these beliefs is wholly mistaken. In modern society we do indeed need to learn how to manipulate institutions. And all of us, particularly but not only the poor and the powerless, find ourselves at the mercy of institutions that control our lives in ways we often do not fully understand. Yet if this is our only conception of institutions we have a very impoverished idea of our common life, an idea that cannot effectively help us deal with our problems but only worsens them.

There is an ambiguity about the idea of institutions that is hard to avoid but that we will try to be clear about. Institutions are normative patterns embedded in and enforced by laws and mores (informal customs and practices). In common usage the term is also used to apply to concrete organizations. Organizations certainly loom large in our lives, but if we think only of organizations and not of institutions we may greatly oversimplify our problems. The corporation is a central institution in American life. As an institution it is a particular historical pattern of rights and duties, of powers and responsibilities, that make it a major force in our lives. Individual corporations are organizations that operate within the legal and other patterns that define what a corporation is. If we do not distinguish between institution and organization, we may think that our only problem with corporations is to make them more efficient or more responsible. But there are problems with how corporations are institutionalized in American society, with the underlying pattern of power and responsibility, and we cannot solve the problems of corporate life simply by improving individual organizations: we have to reform the institution itself. If we confuse organizations and institutions, then when we believe we are being treated unfairly we may retreat into private life or flee from one organization to another—a different company or a new marriage—hoping that the next one will treat us better. But changes in how organizations are conceived, changes in the norms by which they operate—institutional changes—are the only way to get at the source of our difficulties.

The same logic applies throughout our social life. There are certainly better families and worse, happier and more caring families and ones that are less so. But the very way Americans institutionalize family life, the very pressures and temptations that American society presents to all families, are themselves the source of serious problems, so just asking individual families to behave better, important though that is, will not get to the root of the difficulties. Indeed, there is a kind of reductionism in our traditional way of thinking about society. We think in the first place that the problem is probably with the individual; if not, then with the organization. This pattern of thinking hides from us the power of institutions and their great possibilities for good and for evil.

What is missing in this American view of society? Just the idea that in our life with other people we are engaged continuously, through words and actions, in creating and re-creating the institutions that make that life possible. This process is never neutral but is always ethical and political, since institutions (even such an intimate institution as the family) live or die by ideas of right and wrong and conceptions of the good. Conversely, while we in concert with others create institutions, they also create us: they educate us and form us—especially through the socially enacted metaphors they give us, metaphors that provide normative interpretations of situations and actions. The metaphors may be appropriate or inappropriate, but they are inescapable. A local congregation may think of itself as a "family." A corporate CEO may speak of management and workers all being "team players." Democracy itself is not so much a specific institution as a metaphoric way of thinking about an aspect of many institutions.

In short, we are not self-created atoms manipulating or being manipulated by objective institutions. We form institutions and they form us every time we engage in a conversation that matters, and certainly every time we act as parent or child, student or teacher, citizen or official, in each case calling on models and metaphors for the rightness and wrongness of action. Institutions are not only constraining but also enabling. They are the substantial forms through which we understand our own identity of others as we seek cooperatively to achieve a decent society.

The idea that institutions are objective mechanisms that are essentially separate from the lives of the individuals who inhabit them is an ideology that exacts a high moral and political price. The classical liberal view has elevated one virtue, autonomy, as almost the only good, but has failed to recognize that even autonomy depends on a particular kind of institutional structure and is not an escape from institutions altogether. By imagining a world in which individuals can be autonomous not only from institutions but from each other, it has forgotten that autonomy, valuable as it is in itself, is only one virtue among others and that without such virtues as responsibility and care, which can be exercised only through institutions, autonomy itself becomes, as we argued in *Habits of the Heart,* an empty form without substance.

## DEMOCRACY MEANS PAYING ATTENTION

What the metropolis of the American Century has lacked above all was sufficient attention to the whole. Its legacy is environmental damage, social neglect of the least advantaged, and restricted possibilities for all. What is needed for the twenty-first century is not only more and different infrastructure but the sort of "focal structure" that government, the "third sector," and public-private partnerships of business and not-for-profit institutions together can provide. The task of these focal structures is to enhance the capacity of metropolitan citizens and institutions to promote the quality of life for all citizens.

The popularity of urban neighborhood development in the 1970s was strengthened in the 1980s by public-private partnerships, which helped to revive many core cities, though we cannot forget that most of these initiatives benefited the well-to-do and that the position of the urban poor has substantially declined. Today, environmental politics offers an inclusive rallying point that brings together concerns for social justice, economic viability, and environmental integrity. Ecological sustainability as a purpose converges with the desire for safe, diverse, and economically viable communities. As the case of Los Angeles shows, these purposes join in the effort to reverse the indiscriminate sprawl of the postwar decades and aim instead toward more bounded metropolitan environments. The enlargement of our capacity for this will be the office of the democratic public. The public lives through those institutions that cultivate a constituency of conscience and vision. This constituency is the creative matrix from which city, state, and national leaders can arise; its task: to make the interdependency of modern life locally comprehensible so that responsible action is possible.[19]

Americans have pushed the logic of exploitation about as far as it can go. It seems to lead not only to failure at the highest levels, where the pressure for short-term payoff in business and government destroys the capacity for thinking ahead, whether in the nation or in the metropolis, but also to personal and familial breakdown in the lives of our citizens. We have repeatedly suggested the need for a new paradigm, which we can now call the pattern of cultivation. This pattern would not mean a return to the settlement forms of the nineteenth century, but it would be the attempt to find, in today's circumstances, a social and environmental balance, a recovery of meaning and purpose in our lives together, giving attention to the natural and cultural endowment we want to hand down to our children and grandchildren, and avoiding the distractions that have confused us in the past. Again, what has for a long time been dismissed as idealism seems to be the only realism possible today.

But how can we pay attention to all of the problems that beset us? Even the experts feel more comfortable if they can distract themselves by holding on to simple measures of the situation like GNP or comparative military strength. Fortunately, military dangers have lessened—we can expect continuing conflict in the Third World, but hardly of the magnitude of the Soviet military threat. But it would be foolish to replace a military-political fear of the Soviet Union with an economic fear. Indeed, an obsession with competitiveness against Japan or Western Europe can be just as great a distraction from reality as an obsession with communism. The whole argument about whether the United States is in decline or is as strong as ever is also beside the point and fundamentally distracting. Clearly we are headed toward a future in which a number of highly successful national or regional economies will coexist; rather than worrying about where the United States is in the hierarchy, we should be worrying about creating a humane economy that is adequate to our real purposes, and a healthy international economy that operates for the good of all peoples. As Vaclav Havel has been saying, we need to replace a politics of fear with a politics of trust. Trust gives us space for attention, even when what we have to attend to seems baffling, whereas fear drives us to seek distraction, the kind of reassurance that only big numbers can provide.

Money and power are necessary as means, but they are not the proper measures of a good society and a good world. We need to talk about our problems and our future with a richer vocabulary than the indices that measure markets and defense systems alone. Words like "attention" and "distraction," "cultivation" and "exploitation" may begin to encourage conversations in which we can define our priorities, our needs to strengthen existing institutions, and our needs to create new ones.

We need experts and expert opinions, and experts can certainly help us to think about the important issues. But democracy is not the rule of experts. It is basic to the education of citizens that they learn how to evaluate expert opinion. Much of high-school and college education actually does give students help in this matter, but more could be done if it was acknowledged as a central task of education. In any event, evaluating the opinions of experts is only the beginning and not finally the most important problem. Weighing the moral implications of different options is what is fundamental. Here the citizen who has learned to pay attention in the family and the local community can generalize to larger issues. When the family is a school of democracy and the school is a democratic community, then the beginnings of such wisdom have already been learned.

Our institutions are badly functioning and in need of repair or drastic reform, so that if they are to support a pattern of cultivation rather than one of exploitation, we must change them by altering their legal status and the way we think about them, for institutional change involves both laws and mores. More than money and power, these need to be at the center of our attention.

## ATTENTION AND DISTRACTION

We took up the idea of attention as initially a matter of individual psychology. As we followed it, we moved to ever larger social and cultural circles: from self-cultivation, to concern for the family, to our local communities and the vast cities most of us live in, to our national life and life in the world. Attention and distraction, the disturbance and destruction of attention, occurred at every point. Everywhere attention had to do not only with conscious awareness but with the cultivation of human possibilities and purposes, whereas distraction was a response to fear and exhaustion, leading to shallow escapism in some circumstances, to defensive efforts to dominate and control through power or money in others.

Attention and distraction are not merely descriptive but normative terms. Giving attention to a crying infant is something good; working at McDonald's in order to have the money to buy designer jeans rather than studying does little to develop a fuller life or the capacity to contribute to society. Attending and caring or caring for are closely related. Because we have let too much of our lives be determined by processes "going on over our heads," we have settled for easy measures that have distracted us from what needs to be attended to and cared for. One way of defining democracy would be to call it a political system in which people actively attend to what is significant.

It is doubtful whether attention has priority in America today. Much of our current politics seems to be designed to distract us from what is important and seduce us into fantasies that all is well. Worse, these politics offer solutions that only increase our distraction—as, for example, when the only answer to transportation problems is to increase the number of lanes on the freeways, or, more basically, when "growth" is offered as a universal panacea with no attention to what kind of growth or with what consequences. Attending means to concern ourselves with the larger meaning of things in the longer run, rather than with short-term payoffs. The pursuit of immediate pleasure, or the promise of immediate pleasure, is the essence of distraction. A good society is one in which attention takes precedence over distraction.

We have surveyed the problems of many of our large-scale institutions, but in this essay we have returned to the family to illustrate some of the central issues we are concerned with. Among these is what the psychologist Erik Erikson called "generativity," the care that one generation gives to the next.[20] Generativity is a virtue that Erikson initially situates in the concern of parents for children, but he extends it far beyond the family so that it becomes the virtue by means of which we care for all persons and things we have been entrusted with. With what kind of society will we endow our children and our children's children, what kind of world, what kind of natural environment? By focusing on our immediate well-being (are you better off now than you were four years ago?), and by being obsessively concerned with improving our relative income and consumption, we have forgotten that the meaning of life derives not so much from what we have as from what kind of person we are and how we have shaped our lives toward future ends that are good in themselves.

The end of the cold war, and of what may come to be called the Seventy-five Years' War of the Twentieth Century, of which the cold war was the final phase, gives us a chance to step back from these obsessions and think about the future which, perhaps, we unconsciously doubted we had. Now that the threat of the mushroom cloud is receding, we may see that many things we have been ignoring for too long need our attention.

The major problems that come to light require the virtue of generativity to solve—indeed, a politics of generativity. The most obvious problem is the perilous neglect of our own children in America: levels of infant mortality, child poverty, and inadequate schooling put us at or near the bottom in these respects among industrial nations. We fight a "war on drugs," but we do little to fight the despair that leads to the desire for drugs. It might be obvious that meaning is the best antidote to drugs and that there is no meaning if there is no future; but in our theatrical, macho politics more police, more prisons, more military interdiction are more obvious answers.

Poverty and despair fester in our own society, even though in relatively small pockets; but Third World countries know about poverty and despair on a massive scale, and many of them have been slipping backward for a decade or more rather than progressing. Their situation is certainly not "our fault;" although the American banks and the American government have contributed to their problems, particularly in the handling of enormous foreign indebtedness. Nor can we solve their problems for them, though, in accordance with the principle of subsidiarity, we can help where our help will be effectively used. But allowing the current enormous disparities to go on indefinitely runs the risk of a renewal of global conflict that will endanger all our hopes.

Finally, grave threats to the environment are obviously accumulating. To neglect these problems is to make everything else unimportant, for we will have made our planet uninhabitable. But here, too, an emphasis on the short term and the immediate payoff prevents our attending to these problems in a more serious way. For Americans environmental and social problems go hand in hand, although middle-class people are often tempted to think more about the planet than about their less privileged neighbors. The question that both issues raise is whether or not we will ever become settled on this continent. Settlement does not mean static inertia. It means a willingness to cultivate the purposes of individual and common lives rather than be swept along in the fervor of exploitation. A settled people understands its own habitat; it sees the need for wilderness and agriculture as well as cities; and it tries to think of whole regions and their needs and not just the concentrated desires of those with the most wealth and power. A settled people is concerned with the recovery of trust in family and neighborhood; with schools, museums, concert and lecture halls, which enhance its cultural life; and with enabling all its citizens to participate in these goods, so that there is no underclass living in fear and making others fearful. A settled people in the sense we are using the term is not a self-satisfied but an attentive people, concerned with drawing on its multicultural resources for the enrichment of the lives of all. A pattern of settlement and cultivation allows not only the nurturing of ethnic and racial cultures within communities of memory but an open interchange of learning between such communities, a kind of global localism. A settled people is concerned above all with living as fully as possible rather than preparing to live or fearing for their lives. Greed and paranoia, and their giant institutional forms, are enemies of settlement and cultivation.

Needless to say, settlement and cultivation are what Americans need, and they are, in richly diverse form, what troubled peoples all over the globe are also seeking. But settlement in the profound sense in which we use the term will not come as the result of aggregate private decisions; an institutional context must educate and nurture such decisions. Raising consciousness is critical, and creating new institutional patterns, formal and informal, legally and through custom, is equally critical.

Institutional change comes only as a result of the political process. An attentive democratic politics is not some extraneous demand that busy and harried citizens may ignore or attend to fitfully out of "liberal guilt." Our argument is that if we are going to be the kind of persons we want to be, and live the kind of lives we want to live, then attention and not distraction is essential. Concerns that are most deeply personal are closely connected with concerns that are global in scope. We cannot be the caring people whom our children need us to be and ignore the world they will have to live in. We cannot hide from the fact that without effective democratic intervention and institution-building the world economy might accelerate in ways that will tear our lives apart and destroy the environment. Moral discourse is essential in the family; it is also essential in the world. There is no place to hide. "Distracted from distraction by distraction" is how T.S. Eliot characterized our situation. It is time to pay attention.

## THE POLITICS OF GENERATIVITY

At many points we have observed how shortsighted our mechanisms for decision are. Priority in both American economics and American politics has been given to immediate return. Advertising and public rhetoric focus on the individual income, the individual house, the individual car, the individual gun. Except for invoking the ever-present term "freedom" (even when our actual future freedom is being constantly diminished by short-term decisions), our leaders show little concern for the world we are moving into or that our children and grandchildren will have to live in.

In the face of a mass culture and politics dominated by distraction, which offers not only temporary narcotics for anxiety but also a cover for those whose interests are threatened by serious change, there is an urgent need for a new politics of generativity. In recent years the Democratic party has been only half an opposition party, shifting uneasily between trying to outbid the Republicans in offering individual distractions and offering specific policies (such as legislation mandating unpaid parental leave, or national health care, or aid to education) that are at least part of the politics of generativity. But in the absence of an overall philosophy of generative interdependence (as opposed to narrowly self-interested individualism), this liberal laundry list can be taken apart and discarded at will.

The last two decades have been a time of neglect of America's material and social resources, whatever the verdict may finally be on our economic performance of those years. The breakdown during the 1970s of the informal cooperation among government, business, and labor, which had been typical of the "pluralist" politics of the years 1945–68, set in motion a general erosion of social trust. The material consequences of this regression have been profound. Investment in private and public infrastructure has slowed, especially in the public sector, with manifest consequences for our economic life. And the simultaneous disinvestment in "human resources" has already shown itself in the social decay of crime, addiction, cynicism, eroded civility, weakened education, and most shockingly, perhaps, in the pervasive indifference of youth to the world around them.[21]

This withdrawal of responsible attention has spread throughout American society, weakening our economic competitiveness as compared with that of nations such as Germany and Japan, and sapping the energies for social and political attention as well. The pattern of self-seeking indifference was begun and, as the political analyst Kevin Phillips has pointed out, promulgated by many of the wealthiest and most powerful segments of the nation, which defended and partially masked the socially regressive consequences of this generalization of distrust and self-seeking by sponsoring a revival of the nineteenth-century economic ideology of the free market.[22] In the current context of multinational finance, of course, this economic vision cannot mean a return to a world of individual entrepreneurs, however attractive this mirage has proven to some voters: it is simply a carte blanche to the owners and managers of capital to skim profits with even fewer entangling social responsibilities. At the end of the cold war, the great irony is that the Lockean United States may turn out to be more ideologically rigid than the USSR.

We know that the interdependence of modern societies is both complex and fragile. Thus, viability depends, far more than it did in the past, upon the mutual trust and goodwill of all citizens, and notably of the essential functional groups—business, labor, government, the professions, and the "third sector." Viable interdependence, as we have argued repeatedly, requires that participants integrate a cognitive understanding of their interdependence with the practical enactment of goodwill demanded in each institutional context. All-out pursuit of individual or group advantage, which is one consequence of institutional failure in the polity, quickly becomes not only pathological but threatening to the survival of all. Under modern conditions a society's economic and social development hinges essentially on ability to sustain institutions that mediate mutual trust and civic responsibility. Focusing collective attention on this capacity, developing it, and nurturing institutional reforms to promote it is the central theme of the politics of generativity.

In a postindustrial, global economic order, the old categories of (material) "base" and (institutional) "superstructure" are rapidly losing their meaning. Economic development today is the result of a ratio of "inputs" in which raw materials count for less as technological and institutional innovations count for more. It is no longer a matter of mineral deposits and low wages, as in the nineteenth-century model. Not only physical infrastructure but education, socially and environmentally sustainable communities, and managerial and political capacities are the keys to growth and prosperity.

The politics of generativity takes social inclusion and participation as a key theme—for economic no less than for moral and social reasons. Institutions of international cooperation and regulation are necessary for economic growth, even for sustainable competition, within as well as among nations.

And it is the real competition among nations to develop capacities for this kind of political learning that the United States, obsessed by an obsolescent economic ideology, is in danger of losing. The Hayek-Friedman ideology of pristine, Darwinian market competition is practiced nowhere—not in international commerce and least of all by the successful trading and exporting nations, though it may serve the short-term political interests of business and investment bankers. It justifies keeping wages low as it protects the banks' disastrously imprudent international investments, but it will be catastrophic for the United States, and finally for business as well, and in the not so very long run.

We are a society that still denies to many of its citizens the supports of societal membership and dignity that are routinely extended to the privileged—and to all in many of our "competitor" nations—especially health insurance and pensions. The United States is the only advanced nation in which by law nearly all job holders can be dismissed at will.[23] With only a few heartening exceptions, American management has consistently refused to break down the barrier between those whose work allows them some discretion, trust, and the prospect of career advancement and the majority of employees, who lack these things and a secure retirement pension as well. And yet American corporations spend vast sums attempting to improve morale and limit job turnover. A politics of generativity must question and try to overcome these self-defeating failures of social learning. It can no longer assume that a policy of settlement and cultivation is utopian, and must realize that it has become one of enlightened self-interest. But it must realistically attend to the equity and inclusiveness of our institutions. Without morally informed institutional renovation, we are unlikely to develop the trust that is our most valuable social and economic resource.

It may be that, as has happened in the past when the political parties ignore major realities, a new social movement is called for. One thinks of the Green movements which have made some headway in Europe, but much more than environmentalism is required. The politics of generativity includes concerns for a good national society and a good global society as well as a good relation to the environment. A politics of generativity can develop within an existing political party, or through a new social movement, or begin with a social movement and then penetrate a political party. But it would not easily be located on the existing ideological spectrum. It would not favor big government any more than big business. It would favor effective political initiative at the federal and state levels, backed by major commitments of money and expertise, but in the service of local and regional initiatives and institutions—that is the practical meaning of subsidiarity.

Even more important, such a politics is premised on active citizen involvement and discussion—with issues of long-term purpose and consequence taking precedence over the simpler indices upon which current policy analysis focuses—public participation in administrative decisions, constituency involvement in corporate decisions, and a closer public monitoring of legislative action, through review commissions and public debates. The emphasis would be on regulation, setting limits beyond which market and monetary forces are inappropriate and administrative action without review cannot go, and on long-term planning.

The structural changes that a generative politics can produce will anchor our economic and political institutions firmly in the moral discourse of citizens concerned about the common good and the long run. This would make it harder for them to operate over the heads of the people. The achievement of such a generative politics will be to realize Robert Dahl's third democratic transformation. But none of this will happen unless a new moral paradigm—a paradigm of cultivation—replaces the old, outworn Lockean individualist one.

## A PLACE FOR NEW PERSPECTIVES

Walter Lippmann, in his 1937 book *The Good Society,* from which we have taken our title, discussed the "higher law" that he believed Americans had not properly understood when they interpreted it as only the protection of the individual's absolute rights. The higher law, concerned as it is with human rights, is rooted in a fundamentally social understanding of human beings:

> The development of human rights is simply the expression of the higher law that men not deal arbitrarily with one another. Human rights do not mean, as some confused individualists have supposed, that there are certain sterile areas where men collectively may not deal at all with men individually. We are in truth members of one another, and a philosophy which seeks to differentiate the community from the persons who belong to it, treating them as if they were distinct sovereignties having only diplomatic relations, is contrary to fact and can lead only to moral bewilderment. The rights of man are not the rights of Robinson Crusoe before his man Friday appeared.[24]

The higher law that provides the basis for human rights is not a truth complete in itself already known to select philosophers: "To those who ask where this higher law is to be found, the answer is that it is a progressive discovery of men striving to civilize themselves, and that its scope and implications are a gradual revelation that is by no means completed."[25] Nonetheless, classical philosophy and biblical religion give us our best clues as to what the higher law entails. In so arguing, Lippmann for the first time in his work married his own deeply liberal respect for individuality to older Western traditions.

In a closing section entitled "On Designing a New Society," Lippmann argued that we should be moving toward not a single homogeneous system but a society that respects and encourages diversity and attempts to "reconcile the conflicts that spring from this diversity." Such a society will indeed require virtue:

> It requires much virtue to do that well. There must be a strong desire to be just. There must be a growing capacity to be just. There must be discernment and sympathy in estimating the particular claims of divergent interests. There must be moral standards which discourage the quest of privilege and the exercise of arbitrary power. There must be resolution and valor to resist oppression and tyranny. There must be patience and tolerance and kindness in hearing claims, in argument, in negotiation, and in reconciliation.
>
> But these are human virtues; though they are high, they are within the attainable limits of human nature as we know it. They actually exist. Men do have these virtues, all but the most hopelessly degenerate, in some degree. We know that they can be increased. When we talk about them we are talking about virtues that have affected the course of actual history, about virtues that some men have practised more than other men, and no man sufficiently, but enough men in great enough degree to have given mankind here and there and for varying periods of time the intimations of a Good Society.[26]

That Lippmann turned to biblical religion and classical philosophy for elements of the new vision he thought necessary is relevant in our present situation. Recent events in Eastern Europe, as well as past experiences in our own history, suggest that the churches, synagogues, and other religious associations might be one place open to genuinely new possibilities, where cultivation and generativity have clear priority over exploitation and distraction. As an example of fresh thinking about our situation, we call to mind the American Catholic bishops' 1986 letter on the U.S. economy,[27] which argued eloquently that "the dignity of the human person" provides the moral cornerstone for social and economic life. But for the bishops the human person is not an abstract individual but one whose dignity is realized only in community. All persons have rights, but they arise from a mutual bond to care for one another as members of one creation and are rooted in "reverence for God as Creator and fidelity to the covenant." Justice begins with recognition of the need of all persons to take part in the life of a community in order to be fully human, by being united with one another in mutual activity and, finally, mutual love.

The distinctive contribution that the bishops' letter makes to public debate cuts across partisan lines and challenges the conventional bipartisan wisdom that economic well-being is defined in terms of individual levels of material subsistence and consumption, that the economy's success is measured by the aggregate and average amounts of wealth it produces and its efficiency in doing so. Most fundamentally, the bishops challenge the premise that the economy's activities, rules, and relations lie in a social sphere separate from politics and morality. Instead they propose a thick, organic connection in our moral understanding of economic, political, and spiritual life, centered around the necessity of communal solidarity and realizing the dignity and sacredness of all persons. Economic institutions should be judged not by the amount of wealth they produce but by how they produce and distribute it: in doing so do they enable everyone in the community to take part in productive work, learning, and public affairs? Human rights in general, and in particular the rights of once excluded people to take part in a good society, are rooted in a moral matrix of communal solidarity springing from creation and bound by covenant; they do not arise prudentially from the essential self-interest of individuals and their contractual exchange.

In making this argument the bishops recognize that the renewal of a shared vision of a good society must come through critically interrelating the distinctive moral traditions of American culture instead of trying to flatten them into a uniform consensus. So the church seeks to give its own members moral guidance in terms of biblical narrative, theology, and church tradition. But it also seeks to add its voice to public debate through reasoned argument persuasive to those who do not share its own tradition of faith. The confidence that social cooperation can be sustained in public affairs, and that culturally distinctive moral efforts can be carried out compatibly, is itself an expression of faith: "The common bond of humanity that links all persons is the source of our belief that the country can attain a renewed public moral vision."[28]

Like the Protestant Social Gospel, Catholic social teachings in the past century affirm the traditional emphasis on the need to become good persons through the love of God and neighbor and also a commitment to reorder society's institutional arrangements so that people, flawed as they are by "original sin," may live more justly and humanely with one another. A just social system is impossible without people being just. Justice is first and foremost a virtue, and it inheres in individuals and institutions that carry out God's commandment to care for one another—to feed the hungry, heal the sick, and enable the able-bodied to work and contribute to the commonweal.[29]

In defining the institutional conditions that permit genuine communities to flourish, Catholic social thought underlines three principles: (1) that institutions must protect the dignity and inherent sacredness of persons as God's creatures; (2) that social organizations should be ordered in interdependent and cooperative forms, with attention to the natural subsidiarity by which larger and more powerful political and economic institutions sustain smaller communities instead of dominating them; and (3) the necessary existence of social structures, such as the family, church, professional and civic associations, that mediate between the state and its citizens without being controlled by either the will of the state or the interests of the individuals.[30] The purpose of the state, then, is to serve this articulated social order by furthering the cooperation and well-being of all these groupings and institutions.

The principle of subsidiarity favors social cooperation and decentralized power in forms that encourage "a new experiment in participatory democracy" in the American workplace and polity. Its notion of government ordered to aid the flourishing of human beings in community harks back to America's founding ideals as a democratic republic. The principle of subsidiarity offers neither progressives nor neoconservatives a partisan blueprint for political economy. Indeed, one crucial subsidiary function of the state in this understanding is that of encouraging and heeding a moral argument in public life that moves beyond ideological stereotypes.

No political party and few political organizations have put forward so comprehensive a vision, a vision remarkably like Lippmann's analysis in *The Good Society.* In a period when one or another version of savage capitalism is pushed as the answer to our quandary about competitiveness, it is a healthy sign that the bishops' letter generated discussion of the fundamental issues of modern economic life.

## RESPONSIBILITY, TRUST, AND THE GOOD SOCIETY

Another key term in our moral vocabulary that is closely related to attention, and indeed to all issues involved in the effort to create a good society, is "responsibility."

Responsibility must begin with attention. To act responsibly we must ask: What is happening? What is calling us to respond? The theologian H. Richard Niebuhr in his book *The Responsible Self* argued that all our action is a *response* to action upon us, for we are caught in an inescapable web of relationship with other human beings, with the natural world, and with the ultimate reality that includes and transcends all things—what Jews and Christians call God. In many situations we either passively accept what is happening to us or try to evade the implications of what is occurring around us. But, says Niebuhr, we must *interpret* what is happening; especially, we must interpret the intentions of the people we deal with. A third element in responsibility has to do with the effect on others of what we do, a matter that Niebuhr calls "accountability." But our actions usually are not isolated encounters with persons or things with whom we have no continuing relation but, rather, occur in contexts that are already patterned and partake of an element of *social solidarity.* Summing up, Niebuhr wrote: "The idea or pattern of responsibility, then, may summarily and abstractly be defined as the idea of an agent's action as response to an action upon him in accordance with his interpretation of the latter action and with his expectation of response to his response; and all of this is in a continuing community of agents."[31]

So far Niebuhr is being a good sociologist, for sociologists have understood human action in just such a relational context. Indeed, for sociologists, institutions are defined as those patterns which human agents create to regulate action in a "continuing community of agents." But for Niebuhr the idea of the moral life as the responsible life is not just sociologically descriptive but a key to what he calls the "biblical ethos which represents the historic norm of the Christian life."[32] Two aspects of responsibility go beyond purely sociological description: one is trust, and the other is the scope of the responsible action to which we are called.

Trust—and here Niebuhr is being both sociologically realistic and religiously perceptive—is never to be taken for granted. In our relation to the world, trust is always in conflict with mistrust. Because of previous experiences a degree of mistrust is usually realistic; yet if we are dominated by mistrust we cannot attend or interpret adequately, we cannot act accountably, and we will rupture, not strengthen, the solidarity of the community or communities we live in. But how can we trust? Erik Erikson locates what he calls "basic trust" in the child's earliest experience with the mother (perhaps today we would better say "parent") and suggests that if trust has not been warranted then, it is doubtful that it ever will be adequately established in the personality.[33] Theologians such as Niebuhr suggest that behind parental love, essential as that is, lies a deeper question: Is reality, is Being itself, trustworthy? To argue that trust or faith is justified, that God as the very principle of reality is good, is not obvious—not obvious to Christians and Jews, who down through the centuries have been supposed to believe it, and not obvious to anyone who has to live in the world as it is. Trust or faith, like parental love, is a gift. It comes to individuals and groups in particular experiences at particular times and places. Niebuhr did not say that it comes only to Jews and Christians, or that it comes only to people who think of themselves as religious, but that to whomever it comes, it comes as a gift. And when it does come, it brings a great joy and enables us to live responsibly with our fellow beings.

Because so much of the time we are overwhelmed with mistrust, because it is so difficult to believe that Being is good, that, as Christians say, God is love, yet also because to live without trust altogether would be to be close to paranoid schizophrenia, most people try to limit the scope of their trust. They will trust in this person or this occupation or this ethnic group or this religion or this nation, but not in the others. Yet every such limitation impairs the possibility of responsible action. Since we can only attend to those we trust, we cannot interpret accurately, we cannot be accountable to, we cannot grow in solidarity with those we have put outside the circle of our trust. This is no abstract argument. On it hinges the very possibility of whether or not we can create something even partially resembling a good society. When we care only about what Tocqueville called "the little circle of our family and friends" or only about people with skin the same color as ours, we are certainly not acting responsibly to create a good national society. When we care only about our own nation, we do not contribute much to a good world society. When we care only about human beings, we do not treat the natural world with the respect it deserves. If reality itself is for us empty and meaningless, it is hard to see how our lesser commitments can be anything but brittle and transient. But as H. Richard Niebuhr put it:

> In the critical moments we do ask about the ultimate causes . . . and are led to see that our life in response to action upon us, our life in anticipation of response to our reactions, takes place within a society whose boundaries cannot be drawn in space, or time, or extent of interaction, short of a whole in which we live and move and have our being.
>
> The responsible self is driven as it were by the movement of the social process to respond and be accountable in nothing less than a universal community.[34]

Yet for none of us is it easy to override our mistrust and act responsibly in the universal community. Such a possibility is a gift; and when it comes, our response should be gratitude and celebration.

We can indeed try genuinely to attend to the world around us and to the meanings we discover as we interact with that world, and hope to realize in our own experience that we are part of a universal community, making sense of our lives as deeply connect to each other. As we enlarge our attention to include the natural universe and the ultimate ground that it expresses and from which it comes, we are sometimes swept with a feeling of thankfulness, of grace, to be able to participate in a world that is both terrifying and exquisitely beautiful. At such moments we feel like celebrating the joy and mystery we participate in. Religions at their best help us focus that urge to celebrate so that it will include all the meanings we can encompass. The impulse toward larger meaning, thankfulness, and celebration has to have an institutional form, like all the other central organizing tendencies in our lives, so that we do not dissipate it in purely private sentiment.

Institutionalization is always problematic. Socially organized ways of paying attention can become socially organized ways of distraction. Nowhere is the dilemma of institutionalization more poignant than in the realm of religion. Members of biblical religions are under the obligation to listen to what God is saying in the most mundane events of everyday life as well as in the great events of world history, and to respond as conscientiously as they can to the ethical demands raised by those events. Yet it is easier to repeat old formulas, to comfort oneself with the community's familiar practices, than to risk trusting a new response to new conditions.

Yet if we are fortunate enough to have the gift of faith through which we see ourselves as members of the universal community of all being, then we bear a special responsibility to bring whatever insights we have to the common discussion of new problems, not because we have any superior wisdom but because we can be, as Vaclav Havel defines his role, ambassadors of trust in a fearful world. When enough of us have sufficient trust to act responsibly, there is a chance to achieve, at least in part, a good society. In the meantime, even in the world as it is, there are grounds for thankfulness and celebration. Meaning is the living fabric that holds us together with all things. To participate in it is to know something of what human happiness really is.

## NOTES

### Introduction: We Live Through Institutions

1. Eli Sagan, in his book *The Honey and the Hemlock: Democracy and Paranoia in Ancient Athens and America* (New York: Basic Books, 1991), forcibly argues for the importance of psychic trust for democracy and the danger paranoia creates for democratic institutions.

2. George Grant, *English-Speaking Justice* (Notre Dame: University of Notre Dame Press, 1984 [1974]).

3. It was the Berkeley sociologist Kristin Luker who suggested homelessness as an example of the difficulty of knowing how to respond personally to a problem that one knows is institutional in origin.

4. Robert N. Bellah, Richard Madsen, William M. Sullivan, Ann Swidler, and Steven M. Tipton, *Habits of the Heart* (Berkeley and Los Angeles: University of California Press, 1985), p. vi.

5. See the Appendix for a fuller discussion of the sociological conception of institutions.

6. See especially pp. 144–47 of *Habits of the Heart.*

7. See, for example, Bernard Yack, "Liberalism and Its Communitarian Critics: Does Liberal Practice 'Live Down' to Liberal Theory?" and Jeffrey Stout, "Liberal Society and the Language of Morals," in Charles H. Reynolds and Ralph V. Norman, eds., *Community in America: The Challenge of "Habits of the Heart"* (Berkeley and Los Angeles: University of California Press, 1988), pp. 147–69 and 127–46. See also Jeffrey Stout, *Ethics After Babel: The Language of Morals and Their Discontents* (Boston: Beacon Press, 1988).

8. Christopher Lasch in his review of *Habits of the Heart* in *In These Times,* June 26–July 9, 1985, pointed out that *Habits* was about public participation and not simply about community in the traditional American sense of that word. In his new book, *The True and Only Heaven: Progress and Its Critics* (New York: Norton, 1990), Lasch, in chapter 4, "The Sociological Tradition and the Idea of Community," points out in detail the weaknesses of the usual American use of the term "community." In chapter 3, "Nostalgia: The Abdication of Memory," he attacks another characteristic weakness of American thought.

9. Graham Wallas, *The Great Society: A Psychological Analysis* (New York: Macmillan, 1914).

10. John Dewey, *The Public and Its Problems* (1927), in Jo Ann Boydston, ed., *John Dewey: The Later Works,* Vol. 2: 1925–27 (Carbondale and Edwardsville: Southern Illinois University Press, 1984), p. 314.

11. Josiah Royce, *The Hope of the Great Community* (New York: Macmillan, 1916).

12. Walter Lippmann, *The Good Society* (Boston: Little, Brown, 1937).

13. Lipmann, *Good Society,* p. 194.

14. Lipmann, *Good Society,* p. 161.

15. Dennis McCann, "The Good to Be Pursued in Common," in Oliver F. Williams and John W. Houck, eds., *The Common Good and U.S. Capitalism* (Lanham, New York, London: University Press of America, 1987), pp. 158–178.

16. Herbert Fingarette has beautifully analyzed the institutional aspect of shaking hands in our culture in *Confucius: The Secular as Sacred* (New York: Harper and Row, Harper Torchbooks, 1972), pp. 9–10.

Handshaking is an instance of a much more general relation between ceremony and institution. That institutions require ritual reenactment for their survival does not make them, from our point of view, equivalent to nonrational customary behavior. Healthy institutions live in the vital polarity of rational reflection and ritual.

17. David Kirp, *Learning by Heart: AIDS and Schoolchildren in America's Communities* (New Brunswick: Rutgers University Press, 1989).

18. Mary Douglas, *How Institutions Think* (Syracuse: Syracuse University Press, 1986), p. 124.

## Conclusion: Democracy Means Paying Attention

19. Tony Hiss in *The Experience of Place* (New York: Knopf, 1990) describes a number of efforts to make urban and rural patterns of settlement and change intelligible so that responsible action concerning them may be taken. His examples are drawn from New England, New York, and the West Coast. For a description of the problem in the San Francisco Bay area, see Larry Orman and Jim Sayer, *Reviving the Sustainable Metropolis: Guiding Bay Area Conservation and Development in the 21st Century* (San Francisco: Green Belt Alliance, 1989).

20. In *The Life Cycle Completed: A Review* (New York: Norton, 1982), Erik H. Erikson sums up his work on the place of the virtues in the life cycle. Erik H. Erikson, Joan M. Erikson, and Helen Q. Kivnick have much to say about generativity in *Vital Involvement in Old Age: The Experience of Old Age in Our Time* (New York: Norton, 1986).

21. *The New York Times* of June 28, 1990, has extensive coverage of the *Times Mirror* study released that month that shows a significant decline in the interest in and knowledge about national and world events among young people between the ages of eighteen and twenty-four. They are less apt to read newspapers or even watch television news than people of the same age in earlier periods.

22. Kevin Phillips, *The Politics of Rich and Poor: Wealth and the American Electorate in the Reagan Aftermath* (New York: Random House, 1990).

23. "The at will rule—that workers have no rights except those they are able to extract by individual negotiation and agreement—is out of step with the systems of job protection adopted by other industrialized nations, and with international norms. All of our European competitors and Canada have statutes protecting employees against wrongful discharge and establishing tribunals in which claims can be adjudicated. A covenant of the International Labor Organization of the United Nations calls upon

all participating nations to adopt such statutes, but the United States—almost alone among industrial democracies—is not party to that covenant. In this respect we stand isolated within the international community." Joseph Grodin, "Remedy Wrongful Termination by Statute," *California Lawyer,* vol. 10, no. 7, July 1990, p. 120. Grodin is hopeful that legislative action will remedy this situation in the foreseeable future.

24. Walter Lippmann, *The Good Society* (Boston: Little, Brown, 1937), p. 348.

25. Lipmann, *Good Society,* p. 347.

26. Lipmann, *Good Society,* p. 363.

27. National Conference of Catholic Bishops, *Economic Justice for All: Pastoral Letter on Catholic Social Teaching and the U.S. Economy* (Washington, D.C.: National Conference of Catholic Bishops, 1986).

28. *National Conference of Catholic Bishops, Economic Justice for All,* paragraph 27.

29. *National Conference of Catholic Bishops, Economic Justice for All,* paragraph 123.

30. *National Conference of Catholic Bishops, Economic Justice for All,* paragraph 124.

31. H. Richard Niebuhr, *The Responsible Self* (New York: Harper and Row, 1978 [1963]), p. 65; summing discussion on pp. 61–65.

32. Niebuhr, *Responsible Self,* p. 65.

33. On basic trust, see Erik H. Erikson, *Insight and Responsibility* (New York: Norton, 1964).

34. Niebuhr, *Responsible Self,* p. 88.

# 5

# The Demoralization of Society: What's Wrong with the Civil Society

*Gertrude Himmelfarb*

Politics makes for very strange bedfellows, and I've long been troubled by some of those who have rallied to the cause of restoring civil society. But I must say that I was really taken aback when Pat Schroeder decided to become a supporter. That was one bedfellow too many!

I'm not being entirely facetious about this. The *ad hominem* argument is not always as fallacious as it may seem. If people of such diverse views can subscribe to a single idea, that should give us a pause about the nature of that idea. There are some ideas, to be sure, that do command near universal assent—the love of country, for example. But civil society is not that kind of idea. The concept of civil society derives from a very particular view of society and politics, and it has had, in the past, rather particular programmatic consequences. So when liberals and conservatives, libertarians and communitarians, Democrats and Republicans, all profess ardent devotion to this idea, we have to sit back and ask ourselves, "What is this idea that we all seem to affirm?"

The original idea was very simple. It said that civil society consisted of those mediating institutions (families, friends, neighbors, communities, churches, civic organizations, and informal institutions) that intervened between the individual and the state and that served as a corrective both to excessive individualism and to an overweening state. This was all to the good. So long as civil society serves *that* purpose, then I think it is a valuable concept. Unfortunately, the idea is no longer so simple.

You often hear Tocqueville's famous phrase "voluntary associations" quoted to support the idea that liberty is of the essence of civil society. The institutions of civil society are voluntary. They are free, unlike the institutions of the state, which are coercive and obligatory. At least, that is the way it used to be.

One of the anomalies in all this is that the most important institution of civil society is not, in fact, a voluntary association. That institution is the family. What makes the family an effective institution is that it is *not* voluntary, or at least it didn't used to be. Because it was not voluntary it performed the functions and obligations we always associate with the family, which is essentially the care of the most vulnerable, weakest members of society: the young and the old. And those obligations were affirmed not only by all the informal social sanctions—the conventions and customs—associated with the family but by law and government as well. This was decidedly not a voluntary institution.

But in the last few decades the family has become "voluntarized." It has become what we choose to make of it. We will to go in and out of the family, just as we like. That is the meaning of divorce, serial marriages, cohabitation, single-parent families, single-sex parenting. All this has become a matter of choice. To the extent to which the family has become voluntary, it has been deprived of those necessary obligations that once adhered to it. The liberated family no longer serves as an effective, responsible, and reliable force in society.

While the family has been voluntarized, other important institutions of civil society have been devoluntarized, in effect. They retain a nominally voluntary character, but in fact they are no longer that. They are powerful institutions, sometimes semi-monopolistic institutions. They are often funded by the government. They are our large trade unions and trade associations, philanthropies and foundations, educational and cultural institutions, and so on. These institutions are now quasi-governmental. The National Education Association and the Ford Foundation have been more influential in determining the character and quality of our public schools than have the local and state governments that are supposedly responsible for those schools.

The proponents of civil society try to rescue the concept by qualifying and redefining it. They say, "Well, these very large and quasi-governmental institutions are not what we are talking about at all. The heart of civil society consists of small, local, personal, face-to-face institutions." That's all to the good, but it doesn't cover all the contingencies. Some of the face-to-face institutions, some of the local neighborhood institutions are gangs, for example. And surely that is not what we have in mind when we speak about the virtues of civil society.

## CIVIL SOCIETY AND LIBERTY

These voluntary and involuntary institutions that now come together under the rubric of civil society raise another question: the relationship of civil society and individual liberty. All too often civil society is invoked as if it solved the problem of individual liberty: you no longer have a problem because civil society, in itself, affirms the voluntary nature of that relationship.

In the name of civil society (or community: the two terms have become virtually interchangeable), one eminent sociologist proposes: "To restore the family without reviving a 1950s mentality. To stop criminals and drunk drivers without opening the door, even a crack, to a police state. To curb the spread of AIDS while protecting privacy. To discourage divorce without restricting it in any way."

Civil society and individuality are not that easily reconciled. you cannot restore the family without restoring something like a "1950s mentality"—now an invidious term referring to the traditional family. A 1950s family consists of two married, resident parents of different sexes. Even in that retrograde age it was understood that not all families were like this; there were exceptions and deviations from the pattern. But they were understood to be just that—exceptions and deviations. "The family" was assumed to be a traditional family, because only the traditional family could perform the functions that were required of it. And you could not leap in and out of it at will. The liberty of the individual members was restricted. Husband and wife did not have the freedom to divorce without cause or to adopt "alternative lifestyles" that left children without fathers, and mothers without husbands or means of support.

And so with crime, drunk driving, AIDS, and other examples this sociologist cited. In each case, to empower civil society is to diminish the power of the individual within that society.

If some of the proponents of civil society find it difficult to make the hard choices that limit liberty and individuality, others find it equally difficult to make choices that limit the power of the state. For them—and this is true of a large number of those who profess to adhere to the idea of civil society—civil society has become virtually a euphemism for the welfare state. The civic or communitarian influence that sustains civil society is by the same token seen to sustain the welfare state. In this sense, the welfare state becomes the community or the neighborhood writ large—or the "village," as Hillary Clinton understands that word.

This does not cover all the possibilities that are lodged within the concept of civil society these days. There is also the libertarian version. Some libertarians, to be sure, reject any notion of civil society. For them, civil society is as inhibiting and coercive as the state is. This idea has a very respectable heritage. John Stuart Mill, in *On Liberty,* said that social sanctions can be as much an infringement on liberty as legal sanctions. But there are libertarians who accept the idea of civil society, who indeed welcome it. Charles Murray's recent book *What It Means to Be a Libertarian* is a perfect example of this. Murray's libertarianism isn't merely an economic doctrine—it's a social and moral doctrine as well. For him, civil society is a valuable concept because only there can the free individual behave morally in relation to other members of society; individuals can freely choose to be moral.

There are problems, however, with this libertarian view. First, it forgets that civil society has its own kind of coercions, its own social pressures and social sanctions. It is not enough to *encourage* people to be moral; it is also necessary to *shame* them into being moral.

A secondary problem is that within each institution of civil society there is a large limitation on the liberty of its members. An individual is free to enter an institution—to join a church, for example. But once the individual is in that institution, he is bound by its conventions and rules. Institutions do place limitations on liberty and individuality.

Much more important is the degree to which libertarians tend to devalue, sometimes unwittingly, the state. They may accept the legitimacy of the state in the defense of the country. But it is very difficult to argue for an adequate defense budget or a strong foreign policy while at the same time arguing for a drastic reduction in the federal budget and a very minimal government. It's also difficult to retain a sense of national pride if at the same time you view the state with suspicion or disgust.

Of course, there are very good grounds for suspicion and disgust. The state has done a great deal to weaken and delegitimize the institutions of civil society, as well as to subvert individual liberty. The state has deprived families, friends, neighbors, charities, and communities of the social and moral functions they once had. What is even more insidious is that, as currently conceived, the state is itself deprived of a moral function. It is, in effect, demoralized.

## WHAT GOVERNMENTS CAN DO

There are powerful reasons, then, to be suspicious of the state. Nevertheless, there are things of a positive or benign nature that the government can do, beyond the minimal functions that libertarians are prepared to assign to it. Just as bad laws can subvert the social ethic on which civil society rests, so good laws can help sustain that ethic. I'd even go so far as to say that government and laws, used judiciously, modestly, appropriately, can help revitalize and remoralize civil society.

Senator Dan Coats recently introduced a series of bills that seek to use government for just this purpose, to support the family, the community, and private charities, largely through changes in the government's tax codes. I'm not going to argue the merits of the specific proposals, but I would like to support the general proposition that law and government have a proper role in fostering the social ethic upon which civil society rests. We need all the resources available to us, civic and governmental, public and private, religious and secular, in order to sustain that ethic.

I was going to conclude on a positive note, but this is as positive as I can get! If we were to stop thinking of civil society as a mantra that will solve all problems, then it would be a viable and usable concept for all the reasons that Tocqueville explained. But things may have gone too far for it to be salvaged. Maybe the idea has been so badly abused and misused that we should take a different tack. Maybe we should approach our problems in a much more pragmatic way, piecemeal, on a case-by-case basis, without the overarching principle of civil society. I am genuinely of two minds on this subject, and I am very interested in hearing what others have to say about it.

# 6

# Democracy on Trial: The Role of Civil Society in Sustaining Democratic Values

*Jean Bethke Elshtain*

We are blessed, or cursed, to live in interesting times. Even as the nations and peoples formerly under the domination of the Soviet Union proclaim their political ideals in language that inspired and secured the founding of Western democracies, and even as Russia and the various successor states that have sprung up in the wreckage of the terrible Soviet system flail toward democracy or run away from it, our American democracy is faltering. In this chapter I explore warning signs of exhaustion, cynicism, opportunism, and despair using the American experiment as my chief example of the troubles to which democracy is prey. The trials and tribulations of the American republic have a way of setting the agenda for other democratic societies—for better or for worse, and no doubt some of both.

The signs of the times are not encouraging. To interpret those signs is not easy, unless one reacts automatically from a stance of harsh ideological predetermination, whether of the Left or the Right. Let me begin with a few general considerations that flow from the preoccupations of democratic thinkers, past and present. A major concern for all who care about democracy is the everyday actions and spirit of a people. Democracy requires laws, constitutions, and authoritative institutions, yes, but it also depends on what might be called democratic dispositions. These include a preparedness to work with others different from oneself toward shared ends; a combination of strong convictions with a readiness to compromise in the recognition that one can't always get everything one wants; and a sense of individuality and a commitment to civic goods that are not the possession of one person or of one small group alone. But what do we see when we look around? We find deepening cynicism; the growth of corrosive forms of isolation, boredom, and despair; the weakening, in other words, of that world known as democratic civil society, a world of groups and associations and ties that bind.

Many political commentators in the United States have written of the growth of a "culture of mistrust," aided by scandals, a press that feeds off scandals, and a public whose appetite for scandals seems insatiable. The culture of mistrust fuels declining levels of involvement in politics and stokes cynicism about politics and politicians. Journalist E. J. Dionne's book *Why Americans Hate Politics* offers an account of what has gone awry. According to Dionne, both liberals and conservatives are failing America. He laments the false polarization in American politics that has been cast in the form of a cultural civil war: Give no quarter! One mark of this divide is the irony of liberals seeking ways to take the logic of the market in economic life even as they celebrate a nearly untrammeled laissez-faire in cultural and sexual life. Their mirror image is provided by conservatives, who argue for constraints and controls in the cultural and sexual sphere but embrace a nearly unconstrained market.[1] Politicians and citizens get stuck in the *danse macabre* of these two logics and see no clear way out. Needless to say, it is far easier, as Dionne points out, for the media to reinforce the political and cultural divide than to explore ideas that cannot be captured so easily by one logic or the other.

A second perceptive analysis of America's political travail is *Chain Reaction,* an account by Thomas Byrne Edsall and Mary D. Edsall of "the impact of race, rights, and taxes on American politics."[2] The Edsalls describe how numerous programs targeted specifically at black and underclass Americans have lost political legitimacy. Preferential hiring programs, for example, have provoked resentment and have stoked, rather than healed, racial division. Various forms of welfare provision seem to encourage out-of-wedlock births: the rate is around 70 percent for inner-city mothers, many of them teenagers, and is growing rapidly for young white teenagers. Dependence on welfare benefits threatens, over time, to lock these young women into what Mary Jo Bane and David Ellwood, members of the Clinton administration's policy staff, have called a "client-compliance culture" that is much at odds with the possibilities for adult citizenship. A "client" who shows some get-up-and-go may find herself categorized as "error prone"—bureaucratic lingo for a welfare recipient who works more than her eligibility rules permit.[3] She becomes an administrative nuisance, rather than a person with spunk.

In an era of declining resources, resentments cluster around government-sponsored efforts that do not seem to solve the problems they were designed to solve (as voters were told when they signed on to the social contract to make provision for those less fortunate). That is, citizens who pay most of the bills no longer see a benefit flowing from such programs to the society as a whole. Instead, they see a growing dependence on welfare, increased inner-city crime, an epidemic of out-of-wedlock births, and the like. They perceive, therefore, a pattern of redistribution through forms of assistance to people who do not seem to be as committed as they are to following the rules of the game by working hard and not expecting the government to shoulder their burdens. This, at least, is the widespread conviction, and it fuels popular anger and perplexity. As a result, programs geared to particular populations have lost the legitimacy accorded almost automatically to inclusive programs such as social security. Despite their unpopularity, policies that target particular groups are difficult to alter once they are in place, given the phenomenon called "clientele capture." This term refers to the small number of vocal "clients" of such policies—most often the middle-class bureaucrats who administer the programs rather than aid recipients themselves—who have a vested interest in preventing change, even though, over the long run, a policy loses the support of the vast majority of citizens.

The problem goes even deeper than the apparent intractable nature of what Bane and Ellwood called the "basic culture of the welfare system," one that relies on people being weak and having their "needs" defined for them by others. Consider, for example, the working poor who do not flout the rules, try to hold their families together, and are often too proud to ask for assistance even if they may be eligible. Ironically, they are currently the poorest of the poor, severed from the service- and cash-based forms of aid available to those on welfare. These people, hundreds of thousands of our fellow citizens, are finding themselves in increasingly desperate straits as low-paying jobs shrink and wages stagnate. These are people who play by the rules yet appear to be losing nonetheless. This makes it much more difficult to hold up the civic virtues of sobriety, rectitude, hard work, and familial and community responsibility.

## DEMOCRATIC CIVIL SOCIETY

These and other examples of disaffection, including that heart of darkness evoked by American youths from social worlds that are by no means "unprivileged," speak to a deeper matter. As a *civic* question—and it is by no means a civic matter alone—the locus of despair speaks to the loss of civil society. This deepening emptiness, a kind of evacuation of civic spaces, lies in the background of our current discontents, helping to explain why democracy is going through an ordeal of self-understanding as we near the end of the twentieth century. In the associational enthusiasms of civil society, the democratic ethos and spirits of citizens are made manifest. By *civil society,* I mean the many forms of community and association that dot the landscape of a democratic culture, from families to churches to neighborhood groups to trade unions to self-help movements to volunteer assistance to the needy. Historically, political parties, too, were a robust part of this picture. This network lies outside the formal structure of state power. Observers of democracy have long recognized the vital importance of civil society. Some have spoken of "mediating institutions" that lie between the individual and the government or state. These mediating institutions located the child, for example, in his or her little estate, the family, which was itself nested within a wider, overlapping framework of sustaining and supporting civic institutions: churches, schools, and solidaristic organizations, such as unions or mothers' associations. American society was honeycombed by a vast network that offered a densely textured social ecology for the growing citizen.

Curiously, the framers of the American Constitution paid little explicit attention to such institutions, including the family. Perhaps they did not do so because they simply assumed that these associations of civil society were vital and would be long-lasting. They counted on a social deposit of intergenerational trust, neighborliness, and civic responsibility. But we no longer can. That is why political theorists, of whom I am one, must tend explicitly to this matter. We see the ill effects of the loss of civil society all around us.

Think, if you will and if you can bear it, of the growing number of American children for whom not home nor street nor neighborhood affords a safe haven. American children are growing up frightened, and an increasing number of them are being scarred by violence in the schools and streets. The data are overwhelming and consistent. We know that the strongest predictors of domestic situations in which children are likely to be physically abused are stressed-out single-parent households with a teenaged mother, often of several children, and households consisting of a biological mother and her children living with a man who is not related to those children or who does not accept legal responsibility for their well-being. Undersupervised foster care is another recipe for potential disaster; why should this surprise us? These are situations that have been stripped of a dense *sociality,* situations in which the outer world—sometimes that means just outside the door of one's apartment—undermines even the most mature and responsible parents. We further know that a stable, two-parent household is the best protection not only against child abuse but against the possibility that a child will grow up to be an abuser. Again, why should this surprise us? Those who take public responsibility for their stewardship of a private world are more likely to be held accountable and to hold themselves accountable. They are more likely to be sustained by a network of helpful "others"—neighbors, relatives, or associations of all kinds, formal and informal.

Fully 70 percent of juveniles in state reform institutions grew up in homes with a severe "parental deficit," as the sociologists like to call it. I refer to domestic circumstances with fewer helping hands than necessary and less than adequate emotional, economic, and social support. Beyond the tragedy of children assaulted in their homes, an astonishing number die from violence—especially from guns. Homicide by firearms is now the third leading cause of death for fifteen- to nineteen-year-old white Americans (after motor vehicle accidents and suicide). For black Americans in the same age bracket, homicide is the leading cause of death. Why do we tolerate that decimation of African American young people and the sad fact that the suicide rate among young white men has jumped over 200 percent in the past decade? Young white men, aged fifteen to nineteen, are in more danger of self-destruction than any other group. There is more: The prime determinant of drinking or drug use is how many hours a child is left alone during the week. Over the long run, stemming the tide of family collapse is the best protection we can offer a child against becoming either the victim or the perpetrator of violence—or, as it turns out, of poverty.[4]

Seventy-nine percent of children whose parents are unmarried, did not complete high school, and had a first child before age twenty wind up in poverty. Only 8 percent of children with married parents who completed high school and waited until age twenty to bear a child are poor. In other words, married parents who are not high school dropouts are a child's best protection against both poverty and violence.[5] But families cannot do this alone. They need neighbors to turn to; churches to give not only solace but solid, hands-on help; a network of friends; and agencies that assist in time of trouble, such as a serious, prolonged illness. That socially rich world is the world of civil society. If we are to sustain our democratic culture, we must depend on that world. It is not surprising that in areas where the social fabric has most thoroughly come unraveled, we see the most dire and distressing evidence of violence, neglect, babies having babies, desperate grandparents whose children are lost to them trying to raise grandchildren, and all the rest. Neither is it surprising that 67 percent of black adults believe that families and churches will help black families the most, or that only 14 percent believe the government can weave together the warp and woof of their communities at risk. They continue to place their ever more fragile hope in the possibility of civil society.

Civil society is a realm that is neither individualist nor collectivist. It partakes of both the "I" and the "we." Here I think of the many lodges and clubs and party precinct organizations that once dotted the American landscape. It is that world of small-scale social and civic bodies that the Anti-Federalists evoked in debates over ratification of the United States Constitution. The Anti-Federalists were not as confident as the Federalists about the long-term survival of robust civic bodies, and they hoped to ensure that these bodies would flourish. No doubt these Anti-Federalists pushed an idealized image of a self-reliant republic that shunned imperial power and worked, instead, to create a polity modeled on classic principles of civic virtue and the common good. As Ralph Ketcham, a historian of this argument, wrote: "Anti-federalists saw mild, grass-roots, small-scale governments in sharp contrast to the splendid edifice and overweening ambitions implicit in the new Constitution.

. . . The first left citizens free to live their own lives and to cultivate the virtue (private and public) vital to republicanism, while the second soon entailed taxes and drafts and offices and wars damaging to human dignity and thus fatal to self-government."[6]

Despite the often roseate hue with which the Anti-Federalists surrounded their arguments, they were on to something, as we like to say. They hoped to avoid, even to break, a cycle later elaborated by Alexis de Tocqueville in his great nineteenth-century work *Democracy in America.* Tocqueville sketched as a warning a world in decline, a world different from the robust democracy he surveyed. He believed that American democratic citizens needed to take to heart a possible corruption of their way of life. In his worst-case scenario, narrowly self-interested individualists, disarticulated from the saving constraints and nurture of overlapping associations of social life, would require more and more controls "from above" to mute at least somewhat the disintegrative effects of individualism of a narrowly egoistic sort.

To this end, he cautioned, the peripheries must remain vital; political spaces other than or beneath those of the state need to be cherished, nourished, and kept vibrant. Tocqueville had in mind local councils and committees, to forestall concentrations of power at the core or on the top. Too much centralized power is as bad as no power, he believed. Only many small-scale civic bodies would enable citizens to cultivate democratic virtues and to play an active role in the drama of democracy. Such participation turns on meaningful involvement in some form of community. Too much power exercised at a level beyond that which permits and encourages active citizen participation is destructive of civic dignity and may prove fatal to democratic self-government. We see, then, that early Anti-Federalist fears of centralized power presaged Tocqueville's uneasy premonition that imperial greatness bought through force of arms is "pleasing to the imagination of a democratic people" because it sends out lightning bolts of "vivid and sudden luster, obtained without toil, by nothing but the risk of life."[7] This latter course is, despite the expenditure of blood and treasure it requires, far easier than tending to the daily work of democratic civic life.

Tocqueville's worries have been much debated by political and social theorists. Those who follow Tocqueville in this matter believe that American democracy did free individuals from the constraints of older, undemocratic structures and obligations. But, at the same time, it unleashed an individualism of a peculiarly cramped sort. Tocqueville's fear, remember, was not that this development would invite anarchy—as antidemocratic philosophers claim or insist—but that the individualism of an acquisitive commercial republic would engender new forms of social and political domination. He called this bad form of individualism "egoism," to distinguish it from the notions of human dignity and self-responsibility central to a flourishing democratic way of life. All social webs that once held persons intact having disintegrated, the individual finds himself or herself isolated and impotent, exposed and unprotected. Into this power vacuum will likely move a top-heavy, ever more centralized state. Or we will hunker down in defensive "lifestyle enclaves," forbidding others entry. As political theorist Michael Walzer noted:

> We are perhaps the most individualist society that ever existed in human history. Compared certainly to earlier, and Old World societies, we are radically liberated, all of us. Free to plot our own course. To plan our own lives. To choose a career. To choose a partner or a succession of partners. To choose a religion or no religion. To choose a politics or an anti-politics. To choose a lifestyle—any style. Free to do our own thing, and this freedom, energizing and exciting as it is, is also profoundly disintegrative, making it very difficult for individuals to find any stable communal support, very difficult for any community to count on the responsible participation of its individual members. It opens solitary men and women to the impact of a lowest common denominator, commercial culture. It works against commitment to the larger democratic union and also against the solidarity of all cultural groups that constitute our multi-culturalism.[8]

Keep in mind the concern that over time the stripping down of the individual to a hard core of an isolated or a suspended self, the celebration of a version of radical autonomy, casts suspicion on any and all ties of reciprocal obligation and mutual interdependence. What counts in this scheme of things is the individual and his or her choices. If choice is made absolute, it follows that important and troubling questions that arise as one evaluates the distinction between individual right and social obligation are blanked out of existence. One simply gives everything, or nearly so, over to the individualist pole in advance. Ideally, democratic individuality is "not boundless subjectivist or self-seeking individualism," but the worry is that it has, over time, become so.[9] The blessings of democratic life that Tocqueville so brilliantly displayed—especially the spirit of equality, including a certain informality and mixing of peoples of different stations—give way. In their place, other more fearful and self-enclosed, more suspicious and cynical habits and dispositions rise to the fore. We cannot stand isolated for long in the wind with no protective cover. Ironically, the individualism sketched here erodes the possibility of democratic freedom over time, the blessings of liberty to ourselves and our posterity.

In his book *The True and Only Heaven*, historian and cultural critic Christopher Lasch told the tale this way. In the eighteenth century, the founders of modern liberalism embraced an argument that posited human wants and needs as expandable—indeed, nearly insatiable. It followed that indefinite growth of the productive forces of economic life was needed to satisfy and continually fuel the restless cycle of the creation and satiation of needs. This ideology, called Progress, was distinctive, Lasch claimed, in exempting its world from the judgment of time and led to the unqualified and altogether unwarranted optimism that a way of life could persist untarnished, undamaged, and without terrible pressure to its own, most cherished principles.[10]

The joint property of various liberalism and conservatism, twentieth-century purveyors of progress as an ideology celebrated a world of endless growth, which meant, in practice, more and better consumerism. It was essential to move from the glorification of producer to the glorification of the consumer because the conclusion was that underconsumption leads to declining investment. We want more, and we want it now! All of life is invaded by the market and pervaded by market imagery. Perhaps we should not be to surprised that in America's inner cities, young people rob, beat, and even kill one another to steal expensive sneakers and gold chains. Or that in America's suburbs, young people whose families are well off shun school and studies and community involvement to take part-time jobs to pay for extra consumer goods that their parents may be loath to provide.

I take Lasch's argument to be similar to Pope John Paul II's criticism of "liberal capitalism" in "Sollicitudo Rei Socialis," his encyclical on social concerns. Rejecting the self-contained smugness of the ideology of Progress, John Paul scored a phenomenon he called "superdevelopment, which consists in an excessive availability of every kind of material good for the benefit of certain social groups." Superdevelopment "makes people slaves of 'possession' and of immediate gratification, with no other horizon than the multiplication or continual replacement of the things already owned with others still better. This is the so-called civilization of 'consumption' or 'consumerism,' which involves so much 'throwing away' and 'waste.'"[11]

The "sad effects of this blind submission to pure consumerism," John Paul stated, are a combination of materialism and restless dissatisfaction as the "more one possesses the more one wants." Aspirations that cut deeper, that speak to human dignity within a world of others, are stifled. John Paul's name for this alternative aspiration is "solidarity," not "a feeling of vague compassion or shallow distress at the misfortunes of so many people" but a determination to "commit oneself to the common good; that is to say, to the good of all and of each individual because we are really responsible for all." Through solidarity, John Paul said, we *see* "the 'other' . . . not just as some kind of instrument . . . but as our 'neighbor,' a 'helper' . . . to be made a sharer on a par with ourselves in the banquet of life to which all are equally invited by God."[12]

To the extent that John Paul's words strike us as utopian or naive, we have lost civil society. Or so, at least, sociologist Alan Wolfe concluded in *Whose Keeper? Social Science and Moral Obligation.* Wolfe updated Tocqueville, apprising us of how far and how rapidly we have traveled down the road to bad individualism, which requires the greater management, control, and concentration of political and economic power to keep us bounded in our little kingdoms of one. Wolfe suggested that for all our success in modern societies, there is a sense, desperate in some cases, that all is not well, that something has gone terribly awry. We citizens of liberal democratic societies understand and cherish our freedom, but we are, according to Wolfe, "confused when it comes to recognizing the social obligations that make . . . freedom possible in the first place."[13] This confusion permeates all levels, from the marketplace to the home to the academy.

The confusion has a lot to do with a new attitude toward rights that has taken hold in the United States during the past several decades. Americans have been speaking the language of rights for a long time. It is part of our heritage, as American as apple pie. The first noticeable mention of rights, the Bill of Rights, was appended to, and became part of the American Constitution. These rights revolve around civic freedoms—assembly, press, speech—and around what the government cannot do to you, say, unreasonable search and seizure. Rights were designed primarily as immunities, as a way to protect us overweening governmental power, not as entitlements. The rights-bearing individual was a civic creature, a community being, a family man or woman located within the world of civil society I have already described. But as time passed, the rights-bearing individual came to stand alone—"me and my rights"—as if rights were a possession. Rights were construed increasingly in individualistic terms as their civic dimensions withered on the vine. As legal theorist Mary Ann Glendon pointed out in her book *Rights Talk,* the dimensions of sociality and responsibility are missing when the rights-defined self stands alone.[14] The regime of rights cannot be sustained by rights alone.

These ideas help us make sense of the political fallout from "rights talk" that surely puts democracy on trial. Let me elaborate by further developing one of my earlier claims. On the one hand, we witness a morally exhausted Left embracing the logic of the market by endorsing the translation of *wants* into *rights.* Although the political Left continues to argue for taming the market in an economic sense, it follows the market model when social relations are concerned, seeing in any restriction of individual "freedom," or "lifestyle option," as we call it today, an unacceptable diminution of rights and free expression. On the other hand, many on the political Right love the untrammeled (or the less trammeled the better) operations of the market in economic life, but call for a state-enforced restoration of traditional mores, including strict sexual and social scripts for men and women in family and work life. Both rely on either the market or the state to "organize their codes of moral obligation, but what they really need," Wolfe insisted, "is civil society—families, communities, friendship networks, solidaristic workplace ties, voluntarism, spontaneous groups and movements—not to reject, but to complete the project of modernity."[15]

What is needed to speed this cherished end—the revivification of civil society—is a return to a more thoroughly social understanding that rights are always transitive, always involve us with others, cannot stand alone, and cannot come close to exhausting who and what we are. If we were to try to understand through "rights talk" why we stay up all night with a sick child or take our neighbor a pot of soup when she comes home from the hospital or spend hours helping to provide for the victims of a natural disaster, we would seriously distort these socially responsible and compassionate activities. We know this in our bones. Yet each time we feel called upon to justify something politically, we tend to make our concerns far more individualistic and asocial than they really are by reverting to the language of rights as the "first language" of liberal democracy.[16]

None of the thinkers I have mentioned has found a solution to our Tocquevillian anxiety in a more powerful state, including the welfare state as we know it. The most highly developed welfare state in nineteenth-century Europe was Bismarck's "welfare-warfare" state, one in which social benefits were geared explicitly to making the poor loyal dependents of the state. Social control was the aim, welfare the strategy. For most of us in the modern West, the welfare state emerged from a set of ethical concerns and passions that grew as civil society began to succumb to market forces. These concerns ushered in the conviction that the state was the "only agent capable of serving as a surrogate for the moral ties of civil society." But half a century of evidence makes it clear that the logic of the state's provision and creation of classes of long-term dependents in America has further eroded "the very social ties that make government possible in the first place."[17]

Please note well: the argument behind "ending welfare as we know it," when it comes from the direction of a civil society, is not about grinding the faces of the poor into dust from a lack of compassion. Rather, it is about how welfare professionalizes care and counsel and turns citizens into clients. In "Community and Its Counterfeits," a series aired on the Canadian Broadcasting Corporation (CBC), John McKnight, scholar and community activist, claimed that modern institutions are machines that redefine human beings, locating us as entities in a system, rather than as people in a place. When professionals move in on communities to "solve a problem," what happens is that people grow weaker, not stronger, for their "needs" are authoritatively defined by sources outside themselves. The "awakened energies of the community are often dissipated in a maze of government regulations or resources are tied up in social programs which deliver services to people whose real need is income," McKnight argued.

Needs, then, become "the resources of the service sector of contemporary economies—what iron ore is to the steel industry, needs are to those who propose to meet them." According to McKnight, this "never-ending search for new needs . . . is always at the cost of diminished citizenship. So that as these systems of service colonize your life and my life, saying that we are bundles of needs and there are institutionalized services there to meet the needs to make us whole, to make us real, what we become is less and less powerful."

I am not so naive or foolish as to believe we can do without the state. The state, properly chastened, plays a vital role in a democratic society. Rather, I am worried about the *logic* of statism, which looks to the state as the only entity capable of "solving a problem," or responding to a concern. One problem with this logic is that as the state expands its role, the capacities of local institutions are often diminished. Another is what may be called the *ideology* of statism, which is not as prevalent in North American democracy as it was in the civic republican polities imagined by Jean-Jacques Rousseau and implemented in the early-modern and modern epochs by various civic actors, beginning with the French Revolutionaries in the eighteenth century.

The statist wants to thin out the ties of civil society and to erode the force of the plural loyalties and diverse imperatives these ties give rise to and sustain. To the statist, the citizen is unhesitatingly loyal to the state and is prepared to give primacy to it and its purposes. The statist identifies us—we citizens—primarily as creatures who are available for mobilization by a powerful centralized mechanism, rather than as family members, neighbors, participants in a fraternal order or a feminist health cooperative, activists trying to save the African elephant from extinction, members of a reading group, Baptists, Catholics, and so on. The statist wants us to be hemmed in and obliged and homogenized in all sorts of mandated ways.

But the citizen of a democratic civil society understands that government cannot substitute for concrete moral obligations; it can either deplete or nourish them. As our sense of particular, morally grounded responsibilities to an intergenerational web and a world of friends and neighbors falters and the state moves in to treat the dislocations, it may temporarily solve delimited problems. But these solutions may, in time, further thin out the skein of obligation. Eventually, support for the state itself will begin to plummet—people feel anomic and aggrieved, their resentments swell—and one sees the evidence in tax evasion; an upsurge in violence against persons and property; the breakup of social ties, including families, on an unprecedented scale; the rise of political cynicism; and even something akin to despair.

A number of contemporary observers, including several I have already cited, see such signs of civic and social trouble even in the long-established welfare democracies of Western Europe and Scandinavia. It is, alas, the by now familiar story: the loneliness of the aged, the apathy of the young, the withering away of churches and communal organizations, the disentangling of family ties, and the loss of family rituals and rhythms. I do not want to say that the provision of welfare directly caused any of these phenomena. I do want to suggest that a bureaucratic, top-heavy state that numbers among its tasks defining populations by their "needs" and targeting them for various policies based on assumptions about such needs, really cannot help moving in the direction of a "social engineering" that exists in tension with democratic freedom, civic sociality, and individual liberty.

No doubt a distinction should be made between the dominant rhetoric of individualism and the culture of cynicism, on the one hand, and how we actually behave as members of families, communities, churches, and neighborhoods, on the other. But surely it is true that our social practices are under extraordinary pressure and thus that democracy itself is being squeezed. In America today, fearful people rush to arm themselves, believing safety to be a matter of aggressive self-help. Angry people want all the politicians to be kicked out of office, but they believe new ones will be no better. Anxious people fear that their neighbors' children may get some unfair advantage over their own. Despairing people destroy their own lives and the lives of those around them. Careless people ignore their children and then blast the teachers and social workers who must tend to the mess they have made, screaming all the while that folks ought to "mind their own business." Many human ills cannot be cured, of course. All human lives are lived on the edge of quiet desperation. We must all be rescued from time to time from fear and sorrow. But I read the palpable despair and cynicism and violence as dark signs of the times, as warnings that democracy may not be up to the task of satisfying the yearnings it unleashes for freedom and fairness and equality.

## "DEFINING DEVIANCY DOWN"

I spend a lot of time talking to young people, going from campus to campus giving lectures. In April 1994, I gave a talk at a fine institution a good two-and-a-half-hour drive from the nearest airport. Those who fetched me at the airport and returned me there later that day were students. They told me they had no really clear ideas about what lay ahead or what they wanted to be. I was struck by one bright young man, who was perturbed by the recent suicide of Kurt Cobain, front man for the group Nirvana, considered the band that best embodies "Generation X." This student said—and, remember, he is among the privileged—that his generation is cynical: "If you have a thought that doesn't seem cynical, you have to get cynical about your own noncynicism, so you can be safely cynical again and not seem like a dweeb or optimist of some sort." He hailed from a volatile private world of once-feuding parents, then a "broken home"—his words, not mine. He was thoughtful but all at sea, and he envied earlier generations because they seemed to have a "purpose." I told him I thought it was not so much "purpose" as that we middle-aged folks grew up with adult examples of steadiness, competence, and integrity and that these models were fast disappearing. It was a sobering drive.

Let us take a closer look. Counsels of despair are of little help and all too easily descend into bathos and even self-indulgence. One sign that democracy is on trial is the falling away from the firm, buoyant conviction of democrats that a rights-based democratic equality, guaranteed by the vote, will serve over time as the sure and secure basis of a democratic culture. Political theorist George Kateb, for example, celebrates "democratic individuality," reflected in and protected by "the electoral procedure, the set of rules" that embody the "great value of equal respect for persons." Such rules, including the franchise as a right, radiate "a strong influence" that goes much beyond the formal prerogatives themselves, helping to instill a sense of dignity and permanently chastening political authority should it grow overweening.[18] Kateb does well to remind us of the distinction between destructive individualism and the ennobling strengths of the democratic tradition of respect for the human person, taken as a single, unique, and irreplaceable self.

But a striking feature of our epoch is that those very rights, the terms of democratic equality itself, have fallen into disrepute. Rather than rights serving as a frame within which democratic individuality can be shored up—in which a self is made possible by the debates and dialogues a rule-governed democratic culture sustains—we hear ever more cynical appraisals of the rules, regulations, procedures, guarantees, and premises of constitutional democracy. For example, fueled by claims that wildly exaggerate the extent of violence perpetrated against women—for the media's hysteria knows no restraint in this matter—various proposals have been made based on the premise that burdensome democratic procedures, including the presumption of innocence, should be seen for what they are: bourgeois hypocrisy. We should recognize that the presumption of innocence and the need for our accusers to bear the burden of proof will protect us and our loved ones if we are ever called before the bar of justice; instead, we are bombarded with arguments belittling, even trashing, the whole idea of evidentiary requirements that are central to the ideal of equal standing before the law.

This short temper with honoring the rights of the accused and meting out punishment appropriate to fit the concrete, particular crime that may have occurred is powerfully evident in a piece of legislation up for passage in the U.S. Senate. It represents a danger to democratic ideas of fairness and due process and embodies a mind-set that will be around for some time. Called the Violence Against Women Act, the legislation incorporates "gender motivation" into a law that presumes to see in rape—a crime of violence—the paradigmatic, indeed normative, expression of male dominance. This act is an example of what Senator Daniel Patrick Moynihan called "defining deviancy down," on the legislative front in this instance. What is aberrant is suddenly redescribed as normal. Thus one moves away from the guiding presumptions of democratic jurisprudence, namely, that each case must be looked at individually: one must assess what happened to this victim and what was perpetrated by that offender. Instead, the defenders of this new approach assume an undifferentiated class of victimizers (male) of an undifferentiated class of victims (female), raising the specter that the concrete facts of sexual assault will be much less important in establishing guilt or innocence than will some vague "animus based on a victim's gender." The motives police here rely on are the platitudes of radical feminist ideology, a view of the moral and social world that, in the words of Catharine MacKinnon, "stresses the indistinguishability of prostitution, marriage, and sexual harassment."[19] In this scheme of things, sex is what men do *to* women. It follows that men simply *are* rapists, either actual or in situ. What is lost is the truth expressed by our new Supreme Court Justice, Ruth Bader Ginsburg, that "generalizations about the way women or men are . . . cannot guide me reliably in making decisions about particular individuals."[20] One finds, then, at this moment, the distressing spectacle of an assault on civil liberties, coupled with a perfervid ideology of victimization.[21]

Political philosopher Charles Taylor rightly noted the tremendous amount of activity that is discernible in American politics, an incessant hubbub, as a matter of fact, but he described the American political scene as dismal, in part because American society has grown ever more fragmented: "A fragmented society is one whose members find it harder and harder to identify with their political society as a community. This lack of identification may reflect an atomistic outlook, in which people come to see society purely instrumentally. But it also helps to entrench atomism, because the absence of effective common action throws people back on themselves."[22] We are thrown back on ourselves, into the currents of consumer excess or the cold comfort of ever more computerized and centralized bureaucracies.

I think of the words now used to characterize American politics: stalemate, gridlock, cynicism. American politics is a miasma, so argue many experts and journalists, as well as ordinary citizens. This growing cynicism about politics promotes a spiral of delegitimation. How does a spiral of delegitimation get a society in its grip? Over time, the "culture of mistrust" grows, aided, as I already indicated, by public scandals; by an ever more litigious and suspicious society; by a determination to "get mine" no matter what may happen to the other guy; and by salacious snooping into the private lives of public figures, which further fuels cynicism about how untrustworthy our leaders are even as we delight in their downfall.[23]

It is quite a mess, but it is not America's mess alone. Perhaps it is worth noting that the growth of American cynicism about democratic government shifts American toward, not away from, a more generalized norm of disaffection. Most people in other societies, including citizens of the democracies of Western Europe, are cynical about government. As political scientist James Q. Wilson pointed out, we Americans "are less optimistic and less trusting than we once were. And rightly so: if Washington says that we should entrust it to educate our children, to protect our environment, and to regulate our economy, we would be foolish not to be cautious and skeptical."[24] The problem, according to Wilson, is that over the past three to four decades, government has become less effective, not so much as a result of its size per se, but because it has taken on more and more issues that it is simply ill equipped to handle well—including abortion and race relations, to name two of the most volatile.

Too many such "wedge issues," as the pundits and strategists call them, were created not for the most part by cynical demagogues but by well-meaning federal judges who made decisions in the 1960s and 1970s on a whole range of cultural questions without due consideration of how public support for juridically mandated outcomes might be generated. On some questions—for example, school desegregation—the moral mandate was high and consistent with our own perduring principles. For the Supreme Court to come down decisively on one side of the question led to a fierce political struggle, to be sure, but the whole weight of American history since the Civil War has been behind the commitment to inclusion and equality. Many "cultural" and "ethical" matters are not as clear, however.

Dealing with abortion, to take one example of a controversial ethical and cultural issue, cannot be compared to building a great interstate highway system or desegregating the schools. All the cultural questions that now pit democratic citizens against one another—in addition to abortion, I think of family values, drugs and post–civil rights race relations—are guaranteed to continue to divide us, in large part because of the means government has often used to put these issues on the table: judicial fiat. The Supreme Court decision in the deeply contentious *Roe v. Wade* case in 1973 actually preempted a nationwide political debate over abortion, then raging in most states. A grassroots politics to liberalize abortion laws was well under way. Indeed, some sixteen states had already reformed their abortion statutes to make abortion more widely available. In addition, as historian Michael Barone has pointed out, "by the time the *Roe v. Wade* decision was issued, about 70 percent of the nation's population lived within 100 miles—an easy two hours' drive—of a state with a legalized abortion laws. And just as the Supreme Court was speaking, legislatures in almost all of the states were going into session; many would probably have liberalized their abortion laws if the court had not acted."[25]

Regardless of one's personal views on abortion, this case is a good example of juridical moves freezing out citizen debate. Juridical politics is black and white, winner-take-all. The juridical model of politics, first pushed by liberal activists and now embraced by their conservative counterparts—for two can play at this game—preempts democratic contestation and a politics of respect and melioration. When the Supreme Court threw all its weight to one side in a highly fraught situation on which people of goodwill differed, it aroused from the beginning strong and shocked opposition from those who despaired that their government, at its highest level, sanctioned what they took to be the destruction of human life at its most vulnerable stage. By guaranteeing that the forces on either side of the issue need not debate with each other, other than through judges, the court deepened a politics of resentment.

## DEMOCRACY BY PLEBISCITE?

There are, alas, many more examples of this sort. Rather than weary the reader with further recounting of such tales, I will look, instead, at a few proposed solutions and assess whether they promise democratic renewal. A direct, rather than a representative, democratic system is one panacea sought by some who are impatient with the compromises and mediations of democratic civil society and frustrated by governmental inaction or too much action of a sort they oppose. Let the people speak! This populist theme is a recurring refrain in American political life. Historically, populists usually wanted government off their backs and power restored to their own communities. Currently, populists—or those who call themselves such—feed on mistrust and antielitism, and anyone who is unlucky enough to hold any kind of governmental office is subject to their ire.

In the American presidential election of 1992, populist fervor gained surprising strength in the person, and candidacy, of the Texas billionaire Ross Perot. Perot is far less important than the phenomenon he helped to catalyze. Consider, briefly, one of his proposed cures for democratic ills, a cure that has been endorsed, to ends rather different from Mr. Perot's, by some commentators on the Left. Such populists, or strong democrats as they like to be called, would perfect democracy by eliminating barriers between the people's will and its forthright articulation. Pure democracy beckons, whirring and humming in the background of such visions, sometimes called the electronic town hall.

American democracy is in trouble, the proponents of pure democracy believe, because the direct expression of the people's will is thwarted. But technology will come to our rescue through instant plebiscites via interactive television and telepolling. Should we include managed competition in a health-care proposal? Press the yes button or the no button. Should we bomb Baghdad because of yet another blunder or nefarious scheme by Saddam Hussein? Choose your button. What those who push such technosolutions fail to appreciate is that plebiscitary majoritarianism is quite different from a democratic polity sustained by debate and judgment. Plebiscites have been used routinely to shore up antidemocratic regimes—Argentinian Peronism comes to mind.

Even if one could devise a way to "sample" the political responses of America's 120 million households, the plebiscite solution to democratic disillusionment must be criticized no matter who is championing its use. The distinction between a democratic and a plebiscitary system is no idle one. In a plebiscitary system, the views of the majority can more easily swamp minority or unpopular views. Plebiscitarianism is compatible with authoritarian politics carried out under the guise of, or with the connivance of, majority opinion. That opinion can be registered ritualistically, so there is no need for debate with one's fellow citizens on substantive questions. All that is required is a calculus of opinion.

True democracy, Abraham Lincoln's "last, best hope on earth," is a different proposition. It requires a mode of participation with one's fellow citizens that is animated by a sense of responsibility for one's society. The participation of plebiscitarianism is dramatically at odds with this democratic ideal. Watching television and pushing a button are privatizing experiences; they appeal to us as consumers, not as public citizens.

Being asked your opinion and given a chance to register it instantly may at first seem democratic, but the individual in this formulation is the private person enclosed within herself or himself, rather than the public citizen. A compilation of opinions does not make a civic culture; such a culture emerges only from a deliberative process. To see button-pressing as a meaningful act on a par with lobbying, meeting, writing letters to the editor, serving on the local school board, working for a candidate, or helping to forge a coalition to promote or prevent a particular program or policy parallels a crude version of so-called preference theory in economics.

This theory holds that in a free-market-society, the sum total of individual consumer choices results in the greatest benefit to society as a whole even as these choices meet individual needs. The assumption is that each of us is a "preference maximizer." Aside from being a simplistic account of human motivation, preference theory lends itself to the blurring of important distinctions. According to preference maximizers, there is no such thing as a social good—there are only aggregates of private goods. Measuring our opinions through electronic town halls is a variant of this crude but common notion. The cure it promises is more of what ails us. Under the banner of a perfected democratic choice, we become complicit in eroding even further those elements of deliberation, reason, judgment, and shared goodwill that alone make genuine choice, hence democracy, possible. We would turn our representatives into factotums, mouthpieces expressing our electronically generated will. This is a nightmare, not a democratic dream.

## A NEW SOCIAL COVENANT?

Is there any way to break the spiral of mistrust and cynicism? Yes, but it will be difficult. Some, and I include myself in this number, embrace the idea of a new social covenant. But unless Americans, or the citizens of any faltering democracy, can once again be shown that they are all in it together; unless democratic citizens remember that being a citizen is a *civic* identity, not primarily a private sinecure; unless government can find a way to respond to people's deepest concerns, a new democratic social covenant has precious little chance of taking hold. And take hold it must if we are to stem the tide of divisive issues that pit citizen against citizen in what social scientists call a zero-sum game: I win; you lose—that juridical model of politics I have already decried. The social covenant is not a dream of unanimity or harmony, but the name given to a hope that we can draw on what we hold in common even as we disagree.

Let us imagine how a new social covenant might work in America's troubled cities. It would draw whites and blacks together around their shared concern for safe streets and neighborhoods, in part by altering the terms of the public debate. The social covenantee would encourage liberals who espouse untrammeled lifestyle options to be tolerant of the more conservative values and concerns—especially those of family and religious faith.

The interviews I have conducted with mothers and grandmothers who are active in antigang and antidrug politics in their communities show clearly how much at odds their views are with the dogma that refuses to confront the realities of violence and even chaos in housing projects and on dangerous streets. Social provision will not deal with this problem, one that is overwhelmingly a matter of the deterioration and deinstitutionalization of families, churches, and neighborhoods. These institutions must be rebuilt; in the meantime, the violence must be stopped. The mothers I spoke to want more police patrols, more neighborhood power, less freedom for armed teenagers to run amok, and tougher penalties for repeat offenders.

As I write, a debate is taking place over the ability of the police to make unannounced sweeps of housing projects where danger is a pervasive presence. The point is to disarm those who threaten and kill their brothers and sisters in alarming numbers. The people who live in these sites and who are striving with what can only be called heroism to protect their children welcome such police initiatives and can point to their concrete beneficial results. Mike Barnicle, a columnist for the *Boston Globe,* told the story of a thirty-one-year-old mother with three children, who called the police for months with stories of kids on her block "who were dealing daily in guns and drugs and creating a climate of such fear that anyone interested in living normally found it an impossible task."[26] She lined her walls and windows with mattresses to try to hide and perhaps to absorb bullets. When the police implemented a policy called Stop and Search, she and other mothers in the project rejoiced: Maybe, at long last, things would get better.

But, in Barnicle's words, "it ended almost as quickly as it began after lawyers and editorial writers came to the conclusion that it was a tremendous abridgment of the Constitution." So violence prospers, in part, because "simple items like a curfew" get dismissed as inherently coercive. Barnicle listed a few of the rights not currently

> accorded a young black mother and her three children: the right to sit on a stoop or at a playground. The right to walk to a store at any reasonable time . . . without the fear of getting caught in the cross fire. The right to spend a peaceful evening inside their own apartment. The right to stare out a window. The right of free association. The right to use a swing set whenever the whim strikes. The right to complain publicly about gangsters in their midst. The right to be rid of crack and cocaine in the hallway and the vestibule. The right to life.

Kids with 9-millimeter guns—or larger—have their rights, and "a mother of three children has her mattresses in front of the window of her apartment."

The social covenantee recognizes that market strategies are ill designed to speak directly to what concerns people the most in the worst inner-city neighborhoods. He or she would tell gun advocates and libertarians that, yes, murderers do kill people, but they use guns to do it. Surely you favor removing guns from the hands of dangerous people. Can you not assume that a fourteen-year-old drug-using dropout is dangerous, or potentially so? Would his freedom be unduly hampered if we made certain that he did not carry a gun into a school, a schoolyard, or a supermarket? The libertarian might respond that it is against the law for minors to carry loaded firearms. But the tough-minded advocate of a social covenant would parry, "Yes, I know that. But the fact of the matter is that children in America's inner cities are armed and dangerous, primarily to one another. Sure we can begin the process of disarming!"

Take a second case. To those prepared to excuse violent outrages on the grounds that looting, pillaging, burning, beating, and bashing people's heads in with bricks are expressions of rage at social injustice, the social covenant message is to call things by their real names. When I read headlines in certain so-called progressive journals in the aftermath of the 1992 riots in Los Angeles proclaiming L.A. UPRISING! or L.A. REBELLION, I felt real chagrin. A paternalistic attitude that refuses to consider all citizens as responsible is anathema to the democratic ethos. To excuse or even condone random violence—marked not by marches, organizing, issuing manifestos, and cobbling together a political program or vision, however rough-and-ready, but by the brutal destruction of persons and property—is to perpetrate a sickly fascination with violence, as if shedding blood were an inherently political act, and a radical one at that.

Such bewitchment with violence not only ill serves its victims, primarily those in the neighborhoods where the riots occurred, but perpetuates what political philosopher Hannah Arendt found to be one of the most pervasive and dangerous ideas (and she indicted the Left and Right alike for their enchantment with it at different times and in different places): that something good comes out of something evil, that authentic politics flows from the barrel of a gun, a knife blade, or a gasoline bomb. In the words of legal theorist Stephen Carter:

> We must never lose the capacity for judgment, especially the capacity to judge ourselves and our people. . . . Standards of morality matter no less than standards of excellence. There are black people who commit heinous crimes, and not all of them are driven by hunger and neglect. Not all of them turn to crime because they are victims of racist social policy . . . we are not automatons. To understand all may indeed be to forgive all, but no civilization can survive when the capacity for understanding is allowed to supersede the capacity for judgment. Otherwise, at the end of the line lies a pile of garbage: Hitler wasn't evil, just insane.[27]

Government can be effective in lowering the homicide and terror rates in inner-city neighborhoods by helping to stitch community institutions back together. We do not need to abolish the Bill of Rights to accomplish this goal. But we do need, as a first step, to break through cynicism and anomie and to reverse the spiral of delegitimation. The democratic social covenant rests on the presumption that one's fellow citizens are people of goodwill who yearn for the opportunity to work together, rather than to continue to glare at one another across racial, class, and ideological divides. To accomplish this reversal, we must tend to the badly battered institutions of civil society I discussed at the outset.

An enormous task, yes, but worth our best efforts. As we enter the twenty-first century, we may learn, perhaps sooner than we would like, whether Lincoln's expression of the hope of American democracy was an epitaph of the harbinger of a brighter democratic future for America, and hence for the world. For if the American republic falters, it will be the crash heard 'round the world. Our many friends in other countries, especially in the young and fragile democracies, may tremble and perhaps fail without the ballast that America uniquely provides, given her power and her promise. That is the glorious burden of American democracy in the next century.

When I was asked by Jamie Swift, a broadcaster who was putting together a radio series on "The U.S.A. Today" for broadcast on CBC's *Ideas,* "What does it mean to you to be an American?" I stammered and mumbled for a moment before I got my bearings and responded:

> It means that one can share a dream of political possibility, which is to say, a dream of democracy; it means that one can make one's voice heard; it means both individual accomplishment as well as a sense of responsibility; it means sharing the possibility of a brotherhood and sisterhood that is perhaps fractious—as all brotherhoods and sisterhoods are—and yet united in a spirit that's a spirit more of good than ill will; it means that one is marked by history but not totally burdened with it and defined by it; it means that one can expect some basic sense of fair play . . . will be recalled and called upon. I think Americans are committed to a rough-and-ready sense of fair play, and a kind of *social* egalitarianism, if you will, an egalitarianism of manners. I think that's the best I can do.

## NOTES

1. E.J. Dionne, *Why Americans Hate Politics* (New York: Simon and Schuster, 1991).

2. Thomas Byrne Edsall and Mary D. Edsall, *Chain Reaction* (New York: Norton, 1991).

3. Mary Jo Bane and David Ellwood, *Welfare Realities: From Rhetoric to Reform* (Cambridge, Mass.: Harvard University Press, 1994), p. 6.

4. This and other data in this paragraph are summarized in Jean Bethke Elshtain, William Galston, Enola Aird, and Amitai Etzioni, "A Communitarian Position on the Family," *National Civic Review* (Winter, 1993): 25–35. The position paper uses data from such reliable sources as the U.S. Justice Department's Bureau of Justice Statistics, the U.S. Labor Department, the Centers for Disease Control, and *The Kids Count Data Book* (Greenwich, Conn.: Casey Foundation, 1994), among others.

5. The evidence on all this is so overwhelming that it takes a real sleight of hand, sheer intellectual and political malfeasance, to deny it or to try to explain it away. Yet it happens all the time in academic—and many political—discussions. Over the years I have grown more and more perturbed by comfortable upper-middle-class academics blithely celebrating the "diversity"of lifestyles, while inner-city children play out in real life what being unmarried-with-child is more likely to be about than the glamour and glitz of "Murphy Brown." For just a few recent treatments that summarize much of the accumulated date, see Barbara Dafoe Whitehead, "Dan Quayle Was Right," *The Atlantic,* April 1993, pp. 47–84; the special issue of *Fortune,* "Children in Crisis," August 10, 1992; and Daniel Patrick Moynihan, "Defining Deviancy Down," *The American Scholar* (Winter 1993): 17–30.

6. Ralph Ketcham, ed., *The Anti-Federalist Papers and the Constitutional Convention Debates* (New York: New American Library, 1986), p. 18.

7. Alexis de Tocqueville, *Democracy in America,* trans. Henry Reeve, rev. Francis Bowen, ed. Phillips Bradley (New York: Vintage Books, 1945), vol. 2, p. 293.

8. Michael Walzer, *Citizenship and Civil Society* (Rutgers, N.J.: New Jersey Committee for the Humanities Series on the Culture of Community, October 13, 1992), part 1, pp. 11–12.

9. George Kateb celebrates our individualism and finds our worries excessive. The words in quotes are drawn from his *The Inner Ocean* (Ithaca, N.Y.: Cornell University Press, 1992), p. 31.

10. Christopher Lasch, *The True and Only Heaven* (New York: Norton, 1991).

11. Pope John Paul II, "Sollicitudo Rei Socialis," *Origins* 17, no. 33 (1988): 650.

12. Pope John Paul II, "Sollicitudo," pp. 654–55.

13. Alan Wolfe, *Whose Keeper? Social Science and Moral Obligation* (Berkeley: University of California Press, 1989), p. 2.

14. Mary Ann Glendon, *Rights Talk* (New York: Free Press, 1992).

15. Wolfe, *Whose Keeper?,* p. 20.

16. On the matter of civic—or anticivic—languages, see Robert Bellah, Richard Madsen, William Sullivan, Ann Swidler, and Steven Tipton, *Habits of the Heart* (Berkeley: University of California Press, 1985).

17. Bellah et al., *Habits,* p. 30.

18. Kateb, *The Inner Ocean,* pp. 103–4.

19. It is hard to overstate the destructive influence of MacKinnon and the army of MacKinnonites on standards of democratic fairness and due process. For MacKinnon, even to express such concerns is to be a "pimp" for pornographers. MacKinnon has even voiced disappointment that rape is a war crime under international law, since it fails to fit her idea of a simplistic continuum between leers in the workplace and rapes in Bosnia. The terrible irony of her ideology of victimization is that it sees women as abject, helpless, quaking victims or, alternatively, fierce avengers. Neither of these images suits one to democratic citizenship and the give-and-take of democratic policies. But, then, MacKinnon "cannot be overly bothered with the facts" because she prefers "the Big Metaphor." See Kenneth Anderson, "Illiberal Tolerance: An Essay on the Fall of Yugoslavia and the Rise of Multiculturalism in the United States," *Virginia Journal of International Law* 13, no. 2 (1993): 385–431. See also my article "Let's Finally Right the Wrongs: Rape Is a War Crime," *On the Issues* 2, no. 3 (Summer 1993): 36–39.

20. This quote is from my article "Trial by Fury," *The New Republic,* September 6, 1993, pp. 32–36.

21. America is not alone in rushing to embrace new chains in the name of "liberation" for women. In Canada, Bill C-49 embeds the view that it is nearly impossible for a woman to consent to any heterosexual act with a man not of her precise class or occupational status because otherwise there is a "power deferential" involved by definition. One Canadian scholar finds the legislation profoundly condescending to women, denying them any "autonomous, independent female sexuality. . . . I cannot avoid expressing my amazement at the fact that someone who calls herself a feminist should advocate a view which is so condescending towards women." The matter is, remember, not one of violence but of making it nearly impossible for any man at any time to present a case in his own defense that what went on between him and a female partner was not assault but a consensual act. The "special heinousness of rape," paradoxically and horribly, is lost in a general haze of sexual animosity and male bashing. See Robert Martin, "Bill C-49: A Victory for Interest Group Politics," *UNB Law Journal. Revue de Droit de L'Un-B* 42, tome 42 (1993): 371.

22. Charles Taylor, *The Malaise of Modernity* (Concord, Ontario: House of Anansi Press, 1991), p. 117.

23. I first introduced the phrase "spiral of delegitimation" in an essay on the 1992 U.S. presidential election, "Issues and Themes: Spiral of Delegitimation or New Social Covenant?" in Michael Nelson, ed., *The Elections of 1992* (Washington, D.C.: C.Q. Press, 1993), pp. 109–25.

24. James Q. Wilson, "The Government Gap," *The New Republic,* June 3, 1991, p. 38.

25. Cited in Elizabeth Mensch and Alan Freeman, *The Politics of Virtue* (Durham, N.C.: Duke University Press, 1993), p. 128.

26. Mike Barnicle, "A Plea for Family Rights," *Boston Globe,* April 22, 1994, p. 21.

27. Stephen L. Carter, *Reflections of an Affirmative Action Baby* (New York: Basic Books, 1991), pp. 244–45.

# 7

# Communitarianism and the Moral Dimension

*Amitai Etzioni*

A recent, very tempered debate between William A. Galston and Robert P. George brought into relief the importance of a concept neither employed, that of the good society.[1] Galston argued, drawing on Aristotle, that we ought to differentiate between the good *citizen* and the good *person.* The preliberal state, he added, was concerned with the good person; the liberal state is one that limits itself to the cultivation of the good citizen. George, true to his social conservative position, countered that he does not see a great need or compelling merit in drawing a sharp distinction between the good citizen and the good person. Before I suggest a third position, a few more words of background.

Galston is representative of a communitarian variation of classical liberal thinking. Liberals limit themselves to ensuring that individuals develop those *personal* virtues that they need to be good citizens of the liberal state, for instance the ability to think critically.[2] In contrast, social conservatives maintain that it is the role of the state to promote not merely citizenship but also the good person, not only skills needed to participate in the polity, but also *social* virtues—those that make the society a good one.

George Will champions this position, arguing that people are self-indulgent by nature: left to their own devices, they will abuse their liberties, becoming profligate and indolent as a result. People need a "strong national govern-

The author is especially indebted to Robert George for comments on a previous draft. Andrew Wilmar provided research assistance and editorial suggestions. The author additionally is grateful to Andrew Altman, David Anderson, Bruce Douglas, and Thomas Spragens Jr. for their comments on a draft of this paper. He was also helped a great deal by Barbara Fusco and Tim Bloser.

ment" that will be a "shaper" of citizens, and help them cope with the weaker angles of their nature.[3] William Kristol and David Brooks argue that anti-government themes provide too narrow a base for constructing a winning ideological political agenda. Conservatives, they conclude, need to build on the virtue of America, on the ideal of national greatness.[4]

Religious social conservatives have long been willing to rely on the powers of the state to foster behavior they consider virtuous. The measures they favor include banning abortion, banning most kinds of porn, making divorce more difficult, curbing homosexual activities, and institutionalizing prayers in public schools. Additionally, both religious and secular social conservatives have strongly advocated longer, more arduous prison terms for more individuals, for more kinds of crime, favoring especially life-sentences without the possibility of parole and death sentences. These penalties often are applied to people of whose business and consumption the state disapproves (a large proportion of those in jail are there for nonviolent, drug-related crimes) rather than for failing to discharge their citizen duties or actually endangering public safety. These are, on the face of it, not citizen issues but good-person issues.

The term "good state" appropriately summarizes this position because far from being viewed as an institution that if extended inevitably would diminish or corrupt people, the state is treated as an institution that can be entrusted with the task of making people good. That is, while it is not at all suggested that the state is good in itself, it is indicated that the state can be good—provided it acts to foster virtue.

Before moving on, it should be noted that among social conservatives, as among all such large and encompassing schools of thought and belief, there are important differences of opinion. It is relevant for the discussion at hand to note that there are many social conservatives who are less state- and more society-minded, such as Michael Oakeshott and a group associated with the Heritage Foundation called the National Foundation for Civic Renewal. That there are strong and less-strong social conservatives does not, however, invalidate their defining characteristic. To put it differently, thinkers who would rely mainly on the society and on persuasion to promote virtue by my definition are not social conservatives, but rather have one of the defining attributes of communitarians.

Both the liberal and social conservative positions have rich, well-known histories, and profound roots in social philosophy and political theory. While I will not retrace their often-reviewed intellectual foundations here,[5] I refer to one item of the sociology of knowledge: Each of these two positions can be viewed as addressing a particular historical constellation. The liberal position speaks to both the authoritarian and dogmatic environments in which it was first formulated by Locke, Smith, and Mill, as well as the totalitarian experiences of the twentieth century. At its core is a profound concern with the overpowering state and established church, especially if these institutions muster not merely superior and encompassing force but also actually succeed in acquiring an ideological mantle of virtue. The liberal position, which arose as a rejection of the good state, tended to reject all social formulations of the good.

Contemporary social conservative positions, by contrast, address the loss of virtue that modernization and populism have engendered, and reflect a profound concern with rising moral anarchy. While such concerns have been raised since the beginning of industrialization (if not before), they have particularly reintensified since the 1970s. It is this condition that religious fundamentalism seeks to correct, whether the fundamentalists in question are Muslims, Orthodox Jews, or some members of the religious right in the United States.

The third position, the communitarian one, which focuses on the good society, addresses the same sociohistorical conditions that motivate contemporary social conservatives, but provides a fundamentally different response. Much like its liberal cousin, the communitarian position rejects state regulation of moral behavior. Liberals, however, typically take this position because they favor moral pluralism; that is, they hold a broad conception of tolerance that includes the "right to do wrong." In the words of Michael Sandel, they "take pride in defending what they oppose."[6] Communitarians, by contrast, advocate state restraint because they believe that the society should be the agent responsible for promoting moral behavior. Thus, while the communitarian alternative I outline here may seem similar in certain limited respects to both social conservative and liberal positions, it nonetheless should be clear that its focus on the good society is conceptually distinct from both of these.

## THE CORE, NOT THE WHOLE

A good society formulates and promotes shared moral understanding rather than merely pluralism, and hence is far from value-neutral. This does not mean, however, that a good society sets an all-encompassing or even "thick" moral agenda. I discuss first the special nature of the formulation of the good by a communitarian society and then its limited scope.

Much has been written about whether or not there are sociological needs and moral justifications for social formulations of the good. The discussion, it has been stressed, concerns the public realm, namely the formulations that guide the state, which in turn may impose them on those who do not see the goodness of these formulations.[7] I refer here to shared formulations that arise out of moral dialogues among the members of the society, initiated by secular and religious intellectuals and moral authorities, community leaders, other opinion makers, and nourished by the media.[8]

Developing and sustaining a good society does require reaching into what is considered the private realm, the realm of the person. (Indeed, it might be said, that this "is" where the society is in the first place.) A good society, for instance, fosters trust among its members not solely or even primarily to enhance their trust in the government or to reduce burdens on the general public (for example, the problem of litigiousness), but rather to foster what is considered a *better* society. (What is "better" can be accounted for in utilitarian terms—for instance, by observing that in a society with a higher level of trust among its members there will be less white-collar crime—as well as in deontological ones, a notion I do not pursue further in this article.[9]) Other examples: a good society may extol substantive values such as stewardship toward the environment, charity for those who are vulnerable, marriage over singlehood, having children, and showing special consideration to the young and elderly. These are all specific goods with regard to which the society, through its various social mechanisms, prefers *one* basic form of conduct over all others. For instance, contemporary American society considers commitment to the well-being of the environment a significant good. While differences regarding what exactly this commitment entails are considered legitimate, this is not the case for normative positions that are neglectful of, not to mention hostile to, the needs of the environment.

To suggest that the scope of the private realm needs to be reduced, however, does not mean that all or even most private matters need to be subject to societal scrutiny and control. Indeed, one major way the communitarian position differs from its totalitarian, authoritarian, theocratic, and social conservative counterparts (referred to from here on as holistic governments) is that while the good society reaches the person, it seeks to cultivate only a limited set of *core* virtues rather than to be more expansive or holistic. A good society does not seek to ban moral pluralism on many secondary matters. For example, American society favors being religious over being atheist, but is rather "neutral" with regard to what religion a person follows. Similarly, American society expects that its members will show a measure of commitment to the American creed, but is quite accepting of people who cherish their divergent ethnic heritages, as long as such appreciation does not conflict with national loyalties. Unlike totalitarian regimes, American society does not foster one kind of music over others (both Nazis and communists tried to suppress jazz). There are no prescribed dress codes (e.g., no spartan Mao shirts), correct number of children to have, places one is expected to live, and so forth. In short, one key defining characteristic of the good society is that it defines shared formulations of the good, in contrast to the liberal state, while the scope of the good is much smaller than that advanced by holistic governments.

## RELIANCE ON CULTURE; ITS AGENCIES

Aside from limiting the scope of its moral agenda, the good society differs from its alternatives in the principal means by which it nurtures virtue. The basic dilemma that the concept of the good society seeks to resolve is how to cultivate virtue if one views the state as an essentially inappropriate and coercive entity.

In addressing this question, it is important to note that reference is not merely or even mainly to obeying the relevant laws, but rather to those large areas of personal and social conduct that are not governed by law, as well as to those that must be largely voluntarily carried out even if covered by laws, if law enforcement is not to be overwhelmed. At issue are such questions as what obligations parents owe to their children, children to their elderly parents, neighbors to one another, members of communities to other members and to other communities.[10]

The means of nurturing virtue that good societies chiefly rely upon often are subsumed under the term "culture." Specifically, these means include (a) agencies of *socialization* (family, schools, some peer groups, places of worship, and some voluntary associations) that instill values into new members of the society, resulting in an internal moral voice (or conscience) that guides people toward goodness. (b) Agencies of *social reinforcement* that support, in the social psychosocial sense of the term, the values members already have acquired (especially interpersonal bonds, peer relations, communal bonds, public visibility and leadership). These provide an external moral voice. And (c) values fostered because they are built into *societal institutions* (for instance, into marriage). I explore first the moral voice (internal and external) and ask whether it is compatible with liberty, and then the question of how the role societal institutions play in the good society differs from that which they play in the civil society.

## THE MORAL VOICE AND LIBERTY

One main instrument of the good society, the mainstay of "culture," is the moral voice, which urges people to behave in prosocial ways. While there is a tendency to stress the importance of the inner voice, and hence good parenting and moral or character education, communitarians recognize the basic fact that without continual external reinforcement, the conscience tends to deteriorate. The opinion of fellow human beings, especially those to whom a person is attached through familial or communal bonds, carries a considerable weight because of a profound human need to win and sustain the approval of others.[11]

The question has arisen whether compliance with the moral voice is compatible with free choice, whether one's right to be let (or left) alone includes a right to be free not only from state controls but also social pressure. This issue is highlighted by different interpretations assigned to an often-cited line by John Stuart Mill. In *On Liberty,* Mill writes, "The object of this Essay is to assert one very simple principle, as entitled to govern absolutely the dealings of society with the individual in the way of compulsion and control, whether the means used be physical force in the form of legal penalties, or the moral coercion of public opinion."[12] Some have interpreted this statement to suggest on its face that the moral voice is just as coercive as the government. Similarly, Alexis de Tocqueville, years earlier, wrote that "The multitude require no laws to coerce those who do not think like themselves: public disapprobation is enough; a sense of their loneliness and impotence overtakes them and drives them to despair."[13] If one takes these lines as written, the difference between reinforcement by the community and that by the state becomes a distinction without a difference. One notes, though, that de Tocqueville is also known for having highlighted the importance of communal associations in holding the state at bay. As I see it, it is essential to recognize not only that there is a profound difference between the moral voice of the community and coercion, but also that up to a point, the moral voice is the best antidote to an oppressive state.

At the heart of the matter are the assumptions one makes about human nature.[14] If one believes that people are good by nature, and external forces merely serve to pervert them, one correctly rejects all social input. It follows that the freer people are from all pressures, the better their individual and collective condition. If one assumes that people possess frailties that lead to behavior that is damaging not only to self but also others, the question arises of how to foster prosocial behavior (or the "social order"). Classical liberals tend to solve this tension between liberty and order by assuming that rational individuals whose interests are mutually complementary will voluntarily agree to arrangements that provide for the needed order. Communitarians suggest that reasonable individuals cannot be conceived of outside a social order; that the ability to make rational choices, to be free, presumes that the person is embedded in a social fabric. Moreover, communitarians posit that there is an inverse relation between the social order and state coercion: tyrannies arise when the social fabric frays. The moral voice speaks for the social fabric, thereby helping to keep it in good order.

Aside from being an essential prerequisite of social order and hence liberty, the moral voice is much more compatible with free choice than state coercion. The internal moral voice is as much a part of the person's self as the other parts of the self that drive his or her choices, the various tastes that specify the person's pleasures. The external moral voice, that of the community, leaves the final judgment and determination of how to proceed to the acting person—an element that is notably absent when coercion is applied. The society persuades, cajoles, censures, and educates, but that final decision remains the actor's. The state may also persuade, cajole, and censure, but actors realize *a priori* that when the state is not heeded, it will seek to force the actors to comply.

Some have questioned whether the moral voice is never coercive. In part, this is a definitional matter. When the moral voice is backed up by legal or economic sanctions, one must take care to note that it is not the moral voice per se, but rather these added elements that are coercive. Also, it is true in the West that in earlier historical periods, when people were confined to a single village and the community voice was all-powerful, a unified chorus of moral voices could be quite overwhelming even if it is not technically coercive, as physical force is not used or threatened. (It clearly can still be so in some limited parts of the West, and most assuredly in other parts of the world.) However, most people in contemporary free societies are able to choose, to a significant extent, the communities to which they are psychologically committed, and can often draw on one to limit the persuasive power of another. And the voices are far from monolithic. Indeed, it is a principal communitarian thesis that, in Western societies, moral voices often are, by and large, far from overwhelming. In fact, more often than not, they are too conflicted, hesitant, and weak to provide for a good society.[15] In short, highly powerful moral voices exist(ed) largely in other places and eras.

A comparison of the way the United States government fights the use of controlled substances and the way American society fosters parents' responsibilities for their children highlights this issue. The war against drugs depends heavily upon coercive agents; the treatment of children, by contrast, relies primarily upon the moral voice of members of the immediate and extended family, friends, neighbors, and others in the community. Admittedly, the state occasionally steps in. Yet most parents discharge their responsibilities not because they fear jail, but rather because they believe this to be the right way to conduct themselves, notions that are reinforced by the social fabric of their lives.

The difference between the ways societies and states foster values is further highlighted by comparing transferring wealth via charity to taxes; between volunteering to serve one's country and being drafted; and between attending Alcoholics Anonymous meetings and being jailed for alcohol abuse.

The basically voluntaristic nature of the moral voice is the profound reason the good society can, to a large extent, be reconciled with liberty, while a state that fosters good persons cannot. It is the reason the good society requires a clear moral voice, speaking for a set of shared core values, which a civic society and a liberal state do not.

## VIRTUES IN SOCIAL INSTITUTIONS

The other main instrument of the good society are social institutions. While the moral voice often is correctly referred to as "informal," because it is not encoded in law, and is integrated into one's personality and interactions with others,[16] societal institutions are formal and structured. Institutions are societal patterns that embody the values of the particular society or community.[17] A large volume of interactions and transactions are greatly facilitated in that they are predated by social forms upon which actors draw. Contracts are a case in point. Not only can actors often build in whole or in part on texts of contracts prepared by others, but the actors find the very concept of a contract and what this entails in terms of mutual obligations and the moral notion that "contracts ought to be observed" ready-made in their culture. While these institutions change over time, at any one point in time many of them stand by to guide social life, especially in well-functioning societies.[18]

Social institutions are important for the characterization of the difference between the good society and others, because most institutions are neither merely procedural nor value-neutral; in effect, most are the embodiment of particular values. For instance, the family, a major societal institution, is never value-neutral, but always reflects a particular set of values. This reality is highlighted by the reluctance of the Catholic Church to marry divorced people, attempts by several organized religions to encourage people to prepare better for their marriage (e.g., through *pre*marital counseling), and to strengthen their marriages (e.g., by means of counseling, retreats, and renewal of vows). All these institutionalized endeavors reflect the value of marriage—and a particular kind of marriage—that society seeks to uphold.

Similarly, societies do not merely provide public schools as neutral agencies for the purpose of imparting knowledge and skills. Public schools typically foster, despite recent tendencies to deny this fact, a long list of values, including empathy for the poor, interracial and interethnic and other forms of mutual respect (beyond merely tolerance), high regard for science, secularism, patriotism, and stewardship toward the environment. That societies foster specific values, through their institutions, is crucial for the understanding of the limits of conceptions of the civic society.

## A CIVIL AND GOOD SOCIETY

A comparison of the good society with the civil society provides a clearer delineation of both concepts. It should be noted at the outset that these terms are by no means oppositional. The good society is simply a more expansive concept. Thus, far from being uncivil, it fosters additional virtues beyond the merely civil. To put it differently, the two concepts are like concentric circles, with the smaller circle representing the domain of civil society, and the larger that of the good society.[19]

While there is no single, agreed-upon definition of civil society, most usages of the term reflect two institutional features and the values they embody. One is a rich array of voluntary associations that countervails the state and that provides the citizens with the skills and practices that democratic government requires. Another is holding of passions at bay and enhancing deliberative, reasoned democracy by maintaining the civility of discourse.

In a special issue of the *Brookings Review* dedicated to the civil society, editor E. J. Dionne Jr. characterizes the civil society as (a) "a society where people treat each other with kindness and respect, avoiding the nastiness we have come to associate with 30-second political ads and a certain kind of televised brawl." And (b) a collection of voluntary associations that includes Boy and Girl Scouts, Little League, veterans groups, book clubs, Lions and Elks, churches, and neighborhood crime watch groups.[20] Most discussions stress the second feature. "Bowling alone" has become somewhat of a symbol for this line of thinking. Robert Putnam argues that bowling with one's friends (which he terms alone) is less sustaining of civil society than bowling as members of a bowling league because such leagues are part and parcel of the voluntary associations that civil society requires.[21]

From the viewpoint of the discussion at hand, the most important aspect of these characterizations of civil society is that they draw *no difference among voluntary associations with regard to any substantive values* that are fostered by bowling leagues, book clubs, Little Leagues, or any other such voluntary associations. I am not suggesting that these associations are actually without specific normative dispositions. Little Leagues, for instance, may cherish a healthy body and sporting behavior (or—winning at all costs); book clubs foster respect for learning and culture, and so on. But from the viewpoint of their contribution to civil society they all are treated by champions of civil society as basically equivalent; none is, normatively speaking, inherently morally superior to the other. In this particular sense, they are treated as normatively neutral.

Certainly champions of civil society do recognize some differences among voluntary associations, but these are limited to their functions as elements of the civil society rather than their normative content. For instance, voluntary associations that are more effective in developing citizen skills are preferred over those that are less so. But the actual values to which these people apply their skills is not under review nor are other substantive values the associations embody. Thus, the civil society does affirm some values, but only a thin layer of procedural and/or tautological ones; it basically affirms itself. Hence, the civil society (and the associations that constitute its backbone) cherishes reasoned (rather then value-laden) discourse, mutual tolerance, participatory skills, and, of course, volunteerism. Yet these values, upon closer examination, do not entail any particular social formulations of the good. They do not suggest what one best participates in or for, what one should volunteer to support, or which normative conclusions of a public discourse one ought to promote or find troubling.

Particularly telling are recent calls to find *a* common ground and to deliberate in a civil manner—two contentless elements of civility often evoked whenever civil society is discussed. Commonality is celebrated on any grounds as long as it is common. And the proponents of civility seem satisfied as long as one adheres to the rules of engagements (not to demonize the other side, not raise one's voice, etc.), and as long as the dialogue itself is civil, regardless of what actually is being discussed.[22]

For the civil society, an association that facilitates people joining to play bridge has the same basic standing as NARAL or Operation Rescue; members of the Elks share the same status as those of the Promise Keepers; and bowling leagues are indistinguishable from NAMBLA, whose members meet to exchange tips on how to seduce boys who are younger than eight. Indeed, beyond league bowling (and bridge playing), other mainstays of "social capital" that Putnam found in those parts of Italy that are more soundly civil and democratic than others were bird-watching groups and choral societies.[23] Bird-watching groups may enhance respect for nature and choirs may cherish culture (or certain kinds of culture over others), but this is not the reason Putnam praises them. As Putnam puts it, he extols them because "[t]aking part in a choral society or a bird-watching club can teach self-discipline and an appreciation for the joys of successful collaboration."[24] So could most if not all other voluntary associations.

In short, from the basic standpoint of the civil society, one voluntary association is, in principle, as good as any another.[25] They differ greatly, however, from the perspective of the good society, precisely because they embody different values. Thus, to the extent that American society cherishes the notion of interracial integration, it views the Urban League and NAACP as much more in line with its values than the Nation of Islam, and the Ripon Society more so than the Aryan groups—all voluntary associations.[26]

The concept of the good society differs from that of the civil one in that while the former also strongly favors voluntary associations—a rich and strong social fabric, and civility of discourse—it formulates and seeks to uphold some *particular* social conceptions of the good. The good society is, as I have already suggested, centered around a core of substantive, particularistic values. For instance, different societies foster different values or at least give much more normative weight to some values than other societies that exhibit a commitment to the same values. Thus, Austria, Holland, and Switzerland place special value on social harmony, acting only after profound and encompassing shared understandings are achieved. Many continental societies value the welfare state, lower inequality, and social amenities more than American and British societies do, and also put less emphasis upon economic achievements.

Similarly, the question of whether or not religion is disestablished is far from a procedural matter. Many democratic societies that establish one church (e.g., Anglican in the United Kingdom, Lutheran in Scandinavia) also allow much greater and more open inclusion of a specific religion into their institutionalized life than does American society. The presence of crucifixes in Bavarian public schools and the routine pronouncement of Christian prayers in UK schools both illustrate this point. Promoting these religious values is deemed an integral part of what is considered a good society.

I digress to note that none of the societies mentioned are "good" in some perfected sense; they are societies that aspire to promote specific social virtues, and in this sense aspire to be good societies. The extent to which they are successful, and the normative evaluation of the specific virtues one society promotes as compared to others, are subjects not studied here because this would requires an extensive treatment that I have provided elsewhere.[27] All that I argue here is that good societies promote particularistic, substantive formations of the good; that these are limited sets of core values that are promoted largely by the moral voice and not by state coercion. The conditions under which the particular values fostered earn our acclaim is not studied here.

To summarize the difference between a good and a civil society regarding the core institution of voluntary association, one notes that while both kinds of society draw on these associations, these play different roles within these two societies. In civil societies, voluntary associations serve as mediating institutions between the citizen and the state, and help cultivate citizen skills (ways to gain knowledge about public affairs, form associations, gain a political voice, and so on); they develop and exercise the democratic muscles, so to speak. In the good society, voluntary associations *also* serve to introduce members to particularistic values, and to reinforce individuals' normative commitments. Thus, while from the perspective of a civil society a voluntary association is a voluntary association, *from the view of a good society, no two voluntary associations are equivalent.* The regard in which voluntary associations are held ranges from those that are celebrated (because they foster the social virtues the good society seeks to cultivate), to those that are neutral, to those that—while voluntary—sustain values divergent from or even contradictory to those the society seeks to foster.

## THE IMPLICATIONS OF VARYING DEFINITIONS

I now consider briefly the various definitions of civil society offered by particular scholars to further highlight the differentiation between the civil and the good societies.

Michael Novak provides a straightforward, value-neutral definition of the civil society. He writes:

> The term for all these nonstatist forms of social life—those rooted in human social nature, under the sway of reason—is *civil society.* That term includes nat-

> ural associations such as the family, as well as the churches, and private associations of many sorts; fraternal, ethnic, and patriotic societies; voluntary organizations such as the Boy Scouts, the Red Cross, and Save the Whales; and committees for the arts, the sciences, sports and education.[28]

In a book often cited in this context, Berger and Neuhaus view mediating structures as a key element of the civil society and define mediating structures as follows:

> . . . those institutions that stand between the private world of individuals and the large impersonal structures of modern society. They "mediated" by constituting a vehicle by which personal beliefs and values could be transmitted into the mega-institutions. They were thus "Janus-faced" institutions, facing both "upward" and "downward." Their meditations were then of benefit to both levels of social life: the individual was protected from the alienations and "anomie" of modern life, while the large institutions, including the state, gained legitimacy by being related to values that governed the actual lives of ordinary people.[29]

This definition is essentially value-free. It does not distinguish between different mediating structures according to the specific normative foundations or values they extol. A federation of labor unions might fulfill the mediating function as well as one of industrialists; a group of churches as well as a league of atheists; an association of stamp collectors as well as the Sierra Club. At one point, Berger and Neuhaus address this issue of value-neutrality with more directness and candor than any of the other sources examined. The two clearly state that a mediating structure is a mediating structure regardless of its values, even if these might be nefarious, criminal, or otherwise wholly objectionable. Indeed, in the revised edition of their book, Berger and Neuhaus fully concede the limitations of their concept:

> Possibly, though, we were a bit carried away in our enthusiasm for these institutions, overlooking the fact that some of them definitely play nefarious roles in society. Thus, strictly speaking in terms of our definition, the Mafia, the Ku Klux Klan, and the social branch of an organization seeking to get the government to negotiate with visiting aliens in UFOs could also be described as mediating structures. They do, indeed, mediate between individuals and the larger society. It just happens that the beliefs and values thus mediated are criminal, immoral, or just plain crazy. We would suggest now that there are (to put it plainly) both good and bad mediating structures and that social policy will have to make this differentiation in terms of the values being mediated.[30]

While Berger and Neuhaus are best characterized as social conservatives, John Rawls is considered by most to be a liberal. Regarding the issue at hand, however, he seems to hold a compatible view. Indeed, Rawls even seems to go a step further, not only implying that the various mediating institutions are morally equivalent, but also suggesting that the entirety of civil society—not merely the liberal state!—is little more than a neutral zone in which various virtues compete, and in which none is prescribed or even preferred as a matter of societal policy. (I write "seems" to indicate that I do not join here the very elaborate debate concerning what Rawls says, really meant to say, and how he changed his mind from one volume to the next.) The following quote seems to me to speak quite directly to the issue at hand, and it is this Rawls I address here:

> . . . all discussions are from the point of view of citizens in the culture of civil society, which Habermas calls the *public sphere.* There, we as citizens discuss how justice as fairness is to be formulated, and whether this or that aspect of it seems acceptable. . . . In the same way, the claims of the ideal of discourse and of its procedural conception of democratic institutions are considered. Keep in mind that this background culture contains comprehensive doctrines of all kinds that are taught, explained, debated against one another, and argued about—indefinitely without end as long as society has vitality and spirit. It is the culture of daily life with its many associations: its universities and churches, learned and scientific societies; endless political discussions of ideas and doctrines are commonplace everywhere.[31]

This text is compatible with the notion that a civil society is not a good society because it does not promote one "comprehensive doctrine," but rather provides simply the forum in which a plurality of such doctrines can be debated "indefinitely without end," within the numerous voluntary associations. Civil society is thus desirable because it affords and sustains endless debate, thereby precluding any general consensus on the good to which society at large can subscribe and attempt to foster in its members. In that sense, the "endless" element is not merely dismissive but actually essential.

Michael Walzer, often considered a communitarian, espouses the same basic viewpoint very clearly:

> I would rather say that the civil society argument is a corrective to the four ideological accounts of the good life than a fifth to stand alongside them. It challenges their singularity but it has no singularity of its own. The phrase "social being" describes men and women who are citizens, producers, consumers, members of the nation, and much else besides—and none of these by nature or because it is the best thing to be. The associational life of civil society is the actual ground where all versions of the good are worked out and tested . . . and proved to be partial, incomplete, ultimately unsatisfying. . . . Ideally, civil society is a setting of settings: all are included, none is preferred.[32]

Walzer clearly distinguishes the civil society from the good society. Indeed, at one point he makes mocking reference to a potential slogan for civil society, "join the associations of your choice,"[33] arguing that it entails a less than morally compelling and mobilizing vision. Walzer regrets that the anti-ideological nature of the civil society makes it unable to inspire citizens, but implies that this feature is necessary to prevent the idealization of the state. I will return to the importance of this point, which reflects a fear, implicit in Walzer's remarks, that the social formation of the good will lead to authoritarianism, if not totalitarianism.[34]

William Sullivan stresses that the realm of associations and organizations that are part of neither the market nor the state makes up the "much-invoked" idea of the civil society.[35] He points out that these aforementioned bodies are not free-standing, but rather "interwoven" with the state and the market, a point well taken.[36] But Sullivan too sees no apparent need to draw moral distinctions among the various voluntary associations that comprise civil society. Particularly telling is his description of the various civil virtues which these associations are supposed to promote in their members: "public engagement, reciprocity, mutual trust, tolerance within a general agreement about purposes."[37] Once again, while these values certainly are important, they serve to sustain good citizens and make the civic society work, rather than promote a particular moral vision that a good society seeks to foster.

The definition of civil society, it should be reiterated, is anything but conclusive. And there are some commentators—most of them social conservatives—who pack into their notions of civil society elements of what I have referred to as the good society. Gertrude Himmelfarb, for example, argues that only a renewed and remoralized civil society can effectively curb such immoral behaviors as drug addiction, illegitimacy, neglect of the elderly, and the like.[38]

But the definition of civil society seems to resist such expansions. As the preceding examples suggest, when commentators invoke the concept, they typically do so in a more restrictive manner. Indeed, the very effort by Himmelfarb and others to expand the scope of civil society highlights the need for an additional concept that can capture this added normative element. The good society can well serve in this capacity.

We often can learn a great deal about social doctrines and political theories by examining the alternatives they seek to engage. (For instance, Max Weber's volumes on comparative religion clearly speak to the economic determinism associated with Karl Marx.) The civil society thesis addresses the fear that social formations of the good will be imposed by the state on a wide front. It does so by advocating a great restriction of the public realm, and by opposing collective fostering of virtues (all those not directly subservient to the civic society or liberal state). The crisis that modern societies increasingly have had to face for the last generation is that of the moral vacuum, an emptiness that religious fundamentalism has sought to fill. This challenge is variously referred to as the loss of meaning or virtue, the crisis of culture, and the deterioration of values. This spiritual void, however, cannot long be left unfilled.

If not addressed by values that arise out of shared moral dialogue, it will be filled, as we have already seen in large segments of the world, by command and control theocracies. Democratic societies can be expected to continue to be vigilant against the return of overpowering secular governments—a threat countered by a rich fabric of civil institutions. However, given the challenges posed by fundamentalism in the Moslem world, in Israel, and by various Christian, right-wing movements, concerns for the civil society may well need to be supplemented by concern about the nature of the good society. If societies must uphold some substantive values, what will these be beyond the narrow band of largely procedural commitments that civil society presently entails? This is the question the next generation faces, a question flagged by the concept of a good society, a society that fosters a limited set of core values and relies largely on the moral voice rather than upon state coercion.

## NOTES

1. The debate took place at a meeting organized by David Blankenhorn at the Institute for American Values.

2. Galston differs with many liberal colleagues, for instance Amy Gutmann, in terms of the scope of such citizen-virtues that he would have the state promote if such cultivation violates the values of a community. Thus, he would respect the Amish culture and not make their children attend public high schools, while Gutmann would override it in the name of the citizen requirements of the liberal state. There is much more to this debate between liberal communitarians and liberal-liberals but all I seek to highlight here is that both sides presume that the state limits its virtue-cultivating concerns to citizenship; the difference between the sides is limited to the scope of personal virtues that good citizenship requires. See William Galston, *Liberal Purposes* (Cambridge: Cambridge University Press, 1991) and Amy Gutmann, *Democratic Education* (Princeton: Princeton University Press, 1987).

3. Will is seconded by Walter Berns of the American Enterprise Institute, who argues that one cannot fold conservatism's ideals into the notion of "freedom," and by Elliot Cohen, who maintains that the last thing the Founders envisioned was a "feeble government." See George Will, "Conservative Challenge," *Washington Post,* 17 August 1997, c7. William J. Bennett stresses that while there is much to lament about big government, he is deeply troubled by conservatives' "increasing and reckless rhetorical attacks against government itself." He draws on Benjamin Franklin, who is said to have understood that "the strength of the nation depends on the general opinion of the goodness of the government," not a phrase often employed by economic conservatives. See William Bennett, "Rekindling Our Passion for America; Cynicism About Government Programs Cannot be Allowed to Quell Our Love of Country," *Los Angeles Times,* 28 October 1997, 7.

4. See David Brooks and William Kristol, "What Ails Conservatism," *Wall Street Journal*, 15 September 1997.

5. See Amitai Etzioni, *The New Golden Rule: Community and Morality in a Democratic Society* (New York: Basic Books, 1996).

6. Quoted in William Lund, "Politics, Virtue, and the Right To Do Wrong: Assessing the Communitarian Critique of Rights," *Journal of Social Philosophy* 28 (1997): 102.

7. See Lund, "Politics," 108–9.

8. Etzioni, *The New Golden Rule,* 85-118.

9. See Etzioni, *The New Golden Rule,* 217–57; Robert Bellah, Richard Madsen, William M. Sullivan, Ann Swidler, and Steven M. Tipton, *The Good Society* (New York: Vintage, 1991); and Walter Lippman, *An Inquiry Into the Principles of the Good Society* (Westport: Greenwood Press, 1943).

10. The difference between states and societies is surprisingly often ignored. When the communitarian platform was translated into German the term "member" was translated as "Bürger." When it was pointed out that bürger means citizen, a participant in the state and not the society per se, it turned out that there is no term that readily allows to express this distinction in German. The word "Mitglieder" refers more to a dues-payer or someone who belongs, but does not have the rich evocative power of the communitarian notion of membership brings to mind.

11. See Dennis Wrong, *The Problem of Order: What Unites and Divides Society* (New York: Free Press, 1994).

12: John Stuart Mill, *On Liberty,* ed. David Spitz (New York: W.W. Norton, 1975), 71.

13. Alexis de Tocqueville, *Democracy in America,* trans. Henry Reeve, ed. Phillips Bradley (New York: Alfred A. Knopf, 1991), volume 2, 261.

14. This is a huge subject mentioned but not examined here. For discussion of the author's views relating to the issue at hand, see *The New Golden Rule: Community and Morality in a Democratic Society* (New York: Basic Books, 1996), 160–88.

15. For futher discussion, see Etzioni, *The New Golden Rule,* 85–159.

16. See, for instance, Robert Sampson, Stephen Raudenbush, and Felton Earls, "Neighborhoods and Violent Crime: A Multilevel Study of Collective Efficacy," *Science*, 15 August 1997.

17. For an excellent analysis of institutions and their role in the good society, see Bellah et al., *The Good Society, op. cit.*

18. This subject recently has received a great deal of attention in legal scholarship, usually under the heading of "social norms." See, for example, Richard Epstein, "Enforcing Norms: When the Law Gets in the Way," *Responsive Community* 7 (1997): 4–15.

19. Seee Avishai Margalit, *The Decent Society,* trans. Naomi Goldblum (Cambridge: Harvard University Press, 1996).

20. E.J. Dionne, Jr., "*Why Civil Society?*" The Brookings Review 15 (1997): 5.

21. Robert Putnam, "Bowling Alone, Revisited," *The Responsive Community* 5 (1995): 18–33.

22. See James Davison Hunter, *Culture Wars: The Struggle to Define America* (New York: Basic Books, 1991).

23. See Robert Putnam, *Making Democracy Work: Civic Traditions in Modern Italy* (Princeton: Princeton University Press, 1993).

24. Putnam, *Making Democracy Work,* 90.

25. The relevant differences are instrumental, rather than principled or normative (for example, the relative size, the level of public education, etc.).

26. See Suzanna Sherry, "Without Virtue There Can Be No Liberty," 78 *Minnesota Law Review* 61 (1993). A somewhat similar point is made by the noted civic theorist Benjamin Barber. While Barber is a fan of voluntary associations generally, he warns against those that are so "privatistic, or parochial, or particularistic" that they undermine democracy. He writes: "Parochialism enhances the immediate tie between neighbors by separating them from alien 'others,' but it subverts the wider ties required by democracy—ties that can be nurtured only by an expanding imagination bound to no particular sect or fraternity." See Benjamin Barber, *Strong Democracy: Participatory Politics for a New Age* (Berkeley: University of California Press, 1984), 234–35.

27. See Etzioni, *The New Golden Rule*, 217–57.

28. Michael Novak, "Seven Tangled Questions," in *To Empower People: From State to Civil Society*, ed. Michael Novak (Washington, D.C.: American Enterprise Institute, 1996), 138.

29. Peter L. Berger and Richard John Neuhaus, "Response," in *To Empower People: From State to Civil Society*, ed. Michael Novak (Washington, D.C.: American Enterprise Institute, 1996), 148–49.

30. Berger and Neuhaus, "Response," 149–50.

31. John Rawls, *Political Liberalism* (New York: Columbia University Press, 1996), 382–83.

32. Michael Walzer, "The Concept of Civil Society," in *Toward a Global Civil Society*, ed. Michael Walzer (Providence: Berghahn Books, 1995), 16–17.

33. Walzer, "Civil Society," 25.

34. For further discussion and criticism of this conception of civil society, see Jean Cohen, "Interpreting the Notion of Civil Society," in *Toward a Global Civil Society*, ed. Michael Walzer (Providence: Berghahn Books, 1995).

35. William Sullivan, "Institutions and the Infrastructure of Democracy," in *New Communitarian Thinking: Persons, Virtues, Institutions, and Communities*, ed. Amitai Etzioni (Charlottesville: University Press of Virginia, 1995), 173.

36. Sullivan, "Institutions," 173.

37. Sullivan, "Institutions," 173.

38. See Gertrude Himmelfarb, "The Renewal of Civil Society," in *Culture in Crisis and the Renewal of Civic Life*, eds. T. Williams Boxx and Gary M. Quinlivan (New York: Rowman & Littlefield, 1996), 67–75.

# Part Three

# Community as a Generator of Social Capital

# 8

# To Empower People: From State to Civil Society

*Peter L. Berger and Richard John Neuhaus*

Two seemingly contradictory tendencies are evident in current thinking about public policy in America. First, there is a continuing desire for the services provided by the modern welfare state. The serious debate is over how and to what extent it should be expanded. The second tendency is one of strong animus against government, bureaucracy, and bigness as such. This animus is directed not only toward Washington but toward government at all levels. Although this essay is addressed to the American situation, it should be noted that a similar ambiguity about the modern welfare state exists in other democratic societies, notably in Western Europe.

Perhaps this is just another case of people wanting to eat their cake and have it too. It would hardly be the first time in history that the people wanted benefits without paying the requisite costs. Nor are politicians above exploiting ambiguities by promising increased services while reducing expenditures. The extravagant rhetoric of the modern state and the surrealistic vastness of its taxation system encourage magical expectations that make contradictory measures seem possible. As long as some of the people can be fooled some of the time, some politicians will continue to ride into office on such magic.

But this is not the whole story. The contradiction between wanting more government services and less government may be only apparent. More precisely, we suggest that the modern welfare state is here to stay, indeed that it ought to expand the benefits it provides—but that *alternative mechanisms are possible to provide welfare-state services.*

The current anti-government, anti-bigness mood is not irrational. Complaints about impersonality, unresponsiveness, and excessive interference, as well as the perception of rising costs and deteriorating service—these are based upon empirical and widespread experience. The crisis of New York

City, which is rightly seen as more than a fiscal crisis, signals a national state of unease with the policies followed in recent decades. At the same time there is widespread public support for publicly addressing major problems of our society in relieving poverty, in education, health care, and housing, and in a host of other human needs. What first appears as contradiction, then, is the sum of equally justified aspirations. The public policy goal is to address human needs without exacerbating the reasons for animus against the welfare state.

Of course there are no panaceas. The alternatives proposed here, we believe, can solve *some* problems. Taken seriously, they could become the basis of far-reaching innovations in public policy, perhaps of a new paradigm for at least sectors of the modern welfare state.

The basic concept is that of what we are calling mediating structures. The concept in various forms has been around for a long time. What is new is the systematic effort to translate it into specific public policies. For purposes of this study, mediating structures are defined as *those institutions standing between the individual in his private life and the large institutions of public life.*

Modernization brings about a historically unprecedented dichotomy between public and private life. The most important large institution in the ordering of modern society is the modern state itself. In addition, there are the large economic conglomerates of capitalist enterprise, big labor, and the growing bureaucracies that administer wide sectors of the society, such as in education and the organized professions. All these institutions we call the megastructures.

Then there is that modern phenomenon called private life. It is a curious kind of preserve left over by the large institutions and in which individuals carry on a bewildering variety of activities with only fragile institutional support.

For the individual in modern society, life is an ongoing migration between these two spheres, public and private. The megastructures are typically alienating, that is, they are not helpful in providing meaning and identity for individual existence. Meaning, fulfillment, and personal identity are to be realized in the private sphere. While the two spheres interact in many ways, in private life the individual is left very much to his own devices, and thus is uncertain and anxious. Where modern society is "hard," as in the megastructures, it is personally unsatisfactory; where it is "soft," as in private life, it cannot be relied upon. Compare, for example, the social realities of employment with those of marriage.

The dichotomy poses a double crisis. It is a crisis for the individual who must carry on a balancing act between the demands of the two spheres. It is a political crisis because the megastructures (notably the state) come to be devoid of personal meaning and are therefore viewed as unreal or even malignant. Not everyone experiences the crisis in the same way. Many who handle it more successfully than most have access to institutions that *mediate* between the two spheres. Such institutions have a private face, giving private life a measure of stability, and they have a public face, transferring meaning and value to the megastructures. Thus, mediating structures alleviate each facet of the double crisis of modern society. Their strategic position derives from their reducing both the anomic precariousness of individual existence in isolation from society and the threat of alienation to the public order.

Our focus is on four such mediating structures—neighborhood, family, church, and voluntary association. This is by no means an exhaustive list, but these institutions were selected for two reasons: first, they figure prominently in the lives of most Americans and, second, they are most relevant to the problems of the welfare state with which we are concerned. The proposal is that, if these institutions could be more imaginatively recognized in public policy, individuals would be more "at home" in society, and the political order would be more "meaningful."

Without institutionally reliable processes of mediation, the political order becomes detached from the values and realities of individual life. Deprived of its moral foundation, the political order is "delegitimated." When that happens, the political order must be secured by coercion rather than by consent. And when that happens, democracy disappears.

The attractiveness of totalitarianism—whether instituted under left-wing or right-wing banners—is that it overcomes the dichotomy of private and public existence by imposing on life one comprehensive order of meaning. Although established totalitarian systems can be bitterly disappointing to their architects as well as their subjects, they are, on the historical record, nearly impossible to dismantle. The system continues quite effectively, even if viewed with cynicism by most of the population—including those who are in charge.

Democracy is "handicapped" by being more vulnerable to the erosion of meaning in its institutions. Cynicism threatens it; wholesale cynicism can destroy it. That is why mediation is so crucial to democracy. Such mediation cannot be sporadic and occasional; it must be institutionalized in *structures.* The structures we have chosen to study have demonstrated a great capacity for adapting and innovating under changing conditions. Most important, they exist where people are, and that is where sound public policy should always begin.

This understanding of mediating structures is sympathetic to Edmund Burke's well-known claim: "To be attached to the subdivision, to love the little platoon we belong to in society, is the first principle (the germ as it were) of public affections." And it is sympathetic to Alexis de Tocqueville's conclusion drawn from his observation of Americans: "In democratic countries the science of association is the mother of science; the progress of all the rest depends upon the progress it has made." Marx too was concerned about the destruction of community, and the glimpse he gives us of postrevolutionary society is strongly reminiscent of Burke's "little platoons." The emphasis is even sharper in the anarcho-syndicalist tradition of social thought.

In his classic study of suicide, Emile Durkheim describes the "tempest" of modernization sweeping away the "little aggregations" in which people formerly found community, leaving only the state on the one hand and a mass of individuals, "like so many liquid molecules," on the other. Although using different terminologies, others in the sociological tradition—Ferdinand Tönnies, Max Weber, Georg Simmel, Charles Cooley, Thorstein Veblen—have analyzed aspects of the same dilemma. Today Robert Nisbet has most persuasively argued that the loss of community threatens the future of American democracy.

Also, on the practical political level, it might seem that mediating structures have universal endorsement. There is, for example, little political mileage in being anti-family or anti-church. But the reality is not so simple. Liberalism—which constitutes the broad center of American politics, whether or not it calls itself by that name—has tended to be blind to the political (as distant from private) functions of mediating structures. The main feature of liberalism, as we intend the term, is a commitment to government action toward greater social justice within the existing system. (To revolutionaries, of course, this is "mere reformism," but the revolutionary option has not been especially relevant, to date, in the American context.) Liberalism's blindness to mediating structures can be traced to its Enlightenment roots. Enlightenment thought is abstract, universalistic, addicted to what Burke called "geometry" in social policy. The concrete particularities of mediating structures find an inhospitable soil in the liberal garden. There the great concern is for the individual ("the rights of man") and for a just public order, but anything "in between" is viewed as irrelevant, or even an obstacle, to the rational ordering of society. What lies in between is dismissed, to the extent it can be, as superstition, bigotry, or (more recently) cultural lag.

American liberalism has been vigorous in the defense of the private rights of individuals, and has tended to dismiss the argument that private behavior can have public consequences. Private rights are frequently defended *against* mediating structures—children's rights against the family, the rights of sexual deviants against neighborhood or small-town sentiment, and so forth. Similarly, American liberals are virtually faultless in their commitment to the religious liberty of individuals. But the liberty to be defended is always that of privatized religion. Supported by a very narrow understanding of the separation of church and state, liberals are typically hostile to the claim that institutional religion might have public rights and public functions. As a consequence of this "geometrical" outlook, liberalism has a hard time coming to terms with the alienating effects of the abstract structures it has multiplied since the New Deal. This may be the Achilles heel of the liberal state today.

The left, understood as some version of the socialist vision, has been less blind to the problem of mediation. Indeed the term alienation derives from Marxism. The weakness of the left, however, is its exclusive or nearly exclusive focus on the capitalist economy as the source of this evil, when in fact the alienations of the socialist states, insofar as there are socialist states, are much more severe than those of the capitalist states. While some theorists of the New Left have addressed this problem by using elements from the anarcho-syndicalist tradition, most socialists see mediating structures as something that may be relevant to a postrevolutionary future, but that in the present only distracts attention from the struggle toward building socialism. Thus the left is not very helpful in the search for practical solutions to our problem.

On the right of the political broad center, we also find little that is helpful. To be sure, classical European conservatism had high regard for mediating structures, but, from the eighteenth century on, this tradition has been marred by a romantic urge to revoke modernity—a prospect that is, we think, neither likely nor desirable. On the other hand, what is now called conservatism in America is in fact old-style liberalism. It is the laissez-faire ideology of the period before the New Deal, which is roughly the time when liberalism shifted its faith from the market to government. *Both* the old faith in the market *and* the new faith in government share the abstract thought patterns of the Enlightenment. In addition, today's conservatism typically exhibits the weakness of the left in reverse: it is highly sensitive to the alienations of big government, but blind to the analogous effects of big business. Such one-sidedness, whether left or right, is not helpful.

As is now being widely recognized, we need new approaches free of the ideological baggage of the past. The mediating structures paradigm cuts across current ideological and political divides. This proposal has met with gratifying interest from most with whom we have shared it, and while it has been condemned as right-wing by some and as left-wing by others, this is in fact encouraging. Although the paradigm may play havoc with the conventional political labels, it is hoped that, after the initial confusion of what some social scientists call "cognitive shock," each implication of the proposal will be considered on its own merits.

The argument of this essay—and the focus of the research project it is designed to introduce—can be subsumed under three propositions. The first proposition is analytical: *Mediating structures are essential for a vital democratic society.* The other two are broad programmatic recommendations: *Public policy should protect and foster mediating structures,* and *Wherever possible, public policy should utilize mediating structures for the realization of social purposes.* The research project will determine, it is hoped, whether these propositions stand up under rigorous examination and, if so, how they can be translated into specific recommendations.

The analytical proposition assumes that mediating structures are the value-generating and value-maintaining agencies in society. Without them, values become another function of the megastructures, notably of the state, and this is a hallmark of totalitarianism. In the totalitarian case, the individual becomes the object rather than the subject of the value-propagating processes of society.

The two programmatic propositions are, respectively, minimalist and maximalist. Minimally, public policy should cease and desist from damaging mediating structures. Much of the damage has been unintentional in the past. We should be more cautious than we have been. As we have learned to ask about the effects of government action upon racial minorities or upon the environment, so we should learn to ask about the effects of public policies on mediating structures.

The maximalist proposition ("utilize mediating structures") is much the riskier. We emphasize, "wherever possible." The mediating structures paradigm is not applicable to all areas of policy. Also, there is the real danger that such structures might be "co-opted" by the government in a too eager embrace that would destroy the very distinctiveness of their function. The prospect of government control of the family, for example, is clearly the exact opposite of our intention. The goal in utilizing mediating structures is to expand government services without producing government oppressiveness. Indeed it might be argued that the achievement of that goal is one of the acid tests of democracy.

It should be noted that these propositions differ from superficially similar proposals aimed at decentralizing governmental functions. Decentralization is limited to what can be done *within* governmental structures; we are concerned with the structures that stand *between* government and the individual. Nor, again, are we calling for a devolution of governmental responsibilities that would be tantamount to dismantling the welfare state. We aim rather at rethinking the institutional means by which government exercises its responsibilities. The idea is not to revoke the New Deal but to pursue its vision in ways more compatible with democratic governance.

Finally, there is a growing ideology based upon the proposition that "small is beautiful." We are sympathetic to that sentiment in some respects, but we do not share its programmatic antagonism to the basic features of modern society. Our point is not to attack the megastructures but to find better ways in which they can relate to the "little platoons" in our common life.

The theme is *empowerment.* One of the most debilitating results of modernization is a feeling of powerlessness in the face of institutions controlled by those whom we do not know and whose values we often do not share. Lest there be any doubt, our belief is that human beings, whoever they are, understand their own needs better than anyone else—in, say, 99 percent of all cases. The mediating structures under discussion here are the principal expressions of the real values and the real needs of people in our society. They are, for the most part, the people-sized institutions. Public policy should recognize, respect, and, where possible, empower these institutions.

A word about the poor is in order. Upper-income people already have ways to resist the encroachment of megastructures. It is not their children who are at the mercy of alleged child experts, not their health which is endangered by miscellaneous vested interests, nor their neighborhoods which are made the playthings of utopian planners. Upper-income people may allow themselves to be victimized on all these scores, but they do have ways to resist if they choose to resist. Poor people have this power to a much lesser degree. The paradigm of mediating structures aims at empowering poor people to do the things that the more affluent can already do, aims at spreading the power around a bit more—and to do so where it matters, in people's control over their own lives. Some may call this populism. But that term has been marred by utopianism and by the politics of resentment. We choose to describe it as the empowerment of people.

## NEIGHBORHOOD

"The most sensible way to locate the neighborhood," writes Milton Kotler in *Neighborhood Government* (Bobbs-Merrill, 1969) "is to ask people where it is, for people spend much time fixing its boundaries. Gangs mark its turf. Old people watch for its new faces. Children figure out safe routes between home and school. People walk their dogs through their neighborhood, but rarely beyond it."

At first blush, it seems the defense of neighborhood is a motherhood issue. The neighborhood is the place of relatively intact and secure existence, protecting us against the disjointed and threatening big world "out there." Around the idea of neighborhood gravitate warm feelings of nostalgia and the hope for community. It may not be the place where we are entirely at home, but it is the place where we are least homeless.

While no doubt influenced by such sentiments, the interest in neighborhoods today goes far beyond sentimentality. The neighborhood should be seen as a key mediating structure in the reordering of our national life. As is evident in fears and confusions surrounding such phrases as ethnic purity or neighborhood integrity, the focus on neighborhood touches some of the most urgent and sensitive issues of social policy. Indeed, many charge that the "rediscovery" of the neighborhood is but another, and thinly veiled, manifestation of racism.

Against that charge we contend—together with many others, both black and white, who have a strong record of commitment to racial justice—that strong neighborhoods can be a potent instrument in achieving greater justice for all Americans. It is not true, for example, that all-black neighborhoods are by definition weak neighborhoods. As we shall see, to argue the contrary is to relegate black America to perpetual frustration or to propose a most improbable program of social revolution. To put it simply, real community development must begin where people are. If our hopes for development assume an idealized society cleansed of ethnic pride and its accompanying bigotries, they are doomed to failure.

While social policy that can be morally approved must be attuned to the needs of the poor—and in America that means very particularly the black poor—the nonpoor also live in and cherish the values of neighborhood. The neighborhood in question may be as part-time and tenuous as the many bedroom communities surrounding our major cities; it may be the ethnic and economic crazy-quilt of New York's East Village; it may be the tranquil homogeneity of the east side of Cisco, Texas. Again, a neighborhood is what the people who live there say is a neighborhood.

For public policy purposes, there is no useful definition of what makes a good neighborhood, though we can agree on what constitutes a bad neighborhood. Few people would choose to live where crime is rampant, housing deteriorated, and garbage uncollected. To describe these phenomena as bad is not an instance of imposing middle-class, bourgeois values upon the poor. No one, least of all the poor, is opposed to such "middle-class" values as safety, sanitation, and the freedom of choice that comes with affluence. With respect to so-called bad neighborhoods, we have essentially three public policy choices: we can ignore them, we can attempt to dismantle them and spread their problems around more equitably, or we can try to transform the bad into the better on the way to becoming good. The first option, although common, should be intolerable. The second is massively threatening to the nonpoor, and therefore not feasible short of revolution. The third holds most promise for a public policy that can gain the support of the American people. And, if we care more about consequence than about confrontation, the third is also the most radical in long-range effect.

Because social scientists and planners have a penchant for unitary definitions that cover all contingencies, there is still much discussion of what makes for a good neighborhood. Our approach suggests that the penchant should be carefully restrained. It is not necessarily true, for example, that a vital neighborhood is one that supplies a strong sense of social cohesion or reinforces personal identity with the group. In fact many people want neighborhoods where free choice in association and even anonymity are cherished. That kind of neighborhood, usually urban, is no less a neighborhood for its lack of social cohesion. Cohesion exacts its price in loss of personal freedom; freedom may be paid for in the coin of alienation and loneliness. One pays the price for the neighborhood of one's choice. Making that choice possible is the function of the *idea* of neighborhood as it is embodied in many actual neighborhoods. It is not possible to create the benefits of each kind of neighborhood in every neighborhood. One cannot devise a compromise between the cohesion of a New England small town and the anonymity of the East Village without destroying both options.

Nor is it necessarily true that progress is marked by movement from the neighborhood of cohesion to the neighborhood of elective choice. Members of the cultural elite, who have strong influence on the metaphors by which public policy is designed, frequently feel they have escaped from the parochialisms of the former type of neighborhood. Such escapes are one source of the continuing vitality of great cities, but this idea of liberation should not be made normative. The Upper West Side of New York City, for example, the neighborhood of so many literary, academic, and political persons, has its own forms of parochialism, its taboos and restrictions, approved beliefs and behavior patterns. The urban sophisticate's conformity to the values of individual self-fulfillment and tolerance can be as intolerant of the beliefs and behavior nurtured in the community centered in the St. Stanislaus American Legion branch of Hamtramck, Michigan, as the people of Hamtramck are intolerant of what is called liberation on the Upper West Side.

Karl Marx wrote tellingly of "the idiocy of village life." Important to our approach, however, is the recognition that what looks like idiocy may in fact be a kind of complexity with which we cannot cope or do not wish to be bothered. That is, the movement from the community of cohesion to cosmopolitanism, from village to urban neighborhood, is not necessarily a movement from the simple to the complex. In fact, those who move toward the cosmopolitan may be simplifying their lives by freeing themselves from the tangled associations—family, church, club, and so forth—that dominate village life. It is probably easier for an outsider to become a person of political and social consequence in New York City than in most small towns. In a large city almost everyone is an outsider by definition. To put it another way, in the world of urban emigres there are enough little worlds so that everyone can be an insider somewhere. Against the urban and universalizing biases of much social thought, the mediating structures paradigm requires that we take seriously the structures, values, and habits by which people order their lives in neighborhoods, wherever those neighborhoods may be, and no matter whether they are cohesive or individualistic, elective or hereditary. There is no inherent superiority in or inevitable movement toward the neighborhood whose life gravitates around the liberal Democratic club rather than around the parish church or union hall. The goal of public policy should be to sustain the diversity of neighborhoods in which people can remain and to which they can move in accord with what "fits" their self-understanding and their hopes for those about whom they care most.

The empowerment of people in neighborhoods is hardly the answer to all our social problems. Neighborhoods empowered to impose their values upon individual behavior and expression can be both coercive and cruel. Government that transcends neighborhoods must intervene to protect elementary human rights. Here again, however, the distinction between public and private spheres is critically important. In recent years an unbalanced emphasis upon individual rights has seriously eroded the community's power to sustain its democratically determined values in the public sphere. It is ironic, for example, to find people who support landmark commissions that exercise aesthetic censorship—for example, by forbidding owners of landmark properties to change so much as a step or a bay window without legal permission and who, at the same time, oppose public control of pornography, prostitution, gambling, and other "victimless crimes" that violate neighborhood values more basic than mere aesthetics. In truth, a strong class factor is involved in this apparent contradiction. Houses in neighborhoods that are thought to be part of our architectural heritage are typically owned by people to whom values such as architectural heritage are important. These are usually not the people whose neighborhoods are assaulted by pornography, prostitution, and drug trafficking. In short, those who have power can call in the police to reinforce their values while the less powerful cannot.

This individualistic and neighborhood-destroying bias is reinforced by court judgments that tend to treat all neighborhoods alike. That is, the legal tendency is to assume that there is a unitary national community rather than a national community composed of thousands of communities. Thus, the people of Kokomo, Indiana, must accept public promotions of pornography, for instance, because such promotions are protected by precedents established in Berkeley, California, or in Times Square. It is just barely arguable that the person who wants to see a live sex show in downtown Kokomo would be denied a constitutional right were such shows locally prohibited. It is a great deal clearer that the people of Kokomo are now denied the right to determine democratically the character of the community in which they live. More careful distinctions are required if we are to stay the rush toward a situation in which civil liberties are viewed as the enemy of communal values and law itself is pitted against the power of people to shape their own lives. Such distinctions must reflect a greater appreciation of the differences between public and private behavior.

One reason for the present confusion about individual and communal rights has been the unreflective extension of policies deriving from America's racial dilemma to other areas where they are neither practicable nor just. That is, as a nation, and after a long, tortuous, and continuing agony, we have solemnly covenanted to disallow any public regulation that discriminates on the basis of race. That national decision must in no way be compromised. At the same time, the singularity of America's racial history needs to be underscored. Public policy should be discriminating about discriminations. Discrimination is the essence of particularism and particularism is the essence of pluralism. The careless expansion of antidiscrimination rulings in order to appease every aggrieved minority or individual will have two certain consequences: first, it will further erode local communal authority and, second, it will trivialize the historic grievances and claims to justice of America's racial minorities.

In terms of communal standards and sanctions, deviance always exacts a price. Indeed, without such standards, there can be no such thing as deviance. Someone who engages in public and deviant behavior in, say Paducah, Kentucky, can pay the social price of deviance, can persuade his fellow citizens to accept his behavior, or can move to New York City. He should not be able to call in the police to prevent the people of Paducah from enforcing their values against his behavior. (Obviously, we are not referring to the expression of unpopular political or religious views, which, like proscriptions against racial discrimination, is firmly protected by national law and consensus.) The city—variously viewed as the cesspool of wickedness or the zone of liberation—has historically been the place of refuge for the insistently deviant. It might be objected that our saying "he can move to the city" sounds like the "love it or leave it" argument of those who opposed anti-war protesters in the last decade. The whole point, however, is the dramatic difference between a nation and a neighborhood. One is a citizen of a nation and lays claim to the rights by which that nation is constituted. Within that nation there are numerous associations such as neighborhoods more or less freely chosen—and membership in those associations is usually related to affinity. This nation is constituted as an exercise in pluralism, as the *unum* within which myriad *plures* are sustained. If it becomes national policy to make the public values of Kokomo or Salt Lake City indistinguishable from those of San Francisco or New Orleans, we have as a nation abandoned the social experiment symbolized by the phrase "E Pluribus Unum."

Viewed in this light, the national purpose does not destroy but aims at strengthening particularity, including the particularity of the neighborhood. It would be naive, however, to deny that there are points at which the *unum* and the *plures* are in conflict. It is patently the case, for example, that one of the chief determinants in shaping neighborhoods, especially in urban areas, is the racism that marks American life. The problem, of course, is that racial discrimination is often inseparable from other discriminations based upon attitudes, behavior patterns, and economic disparities. One may sympathize with those who are so frustrated in their effort to overcome racial injustice that they advocate policies aimed at wiping out every vestige and consequence of past racial discrimination. In fact, however, such leveling policies are relentlessly resisted by almost all Americans, including the black and the poor who, rightly or wrongly, see their interests attached to a system of rewards roughly associated with "free enterprise." The more practicable and, finally, the more just course is advanced by those who advocate massive public policy support for neighborhood development as development is defined by the people in the neighborhoods. As people in poor neighborhoods realize more of the "middle class" goals to which they undoubtedly aspire, racial discrimination will be reduced or at least will be more readily isolated than now and thus more easily reachable by legal proscription. The achievement of the poor need not mean that achievers move out of poor neighborhoods, thus leaving behind a hard core or more "ghettoized" residents. It is often overlooked, for example, that many middle-class and wealthy blacks *choose* to live in Harlem, creating "good neighborhoods" within an area often dismissed as hopeless. The dynamics of such community maintenance deserve more careful study and wider appreciation.

The pervasiveness of racial prejudice among whites means that blacks cannot depend upon economic mobility alone to gain freedom in choosing where to live and how to live. The communications media, churches, schools, government, and other institutions with some moral authority must continue and indeed intensify efforts to educate against racial bias. Where instances of racial discrimination can be reasonably isolated from other factors, they must be rigorously prosecuted and punished. It remains true, however, that economics and the values associated with middle-class status are key to overcoming racism. The public policy focus must therefore be on the development of the communities where people are. To the objection that this means locking the black and poor into present patterns of segregation, it must be answered that nothing would so surely lock millions of black Americans into hopelessness as making progress contingent upon a revolution in American racial attitudes or in the economic system. It is not too much to say that the alternative to neighborhood development is either neglect or revolution. Neglect is morally intolerable and, in the long run, probably too costly to the whole society to be viable even if it were acceptable morally. Revolution is so utterly improbable that it would be an unconscionable cruelty to encourage the poor to count on it.

The current attack on the existing pattern of housing and zoning regulations is, we believe, wrongheaded in several respects. Unless such regulations are almost totally dismantled, the attack is hardly worth pressing; and, if they are dismantled, the likely result would be great injustice to the poor whom the changes were designed to benefit and to the nonpoor who would certainly resist such changes. Those who propose to overcome poverty by spreading the poor more evenly seldom consider whether the burden of poverty might not be increased by virtue of its stark contrast with the affluence it would then be forced to live with. Even were it logistically and politically possible to distribute South Chicago's welfare families throughout the metropolitan area, it is doubtful their lot would be improved by living in projects, large or small, next to the $80,000 homes of the more prosperous suburbs. The people who live in those suburbs now do so quite deliberately in order to get away from the social problems associated with poverty—and, in fashion too often related to racism, to get away from the minorities most commonly associated with those problems. It is one thing to make white Americans feel guilty about racism; it is quite another (and both wrong and futile) to make them feel guilty about their middle-class values—values also enthusiastically endorsed by the poor. These considerations aside, the great wrong in proposals to overcome poverty by dispersing the poor is that they would deprive the poor, whether black or white, of their own communities. Again, the proposition implicit in so much well-intended social advocacy—the proposition that an all-black neighborhood or all-black school is of necessity inferior—is aptly described as reverse racism. To the extent the proposition is internalized by the black poor, it also tends to become a self-fulfilling prophecy.

In sum, with respect to the connection between the neighborhood and race, we would draw a sharp distinction between a society of *pro*scription and a society of *pre*scription. We have as a society covenanted to proscribe racial discrimination in the public realm. That proscription must be tirelessly implemented, no matter how frustrating the efforts at implementation sometimes are. But it is quite another matter to pursue policies of prescription in which government agencies prescribe quotas and balances for the redistribution of people and wealth. Pushed far enough, the second course invites revolutionary reaction, and it would almost certainly be revolution from the right. Pushed as far as it is now being pushed, it is eroding community power, distracting from the tasks of neighborhood development, and alienating many Americans from the general direction of domestic public policy.

If it is to make a real difference, neighborhood development should be distinguished from programs of decentralization. From Honolulu to Newton, Massachusetts, the last ten years have witnessed an explosion of neighborhood councils, "little city halls" dispersed through urban areas, and the like. Again, the decentralized operation of megastructures is not the same thing as the creation of vital mediating structures—indeed, it can be quite the opposite. Decentralization can give the people in the neighborhoods the feeling that they are being listened to, and even participating, but it has little to do with development and governance unless it means the reality as well as the sensations of power. Neighborhood governance exists when—in areas such as education, health services, law enforcement, and housing regulation—the people democratically determine what is in the interest of their own chosen life styles and values.

Many different streams flow into the current enthusiasms for neighborhood government. Sometimes the neighborhood government movement is dubbed "the new Jeffersonianism." After two centuries of massive immigration and urbanization, we cannot share Jefferson's bucolic vision of rural and small-town America, just as we do not indulge the re-medievalizing fantasies associated in some quarters with the acclaim for smallness. We believe the premise on which to devise public policy is that the parameters of modern, industrial, technological society are set for the foreseeable future. Our argument is not against modernity but in favor of exploring the ways in which modernity can be made more humane. With respect to neighborhood government, for example, it was widely assumed fifty and more years ago that modernity required the "rationalization" of urban polity. This was the premise of the "reform" and "good government" movements promoting the managerial, as distinct from partisan political, style of urban governance. The limitations of that approach are more widely recognized today.

It is recognized, for example, that the managerial model, however well-intended in many instances, served certain vested interests. Black writers and politicians have noted, and with some justice, an apparent racial component in the movement away from what some consider the irrationalities of local control. As urban populations become more black, some reformers put more emphasis upon regional planning and control, thus depriving blacks of their turn at wielding urban power. In 1976, during New York City's fiscal crisis, when more and more power was transferred to the state government, to the banks, and to Washington, it was widely and ruefully remarked that the power brokers were getting ready for the election of the first black or Puerto Rican mayor, who would be endowed with full authority to cut ceremonial ribbons.

In addition, there are today hundreds of thousands of public employees, politicians, planners, and theorists who have deep vested interest in maintaining the dike of "national organization" against what they allege is the threatening chaos of community control. The prospect of neighborhood government must be made to seem less threatening to these many dependents of centralization. Their legitimate interests must be accommodated if neighborhood government is to mature from a protest movement to a guiding metaphor of public policy. A distinction should be made, for example, between unionized professionals and professional unionists. The former need not be threatened by the role we propose for the neighborhood and other mediating structures in public policy. In fact many new opportunities might be opened for the exercise of truly professional imagination in greater responsiveness to the felt needs of people. With many more institutional players in the public realm, professionals could have greater choice and freedom for innovation. The protection of professional interests through unions and other associations need not be dependent upon the perpetuation of the monolithic managerial models for ordering society.

One factor sparking enthusiasm for community control and neighborhood government is the growing realization that localities may not be receiving a fair break when it comes to tax monies. That is, some studies suggest that even poor neighborhoods, after everything is taken into account, end up sending considerably more out of the neighborhood in taxes than is returned. We do not suggest that the income tax, for instance, should be administered locally. It is reasonable to inquire, however, whether the tax-collecting function of the federal and state governments could not be maintained, while the spending function is changed to allow tax monies to be returned in a noncategorical way to the places where they were raised to begin with. Needless to say, this suggestion goes far beyond what is currently called revenue sharing. Nor does it ignore the fact that sizable funds are required for functions that transcend the purview of any neighborhood, such as transportation or defense. But again—focusing on activities of the kind carried on by the Department of Health, Education and Welfare (HEW)—it does imply that the people in communities know best what is needed for the maintenance and development of those communities.

If neighborhoods are to be key to public policy, governmental action is necessary to fund neighborhood improvement. As is well known, practices such as red-lining deteriorating neighborhoods are today very common. It may be that there is no effective way to force private financial institutions to make monies available for home improvement and other investments in "ghetto" neighborhoods. Without a direct assault upon the free enterprise system, the possibilities of evasion and subterfuge in order to invest money where it is safest or most profitable are almost infinite. To strengthen the mediating role of neighborhoods we need to look to new versions of the Federal Housing Administration assistance programs that played such a large part in the burgeoning suburbs after World War II. Such programs can, we believe, be developed to sustain and rehabilitate old communities, as they have been used to build new ones. The idea of urban homesteading, for example, although afflicted with corruption and confusion in recent years, is a move in the right direction. At a very elementary level, property tax regulations should be changed to encourage rather than discourage home improvement. Especially in large metropolitan areas, granting the most generous tax "breaks" might in the not-so-long run yield more revenue than the current system, especially since in many places the abandonment of buildings means that present taxation levels yield little. In short, the tax structure should be changed in every way that encourages the tenant to become a homeowner and the landlord to improve his property.

Neighborhoods will also be strengthened as people in the neighborhood assume more and more responsibility for law enforcement, especially in the effort to stem the tide of criminal terrorism. In this area, too, we have become so enamored of professionalism and so fearful of vigilantism that we have forgotten that community values are only operative when the people in the community act upon them. We should not limit ourselves to thinking about how communities might control conventional police operations and personnel. Rather, we should examine the informal "law enforcement agents" that exist in every community—the woman who runs the local candy store, the people who walk their dogs, or the old people who sit on park benches or observe the streets from their windows. This means new approaches to designing "defensible space" in housing, schools, and the like. It certainly suggests the need to explore the part-time employment, through public funding, of parents and others who would police schools and other public spaces. We have been increasingly impressed, in conversation with people knowledgeable about law enforcement, with the point that there are probably few fields of law enforcement requiring the kind of metropolitan, comprehensive, and professional police force which have come to be taken for granted as an urban necessity. The fact is that there is probably no neighborhood in which the overwhelming majority of residents do not wish to see the laws enforced. Yet the residents feel impotent and therefore the neighborhoods often are impotent in doing anything about crime. The ways in which public policies have fostered that feeling of impotence must be examined, and alternatives to such policies found.

Finally, no discussion of neighborhood can ignore the homogenizing role of the mass communications media in creating a common culture. We suspect, and frankly hope, that the influence of the mass media in destroying the particularisms of American society is frequently overestimated. Television certainly is a tremendous force in creating something like a national discourse regarding current affairs and even values. We do not advocate the dismantling of the national networks. We do propose, however, that it be public policy to open up many unused channels, now technically available, for the use of regional, ethnic, and elective groups of all sorts. Similarly, taxation policies, postal regulations, and other factors should be reexamined with a view toward sustaining neighborhood newspapers and other publications.

All of which is to say that the goal of making and keeping life human, of sustaining a people-sized society, depends upon our learning again that parochialism is not a nasty word. Like the word parish, it comes from the Greek, *para* plus *oikos,* the place next door. Because we all want some choice and all have a great stake in the place where we live, it is in the common interest to empower our own places and the places next door.

## FAMILY

There are places, especially in urban areas, where life styles are largely detached from family connections. This is, one hopes, good for those who choose it. Certainly such life styles add to the diversity, the creativity, even the magic, of the city. But since a relatively small number of people inhabit these areas, it would be both foolish and undemocratic to take such life styles as guidelines for the nation. For most Americans, neighborhood and community are closely linked to the family as an institution.

The family may be in crisis in the sense that it is undergoing major changes of definition, but there is little evidence that it is in decline. High divorce rates, for example, may indicate not decline but rising expectations in what people look for in marriage and family life. The point is underscored by high remarriage rates. It is noteworthy that the counterculture, which is so critical of the so-called bourgeois family, uses the terminology of family for its new social constructions, as do radical feminists pledged to "sisterhood." For most Americans, the evidence is that involvement in the bourgeois family, however modified, will endure.

Of course, modernization has already had a major impact on the family. It has largely stripped the family of earlier functions in the areas of education and economics, for example. But in other ways, modernization has made the family more important than ever before. It is the major institution within the private sphere, and thus for many people the most valuable thing in their lives. Here they make their moral commitments, invest their emotions, plan for the future, and perhaps even hope for immortality.

There is a paradox here. On the one hand, the megastructures of government, business, mass communications, and the rest have left room for the family to be the autonomous realm of individual aspiration and fulfillment. This room is by now well secured in the legal definitions of the family. At the same time, the megastructures persistently infringe upon the family. We cannot and should not eliminate these infringements entirely. After all, families exist in a common society. We can, however, take positive measures to protect and foster the family institution, so that it is not defenseless before the forces of modernity.

This means public recognition of the family *as an institution.* It is not enough to be concerned for individuals more or less incidentally related to the family as institution. Public recognition of the family as an institution is imperative because every society has an inescapable interest in how children are raised, how values are transmitted to the next generation. Totalitarian regimes have tried—unsuccessfully to date—to supplant the family in this function. Democratic societies dare not try if they wish to remain democratic. Indeed they must resist every step, however well intended, to displace or weaken the family institution.

Public concern for the family is not antagonistic to concern for individual rights. On the contrary, individuals need strong families if they are to grow up and remain rooted in a strong sense of identity and values. Weak families produce uprooted individuals, unsure of their direction and therefore searching for some authority. They are ideal recruits for authoritarian movements inimical to democratic society.

Commitment to the family institution can be combined, although not without difficulty, with an emphatically libertarian view that protects the private lives of adults against public interference of any kind. Public interest in the family is centered on children, not adults; it touches adults insofar as they are in charge of children. The public interest is institutional in character. That is, the state is to view children as members of a family. The sovereignty of the family over children has limits—as does any sovereignty in the modern world—and these limits are already defined in laws regarding abuse, criminal neglect, and so on. The onus of proof, however, must be placed on policies or laws that foster state interference rather than on those that protect family autonomy. In saying this we affirm what has been the major legal tradition in this country.

Conversely, we oppose policies that expose the child directly to state intervention, without the mediation of the family. We are skeptical about much current discussion of children's rights—especially when such rights are asserted *against* the family. Children do have rights, among which is the right to a functionally strong family. When the rhetoric of children's rights means transferring children from the charge of families to the charge of coteries of experts ("We know what is best for the children"), that rhetoric must be suspected of cloaking vested interests—ideological interests, to be sure, but, also and more crudely, interest in jobs, money, and power.

Our preference for the parents over the experts is more than a matter of democratic conviction—and does not ignore the existence of relevant and helpful expertise. It is a bias based upon the simple, but often overlooked, consideration that virtually all parents love their children. Very few experts love, or can love, most of the children in their care. Not only is that emotionally difficult, but expertise generally requires a degree of emotional detachment. In addition, the parent, unlike the expert, has a long-term, open-ended commitment to the individual child. Thus the parent, almost by definition, is way ahead of the expert in sheer knowledge of the child's character, history, and needs. The expert, again by definition, relates to the child within general and abstract schemata. Sometimes the schemata fit, but very often they do not.

We have no intention of glorifying the bourgeois family. Foster parents, lesbians and gays, liberated families, or whatever—all can do the job *as long as* they provide children the loving and the permanent structure that traditional families have typically provided. Indeed, virtually any structure is better for children than what experts of the state can provide.

Most modern societies have in large part disfranchised the family in the key area of education. The family becomes, at best, an auxiliary agency to the state, which takes over the child's education at age five or six coercively (compulsory school laws) and monopolistically (for the most part). Of course there are private schools, but here class becomes a powerful factor. Disfranchisement falls most heavily on lower-income parents who have little say in what happens to their children in school. This discrimination violates a fundamental human right, perhaps the most fundamental human rights—the right to make a world for one's children.

Our purpose is not to deprive upper-income families of the choices they have. The current assault on private schools in Britain (there called public schools) is not a happy example. Our purpose is to give those choices to those who do not now have decision-making power. When some are freezing while others enjoy bright fires, the solution is not to extinguish all fires equally but to provide fires for those who have none.

There is yet a further class discrimination in education. By birth or social mobility, the personnel of the education establishment are upper middle class, and this is reflected in the norms, the procedures, and the very cultural climate of that establishment. This means the child who is not of an upper-middle-class family is confronted by an alien milieu from his or her first day at school. In part this may be inevitable. The modern world is bourgeois and to succeed in a bourgeois world means acquiring bourgeois skills and behavior patterns. We do not suggest, as some do, that the lower-class child is being culturally raped when taught correct English. But there are many other, sometimes unconscious, ways in which the education establishment systematically disparages ways of life other than those of the upper middle class. Yet these disparaged ways of life are precisely the ways in which parents of millions of American children live. Thus schools teach contempt for the parents and, ultimately, self-contempt.

In a few metropolitan areas, the education establishment has responded to these problems, sometimes creatively. But monopolies endowed with coercive powers do not change easily. The best way to induce change is to start breaking up the monopoly—to empower people to *shop elsewhere.* We trust the ability of low-income parents to make educational decisions more wisely than do the professionals who now control their children's education. To deny this ability is the worst class bias of all, and in many instances it is racism as well.

To affirm empowerment against tutelage, irrespective of economic or social status, is hardly a wildly radical position. That this may seem so to some is a measure of the elitist and essentially anti-democratic effects of the bureaucratization and professionalization of American society.

Against the politics of resentment, empowerment is not a zero-sum game. That is, lower-income people can be enfranchised without disfranchising or impoverishing the better off. But this process does assume a lower limit of poverty beyond which efforts at empowerment are futile. Any humane and effective social policy must place a floor of decency under everyone in the society. The relative merits of income maintenance programs—guaranteed income, negative income tax, and so forth—are beyond the scope of this essay, but the whole argument assumes that a floor of decency must be established. Aside from moral imperatives, such a floor can strengthen mediating structures, notably here poor families, by helping them break out of present patterns of dependency upon a confused and confusing welfare system.

The implications of our policy concept may be clarified by looking briefly at three currently discussed issues—education vouchers, day care, and the care of the handicapped. The idea of education vouchers has been around for a while and has had its ups and downs, but it remains one of the most intriguing possibilities for radical reform in the area of education. In this proposal, public funding of education shifts from disbursement to schools to disbursement to individuals. Parents (or, at a certain age, their children) choose the schools where they will cash in their vouchers, the schools then being reimbursed by the state. Essentially the proposal applies the paradigm of the GI Bill to younger students at earlier periods of education. This proposal would break the coercive monopoly of the present education system and empower individuals in relating to the megastructures of bureaucracy and professionalism, with special benefits going to lower-income people. In addition, it would enhance the diversity of American life by fostering particularist communities of value—whether of life style, ideology, religion, or ethnicity. And all this without increasing, and maybe decreasing, costs to the taxpayer since, at least at the primary levels of education, the evidence suggests that economies of scale do not operate.

Politically, education vouchers have advocates on the right and on the left, notably Milton Friedman and Christopher Jencks, respectively. The chief difference is whether vouchers should be basic or total—that is, whether upper-income parents should have the right to supplement vouchers with their own money. Friedman says they should because they have a right to the benefits of their taxes without surrendering the free use of their income. Jencks, for egalitarian reasons, says they should not. On this we incline toward Friedman's position for two reasons: first, the purpose of schools is to educate children, not to equalize income; and second, as stated before, lower-income people can be empowered without penalizing others. Needless to say, the second consideration has much to do with the political salability of education vouchers and, indeed, of the mediating structures paradigm in other policy areas.

There have been limited experiments with the voucher idea within existing public school systems (Seattle; Alum Rock, California; and Gary, Indiana). The results are still being analyzed, but already certain cautions have been raised. An urgent caution is that under no circumstances should vouchers be used to subsidize schools that practice racial exclusion. Another caution is that vouchers are not given a fair trial unless the experiment includes schools outside the public school system. (Of course this raises certain church-state considerations, and we will address them in the next section.)

Among other questions still unanswered: Should vouchers be uniform or graded by income? Should the state insist on a core curriculum, and, if so, should compliancy be ensured by inspection or by examination? Should present methods of teacher certification be extended to schools now considered private? What are the other implications of, in effect, making all schools public schools? And, of course, what would be the effect of a voucher system on teachers unions? Although the unions have tended to be antagonistic to the idea so far, we believe that both bread-and-butter interests and professional interests can be secured, and in some ways better secured than now, within a voucher framework.

Obviously we cannot address all these questions here. We are struck, however, by the fact that almost all the objections to the voucher idea have been on grounds *other than educational.* And education, after all, is what schools are supposed to be about.

Turning to our second example, we note that day care has become a public issue, as more and more mothers of small children have entered the labor force and as many people, spurred by the feminist movement, have begun to claim that working mothers have a right to public services designed to meet their special needs. Both factors are likely to continue, making day care a public issue for the foreseeable future.

Three positions on national day-care policy can be discerned at present. One is that the government should, quite simply, stay out of this area. Financially, it is said, any program will be enormously costly and, ideologically, the government should refrain from intruding itself so massively into the area of early childhood. Another position endorses a federally funded, comprehensive childcare system attached to the public schools. This is the view of the American Federation of Teachers. A third position is much like the second, except that the national program would be less closely linked to the public school system. (This position was embodied in the Mondale-Brademas bill which President Ford vetoed in 1976.) As in the Head Start program, this plan would work through prime sponsors. These sponsors could be private or public, voluntary associations, neighborhood groups, or simply parents getting together to run a day-care center—the only condition being that sponsors be nonprofit in character.

It should come as no surprise that we favor the third position. We do so because there is a real need and because the need should be met in a way that is as inexpensive and as unintrusive as possible. The mediating structures concept is ideally suited to the latter purpose and may also advance the former. As to the second position mentioned above, we are sympathetic to the teachers union's desire for new jobs in a period of educational retrenchment. But, again, providing jobs should not be the purpose of education and child care.

The voucher approach can be the more readily used in day care since there are not as yet in this area the powerful vested interests so firmly established in primary and secondary education. Vouchers would facilitate day-care centers that are small, not professionalized, under the control of parents, and therefore highly diversified. State intervention should be strictly limited to financial accountability and to safety and health standards (which, perhaps not incidentally, are absurdly unrealistic in many states). Considerable funds can be saved through this approach since it is virtually certain that economies of scale do not apply to day-care centers. Imaginative proposals should be explored, such as the use of surrogate grandparents—which, incidentally, would offer meaningful employment to the growing numbers of elderly persons in our society. (We realize that we argued above that employment should not be the purpose of education, but presumably teachers *can* do something other than teach school, while surrogate grandparents may be restricted to grandparenting.)

The third issue mentioned is care of the handicapped. An important case in this area is the so-called special child—special children being those who, for a broad range of nonphysical reasons, are handicapped in their educational development. The field of special education has grown rapidly in recent years and many of its problems (medical and educational as well as legal) are outside our present scope. One problem within our scope is the recurring choice between institutionalizing the severely handicapped and dealing with their problems within the family setting.

Apart from the inability of the normal family to deal with some severe handicaps, the trend toward institutionalization has been propelled by considerations such as the convenience of parents, the vested interests of professionals, and the alleged therapeutic superiority of institutional settings. Because the therapeutic claims of these institutions have been shown to be highly doubtful, and because institutional care is immensely expensive, innovative thinking today moves toward using the family as a therapeutic context *as much as possible.* This means viewing the professional as *ancillary* to, rather than as a substitute for, the resources of the family. It may mean paying families to care for a handicapped child, enabling a parent to work less or not at all, or to employ others. Such an approach would almost certainly reduce costs in caring for the handicapped. More important, and this can be amply demonstrated, the best therapeutic results are obtained when children remain in their families—or, significantly, in institutional settings that imitate family life. ( We will not repeat what we said earlier about the relative merits of love and expertise.) And, of course, there is no reason why this proposal could not be extended to the care of handicapped adults.

Again, we are well aware of current misgivings about the traditional family, misgivings pressed by feminists but not by feminists alone. As far as adults are concerned, we favor maximizing choices about life styles. The principal public policy interest in the family concerns children, not adults. This interest is common to all societies, but in democratic society there is an additional and urgent interest in fostering socialization patterns and values that allow individual autonomy. That interest implies enhanced protection of the family in relation to the state, and it implies trusting people to be responsible for their own children in a world of their own making.

## CHURCH

Religious institutions form by far the largest network of voluntary associations in American society. Yet, for reasons both ideological and historical, their role is frequently belittled or totally overlooked in discussions of social policy. Whatever may be one's attitude to organized religion, this blind spot must be reckoned a serious weakness in much thinking about public policy.

The churches and synagogues of America can no more be omitted from the responsible social analysis than can big labor, business corporations, or the communications media. Not only are religious institutions significant "players" in the public realm, but they are singularly important to the way people order their lives and values at the most local and concrete levels of their existence. Thus they are crucial to understanding family, neighborhood, and other mediating structures of empowerment.

The view that the public sphere is synonymous with the government or the formal polity of the society has been especially effective in excluding religion from considerations of public policy. We shall return to some of the church/state controversies that have reflected and perpetuated this view; but for the moment it should be obvious that our whole proposal aims at a complex and nuanced understanding of the public realm that includes many "players" other than the state. Also, much modern social thought deriving from Enlightenment traditions has operated on one or two assumptions that tend to minimize the role of religion. The first assumption is that education and modernization make certain the decline of allegiance to institutional religion. That is, there is thought to be an inevitable connection between modernization and secularization. The second assumption is that, even if religion continues to flourish, it deals purely with the private sphere of life and is therefore irrelevant to public policy. Both assumptions need to be carefully reexamined.

The evidence, at least in America, does not support the hypothesis of the inevitable decline religion. Although the decline is perennially announced—its announcement being greeted with both cheers and lamentations—it is likely that religion is at least as institutionally intact as some other major institutions (such as, for example, higher education). It is worth noting that in recent years the alleged decline of religion has been measured by comparison with the so-called religious boom of the late 1950s. The comparison with that unprecedented period of institutional growth offers a very skewed perspective. But, even when the vitality of religion is measured by that misleading comparison, it is notable that in the past few years the indexes are again on the upswing. Church attendance, claimed affiliation, financial contributions, and other indicators all suggest that whatever decline there was from the apex of the late 1950s has now stopped or been reversed. It is perhaps relevant to understanding American society to note that on any given Sunday there are probably more people in churches than the total number of people who attend professional sports events in a whole year—or to note that there are close to 500,000 local churches and synagogues voluntarily supported by the American people.

This is not the place for a detailed discussion of various secularization theories. We are keenly aware of the need to distinguish between institutions of religion and the dynamic of religion as such in society. Let it suffice that our approach raises a strong challenge to the first assumption mentioned above, namely, that in the modern world allegiance to institutional religion must perforce decline. Public policies based upon that highly questionable, if not patently false, assumption will continue to be alienated from one of the most vital dimensions in the lives of many millions of Americans.

The second assumption—that religion deals purely with the private sphere and is therefore irrelevant to public policy—must also be challenged. Although specifically religious activities have been largely privatized, the first part of the proposition overlooks the complex ways in which essentially religious values infiltrate and influence our public thought. But even to the extent that the first part of the proposition is true, it does not follow that religion is therefore irrelevant to public policy. The family, for example, is intimately involved in the institution of religion, and since the family is one of the prime mediating structures (perhaps the prime one), this makes the church urgently relevant to public policy. Without falling into the trap of politicizing all of life, our point is that structures such as family, church, and neighborhood are all public institutions in the sense that they must be taken seriously in the ordering of the polity.

The church (here meaning all institutions of religion) is important not only to the family but also to families and individuals in neighborhoods and other associations. For example, the black community, both historically and at present, cannot be understood apart from the black church. Similarly, the much discussed ethnic community is in large part religiously defined, as are significant parts of American Jewry (sometimes, but not always, subsumed under the phenomenon of ethnicity). And of course the role of religion in small towns or rural communities needs no elaboration. In none of these instances should the religious influence be viewed as residual. Few institutions have demonstrated and continue to demonstrate perduring power comparable to that of religion. It seems that influence is residual only to the extent that the bias of secularizing culture and politics is determined to act as though it is residual. Again, these observations seem to us to be true quite apart from what we may or may not *wish* the influence of religion to be in American society. We are convinced that there is a profoundly antidemocratic prejudice in public policy discourse that ignores the role of religious institutions in the lives of most Americans.

In the public policy areas most relevant to this discussion—health, social welfare, education, and so on—the historical development of programs, ideas, and institutions is inseparable from the church. In some parts of the country, notably in the older cities of the Northeast, the great bulk of social welfare services function under religious auspices. For reason to be discussed further in the next section, the religious character of these service agencies is being fast eroded. Where government agencies are not directly taking over areas previously serviced by religious institutions, such institutions are being turned into quasi-governmental agencies through the powers of funding, certification, licensing, and the like. The loss of religious and cultural distinctiveness is abetted also by the dynamics of professionalization within the religious institutions and by the failure of the churches either to support their agencies or to insist that public policy respect their distinctiveness. The corollary to the proposition that government responsibilities must be governmentally implemented—a proposition we challenge—is that public is the opposite of sectarian. In public policy discourse sectarian is usually used as a term of opprobrium for anything religious. We contend that this usage and the biases that support it undermine the celebration of distinctiveness essential to social pluralism.

The homogenizing consequences of present patterns of funding, licensing, and certification are intensified by tax policies that have a "chilling effect" upon the readiness of religious institutions to play their part in the public realm. The threatened loss of tax exemption because of excessive "political activity" is a case in point. Even more ominous is the developing notion of tax expenditures (on which more in the next section). Most recently what has been called tax reform has aimed at driving a wedge between churches as such and their church-related auxiliaries, making the latter subject to disclosure, accountability, and therefore greater control by the state. These directions are, we believe, fundamentally wrongheaded. Pushed far enough, they will likely provoke strong reaction from a public that will not countenance what is perceived as an attack on religion. But public policy decision makers should not wait for that reaction to supply a corrective to present tendencies. It is precisely in the interest of public policy to advance a positive approach to the church as a key mediating structures.

Obviously all these questions touch on the complex of issues associated with separation of church and state. We believe, together with many scholars of jurisprudence, that the legal situation of church/state questions is today bogged down in conceptual confusions and practical contradictions. "The wall of separation between church and state" (Jefferson's phrase, not the Constitution's) is a myth long overdue for thorough rethinking. We are deeply committed to the religion clauses of the First Amendment. They should not be understood, however, as requiring absolute separationism; such absolute separationism is theoretically inconceivable and practically contrary to the past and present interaction of church and state. It is yet another of those grand abstractions that have had such a debilitating effect upon the way society's institutions relate to one another and upon the way in which people actually order their lives.

In brief, "no establishment of religion" should mean that no religious institution is favored by the state over other religious institutions. "Free exercise of religion" should mean that no one is forced to practice or profess any religion against his will. Where there is neither favoritism nor coercion by the state there is no violation of the separation of church and state. While the subject is more complicated than suggested here, and while the courts will no doubt take time to disentangle themselves from the confusions into which they have been led, it is to be hoped that public policy will, in general, more nearly approximate "the Kurland rule" (named after Philip Kurland of the University of Chicago), namely, that if a policy furthers a legitimate secular purpose it is a matter of legal indifference whether or not that policy employs religious institutions. Clearly, this has far-ranging implications in the areas of education, child care, and social services generally.

The danger today is not that the churches or any one church will take over the state. The much more real danger is that the state will take over the functions of the church, except for the most narrowly construed definition of religion limited to worship and religious instruction. It is not alarmist but soberly necessary to observe that the latter has been the totalitarian pattern of modern states, whether of the left or of the right. Pluralism, including religious pluralism, is one of the few strong obstacles to that pattern's success. While those who advance this pattern may often do so inadvertently, it would be naive to ignore the fact that many of them—sundry professionals, bureaucrats, politicians—have a deep vested interest in such state expansion. The interest is not only ideological, although that is no doubt the primary interest in many cases; it is also and very practically an interest in jobs and power.

From the beginning, we have emphasized the importance of mediating structures in generating and maintaining values. We have already discussed the function of the family in this connection. Within the family, and between the family and the larger society, the church is a primary agent for bearing and transmitting the operative values of our society. This is true not only in the sense that most Americans identify their most important values as being religious in character, but also in the sense that the values that inform our public discourse are inseparably related to specific religious traditions. In the absence of the church and other mediating structures that articulate these values, the result is not that the society is left without operative values; the result is that the state has an unchallenged monopoly on the generation and maintenance of values. Needless to say, we would find this a very unhappy condition indeed.

With respect to our minimalist proposition, that public policy should not undercut mediating structures, a number of implications become evident. Already mentioned are aspects of taxation and regulation, which we will treat more fully in the next section because they affect not only the church but all voluntary associations. More specific to religious institutions is the demand for "right to equal access," a notion that cannot help but undercut particularism. Here again we run into the problem of not being discriminating about discriminations or, to put it differently, of failing to distinguish between discrimination and discretion. It seems to us, for example, there is nothing wrong with an elderly Italian Roman Catholic woman wanting to live in a nursing home operated and occupied by Italian Roman Catholics. To challenge that most understandable desire seems to us, quite frankly, perverse. Yet challenged it is—indeed, it is made increasingly impossible—by depriving such a "sectarian" or "discriminatory" institution of public funds. The same obviously holds true for Methodists, atheists, Humanists, and Black Muslims. Public policy's legitimate secular purpose is to ensure that old people have proper care. It should also be public policy that such care by available as much as possible within the context that people desire for themselves and for those whom they care most about. Again, the unique proscription relevant to public policy is against racial discrimination. (To contend that, since there are few black Italian Roman Catholics or few white Black Muslims, this constitutes racial discrimination *in result* is the kind of absurd exercise in social abstraction that plagues too much policy thinking today.)

A most poignant instance of public policy's undercutting the mediating structure of religion is that of present litigation aimed at prohibiting adoption and foster-care agencies from employing a religious criterion. That is, it is proposed to outlaw agencies designed to serve Jewish, Protestant, or Catholic children, if those agencies receive public funds (which of course they do). The cruel and dehumanizing consequences of this are several. First, the parent putting a child up for adoption or surrendering a child to foster care is deprived of the most elementary say in how that child is to be reared. As mentioned in the last section, this is among the most basic of human rights and should not be denied except under the most pressing necessity, especially when one considers that the surrender of children to such agencies is not always entirely voluntary. Another consequence is that the motivation of paid and volunteer workers in such agencies is severely undercut. In many, if not most, instances that motivation is to live out and explicitly transmit religious conviction. Yet a further consequence, perhaps the most important, is that the child is deprived of religious training. This may well be construed as a denial of free exercise of religion. The state has no rightful authority to decide that this is not a serious deprivation. What is necessary to rearing the child should be left to those who bear the children and those who care for them. Except for cases of criminal neglect or other injury, the state should have no authority to intervene. Again, the legitimate secular purpose is that the children be cared for.

It might be objected that leaving such a wide range of social services to religious and other voluntary associations would mean that the many people who did not belong to such groups would go unserved. The objection is revealed as specious, however, when it is recalled that public funds would be made available to almost every conceivable kind of group so long as it were prepared to carry out the public policy purpose. Such agencies might espouse one religion, all religions, or none. Almost everyone belongs to some group that can, with public funds, facilitate public policy in the area of social services. In truth, if we are really concerned for those individuals who fall between the cracks, it is worth noting that the most anomic individuals in our society, the denizens of skid row for example, are cared for almost exclusively by voluntary associations, usually religious in character. Government bureaucracies—indeed, by definition, all bureaucracies—demonstrate little talent for helping the truly marginal who defy generalized categories. The Salvation Army needs no lessons from the state on how to be nonsectarian in its compassion for people. The raison d'être of the Salvation Army is seriously undercut, however, if its workers cannot preach to those to whom they minister.

Still on the minimalistic side of the proposition, the mediating structures paradigm opposes the growing trend toward legally enforced symbolic sterility in public space. A Christmas tree or Hanukkah lights on the town common is a good case in point. Voluntary prayer in public schools is another. "In God We Trust" inscribed on coins is another. Little things these may be, perhaps, but of myriad such little things the public ethos is formed. Reaching toward absurdity, a California court recently ruled that it was unconstitutional to have a state holiday on Good Friday. Presumably there is no objection to the previous Friday, since the secular purpose is to give another day off to state workers. But when secular purpose is combined with religious significance it is apparently beyond the pale of constitutionality.

Our proposition assumes that nobody has a right to be unaffected by the social milieu of which he or she is part. In the second section we touched on the tensions between individual and communal rights. If someone walks naked down Main Street, citizens now have the right to call in the police and have the offensive behavior stopped. Such regulations dealing with community values are of course undergoing change in many places. Change is a constant in the definition of community standards, and the authors probably tend to be more libertarian than most on the question of tolerating deviant behavior in public. The point here is that there must also be limits on the ability of individuals to call in the police to prevent behavior that is communally approved—for example, the Christmas tree on the town common. Nobody has a legal right not to encounter religious symbols in public places and thus to *impose his aversion* to such symbols on the community that cherishes them. As long as public space is open to the full range of symbols cherished in that community, there is no question of one religion being "established" over another. Public policy is presently biased toward what might be called the symbolic nakedness of the town square. Again, social abstractions have resulted in antidemocratic consequences, antidemocratic because they deny the democratically determined will of the people to celebrate themselves—their culture and their beliefs—in public, and, just as important, consequences that are antidemocratic because they give to the state a monopoly on public space and on the values to be advanced in that space.

In a public housing project in Brooklyn a deal has been struck between the leaders of a Hassidic Jewish community and of the Hispanic community to rent apartments in a way that will concentrate both communities in a more or less intact manner. The deal is probably illegal, on grounds both of racial and religious discrimination. In this particular case, it is also eminently sensible and fair, and therefore ought to be legal. No one is hurt, unless it be the "strict separationist" and "geometrical integrationist" who may be offended by the violations of their abstractions. But they are not renting apartments in public housing. We stress "in this particular case"—because public policy, especially in the area of religion and communal values, should show more respect for particular cases.

Finally, on the maximalist side of our proposition (public policy should utilize mediating structures as much as feasible) the implications spelled out throughout this essay apply also to churches. Our proposal is that the institutions of religion should be unfettered to make their maximum contribution to the public interest. In some areas of social service and education, this means these institutions should be free to continue doing what they have historically done.

Again, and in accord with our maximalist proposition, we expect increased public funding for the meeting of human needs in a wide range of policy areas; our particular contention is that mediating institutions, including religious institutions, be utilized as much as possible as the implementing agencies of policy goals. Contrary to some public policy and legal thinking today, such increased funding need not require an increase in governmental control and a consequent war on pluralism. With respect to the church and other mediating structures, the hope of the New Deal will be more nearly fulfilled when policies do not advance public compassion and responsibility at the price of conformity and repression.

## VOLUNTARY ASSOCIATION

The discussion of the church leads logically to the subject of the voluntary association. Of course the church is—in addition to whatever else it may be—a voluntary association. But the category of voluntary association includes many other structures that can play a crucial mediating role in society.

There is a history of debate over what is meant by a voluntary association. For our present purposes, a voluntary association is a body of people who have voluntarily organized themselves in pursuit of particular goals. (Following common usage, we exclude business corporations and other primarily economic associations.) Important to the present discussion is the subject of volunteer service. Many voluntary associations have both paid and volunteer staffing. For our purposes, the crucial point is the free association of people for some collective purpose, the fact that they may pay some individuals for doing work to this end not being decisive.

At least since de Tocqueville the importance of voluntary associations in American democracy has been widely recognized. Voluntarism has flourished in America more than in any other Western society and it is reasonable to believe this may have something to do with American political institutions. Associations create statutes, elect officers, debate, vote courses of action, and otherwise serve as schools for democracy. However trivial, wrongheaded, or bizarre we may think the purpose of some associations to be, they nonetheless perform this vital function.

Apart from this political role, voluntary associations are enormously important for what they have actually done. Before the advent of the modern welfare state, almost everything in the realm of social services was under the aegis of voluntary associations, usually religious in character. Still today there are about 1,900 private colleges and universities, 4,600 private secondary schools, 3,600 voluntary hospitals, 6,000 museums, 1,100 orchestras, 5,500 libraries, and no less than 29,000 nongovernmental welfare agencies. Of course not all of these are equally important as mediating structures. Orchestras and groups promoting stamp-collecting or the preservation of antique automobiles are, however important in other connections, outside our focus here. We are interested in one type within the vast array of voluntary associations—namely, associations that render social services relevant to recognized public responsibilities.

Assaults on voluntary associations come from several directions, from both the right and left of the political spectrum. Some condemn them as inefficient, corrupt, divisive, and even subversive. Many subscribe to the axiom that public services should not be under private control. From the far left comes the challenge that such associations supply mere palliatives, perpetuate the notion of charity, and otherwise manipulate people into acceptance of the status quo.

Such assaults are not merely verbal. They reflect a trend to establish a state monopoly over all organized activities that have to do with more than strictly private purposes. This trend has borne fruit in outright prohibition, in repressive taxation, and in the imposition of licensing and operating standards that have a punitive effect on nongovernmental agencies.

Of course there are instances of corruption and inefficiency in voluntary agencies. A comparison of governmental and nongovernmental social services on these scores, however, hardly supports the case for governmental monopoly. It should be obvious that government bureaucrats have a vested interest in maintaining and expanding government monopolies. Similarly, politicians have an interest in setting up services for which they can claim credit and over which they can exercise a degree of power. In short, social services in the modern welfare state are inescapably part of the political pork barrel.

Pork barrels may be necessary to political democracy. The problem confronting us arises when the vested interests in question use coercive state power to repress individual freedom, initiative, and social diversity. We are not impressed by the argument that this is necessary because voluntary associations often overlap with the functions of government agencies. Overlap may in fact provide creative competition, incentives for performance, and increased choice. But our more basic contention is against the notion that anything public must *ipso facto* be governmental. That notion is profoundly contrary to the American political tradition and is, in its consequences, antidemocratic. It creates clients of the state instead of free citizens. It stifles the initiative and responsibility essential to the life of the polity.

Our present problem is also closely linked with the trend toward professionalization. Whether in government or nongovernment agencies, professionals attack allegedly substandard services, and substandard generally means nonprofessional. Through organizations and lobbies, professionals increasingly persuade the state to legislate standards and certifications that hit voluntary associations hard, especially those given to employing volunteers. The end result is that the trend toward government monopoly operates in tandem with the trend toward professional monopoly over social services. The connection between such monopoly control and the actual quality of services delivered is doubtful indeed.

Professional standards are of course important in some areas. But they must be viewed with robust skepticism when expertise claims jurisdiction, as it were, over the way people run their own lives. Again, ordinary people are the best experts on themselves. Tutelage by certified experts is bad enough when exercised by persuasion—as, for example, when parents are so demoralized that they feel themselves incapable of raising their children without ongoing reference to child-raising experts. It is much worse, however, when such tutelage is imposed coercively. And, of course, lower-income people are most effectively disenfranchised by the successful establishment of expert monopolies.

Professionalization is now being exacerbated by unionization of professionals. In principle, employees of nongovernment agencies can be unionized as readily as government employees. In practice, large unions prefer to deal with the large and unified management that government offers. Standards and certification become items of negotiation between union and management, thus reinforcing the drive toward professional monopolies. In addition, unions would seem to have an intrinsic antagonism toward volunteer work. It is alleged that the volunteer is an unpaid laborer and is therefore exploited. This argument has been recently advanced also by some feminists, since many volunteers are women.

In protesting the use of labor and feminist rhetoric to camouflage the establishment of coercive monopolies and the disenfranchisement of people in the running of their own lives, our position is neither anti-union nor anti-feminist. Who defines exploitation? We trust people to know when they are being exploited, without the benefits of instruction by professionals, labor organizers, or feminist authors. So long as voluntary work is genuinely voluntary—is undertaken by free choice—it should be cherished and not maligned. It is of enormous value in terms of both the useful activity offered to volunteers and the actual services rendered. In addition, because of their relative freedom from bureaucratic controls, voluntary associations are important laboratories of innovation in social services; and, of course, they sustain the expression of the rich pluralism of American life.

Attacks on the volunteer principle also aid the expansion of the kind of capitalist mentality that would put a dollar sign on everything on the grounds that only that which has a price tag has worth. We believe it proper and humane (as well as "human") that there be areas of life, including public life, in which there is not a dollar sign on everything. It is debilitating to our sense of the polity to assume that only private life is to be governed by humane, nonpecuniary motives, while the rest of life is a matter of dog-eat-dog.

An additional word should be said about the development of paraprofessional fields. To be sure, people who make their living in any socially useful occupation should be given respectful recognition and should be paid a decent wage. However, much of the paraprofessional development is in fact empire-building by professional and union monopolists who would incorporate lower-status occupations into their hierarchy. At least in some instances, the word that best describes this development is exploitation. This is the case, for example, when parents and other lay people can no longer hold professionals to account because they have themselves been co-opted into the vested interests of the professionals.

With the immense growth of knowledge and skills in modern society, professions are necessary and it is inevitable that there be organizations and unions to defend their interests. This development cannot be, and should not be, reversed. It can, however, be redirected. The purpose of the professions is to serve society—not the other way around. Too often professionals regard those they serve as clients in the rather unfortunate sense the Latin word originally implied. The clients of a Roman patrician were one step above his slaves in the social hierarchy, not entirely unlike some of today's servile dependents upon professionals. Such a notion has no place in a democratic society.

Professionals should be ancillary to the people they serve. Upper-income people refer to "our" doctor or "my" doctor, and whatever patterns of dependency they develop are largely of their own choosing. It should be possible for lower-income people to use the possessive pronoun in referring to professionals.

The policy implications of our approach touch also on the role of nonprofit foundations in our society. Technically, there are different kinds of foundations—strictly private, publicly supported, operating, and so on—but the current assault applies to all of them. The argument is summed up in the words of the late Wright Patman whose crusade against foundations led to Title I of the Tax Reform Act of 1969:

> Today I shall introduce a bill to end a gross inequity which this country and its citizens can no longer afford: the tax-exempt status of the so-called privately controlled charitable foundations, and their propensity for domination of business and accumulation of wealth. . . . Put most bluntly, philanthropy—one of mankind's more noble instincts—has been perverted into a vehicle for institutionalized deliberate evasion of fiscal and moral responsibility to the nation. (*Congressional Record,* August 6, 1969)

Of course, foundations have engaged in abuses that need to be curbed, but the resentment and hostility manifested by the curbers also needs to be curbed if we are not to harm the society very severely. The curbers of foundations make up an odd coalition. Right-wing forces are hostile to foundations because of their social experimentation (such as the Ford Foundation's programs among inner-city blacks), while others are hostile because of the role of big business ("the establishment") in funding foundations. The most dangerous part of the 1969 legislation is the new power given to the Internal Revenue Service to police foundation activities. The power to revoke or threaten to revoke tax exemption is a most effective instrument of control. (In recent years such threats have been made against religious organizations that opposed the Vietnam War and advocated sundry unpopular causes.) More ominous than the prospect that a few millionaires will get away with paying less taxes is the prospect of government control over officially disapproved advocacy or programs.

Directly related to this concern is the relatively new concept of tax expenditure that has been infiltrated into public policy. It is calculated, for example, that a certain amount of revenue is lost to the government because a private college is tax exempt. The revenue lost is called a tax expenditure. This may seem like an innocuous bit of bookkeeping, but the term expenditure implies that the college is in fact government-subsidized (a tax expenditure is a kind of government expenditure) and therefore ought to be governmentally controlled. This implication, which is made quite explicit by some bureaucrats, is incipiently totalitarian. The logic is that all of society's wealth *really* belongs to the government and that the government should therefore be able to determine how all wealth—including the wealth exempted from taxation—should be used. The concept of tax expenditure should be used, if at all, as a simple accounting device having no normative implications.

While large foundations would seem to be remote from the mediating structures under discussion, in fact they are often important to such structures at the most local level, especially in the areas of education and health. Were all these institutions taken over by the government, there might be a more uniform imposition of standards and greater financial accountability than now exists (although the monumental corruption in various government social services does not make one sanguine about the latter), but the price would be high. Massive bureaucratization, the proliferation of legal procedures that generate both public resentment and business for lawyers, the atrophying of the humane impulse, the increase of alienation—these would be some of the costs. Minimally, it should be public policy to encourage the voluntarism that, in our society, has at least slowed down these costs of modernity.

As always, the maximalist side of our approach—that is, using voluntary associations as agents of public policies—is more problematic than the minimalist. One thinks, for example, of the use of foster homes and half-way houses in the treatment and prevention of drug addiction, juvenile delinquency, and mental illness. There is reason to believe such approaches are both less costly and more effective than using bureaucratized megastructures (and their local outlets). Or one thinks of the successful resettlement of more than 100,000 Vietnam refugees in 1975, accomplished not by setting up a government agency but by working through voluntary agencies (mainly religious). This instance of using voluntary associations for public policy purposes deserves careful study. Yet another instance is the growth of the women's health movement, which in some areas is effectively challenging the monopolistic practices of the medical establishment. The ideas of people such as Ivan Illich and Victor Fuchs should be examined for their potential to empower people to reassure responsibility for their own health care. Existing experiments in decentralizing medical delivery systems should also be encouraged, with a view toward moving from decentralization to genuine empowerment.

We well know that proposals for community participation are not new. The most obvious example is the Community Action Program (CAP), a part of the War Against Poverty of the 1960s. CAP led to much disillusionment. Some condemned it as a mask for co-opting those who did, or might, threaten local power elites. Thus, community organizations were deprived of real potency and turned into government dependents. From the other side of the political spectrum, CAP was condemned for funding agitators and subversives. Yet others charged that CAP pitted community organizations against the institutions of representative government. To some extent these criticisms are mutually exclusive—they cannot all be true simultaneously. Yet no doubt all these things happened in various places in the 1960s.

That experience in no way invalidates the idea of community participation. First, the peculiar developments of the 1960s made that decade the worst possible time to try out the idea (and the same might be said about experiments in the community control of schools during the same period). Second, and much more important, the institutions used to facilitate community participation were not the actual institutions of the community but were created by those in charge of the program. This was especially true in inner-city black areas—the chief focus of the program—where religious institutions were, for the most part, neglected or even deliberately undercut. So, to some extent, were the family structures of the black community. In short, the program's failures resulted precisely from its failure to utilize existing mediating structures.

This said, it remains true that mediating structures can be co-opted by government, that they can become instruments of those interested in destroying rather than reforming American society, and that they can undermine the institutions of the formal polity. These are real risks. On the other side are the benefits described earlier. Together they constitute a major challenge to the political imagination.

## EMPOWERMENT THROUGH PLURALISM

The theme of pluralism has recurred many times in this essay. This final section aims simply to tie up a few loose ends, to anticipate some objections to a public policy designed to sustain pluralism through mediating structures, and to underscore some facts of American society that suggest both the potentials and limitations of the approach advanced here.

It should be obvious that by pluralism we mean much more than regional accents, St. Patrick's Day, and Black Pride Days, as important as all these are. Beyond providing the variety of color, costume, and custom, pluralism makes possible a tension within worlds and between worlds of meaning. Worlds of meaning put reality together in a distinctive way. Whether the participants in these worlds see themselves as mainline or subcultural, as establishment or revolutionary, they are each but part of the cultural whole. Yet the paradox is that wholeness is experienced through affirmation of the part in which one participates. This relates to the aforementioned insight of Burke regarding "the little platoon." In more contemporary psychological jargon it relates to the "identity crisis" which results from an "identity diffusion" in mass society. Within one's group—whether it be racial, national, political, religious, or all of these—one discovers an answer to the elementary question, "Who am I?" and is supported in living out of that answer. Psychologically and sociologically, we would propose the axiom that any identity is better than none. Politically, we would argue that it is not the business of public policy to make value judgments regarding the merits or demerits of various identity solutions, so long as all groups abide by the minimal rules that make a pluralistic society possible. It is the business of public policy not to undercut, and indeed to enhance, the identity choices available to the American people (our minimalist and maximalist propositions throughout).

This approach assumes that the process symbolized by "E Pluribus Unum" is not a zero-sum game. That is, the *unum is* not to be achieved at the expense of the *plures.* To put it positively, the national purpose indicated by the *unum is* precisely to sustain the *plures.* Of course there are tensions, and accommodations are necessary if the structures necessary to national existence are to be maintained. But in the art of pluralistic politics, such tensions are not to be eliminated but are to be welcomed as the catalysts of more imaginative accommodations. Public policy in the areas discussed in this essay has in recent decades, we believe, been too negative in its approach to the tensions of diversity and therefore too ready to impose uniform solutions on what are perceived as national social problems. In this approach, pluralism is viewed as an enemy of social policy planning rather than as a source of more diversified solutions to problems that are, after all, diversely caused and diversely defined.

Throughout this essay, we have emphasized that our proposal contains no animus toward those charged with designing and implementing social policy nor any indictment of their good intentions. The reasons for present pluralism-eroding policies are to be discovered in part in the very processes implicit in the metaphors of modernization, rationalization, and bureaucratization. The management mindset of the megastructure—whether of HEW, Sears Roebuck, or the AFL-CIO—is biased toward the unitary solution. The neat and comprehensive answer is impatient of "irrational" particularities and can only be forced to yield to greater nuance when it encounters resistance, whether from the economic market of consumer wants or from the political market of organized special interest groups. The challenge of public policy is to anticipate such resistance and, beyond that, to cast aside its adversary posture toward particularism and embrace as its goal the advancement of the multitude of particular interests that in fact constitute the common weal. Thus, far from denigrating social planning, our proposal challenges the policy maker with a much more complicated and exciting task than today's approach. Similarly, the self-esteem of the professional in all areas of social service is elevated when he or she defines the professional task in terms of being helpful and ancillary to people rather than in terms of creating a power monopoly whereby people become dependent clients.

Of course, some critics will decry our proposal as "balkanization," "retribalization," "parochialization," and such. The relevance of the Balkan areas aside, we want frankly to assert that tribe and parochial are not terms of derision. That they are commonly used in a derisive manner is the result of a world view emerging from the late eighteenth century. That worldview held, in brief, that the laws of Nature are reflected in a political will of the people that can be determined and implemented by rational persons. Those naive notions of Nature, Will, and Reason have in the last hundred years been thoroughly discredited in almost every discipline, from psychology to sociology to physics. Yet the irony is that, although few people still believe in these myths, most social thought and planning continues to act as though they were true. The result is that the enemies of particularism ("tribalism") have become an elite tribe attempting to impose order on the seeming irrationalities of the real world and operating on premises that most Americans find both implausible and hostile to their values. Social thought has been crippled and policies have miscarried because we have not developed a paradigm of pluralism to replace the discredited assumptions of the eighteenth century. We hope this proposal is one step toward developing such a paradigm.

Throughout this essay we have frequently referred to democratic values and warned against their authoritarian and totalitarian alternatives. We are keenly aware of the limitations in any notion of "the people" actually exercising the *kratein*, the effective authority, in public policy. And we are keenly aware of how far the American policy is from demonstrating what is possible in the democratic idea. The result of political manipulation, media distortion, and the sheer weight of indifference is that the great majority of Americans have little or no political will, in the sense that term is used in democratic theory, on the great questions of domestic and international policy. Within the formal framework of democratic polity, these questions will perforce be answered by a more politicized elite. But it is precisely with respect to mediating structures that most people do have, in the most exact sense, a political will. On matters of family, church, neighborhood, hobbies, working place, and recreation, most people have a very clear idea of what is in their interest. If we are truly committed to the democratic process, it is their political will that public policy should be designed to empower. It may be lamentable that most Americans have no political will with respect to U.S. relations with Brazil, but that is hardly reason to undercut their very clear political will about how their children should be educated. Indeed policies that disable political will where it does exist preclude the development of political will where it does not now exist, thus further enfeebling the democratic process and opening the door to its alternatives.

As difficult as it may be for some to accept, all rational interests do not converge—or at least there is no universal agreement on what interests are rational. This means that public policy must come to terms with perduring contradictions. We need not resign ourselves to the often cynically invoked axiom that "politics is the art of the possible." In fact politics is the art of discovering *what* is possible. The possibility to be explored is not how far unitary policies can be extended before encountering the backlash of particularity. Rather, the possibility to be explored is how a common purpose can be achieved through the enhancement of myriad particular interests. This requires a new degree of modesty among those who think about social policy—not modesty in the sense of lowering our ideals in the search for meeting human needs and creating a more just society, but modesty about *our* definitions of need and justice. Every world within this society, whether it calls itself a subculture or a supraculture or simply the American culture, is in fact a subculture, is but a part of the whole. This fact needs to be systematically remembered among those who occupy the world of public policy planning and implementation.

The subculture that envisages its values as universal and its style as cosmopolitan is no less a subculture for all that. The tribal patterns evident at an Upper West Side cocktail party are no less tribal than those evident at a Polish dance in Greenpoint, Brooklyn. That the former is produced by the interaction of people trying to transcend many particularisms simply results in a new, and not necessarily more interesting, particularism. People at the cocktail party may think of themselves as liberated, and indeed they may have elected to leave behind certain particularisms into which they were born. They have, in effect, elected a new particularism. Liberation is not escape from particularity but discovery of the particularity that fits. Elected particularities may include life style, ideology, friendships, place of residence, and so forth. Inherited particularities may include race, economic circumstance, region, religion, and, in most cases, politics. Pluralism means the lively interaction among inherited particularities and, through election, the evolution of new particularities. The goal of public policy in a pluralistic society is to sustain as many particularities as possible, in the hope that most people will accept, discover, or devise one that fits.

It might be argued that the redirection of public policy proposed here is in fact naive and quixotic. A strong argument can be made that the dynamics of modernity, operating through the megastructures and especially through the modern state, are like a great leviathan or steamroller, inexorably destroying every obstacle that gets in the way of creating mass society. There is much and ominous evidence in support of that argument. While we cannot predict the outcome of this process, we must not buckle under to alleged inevitabilities. On the more hopeful side are indications that the political will of the American people is beginning to assert itself more strongly in resistance to "massification." In contradiction of social analysts who describe the irresistible and homogenizing force of the communications media, for example, there is strong evidence that the media message is not received uncritically but is refracted through myriad world views that confound the intentions of would-be manipulators of the masses. (Happily, there are also many often-contradictory media messages.) New "Edsels" still get rejected (though the Edsel itself is a collector's item). The antiwar bias of much news about the Vietnam War (a bias we shared) was, studies suggest, often refracted in a way that reinforced support of official policy. Promotion of diverse sexual and life-style liberations seems to be doing little empirically verifiable damage to devotion to the family ideal. Thirty years of network TV English (not to mention thirty years of radio before that) has hardly wiped out regional dialect. In short, and to the consternation of political, cultural, and commercial purveyors of new soaps, the American people demonstrate a robust skepticism toward the modern peddlers of new worlds and a remarkable inclination to trust their own judgments. We do not wish to exaggerate these signs of hope. Counter-indicators can be listed in abundance. We do suggest there is no reason to resign ourselves to the "massification" that is so often described as America today.

America today—those words are very important to our argument. While our proposal is, we hope, relevant to modern industrialized society in general, whether socialist or capitalist, its possibilities are peculiarly attuned to the United States. (We might say, to North America, including Canada, but some aspects of particularism in Canada—for example, binationalism between French- and English-speaking Canadians—are beyond the scope of this essay.) There are at least five characteristics of American society that make it the most likely laboratory for public policy designed to enhance mediating structures and the pluralism that mediating structures make possible. First is the immigrant nature of American society. The implications of that fact for pluralism need no elaboration. Second, ours is a relatively affluent society. We have the resources to experiment toward a more humane order—for example, to place a floor of economic decency under every American. Third, this is a relatively stable society. Confronted by the prospects of neither revolution nor certain and rapid decline, we do not face the crises that call for total or definitive answers to social problems. Fourth, American society is effectively pervaded by the democratic idea and by the sense of tolerance and fair play that make the democratic process possible. This makes our society ideologically hospitable to pluralism. And fifth, however weakened they may be, we still have relatively strong institutions—political, economic, religious, and cultural—that supply countervailing forces in the shaping of social policy. Aspirations toward monopoly can, at least in theory, be challenged. And our history demonstrates that the theory has, more often than not, been acted out in practice.

Finally, we know there are those who contend that, no matter how promising all this may be for America, America is very bad for the rest of the world. It is argued that the success of America's experiment in democratic pluralism is at the expense of others, especially at the expense of the poorer nations. It is a complicated argument to which justice cannot be done here. But it might be asked, in turn, whether America would in some sense be better for the world were we to eliminate any of the five characteristics mentioned above. Were the American people more homogeneous, were they as poor as the peasants of Guatemala, were their institutions less stable and their democratic impulses less ingrained—would any of these conditions contribute concretely to a more just global order? We think not.

Neither, on the other hand, are we as convinced as some others seem to be that America is the "advance society" of human history, or at least of the modern industrialized world. Perhaps it is—perhaps not. But of this we are convinced: America has a singular opportunity to contest the predictions of the inevitability of mass society with its anomic individuals, alienated and impotent, excluded from the ordering of a polity that is no longer theirs. And we are convinced that mediating structures might be the agencies for a new empowerment of people in America's renewed experiment in democratic pluralism.

# 9

# Professionalized Services: Disabling Help for Communities and Citizens

*John L. McKnight*

The business of modern society is service. Social service in modern society is business.

This fact is reflected in the language employed. Professionals and their managers now speak of educational "products," health "consumers," and a legal "industry." Clients are defined as "markets," and technocrats—an entirely new breed of professionals—are developing methods to "market" services, using business accounting systems. Computers measure and store psychological "inputs" and family "outputs." There are "units served" and "units of service," and sophisticated economists, statisticians, and planners deal with the production and consumption of social services in the same way as the production, consumption, and maintenance of physical goods is accounted for. Furthermore, and this is of central importance, every modernized society, whether socialist or capitalist, is marked by the growing percentage of service in its gross national product, not only of services such as postal deliveries, catering, and car repairs, but social services such as marriage guidance, birth control counseling, education, legal arbitration, care of the young, the adult, and the old in all its ramifications, and all that falls under the general heading of social help.

This stage of economic development is distinguished by its unlimited potential, since service production has none of the limits imposed by goods production—limits such as natural resources, capital, and land. Therefore, the social service business has endless possibilities for expansion, as there seems to be no end to the needs for which services can be manufactured.

Modernized nations are therefore best defined as service economies. They are serviced societies and they are peopled with service producers and service consumers—professionals and clients.

The politics of serviced societies are gradually being clarified. Public budgets are becoming strained under the service load. Many national and local governments find themselves involved in the unprecedented politics of deciding between competing services—should we give more to education and less to medicine? Within the service sectors there are equally difficult dilemmas. Should we cut back on tax-paid abortions or should the available money be used for free flu vaccine?

These dilemmas are often resolved by the apolitical ideology of service. While old-fashioned politics, rooted in a goods economy, allowed a civic debate as to whether a nation needed more wheat or more steel, more automobiles or more houses, the new service politics is a debate as to whether we should have more doctors or more teachers, more lawyers or more social workers. Politically the question becomes whether we should trade health for learning, or justice for family well-being. These choices create an impossible politics in traditional terms.

While our political traditions make it possible to decide between wheat and steel, it seems politically impossible to decide between health and education because health and education are not alternatives amenable to choices, they are services. Indeed, the allocation of services is so immune to political debate that many governments resolve the dilemma by deciding that we will have less wheat and more education, less steel and more medicine.

This is not to suggest that these choices are correct or incorrect, or even that they define appropriateness. Rather, it is to say that the apolitical nature of service is so pervasive that it is difficult for the public and policymakers to recognize that the creation and allocation of services are the central political issue in many modernized economies.

The political immunity of the services is best understood in terms of the symbolic referent of service:

Services are something one pays for.

The "good" that is paid for is care.

Care is an act that is an expression of love. We say "I care for her more than anyone" or "I am taking care of my mother and father."

Thus, *service* is to *care* which is to *love* and love is the universal, apolitical value.

Symbolically, then, the apolitical nature of service depends on its association with the unlimited universality of love. Ask any servicer what is ultimately satisfying about his work and the answer will most commonly be framed in terms of wanting to care for and help people. Press on and the answer is usually that the individual "loves people."

Since love is not a political issue, care is not a policy question and service becomes the one business that is an unlimited, unquestionable, and nonpolitical "good."

While this analysis may seem overly symbolic, consider the political use of the language of social service in the United States. When the first major program to provide governmentally insured medicine was proposed, it was not described as a policy to expand access to and income for the medical system. It was called Medi*care.*

The president of the American Federation of Teachers noted in an address that there are thousands of unemployed teachers and a large new supply graduating from teacher training institutions. He dealt with the economic dilemma by noting that large sectors of the society need education—the preschool, adult, and elderly populations. In order to meet this "need," he called for a new government program to guarantee the lifelong educational rights of all Americans. He called it Edu*care.*

In the law schools of the United States, law students number 40 percent of all the practicing lawyers in the country. A recent study asked the leaders of the American bar what they thought could be done to ensure that this flood of new lawyers could provide their service and have an adequate income. The most common response was to suggest the need for a publicly supported program that would guarantee the rights of all people to legal services. The name that was universally applied to such a program was Judi*care.*

It is clear, therefore, that the word "care" is a potent political symbol. What is not so clear is that its use masks the political interests of servicers. This fact is further obscured by the symbolic link between care and love. The result is that the politico-economic issues of service are hidden behind the mask of love.

Behind that mask is simply the servicer, his systems, techniques, and technologies—a business in need of markets, an economy seeking new growth potential, professionals in need of an income.

It is crucial that we understand that this mask of service is *not* a false face. The power of the ideology of service is demonstrated by the fact that most servicers cannot distinguish the mask from their own face. The service ideology is *not* hypocritical because hypocrisy is the false pretense of a desirable goal. The modernized servicer believes in his care and love, perhaps even more than in the services. The mask is the face. The service ideology is *not* conspiratorial. A conspiracy is a group decision to create an exploitative result. The modernized servicer honestly joins his fellows to create a supposedly beneficial result. The masks are the faces.

In order to distinguish the mask and the face it is necessary to consider another symbol—need.

We say love is a need. Care is a need. Service is a need. Servicers meet needs. People are a collection of needs. Society has needs. The economy should be organized to meet needs.

In a modernized society where the major business is service, the political reality is that the central "need" is an adequate income for professional servicers and the economic growth they portend. The masks of love and care obscure this reality so that the public cannot recognize the professionalized interests that manufacture needs in order to rationalize a service economy. Medicare, Educare, Judicare, Socialcare, and Psychocare are portrayed as systems to meet need rather than programs to meet the needs of servicers and the economies they support.

Removing the mask of love shows us the face of servicers who need income, and an economic system that *needs* growth. Within this framework, the client is less a person in need than a person who is needed. In business terms, the client is less the consumer than the raw material for the servicing system. In management terms, the client becomes both the output and the input. His essential function is to meet the needs of servicers, the servicing system, and the national economy. The central political issue becomes the servicers' capacity to manufacture needs in order to expand the economy of the servicing system.

Within this analytical framework, pejoratives are inappropriate. After all, a serviced society provides an economy, a structure for social organization, and service workers motivated by the ethical values of care and love. If these service system needs are legitimate, clients can be viewed as needed, rather than in need, and we can get on with the business of researching, developing, manufacturing, and marketing services without the necessity to project professional need upon citizens. We can deal in political and economic terms with the needs of servicers, freed of the apolitical mask of love.

The problem with this political resolution is political reality. Throughout modernized societies a troublesome question is being raised by the citizenry. In popular terms, it is:

> Why are we putting so much resource into medicine while it is not improving our health?
>
> Why are we putting so much resource into education and our children seem to be learning less?
>
> Why are we putting so much resource into criminal justice systems and society seems less just and less secure?
>
> Why are we putting so much more resource into mental health systems and we seem to have more mental illness?

As if these questions were not troubling enough, a new group of service system critics are asking whether we are putting more resources in and getting out the very opposite of what the system is designed to "produce." In medicine, this question is most clearly defined as iatrogenesis—doctor-created disease. The new critics' question is not whether we get less service for more resources. Rather, it is whether we get the reverse of what the service system is supposed to "produce." In the terms of Ivan Illich, the question is whether the systems have become counterproductive. Do we get more sickness from more medicine? Do we get more injustice and crime with more lawyers and police? Do we get more ignorance with more teachers and schools? Do we get more family collapse with more social workers?

This is the question that is most threatening to the previously apolitical service systems, because while services defined as embodiments of care and love are a political platform; while services that are understood as being less effective than they have been in the past are a political possibility; while it is even politically feasible to remove the mask of love and recognize services as systems in need of resources in order that economies may grow, it is politically *impossible* to maintain a service economy if the populace perceives that the service system hurts more than it helps—that professionalized service can become disabling help.

In the last few years, the progressive leaders of the service business have recognized the counterproductive threat. Their response has been to develop new strategies to deal with the counterproductivity of service systems. They have called upon the skills of another profession—the managers. Their assumption is that although professional servicers are unable to control the harm they induce, the managerial profession can become the modern reformer, controlling and directing the systems so that counterproductivity is neutralized, while at the same time protecting the political support for the growth of the service system.

The new service manager, translating his skills from the goods production sector, sees four elements to be manipulated in rationalizing the service system: budgets, personnel, organizational structure, and technology. Therefore, the service manager is now busily at work instituting cost-control systems, developing personnel-training systems, restructuring delivery systems, and introducing new technologies.

The most progressive managers have used their advanced marketing skills to develop a fifth manipulation—preparing the client. They recognize that if there is no need for service, it is possible to manufacture a need. If the popular perceptions of need do not fit the service, social service managers have developed techniques that can persuade people to fit the service through advanced marketing systems.

Will these professional management techniques stabilize the service business by eliminating counterproductive effects? Certainly the capacities of modern management systems are impressive. Aided by the apolitical ideology of the services, one might well prophesy a collaboration between the servicers and their managers to coalesce into an irresistible force that will henceforth direct the economic policies of modernized economies.

An alternative view suggests that there may be an immovable object that faces the irresistible force: a new ideology that assigns to the state the coordination of total disservice.

If such an object exists, it is found in the human necessity to act rather than be acted upon; to be citizen rather than client. It is this human imperative that suggests that even the best-managed service systems will be unable to overcome popular recognition of the disabling impacts of modernized professional service.

The remainder of this chapter attempts to identify the disabling effects of modernized service systems and to suggest the political consequences of the conflict between the irresistible force of client-making and the immovable object of citizen action.

## PROFESSIONALIZED ASSUMPTION REGARDING NEED

Three disabling effects grow from professionalized assumption of need.

*First* is the translation of a need into a deficiency. A need could be understood as a condition, a want, a right, an obligation of another, an illusion, or an unresolvable problem. Professional practice consistently defines a need as an unfortunate absence or emptiness in another.

One is reminded of the child's riddle asking someone to describe a glass that has water in its lower half. Is it half-full—or half-empty? The basic function of modernized professionalism is to legitimize human beings whose capacity is to see their neighbor as half-empty. Professionalized research increasingly devotes its efforts to extending the upper rim of the glass in order to ensure that it will never be filled—even by the results of "effective service."

In a servicing economy where the majority of the people derive their income from professionalized "helping" and GNP is measured by services rendered, nations need an increased supply of *personal* deficiency. Thus, a society that purports to meet need defined as personal deficiency is more accurately understood as an economy in need of need. The comic distortion could be societies of neighbors whose income depends upon finding the deficiency in each other. The political consequence is neighbors unable to act as communities of competence with the capacity to perceive or act upon solvable problems.

The *second* disabling characteristic of professionalized definitions of need is the professional practice of placing the perceived deficiency *in* the client. While most modernized professionals will agree that individual problems develop in a socioeconomic-political context, their common remedial practice isolates the individual from the context. The effect of this individualization leads the professional to distort even his own contextual understanding. Because his remedial tools and techniques are usually limited to individualized interaction, the interpretation of the need necessarily becomes individualized. The tool defines the problem rather than the problem defining the tool.

A study of children who became state wards exemplifies the process. The children were legally separated from their families because the parents were judged to be unable to provide adequate care for the children. Therefore, the children were placed in professional service institutions. However, the majority of the professional case records portrayed the children as the problem. Quite correctly, officials who were involved in removing the children from their homes agreed that a common reason for removal was the economic poverty of the family. Obviously, they had no resources to deal with poverty. But there were many resources for professionalized institutional service. The service system met the economic need by institutionalizing an individualized definition of the problem. The negative side effect was that the poverty of the families was intensified by the resources consumed by the "caring" professional services. In counterproductive terms, the servicing system "produced" broken families.

The individualizing, therapeutic definition of need has met a counteracting force in some of the "liberation" movements. The civil rights and women's liberation movements are cases in point. Their essential ideological function is to persuade minorities and women that they are human beings who are neither deficient nor dependent upon systems purporting to meet their "needs" through individualized professional help. Instead, these movements struggle to overcome the individualized-deficiency-oriented "consciousness" communicated by the professional service ideology by affirming individual competence and collective action.

The *third* disabling effect of professionalized definitions of need results from specialization—the major "product" of advanced systems of technique and technology. We all know that this process creates highly specialized, intricately organized service systems that provide magnificent organizational problems for the new service managers. Vast human and financial resources are now devoted to the rationalization of these systems, providing politically acceptable criteria justifying economic growth through the service sector.

What is less clearly understood is that these systems impose their mirror image on the citizenry. As the systems are a set of managed parts, so the client is necessarily understood and processed as a set of manageable parts, each with its own service mechanic. These complex service systems remind one of those table mats in some restaurants that show a cow divided into parts locating the steak, the roast, the ribs, and the tongue.

In like manner, professionalized service definitions increasingly translate need in terms of people in pieces. We need podiatrists for our hooves and eye, ear, nose, and throat men for our snouts. Our psyche, marriage, relationship with our children, in fact our most intimate and personal activities are divided into separate bits and pieces.

Modernized professions also piece us out in time. Service professionals now assure us that we live through a set of needs defined by age. Professionals have "found" seven life crises (formerly known as the seven ages of man) from infancy to death, each requiring its helping professional. Elizabeth Kubler-Ross has advanced the process by giving us five phases of death. Her work ensures a new set of helpers for stage one of dying, stage two of dying, and so on. Following these dying therapists will be research professionals attempting to decide why some people skip, say, stage two or three of dying.

While individualizing need may disable by removing people from the social context, the compartmentalization of the person removes even the potential for individual action. People are, instead, a set of pieces in need, in both time and space. One hopes that the pieces can be put together again to make a human unit of sufficient residual effectiveness to pay for "its" servicing.

To sum up, professionalized services define need as a deficiency and at the same time individualize and compartmentalize the deficient components. The service systems communicate three propositions to the client:

- You are deficient.
- You are the problem.
- You have a collection of problems.

In terms of the interest of service systems and their needs, the propositions become:

- We *need* deficiency.
- The economic unit we *need* is individuals.
- The productive economic unit we *need* is an individual with multiple deficiencies.

## THE PROFESSIONALIZED ASSUMPTIONS REGARDING THE REMEDY OF NEED

These professionalized definitions of need produce a logical and necessary set of remedial assumptions, each with its own intrinsically disabling effects.

The *first* of these assumptions is the mirror image of the individualized definition of need. As *you* are the problem, the assumption is that I, the professional servicer, *am the answer. You* are not the answer. *Your peers* are not the answer. *The political, social, and economic environment* is not the answer. Nor is it possible that there is no answer. I, the professional, am the answer. The central assumption is that service is a unilateral process. I, the professional, produce. You, the client, consume.

These are, of course, an impressive set of professionalized coping mechanisms that have been developed by sensitive servicers to deny the unilateral nature of professionalized service. They are described as group-oriented services, peer-oriented services, client-oriented services, and community-oriented services. Each of these rhetorical devices is a symbolic attempt to deal with the anxieties of servicers who *need* to deny the unilateral nature of their relationships.

While it is clear that many humanistic professionals seek a democratic definition for their role, it is difficult to perceive the bilateral component beyond the client's payment, whether out of pocket or through taxation. Indeed, a basic definition of "unprofessional conduct" is "becoming involved with the client." To be professional is to distance—to ensure that the relationship is defined in terms that allow the client to understand who is *really* being serviced.

In spite of the democratic pretense, the disabling function of unilateral professional help is the hidden assumption that "you will be better because I, the professional, know better."

The political implications of this assumption are central to antidemocratic systems. Indeed, it is possible that societies dependent on economies of unilateral professional servicing are systematically preparing their people for antidemocratic leaders who can capitalize upon the dependencies created by expert, professionalized helpers, who teach people that "they will be better because we, the professional helpers, know better."

A *second* disabling characteristic of professionalized remedial assumptions is the necessity for the remedy to define the need. As professionalized service systems create more elegant techniques and magnificent tools, they create an imperative demanding their use.

The problem with these beautiful, shiny, complex, professional tools and techniques is that their "benefits" are not easily comprehended by the public. We see the professions developing internal logics and public marketing systems that assure use of the tools and techniques by assuming that the client doesn't understand what he needs. Therefore, if the client is to have the benefit of the professional remedy, he must also understand that the professional not only knows what he needs but also knows how the need is to be met.

Thus the complex professional remedial tools have come to justify the professional power to define the need—to decide not only the appropriate remedy but the definition of the problem itself. Increasingly, professions assume that in order to deal with deficiency, they must have the prerogative to decide what is deficient.

There is no greater power than the right to define the question. From that right flows a set of necessary answers. If the servicer can effectively assert the right to define the appropriate question, he has the power to determine the need of his neighbor rather than to meet his neighbor's need.

While this power allows the professional to use his shiny new remedy, it also defines citizens as people who can't understand whether they have a problem—much less what should be done about it.

Modernized societies are now replete with need-defining research. Professionals have recently "discovered" tool-using needs called child abuse, learning disabilities, and "removal trauma" (the need for therapy for children who are traumatized because they are removed from their allegedly traumatic families).

Brigitte Berger suggests, in a recent article, that baldness will soon be defined as a disease because underemployed dermatologists will decree it to be one. The final institutionalization of the process is a new program developed by a famous clinic in the United States: the program provides a costly opportunity for people who don't feel anything is wrong to find out what problems they have that meet the needs of new tools.

When the capacity to define the problem becomes a professional prerogative, citizens no longer exist. The prerogative removes the citizen as problem-definer, much less problem-solver. It translates political functions into technical and technological problems.

Once the service professional can define remedy and need, a *third* disabling remedial practice develops. It is the coding of the problem and the solution into languages that are incomprehensible to citizens.

While it is clearly disabling to be told you can't decide whether you have a problem and how it can be dealt with, the professional imperative compounds the dilemma by demonstrating that you couldn't understand the problem or the solution anyway. The language of modernized professional services mystifies both problem and solution so that citizen evaluation becomes impossible. The only people "competent" to decide whether the servicing process has any merit are professional peers, each affirming the basic assumptions of the other.

While there are fascinating interjurisdictional disputes among servicing peers, these conflicts rarely break the rule that it is only the professional who understands the problem and the solution. The internal conflicts are power struggles over which professionals shall be dominant. A professional who breaks the rule of professional dominance will be stigmatized by all the disputants and lose his place on the rungs of the ladder to success. The politics of modernized professional power are bounded by peer review. Modern heretics are those professional practitioners who support citizen competence and convert their profession into an understandable trade under the comprehensible command of citizens.

The critical disabling effect of professional coding is its impact upon citizen capacities to deal with cause and effect. If I cannot understand the question or the answer—the need or the remedy—I exist at the sufferance of expert systems. My world is not a place where I do or act with others. Rather, it is a mysterious place, a strange land beyond my comprehension or control. It is understood only by professionals who know *how* it works, *what* I need, and *how* my need is met. I am the object rather than the actor. My life and our society are technical problems rather than political systems.

As the service professions gain the power to unilaterally define remedy and need and to code the service process, a *fourth* disabling characteristic develops. It is the capacity of servicers to define the output of their service in accordance with their own satisfaction with the result. This fourth capacity develops in a service professional just as the citizen is totally and definitely transmogrified into a *critical* addict.

Increasingly, professionals are claiming the power to decide whether their "help" is effective. The important, valued, and evaluated outcome of service is the professional's assessment of his own efficacy. The client is viewed as a deficient person, unable to know whether he has been helped.

This developing professional premise is contested by the consumer movement. The movement is a valiant last stand of those disabled citizens who lay final claim to the right to evaluate the effects or "outputs" of professionalized service.

The basic assumption of the movement is that citizens are enabled because they have become powerful consumers. In this assumption the movement is a handmaiden of the serviced society. It implicitly accepts the service ideology. Citizens are as they consume. Citizen welfare is defined by equitable, efficacious consumption. The service system is a given good. The citizen role is in evaluating the output. While citizens may not understand the service system, the consumer movement assumes they do know whether the system's output helps or hurts.

Professionally managed service systems are now dealing with this remnant citizen role as a consumer. The result has been an increasing professional focus on manipulating consumer perceptions of outcomes. Thomas Dewar, in an article titled "The Professionalization of the Client," describes how the service systems are training citizens to understand that their satisfaction is derived from being effective clients rather than people whose problems are solved.

The paradigm of this process is the school. Unlike most servicing systems, the school is transparent in its institutional definition of the client's role. The school client is evaluated in terms of his ability to satisfy the teacher. The explicit outcome of the system is professional approval of behavior and performance.

The professional imperative is now universalizing the ideology of the school, communicating the value of effective clienthood. Negating even the client "output" evaluation, modernized professional services increasingly communicate the value of being an effective client as the proof of the system's efficacy.

Once effective "clienthood" becomes a central value in society, the consumer movement as we know it now will be stifled and will wither away.

The service ideology will be consummated when citizens believe that they cannot know whether they have a need, cannot know what the remedy is, cannot understand the process that purports to meet the need or remedy, and cannot even know whether the need is met unless professionals express satisfaction. The ultimate sign of a serviced society is a professional saying, "I'm so pleased by what you've done." The demise of citizenship is to respond, "Thank you."

We will have reached the apogee of the modernized service society when the professionals can say to the citizen:

- We are the solution to your problem.
- We know what problem you have.
- You can't understand the problem or the solution.
- Only we can decide whether the solution has dealt with your problem.

Inverted, in terms of the needs of professionalized service systems, these propositions become:

- We *need* to solve your problems.
- We *need* to tell you what they are.
- We *need* to deal with them in our terms.
- We *need* to have you respect our satisfaction with our own work.

The most important research issues in modernized societies involve an understanding of the *needs* of servicers and the mechanics of their systems. These systems are obviously important. They provide incomes for a majority of the people. They support national economies. It is, of course, no secret that they are consistently failing to meet their own goals in spite of magnanimous applications of money and personnel. It is becoming more and more evident that rather than *producing* "services," they are creating sensitive but frustrated professionals, unable to understand why their love, care, and service do not re-form society, much less help individuals to function.

We should, therefore, reorient our research efforts toward the needs of servicers. After all, they are a growing majority of people employed in modernized societies and they are an increasingly sad, alienated class of people in *need* of support, respect, care, and love. Modernized societies *need* to determine how we can help these professionalized servicers while limiting their power to disable the capacities of citizens to perceive and deal with issues in political terms.

And if we cannot do that, we should at least understand the political impact of the disabling nature of professionalized definitions of need and remedy.

Professionalized services communicate a worldview that defines our lives and our societies as a series of technical problems. This technical definition is masked by symbols of care and love that obscure the economic interests of the servicers and the disabling characteristics of their practices.

# 10

# Culture, Incentives, and the Underclass

*James Q. Wilson*

Policy elites, liberal and conservative, usually explain the problems of the urban underclass as the result of misguided incentives. Liberals may blame poverty and dependency on a lack of benefits and opportunities while conservatives may blame it on overly generous benefits offered without corresponding obligations, but the argument is about benefits. Liberals may blame crime on poverty or joblessness and conservatives may blame it on indefinite or lenient criminal sanctions, but the dispute is about rewards and penalties.

This is not the way ordinary citizens see the matter. Though acknowledging that schooling may be poor, jobs scarce, and the criminal justice system ineffective, they tend to stress the overriding importance of the attitudes of the permanently poor and the habitually criminal, attitudes formed in the family (or, increasingly, the nonfamily) and reinforced by culture. Those attitudes are characterized as a belief in rights but not in responsibilities, an emphasis on "me" and a neglect of "we," a preference for immediate gratification over investments for the future, and an expectation that if one is lucky or clever enough one can get something for nothing.

The public believes that whatever incentives or problems a family may face, it has a choice as to how to respond. A good family will respond by inculcating constructive habits and decent principles in its children. In recent years, however, these habits and principles have become less common in part because the family has become weaker and in part because rivals for its influence—notably television and the movies—have become stronger. More and more children are being raised by one parent, who is typically a teenage girl. Parents overall are spending less time with their children and disciplining them less. Overwhelmingly, Americans think that it is better for children if one parent stays home, even if it means having less money.[1]

Elite views, not popular views, tend to drive public policy. This is the case because the former have clear policy implications while the latter have vague ones, because changing the former acknowledges individual autonomy while changing the latter seems preachy or invasive, and because one can marshal countless facts bearing on the incentives issue but not many bearing on the culture one. We debate incentive effects by measuring unemployment rates, poverty levels, crime trends, welfare payments, and arrest probabilities and feeding these numbers into equations. By contrast, we debate cultural effects by shouting slogans, offering anecdotes, and interpreting history.

In this chapter I hope to do two things. First, I want to argue that some significant part of what is popularly called the "underclass problem" exists not simply because members of this group face perverse incentives but because they have been habituated in ways that weaken their self-control and their concern for others. Second, I want to speculate about what, if anything, can be done to change that pattern of habituation so that, given whatever incentives people face, they will be more likely to behave in a morally correct fashion.

Before going on, let me clarify some terms, admit to some uncertainties, and respond to some preemptive criticisms. I use the term *habituation* to refer to the process whereby people acquire a constant, often unconscious, way of doing something, a regular inclination to behave in ways that are either impulsive or reflective, self-indulgent or other-regarding, decent or indecent. Not all behavior, of course, is habitual, but to say that someone has a "good" or "bad" character means that, as opportunities arise, that person ordinarily behaves in a good or bad way.

I do not wish to deny the importance of incentives, such as jobs, penalties, or opportunities, but I do wish to call attention to the fact that people facing the same incentives often behave in characteristically different ways because they have been habituated to do so. That habituation was shaped in large part by the incentives confronting people earlier in their lives. "Incentives" and "culture" are different explanations of behavior at any one time, but if we trace back someone's life history, we shall surely discover that what we now call culture was instilled by incentives (for example, parental admonitions or peer-group expectations), and those earlier incentives were offered to a person because those doing the offering were, in part, culturally disposed to do so, and they in turn were so disposed because of incentives that they had once encountered, and so on. A complete explanation of human development, were that possible, would make the customary distinction between incentives and culture rather unclear, however important it may be to any contemporary policy debate. For policy purposes I am simply asserting that changing incentives will not alter the behavior of poorly habituated persons as much as we would like, at least in the near term.

I write unabashedly about "morally correct" or "moral" behavior. In this context, I mean simply that moral people do not lie, cheat, steal, rape, assault, murder, or abuse drugs. Immoral people do these things regularly and often without remorse.

Though I am here arguing for the importance of culture, I have elsewhere argued for the importance of incentives. In 1975 I published a book in which I took issue with the effort of criminologists to ground crime-control policies on an understanding of the root causes of crime.[2] At that time, those causes were thought to be the attitudes, values, and aspirations of criminals—in short, their culture. I suggested that our understanding of these cultural factors was so poor and our capacity to alter them by plan so weak that any crime-reduction policy based on them was bound to fail. I argued instead for a policy based on the assumption that would-be offenders were rationally self-interested. Given that view, the most effective response to crime would be to reduce its net benefits relative to legitimate work by increasing both the certainty of sanctions and the availability of jobs.

Lest any readers think that I am here repudiating my previous view, let me remind them that at the end of the book I suggested that an incentives-based attack on crime would be fortunate if it led to even a 20 percent reduction in the rate of serious crime. A reduction larger than this was unlikely because, while sanctions had become less certain, crime had become less shameful. One of the main reasons it had become less shameful—that is, less likely to be inhibited by internal constraints—was because of the weakening of the family.[3] Since the book was published in 1975, the probability of going to prison, given an arrest, has risen (except, after 1985, for drug offenders) and prison has increasingly been reserved for serious career criminals instead of petty or one-time offenders. These changes probably contributed to the decline in victimization rates that has taken place since the early 1980s. But while the criminal justice system has become somewhat tougher, the family unit has become much weaker. This helps explain why the average young person is much more likely to commit a crime today than in the 1950s.[4]

## WHAT INCENTIVES CANNOT EXPLAIN

The rise in the number of out-of-wedlock births and participation in the former Aid to Families with Dependent Children (AFDC) program cannot be explained by economic conditions of the level of welfare benefits. Irwin Garfinkel and Sara McLanahan estimate that rising government benefits accounted for no more than about 14 percent of the increase in the prevalence of unwed mothers that occurred between 1960 and 1974.[5] Robert Moffitt has reviewed the evidence on the effects of welfare benefits on work and family structure and concluded that, while benefits make a difference, they do not explain more than a modest amount of the decline in work levels or the increase in single-parent families.[6] One of the reasons that welfare benefits do not correlate with welfare participation is that for some people participation carries a stigma. The fear of losing self-respect or social esteem helps explain why in 1970 only 69 percent of the families eligible for AFDC enrolled in it. One explanation of the increase in the percentage of eligibles who actually enroll to over 90 percent may be a change in the stigma attached to participation.

We have become accustomed to the sight of inner-city males on the streets, out of school and out of work, but this was not always the case. Black and white teenage unemployment rates were much lower in the 1950s than they were in the 1980s. There has been a dramatic increase in the percentage of young urban males who are not in the labor force and in the proportion who report no income,[7] an increase that has occurred during a period of generally rising incomes and educational levels and a decline in the proportion of children failing to complete high school.[8] The number of jobs has grown faster than the population. Despite this growth a large fraction of inner-city residents have dropped out of the labor force.

Some scholars, such as William Julius Wilson, explain the paradox of rising inner-city unemployment in the midst of long-term job growth by the spatial mismatch theory. In this view, jobs have moved out of the inner city and the people living there have been unable to follow. This mismatch may discourage labor force participation, especially if it lasts for several generations.[9] But evidence for the mismatch theory is not clear. Christopher Jencks and Susan E. Moyers conclude that the evidence supporting mismatch suggests that it has some effect, but "the support is so mixed that no prudent policy analyst should rely on it."[10] Wilson has responded vigorously to these criticisms with a different reading of the evidence.[11]

In my view, mismatch probably explains part of the rise in idleness, but not all. In particular it cannot explain the fact that many inner-city jobs go unfilled because of what appears to be a high reservation wage,[12] nor can it explain why Latinos (including recent immigrants) have had greater success in finding and holding inner-city jobs than have blacks, even though both groups tend to live in impoverished neighborhoods and Latinos have less formal education than blacks.[13] The black-Latino contrast is noteworthy in another respect. Though Latinos in California have very high poverty rates, Latino children are much more likely than black children to grow up in a two-parent family, Latino adults are much more likely than black adults to be in the labor force, and poor Latino families are only one-fifth as likely as black families to receive welfare payments. So marked is this contrast that the scholars reporting these findings question whether California Latinos should be considered part of the urban underclass at all.[14] Nationally, from 1977 to 1991, when the percentage of white and black men with no income was going up, the percentage of Latino men in that predicament was going down.[15]

Finally there is the case of crime. I do not propose to give a full explanation of why either individuals or societies differ in their rates of crime. Richard Herrnstein and I have tried to provide such an explanation.[16] I will say nothing about gun ownership, television viewing, peer pressures, or some of the other possible influences on crime rates. I omit them in part because the concept of habituation already embraces most of them: millions of people watch television, own guns, or have friends, but the vast majority do not regularly commit crimes.

The increase in crime cannot be explained fully by changes in the objective features of the situation. The rate of street crime is today much higher—by three to four times—than it was in the late 1950s and early 1960s. This increase has occurred despite, some might say because of, a dramatic increase in per capita income and average educational attainment, a decrease in the proportion of students dropping out of high school, and a substantial growth in government expenditures aimed at preventing delinquency and controlling crime. Nor can this increase in crime rate be explained by the changing age structure of the population. Scarcely any expert believes that the increase in the number of young people can account for more than half of the increase in crime, and many estimate the proportion of explained variance to be as low as one-fourth.[17] If the age-specific crime rate (that is, the number of crimes committed per person of a given age, say eighteen) had remained constant during the 1960s and 1970s, violent crime would have increased by about 8 percent. In fact it doubled.[18] A study of the officially recorded criminality of two groups of Philadelphia boys—those born in 1945 and those born in 1958—found that the group born in 1958 was three times more likely to commit violent crimes and five times more likely to commit robberies than the group born in 1945.[19]

Part of the crime increase was the result of the drop in its costs: the magnitude of punishment discounted by its probability was lower in 1980 than it had been in 1960. During the early years of the crime boom, the aggregate probability of imprisonment for a reported crime declined. In 1960 there were sixty-two prison commitments per 1,000 serious offenses.[20] ("Serious" crimes are those that the FBI includes in its uniform crime reports (UCR): murder, rape, assault, robbery, burglary, and auto theft.) The length of time served in prison for the median inmate also declined from twenty-one months in 1960 to seventeen months in 1981.[21] The combined effect of fewer and shorter imprisonments was a drop in the expected days of imprisonment per UCR crime from ninety-three in 1959 to fourteen in 1975. This drop in the deterrent and incapacitative potential of prison was, I believe, partly responsible for the sharp increase in the crime rate.

Beginning around 1974, the absolute number of prison inmates began to rise at an accelerating rate. Between 1974 and 1989, it more than tripled. Contrary to what many people believe, this increase was not simply the result of prisoners serving longer sentences—on the average, time served continued to decline. Until the late 1980s, the growth in prison populations was mostly explained by the fact that beginning in the mid-to-late 1970s, arrests were more likely to lead to imprisonment. In 1974 an arrested robber had about one chance in five of going to prison; by 1986 he had more than one chance in four.[22] By 1986, the expected days of imprisonment per UCR offense was nineteen, a third higher than it had been in 1975 but still less than a fifth of what it was in 1959. At the same time, in the years following 1974 there was a flattening out and even a decline in the rate of most crimes, at least as measured by victimization surveys.

These national data are consistent with the view—though clearly they do not prove it—that between 1960 and 1974 society may have unintentionally encouraged the idea that crime paid. This view may help explain why the age-specific crime rate increased during this period. Since 1974, society has been trying, with limited success, to unteach that lesson.

The linkage, if any, between the changing probabilities of punishment and offense rate of any given young male is not known and probably unknowable. Even if society were willing to pay for further increases in the expected days of imprisonment per crime (a big assumption), we can only speculate on whether it would lower the age-specific crime rate, especially since the people we most wish to affect are not the small number of high-rate, hard-core criminals but the much larger number of moderate-to-low-rate offenders. We want to affect the latter because they constitute a more numerous group and because high-rate offenders already spend a very large fraction of any given year in prison. One study estimates that the average high-rate robber in California, Michigan, and Texas spends 216 days out of the typical year in prison. In compensation, he earns about $9,500 per year for the time he is free on the street.[23] Not a very attractive deal, but that is exactly my point: high-rate offenders have such poor impulse control that they are neither very rational about how they spend their time nor very likely to notice small shifts in the costs of committing a crime. This probably helps explain why changes in the unemployment rate and the business cycle have so weak a connection with the crime rate.[24]

The total amount of variance in crime rates explained by cross-section regression equations with the relevant objective factors entered—age, income, unemployment, and the probability and severity of sanctions—is relatively modest.[25] Some unknown, but I suspect large, fraction of the unexplained variance can be attributed to changes in tastes, preferences, and attitudes toward risk.

We have rather little direct evidence of such changes. One of the few tests of changes in impulsiveness compared the time preferences (that is, the willingness to postpone gratification) of a group of Rhode Island delinquents in 1959 with a similar group in 1974 and concluded that the latter had become much more present-oriented.[26] This finding, while indicative of a change, suffers from sample selection bias and other problems. The existence of a cultural explanation for crime must rest largely on inference, particularly on the inference that high rates of criminality and drug usage cannot easily be reconciled to any theory that people are maximizing their incomes. If criminals in prison are like those on the street, crime pays very little to its practitioners. If repeated thefts can be explained at all, it is only on the assumption that for some people the prospect of a small, immediate gain dominates the prospect of a later, larger benefit. Similarly, drug abusers sooner or later come to a crossroad where they would like to reform their lives, but the lure of drugs outweighs the benefits of abstinence, whatever the cost of continuing the drug-abuser lifestyle.[27] In short, many criminal offenders and drug abusers are very impulsive and (in the case of crime) have a low regard for the rights and well-being of others. It is likely that impulsivity has become more common in our society (and in most industrialized societies) in recent decades.

The evidence linking criminality with weak impulse control and lack of empathy with others is very strong.[28] If impulsiveness and self-regardingness are highly predictive of criminality, and if rates of criminality have increased far beyond what can be explained by the expected utility of their material returns, we are left with a presumptive case for a change in the degree to which habitual self-control and sympathy rule our lives.

## FAMILIAL HABITUATION

Familial habituation is the chief method by which every society induces its members to exercise a modicum of self-control and to assign a reasonable value to the preferences of others. There is a broad consensus among developmental psychologists as to the parental practices that are most likely to achieve these goals. They involve a combination of affection and discipline such that the child's attachment to the parents is strong and the rules of everyday behavior are clearly understood and consistently enforced.[29] This vital socializing task, which is the foundation of human society, would be impossibly difficult were it not for two facts: babies are biologically eager for attachment and predisposed to socialization, and parents love their babies and invest without compensation in their rearing.

But individuals differ in the extent to which they have (or reveal) prosocial impulses, and so some babies are difficult and some parents are incompetent. Unfortunately, since temperament is to a significant degree under genetic control, there is an elevated probability that difficult babies will be born to incompetent parents. At one time, natural selection worked against any dysgenic trends by exposing marginal families to higher infant mortality rates. Nobody wants dead babies to be a solution to socialization failures. But these failures, if uncorrected, can breed, literally, more failures. Crime, alcoholism, and impulsive, sensation-seeking behavior run in the family.

Matters become worse if families cease to exist or are transformed into pseudofamilies. Poverty has now become a children's problem owing chiefly to the fact that an increased proportion of children live for long periods—sometimes for their entire childhood—in mother-only families, a large fraction of which are also poor. There is mounting evidence that mother-only families do not do as well as two-parent families.[30] For example, in 1988 the Department of Health and Human Services surveyed the family arrangements and personal problems of more than 60,000 children living in households all over the country. The results were striking. At every income level save the very highest (more than $50,00 a year), for both sexes and for whites, blacks, and Latinos, children living with never-married mothers were substantially worse off than those living in two-parent families. Children living with never-married mothers were more likely to have been expelled or suspended from school, to display emotional problems, and to engage in anti-social behavior.[31]

Sara McLanahan at Princeton and Gary Sandefur at Wisconsin have been analyzing the best available data—the National Longitudinal Study of Youth, the Panel Study of Income Dynamics, the High School and Beyond Study, and the National Survey of Families and Households. Their findings are that, even after controlling for race, income, and education, being a child in a mother-only family decreases a child's chances of graduating from high school, increases a girl's chances of becoming a teenage mother, and increases a boy's chances of being idle (that is, neither working nor in school).[32]

If the family is headed by a teenage mother, the risks are even greater. Children of teenage black mothers compared to those of older mothers are less able to control their impulses, have a lower tolerance for frustration, are more likely to be hyperactive, have more difficulty in adapting to school and, if boys, are more likely to be hostile, assertive, and willful.[33] If the single, teenage mother is a heavy user of drugs or alcohol, the risks increase catastrophically.

The average American fully understands this without benefit of scientific studies. As Daniel Yankelovich points out, Americans believe by overwhelming majorities that families have become weaker in ways that severely threaten human well-being and by large majorities think that this weakening results from parents spending too little time with their children. It stands to reason that one parent spends less time than two and two working parents less time than one working and one nonworking parent.[34]

## WHAT IS CULTURE?

To the extent that certain bad behaviors—criminality, drug abuse, welfare dependency, producing illegitimate children—are in part the result of cultural factors, one must clarify what one means by "culture" before asking whether it can be changed. The term has at least three meanings that are relevant to these behaviors. First, culture refers to a widely shared integrating perspective or worldview by which people interpret their experiences, a perspective that is passed on from one generation to the next by precept, myth, and ritual and accepted by most, if not all, of society. A culture in this sense is what gives a particular society its identity and meaning; it will change very slowly, if at all, and never by plan. We have this meaning in mind when we speak of "American," "Southern," or "Yankee" culture.

A culture can also be a subjective adaptation to the circumstances of one's life. If one is poor, and the poverty extends over several generations, one might adapt to that reality by being fatalistic and pessimistic or by increasing the value one attaches to immediate pleasures at the expense of long-term investments. This is what many people have in mind when they speak of the "culture of poverty." Presumably this culture would change, albeit slowly, if objective reality changed.

Finally, a culture can be the set of standards and values held up and prized by some social elite: the rich, the powerful, the beautiful, the celebrated. These values are an elite endorsement of certain ways of acting and thinking, an endorsement that acquires causal power insofar as people seek to emulate those ways of acting and thinking. Because elites are sometimes divided, there may be more than one such culture. Beginning in the 1960s there was a conflict between bourgeois culture, with its emphasis on propriety, property and progress, and the counterculture, with its emphasis on sincerity, spontaneity, and self-expression. This kind of culture is capable of relatively rapid change because it entails an element of fashion.

Cultural interpretations of the underclass involved a competition among all three meanings. Those who believe that the underclass consists mainly of marginal people—the indolent, the impulsive, the drug-dependent, the thrill-seekers—feel that there will always be an underclass, it will always be a small fraction of the whole society (because people in it are at the extremes of the distribution of impulse control), and the main problem is to prevent it from getting out of hand.[35] The disreputable poor have always been among us; we pay more attention to them today because they are centrally located, heavily armed, and threats to those institutions, for example, schools, in which they now participate. One can only cope with the symptoms of the underclass—its location, firepower, and institutional involvement. In this view, such people ought to be segregated or dispersed so as to reduce their numbers at any-one location below a critical mass, disarmed or incarcerated, and kept out of mainstream institutions or put in specialized ones.

Those who believe in the culture of poverty have, of course, a very different view. If circumstances are changed, culture will change. The magnitude of the change varies with the radicalism of the author. For some it means simply more jobs, better schooling, and less discrimination; for others it means wholesale and fundamental changes in the economic system.[36]

Those who believe that the fault lies with elite culture call attention to the vast shift that has occurred in the mores conveyed by judges, political leaders, the mass media, and popular entertainment. It is a shift away from an ethic of self-reliance, self-control, and delicate modesty and toward one of social dependence, self-expression, and the celebration of alternative lifestyles. People holding this view interpret the underclass as simply that group in our society most vulnerable to false prophecies. For all its idiosyncratic inflections, underclass culture is, in the words of Myron Magnet, a "dialect" of the elite culture that celebrates personal liberation, denounces conformity, values the avant-garde, and regards the core traditions of the republic as nothing more than a camouflage for repression and greed. Elite culture is a curse inflicted by the haves on the have-nots.[37]

## CHANGING CULTURE

It is very difficult, perhaps impossible, to choose which among these theories is the most accurate. Cultural explanations by their very nature defy experimental or mathematical tests. The best one can do is ask what we have learned from efforts to act on one or the other theory.

By that standard the news is fairly grim. The first theory implies that change is impossible. The third suggests that it is all but impossible, the logic being that if elites are the problem, and elites like their culture, and elites—by definition—control social and political resources, then there is not much chance that this culture can be changed. The second theory is easier to test, but the tests are not encouraging. The growth of the underclass during a period of unparalleled prosperity does not disprove the possibility that changing incentives will induce a change in behavior, but it does make one pessimistic about the chances of any planned improvement. Since society can only manipulate incentives in the aggregate, and cope, by lecturing and example, with culture as a whole, the likelihood of altering individual preferences by plan in the face of powerful, long-term forces operating in the opposite direction seems remote. If the underclass culture grew despite prosperity, then it stands to reason that only a radical change in the economic and social order would break the culture; however, radical changes are by definition unlikely ones. But perhaps those who hold this view have overlooked the interaction between culture and poverty: though poverty may create its own culture, that culture may perpetuate poverty. Perhaps what is needed is a concerted effort to change the fatalistic or self-indulgent attitudes of the poor so that they will take better advantage of whatever opportunities are available to them.

There is nothing in principle wrong with such a view; indeed, it is the governing assumption of every religious and of many secular efforts that attempt to help social outcasts such as alcoholics, drug abusers, and school dropouts. There are countless success stories to be found among these spiritual and worldly enterprises. The problem arises when one tries to imagine a program that by plan and in the hands of ordinary managers achieves this necessary personal redemption for large numbers of people.

Efforts to do this on a large scale and by bureaucratic processes have not, on the whole, proven very successful. Though here and there one can find promising projects, most efforts to rehabilitate large numbers of delinquents or criminals have met with more failures than successes.[38]

Using the military to improve the character of the most disadvantaged has not been a very promising solution either. In 1966, Secretary of Defense Robert McNamara began Project 100,000 as a way of contributing to the War on Poverty. Over a five-year period, 320,000 low-aptitude recruits entered military service. From 1976 to 1980, as a result of the misnorming of the military enlistment test, low-aptitude individuals were inadvertently recruited. These two occasions provided a natural, quasi-experiment in the use of intensive training and strict discipline as means of improving the self-control and expanding the other-regardingness of difficult boys.

To evaluate these quasi-experiments, investigators studied veterans of Project 100,000 and of the misnorming episode, comparing their economic, educational, and family status to that of persons of similarly low aptitude who had never served in the military. When interviewed, a majority of the low-aptitude veterans aid that their military experience had been good for them, primarily because it taught them discipline and made them more mature. Unfortunately, the belief did not correspond to the reality. Project 100,000 veterans were worse off in employment status, educational achievement, and income than those presumably similar persons who had never been in the military; misnormed veterans were no better off than their nonveteran counterparts. The veterans were more likely to be divorced than the nonveterans. (There were, of course, no data on crime for the two groups.) The authors of the study concluded that "the military doesn't appear to be a panacea for struggling youth."[39]

Altering the time preferences or improving the achievements of temperamentally difficult or low-aptitude youth is not easily done if one waits until they have reached their teens or become young adults. Evidence from criminal rehabilitation programs and military experiences is not very encouraging. Evidence from early childhood programs is more encouraging but still very fragmentary and in some cases inconsistent.

These familiar facts are what give so much impetus to efforts to find supplements for family care, such as day care and preschool education. There is no governmental program more popular today than Head Start, nor any for which more inflated claims have been made. This is not to say that Head Start or similar preschool education programs for three- and four-year-olds have no effect. After it was shown that there were no lasting improvements in cognitive abilities (specifically, in IQ) resulting from Head Start participation, attention shifted to whether such participation facilitated a child's entry into kindergarten and the first grade. The evidence seems clear that it does.[40]

But the long-term effect of preschool education is not so clear. The strongest evidence of a positive effect comes from one program, the Perry Preschool in Ypsilanti, Michigan, which was not a Head Start project. It enrolled 123 poor black children, half of whom were living in mother-headed households, randomly assigned them to a preschool program or to a control group, and followed them for many years. Those in the preschool program were less likely to drop out before finishing high school, less likely to go on welfare, more likely to be working after leaving school, and less likely to have been arrested.[41]

No other preschool program has produced evidence of such dramatic long-term effects. Evaluations of the many Head Start projects (few of which were as carefully done as the Perry evaluation) fail to find school completion rates as high as those in Perry, and there is hardly any evidence on the effects of Head Start programs on such matters as pregnancy, welfare, and crime. In a 1989 review of Head Start evaluations, Ron Haskins, a staff member of the House Ways and Means Committee, was only able to locate a handful of studies that measure the long-term effects of Head Start on crime, teen pregnancy, and welfare dependency. The two studies that looked at pregnancy found no effect; the two that examined crime found some effect; and the two that considered welfare came to inconsistent conclusions.[42]

Why did the Perry program (and possibly a few other programs) do so well? One reason is that they were model programs conducted by capable people who had received extensive training and ample budgets. At Perry Preschool there was one teacher for every five or six pupils. Another reason is that the Perry project was not limited to providing children with preschool experiences for twelve-and-a-half hours a week; it also involved an extensive program of home visits conducted once a week by the teacher who would visit with the mother for about one-and-a-half hours in her home. There is evidence that such home visitations improve child development.[43]

Something akin to the Perry results, albeit, thus far, only for the short term, has been reported by the infant Health and Development Program. This program provided an intensive array of services to nearly 1,000 premature, low-birth-weight infants in eight cities. Such babies have been found to be at risk for intellectual retardation, behavioral problems, and learning difficulties. As in Ypsilanti, these infants were randomly assigned to treatment and control groups. The infants and parents in the experimental groups were given three services: weekly (later biweekly) home visits by trained counselors, attendance at child development centers five days a week by babies after they had reached their first birthday, and biweekly meetings at which parents were given information and could share experiences. At age three, the babies in the experimental group had significantly higher measured IQs and significantly fewer behavioral problems than those in the control groups, and the gains were greatest for infants who had the most disadvantaged mothers.[44] It will be some years before we know whether these gains persist.

Suppose that the long-term results from the premature baby project parallel those of the Perry project. What lessons can we infer? The most obvious and, to some, perhaps the most troubling is that intervention programs produce more benefits the more deeply they intervene. For at-risk children, the more the programs either assume parental functions or alter the behavior of parents (by home visits, parent training, and close preschool supervision), the greater the benefit to the child.[45]

Another possibility, albeit one that has as yet only fragmentary evidence, is that long-lasting interventions are likely to make more of a difference than short-term ones.[46] Children cannot be inoculated against behavioral problems as they are against smallpox. Yet beginning at age five or six the only intervention program aimed at children and generally under government control is the school, a state of affairs that continues until they enter the labor force, are arrested for a crime, or enlist in the armed services.

The central role of the school has led Americans to focus their hopes for character formation on it, hopes that receive some support from studies suggesting that the schools doing the best job of educating children are also, and of necessity, those that do the best job of controlling their behavior.[47] Learning is easier when students are more orderly. But in the past, the problem of improving the character of what we delicately term antisocial people was never left wholly to the schools but was given in addition to a host of home visitation and mothers' aid societies that were charged with instructing mothers on how to raise their children.[48] We do not know what effect these efforts had on family life, but we do know that the most successful contemporary programs aimed at young children include home visits and parental training. Missouri, followed by other states, has built on this insight with its Parents as Teachers plan that makes available in-home training for parents and babies.

Families with the necessary financial resources have always had boarding school as an important way of coping with hard-to-socialize children or of escaping their responsibility for socializing them. The current movement to give parents a meaningful choice among schools may help address many educational problems, but even the best public school occupies a child only six hours a day, half the days of the year.

Schools are character-forming enterprises; public schools were created first and foremost for moral instruction. But even the best school cannot offset the threats of disorderly streets, the neglect of absent parents, or the discord of unhappy homes. Boarding schools are not for everyone, but they are better for some.

If boarding schools were established as a way of shaping character, what would they do? I have a set of guidelines in mind. In the elementary years, a boarding school would simply extend the number of hours the child was under school rather than parental supervision. School might become an all-day affair, breakfast and dinner served and supervised after-class play opportunities provided in addition to regular instruction. In the extreme case of a child with no competent parent at all, sleeping quarters would be provided. As the child got older—say in the junior high years—boarding school would be full time with home visits arranged by mutual agreement. The schools would be operated, I would hope, by private more often than by public agencies; enrollment would be voluntary but encouraged for at-risk children. The object would be to provide a safe, consistent, and enjoyable mechanism for the habituation of the child—that is, for the inculcation of the ordinary virtues of politeness, self-control, and good social skills. What was taught would be less important than the regular and supportive routine by which it was taught. Character is formed by habitual action more than by memorized precepts.

Boarding schools may be especially important for boys growing up in fatherless families. Much has been said about the economic and psychological costs borne by such children. But something also must be said about the equally important communal costs. Neighborhood standards may be set by mothers but they are enforced by fathers, or at least by adult males. Neighborhoods without fathers are neighborhoods without men able and willing to confront errant youth, chase threatening gangs, and reproach delinquent fathers. Mercer Sullivan, in his study of poor neighborhoods in New York, notes that the absence of fathers, especially in black areas, deprives the community of those little platoons that informally but often effectively control boys on the street.[49]

I do not know of any way whereby this generation of errant fathers can be required to take up their responsibilities. The reach of the law has been lengthened, but we should not be optimistic that this will result in more than a modest increase in the size of family support payments received by some mothers, much less any increase in the extent to which fathers would help care for children. Our main goal ought to be reducing the number of errant fathers produced by the next generation. To that end, history supplies presumptive evidence of the value of using public resources to enable families in underclass neighborhoods voluntarily to enroll their children beginning at an early age in boarding schools. These schools then must have as a goal either placing their students into college or qualifying them for entry into an occupation by means of an apprenticeship program.[50]

Perhaps better homes can be supplied without leaving matters entirely to chance or voluntary participation. Supposed that unmarried mothers seeking welfare were given a choice: as a condition of receiving financial aid, they must either live with their parents or in group homes (shelters) where they would be instructed in child care, receive a regular education, and conform to rules governing personal conduct and group resonsiblities.[51] The key elements in this idea are threefold: Welfare should not be used to subsidize independent but dysfunctional households, mothers of small children should not work outside the home, and the best and most structured start in life for the next generation of babies is of utmost importance.

## IMPLICATIONS

The great puzzle for a free society is how it can encourage those traits of character on which the wise exercise of freedom depends. Our Constitution is silent on this matter, and so were, for the most part, the deliberations of the founders. Creatures of the Enlightenment, these men took for granted the existence of sufficient virtue among the people to make free government possible; victims of what they regarded as the excesses of centralized government, they were in no mood to create a strong central government here, much less to endow it with authority to shape character.

From the time of the founding until well into the twentieth century, their assumptions were reasonable ones. Village life, by its daily routines and face-to-face contacts, was sufficient to reinforce the normal processes of familial habituation; where the latter was lacking, villagers found ample ways to encourage the slack and punish the errant. As large cities were formed, the informal but intimate ties of village life were replaced by the formal and anonymous relationships of urban life, with the result that young men more easily escaped social control or found like-minded companions with whom they could indulge licentious impulses. But society was not powerless to counter this process nor was it inclined to use the government as its principal tool. Apart from state temperance laws that became commonplace after the middle of the nineteenth century, most efforts to inculcate self-control were made under voluntary auspices.

These efforts—temperance meetings, child care programs, home visitations, and YMCAs—involved large numbers of adults and children. There was nothing like a modern program evaluation technology available at the time, and so we can only guess at the effect of these efforts. But, as I have argued elsewhere, it is hard to explain the decline in alcohol consumption and criminality in the face of rapid urbanization, large-scale industrialization, and massive immigration on any basis other than the speculation that these efforts at inducing self-control made a difference.[52]

It is apparent today that many such programs still operate, though rarely with the religious zeal that once gave them such energy. Moreover, neighborhoods can still exist in big cities, and some of the habituation that was once achieved by small towns is now achieved by informal social controls in urban communities. Parents must assume not only individual responsibility for their own children but some measure of collective responsibility for everyone's children, at least when they are at play in public places.

It is a truism that we have transferred to the market or the government many of the responsibilities once exercised by families and neighborhoods. The family, once the chief organization for production, education, self-defense, health care, and welfare, is now an entity limited to procreation, child-rearing, and affectional ties, and it is losing ground in the performance of even these rudimentary tasks.[53] Much has been gained by the decline of the family—greater personal freedom, more economic mobility, enhanced opportunities for women, and the advantages of the division of labor. But something has been lost.

A fundamental change in family structure illustrates what has been lost. At one time children needed parents for care, affection, and nurture, and parents needed children for agricultural or pastoral labor and for support when they were sick or elderly. Today children still need parents but parents do not, in any material sense, need children. Thus the incentive some parents have to care for children has been weakened. (That it has not been weakened to the point of extinction is a measure of the power of elemental love.) When children had economic consequences, the need to care for them, up to a point, was self-enforcing. Now that children are a net economic burden, there is no material incentive to care for them.

This shift has, of course, affected men more than women. A mother's attachment to a child—call it the maternal instinct—is strong enough to ensure some level of care. But there is not an equally strong attachment on the part of the father, made clear by the fact that the overwhelming majority of single-parent families are headed by women.

The goal of public policy and private effort should be to reinforce the obligation, which once was supplied by economic necessity, to care responsibly for children. We do not have a good idea of how to accomplish this. The Family Support Act of 1988 and comparable state laws have placed the government clearly on the side of mothers trying to collect support payments from absent fathers. But getting more money, while important, is far less important than getting more affection and supervision.

Better methods for socializing young men must be discovered. My general view is that this must be done, if it is to be done at all, in the first ten years of life, and perhaps even sooner. We need to know whether some combination of parent training programs, home visitations, preschool education, boarding schools, parental accountability laws, mother-child groups homes, and criminal sanctions will make a significant—and above all, a lasting—difference in the probability of an at-risk boy growing up to be a decent citizen and responsible father.

It is important that jobs be available for such men, but I see little reason for believing that job creation programs (assuming—a whopper—that the government can do this efficiently) will be enough. Not all reliable workers will find jobs in a free market, but it is my general view that good people are scarcer than good jobs.

Our object ought to be to increase the number of urban young men who marry and remain married. Of all the institutions through which people may pass—schools, employers, the military—marriage has the largest effect. For every race and at every age, married men live longer than unmarried men and have lower rates of homicide, suicide, accidents, and mental illness. Crime rates are lower for married than unmarried men and incomes are higher. It is less likely for drug dealers to be married than for young men who are not dealers.[54] Infant mortality rates are higher for unmarried than for married women, whether black or white, and these differences cannot be explained by differences in income or availability of medical care. So substantial is this difference that an unmarried woman with a college education is more likely to have her infant die than is a married women with less than a high-school education.[55]

Though some of these differences can be explained by female selectivity in choosing mates, I doubt that all can. Marriage not only involves screening people for their capacity for self-control, it also provides inducements—the need to support a mate, care for a child, and maintain a home—that increases capacity.

Throughout history, the institutions that have produced effective male socialization have been private, not public. Today we expect "government programs" to accomplish what families, villages, and churches once accomplished. This expectation leads to disappointment, if not frustration. Government programs, whether aimed at farmers, professors, or welfare mothers, tend to produce dependence, not self-reliance. If this is true, then our policy ought to be to identify, evaluate, and encourage those local, private efforts that seem to do the best job at reducing drug abuse, inducing people to marry, persuading parents, especially fathers, to take responsibility for their children, and exercising informal social control over neighborhood streets.

The federal government is a powerful but clumsy giant, not very adept at identifying, evaluating, and encouraging individuals who need help. It is good at passing laws, transferring funds, and multiplying regulations. These are necessary functions, but out of place in the realm of personal redemption. A government program to foster personal redemption will come equipped with standardized budgets, buy-America rules, minority set-asides, quarterly reporting requirements, and environmental impact statements and, in all likelihood, a thinly disguised bias against any kind of involvement with churches.

There may be a better way: public funds sent to private foundations that in turn do the identifying, evaluating, and encouraging, all on the basis of carefully negotiated charters that free these intermediaries from most governmental constraints. I have no example to cite, but people who wish to think seriously about changing the culture of poverty had better start inventing one.

## NOTES

1. Evidence for these beliefs can be found in the poll data reported in "Public Opinion and the Demographic Report," *American Enterprise,* vol. 3 (September-October 1992), pp. 85–86.

2. James Q. Wilson, *Thinking About Crime* (New York: Basic Books, 1975), chap. 3.

3. Wilson, *Thinking About Crime,* pp. 199, 204–7.

4. The rise in the probability of imprisonment is measured in Patrick A. Langan, "America's Soaring Prison Population," *Science,* March 1991, p. 1572. The increase in the incidence of crime among young male cohorts is established in Paul E. Tracy, Marvin E. Wolfgang, and Robert M. Figlio, *Delinquency Careers in Two Birth Cohorts* (New York: Plenum, 1990) p. 276.

5. Irwin Garfinkel and Sara S. McLanahan, *Single Mothers and Their Children: A New American Dilemma* (Washington: Urban Institute Press, 1986). See also William A. Galston, "Causes of Declining Well-Being among U.S. Children: Data and Debates," *Aspen Institute Quarterly,* vol. 5, no. 1 (1993), pp. 52–77.

6. Robert Moffitt, "An Economic Model of Welfare Stigma," *American Economic Review,* vol. 73 (December 1983), pp. 1023–35; Robert Moffitt, "Incentive Effects of the U.S. Welfare System: A Review," *Journal of Economic Literature,* vol. 30 (March 1992), pp. 1–61; and Robert Moffitt, "The Effect of the U.S. Welfare System on Marital Status," *Journal of Public Economics,* vol. 41 (February 1990), pp. 101–24.

7. Douglas J. Besharov, "Poverty, Welfare Dependency, and the Underclass," paper delivered at the Conference on Reducing Poverty in America, University of California at Los Angeles, January 1993.

8. Between 1960 and 1988, per capita disposable income (in constant dollars) increased from $6,036, to $11, 337, median school years completed increased from 10.6 to 12.7, and the percentage of people between the ages of 16 and 24 failing to complete high school declined from 17.0 in 1967 to 12.9 in 1988. Bureau of the Census, *Statistical Abstract of the United States* (Washington, 1963), p. 119, and (1990), pp. 428, 133; and National Center for Educational Statistics, *Digest of Education Statistics,* 1990 (Washington: Department of Education, 1991), p. 110.

9. William Julius Wilson, *The Truly Disadvantaged: The Inner City, the Underclass, and Public Policy* (Chicago: University of Chicago Press, 1987).

10. Christopher Jencks and Susan E. Mayer, "Residential Segregation, Job Proximity, and Black Job Opportunities," in Laurence E. Lynn, Jr., and Michael G. H. McGeary, eds., *Inner-City Poverty in the United States* (Washington D.C.: National Academy Press, 1990), p. 219.

11. William Julius Wilson, "Public Policy Research and *The Truly Disadvantaged,*" in Christopher Jencks and Paul E. Peterson, eds., *The Urban Underclass* (Washington D.C.: Brookings Institution, 1991), pp. 460–81.

12. Richard B. Freeman and Harry J. Holzer, eds., *The Black Youth Employment Crisis* (Chicago: University of Chicago Press, 1986), p. 16.

13. W. J. Wilson has acknowledged the black-Latino difference. See Wilson, "The

Plight of the Inner-City Black Male," *Proceedings of the American Philosophical Society,* vol. 136 (September 1992), p. 321.

14. David E. Hayes-Bautista and others, *No Longer a Minority: Latinos and Social Policy in California* (Los Angeles: UCLA Chicano Studies Research Center, 1992). See Also Aida Hurtado and others, *Redefining California: Latino Social Engagement in a Multicultural Society* (Los Angeles: UCLA Chicano Studies Research Center, 1992).

15. Besharov, "Poverty, Welfare Dependency, and the Underclass," p. 15.

16. James Q. Wilson and Richard Herrnstein, *Crime and Human Nature* (Simon and Schuster, 1985).

17. Jan M. Chaiken and Marcia R. Chaiken, "Crime Rates and the Active Criminal," in James Q. Wilson, ed., *Crime and Public Policy* (San Francisco, Calif.: Institute for Contemporary Studies, 1983), pp. 18–21; James Alan Fox, *Forecasting Crime Data: An Econometric Analysis* (Lexington, Mass.: Lexington Books, 1978); Theodore N. Ferdinand, "Demographic Shifts and Criminality: An Inquiry," *British Journal of Criminology,* vol. 10 (April 1970), pp. 169–75; and Darrell J. Steffensmeier and Miles D. Harer, "Is the Crime Rate Really Falling? An 'Aging' U.S. Population and its Impact on the Nation's Crime Rate, 1980–1984," *Journal of Research in Crime and Delinquency,* vol. 24 (February 1987), pp. 23–48.

18. Christopher Jencks, "Is the American Underclass Growing?" in Jencks and Peterson, *The Urban Underclass,* p. 81.

19. Paul E. Tracy, Marvin E. Wolfgang, and Robert M. Figlio, *Delinquency Careers in Two Birth Cohorts* (New York: Plenum, 1990), p. 276.

20. Robyn L. Cohen, *Prisoners in 1990* (Washington: Bureau of Justice Statistics, 1991), p. 7; Mark A. R. Kleiman and others, "Imprisonment-to-Offense Ratios," Working Paper 89-06-02, Program in Criminal Justice Policy and Management of the John F. Kennedy School of Government (Harvard University, 1988). I am indebted to John J. DiIulio, Jr., and Charles Logan for bringing the calculations in this paragraph to my attention.

21. Stephanie Minor-Harper and Lawrence A. Greenfeld, *Prison Admissions and Releases, 1982* (Washington: Bureau of Justice Statistics, 1985).

22. Patrick A. Langan, "America's Soaring Prison Population," *Science,* March 1991, p. 1572.

23. James Q. Wilson and Allan Abrahamse, "Does Crime Pay?" *Justice Quarterly,* vol. 9 (1993), pp. 359–78.

24. Wilson and Herrnstein, *Crime and Human Nature,* chap. 12; and James Q. Wilson and Philip J. Cook, "Unemployment and Crime: What is the Connection?" *Public Interest,* no. 79 (Spring 1985), pp. 3–8.

25. For example, when Barbara Boland and I estimated the effects of socioeconomic conditions and police arrest rates on robbery rates in thirty-five cities, we were able to explain only 74 percent of the variance; see James Q. Wilson and Barbara Boland, "The Effect of the Police on Crime," *Law and Society Review,* vol. 12 (Spring 1978), pp. 367–90.

26. Anthony Davids, Catherine Kidder, and Melvyn Reich, "Time Orientation in Male and Female Juvenile Delinquents," *Journal of Abnormal and Social Psychology,* vol. 64 (March 1962), pp. 239–40; Anthony Davids and Bradley B. Falkof, "Juvenile Delinquents Then and Now: Comparison of Findings from 1959 and 1974," *Journal of Abnormal Psychology,* vol. 84 (April 1975), pp. 161–64.

27. See, for example, Richard J. Herrnstein and Drazen Prelec, "A Theory of Addiction," in G. F. Lowenstein and Jon Elster, eds., *Choice Over Time* (New York: Russell Sage Foundation, 1992), pp. 331–60; and Thomas Schelling, "The Intimate Contest for Self-Command," *Public Interest,* no. 60 (Summer 1980), pp. 94–118.

28. The evidence is reviewed in Wilson and Herrnstein, *Crime and Human Nature,* chap. 7; Terrie E. Moffitt, "Juvenile Delinquency and Attention Deficit Disorder: Boys' Developmental Trajectories from Age 3 to Age 15," *Child Development,* vol. 61 (June 1990), pp. 893–910; and David P. Farrington, Rolf Loeber, and W. B. Van Kammen, "Long-term Criminal Outcomes of Hyperactivity-Impulsivity-Attention Deficit an Conduct Problems in Childhood," in Lee N. Robins and Michael Rutter, eds., *Straight and Devious Pathways from Childhood to Adulthood* (New York: Cambridge University Press, 1990), pp. 62–81.

29. For summaries, see William Damon, *The Moral Child: Nurturing Children's Natural Moral Growth* (New York: Free Press, 1988); and Wilson and Herrnstein, *Crime and Human Nature,* chaps. 8, 9.

30. Sheppard G. Kellam, Margaret E. Ensminger, and R. Jay Turner, "Family Structure and the Mental Health of Children," *Archives of General Psychiatry,* vol. 34 (1977), pp. 1012–22.

31. Deborah A. Dawson, "Family Structure and Children's Health: United States, 1988," National Center for Health Statistics, *Vital and Health Statistics,* series 10, no. 178 (Hyattsville, Md.: Department of Health and Human Services, June 1991).

32. Sara McLanahan and Gary Sandefur, *Uncertain Childhood, Uncertain Future* (Cambridge, Mass.: Harvard University Press, forthcoming). See also James Q. Wilson, "The Family-Values Debate," *Commentary,* vol. 95 (April 1993), pp. 24–31.

33. J. Brooks-Gunn and Frank F. Furstenberg, Jr., "The Children of Adolescent Mothers: Physical, Academic, and Psychological Outcomes," *Developmental Review,* vol. 6 (September 1986), pp. 224–51; and Frank F. Furstenberg, Jr., J. Brooks-Gunn, and Lindsay Chase-Lansdale, "Teenaged Pregnancy and Childbearing," *American Psychologist,* vol. 44 (February 1989), pp. 313–20.

34. See Sylvia Ann Hewlett, *When the Bough Breaks: The Cost of Neglecting Our Children* (New York: Basic Books, 1991), chap. 3, and the studies summarized therein.

35. On time horizon as the defining characteristic of the urban poor, see Edward C. Banfield, *The Unheavenly City: The Nature and Future of Our Urban Crisis* (Boston: Little Brown, 1970).

36. An example of the more radical view is Michael Harrington, *The Other America: Poverty in the United States* (New York: Macmillan, 1962).

37. Myron Magnet, *The Dream and the Nightmare: The Sixties' Legacy to the Underclass* (New York: William Morrow, 1993), esp. pp. 16–17, 220.

38. Wilson, *Thinking About Crime,* chap. 8. For some promising leads, see Paul Gendreau and Robert R. Ross, "Revivification of Rehabilitation: Evidence from the 1980s," *Justice Quarterly,* vol. 4 (1987), pp. 349–407.

39. Janice H. Laurence, Peter F. Famsberger, and Monica A. Gribben, *Effects of Military Experience on the Post-Service Lives of Low-Aptitude Recruits: Project 100,000 and the ASVAB Misnorming,* Final Report 89–29 to the Office of the Assistant Secretary of Defense for Force Management and Personnel (Alexandria, Va.: Human Resources Research Organization, 1989), p. 170. Veterans' names were selected from among participants in the National Longitudinal Survey, run by Ohio State Uni-

versity for the Department of Labor. There are several limitations to this study that the authors properly note. It was very difficult to locate veterans, and so there may be some sample selection bias (though if the hard-to-find were worse off than the easy-to-find, the bias means that the study underestimated how badly off the veterans were). Low-aptitude recruits who left the military may have been worse off than those who stayed in. Another evaluation of these careerists found that, on the whole, they performed reasonably well, but the authors could only locate about 8,000 such men; since they accounted for only 2.4 percent of the low-aptitude recruits, it is impossible to generalize from their success to the success of the program. See Thomas G. Sticht and others, *Cast-Off Youth: Policy and Training Methods from the Military Experience* (New York: Praeger, 1987), pp. 38, 56–60.

40. Ruth Hubble McKey and others, *The Impact of Head Start on Children, Families, and Communities: Final Report of the Head Start Evaluation, Synthesis, and Utilization Project,* no. OHDS 85–31193 (Department of Health and Human Services, 1985); and Ron Haskins, "Beyond Metaphor: The Efficacy of Early Childhood Education," *American Psychologist,* vol. 44 (February 1989), pp. 274–82.

41. John R. Berrueta-Clement and others, *Changed Lives: The Effects of the Perry Preschool Program on Youths Through Age 19* (Ypsilanti, Mich.: High/Scope, 1984); L.J. Schweinhart, "Can Preschool Programs Help Prevent Delinquency?" in James Q. Wilson and Glenn C. Loury, eds., *Families, Schools, and Delinquency Prevention* (New York: Springer-Verlag, 1987), pp. 135–53.

42. Haskins, "The Efficacy of Early Childhood Education."

43. Phyllis Levenstein, John O'Hara, and John Madden, "The Mother-Child Home Program of the Verbal Interaction Project," in Consortium for Longitudinal Studies, *As the Twig is Bent: Lasting Effects of Preschool Programs* (Hillsdale, N.J.: Erlbaum Associates, 1983), pp. 237–63.

44. The Infant Health and Development Program, "Enhancing the Outcomes of Low-Birth-Weight, Premature Infants," *Journal of the American Medical Association,* vol. 263 (June 13, 1991), pp. 3035–42.

45. I say "for at-risk children" because it is not clear that there are any benefits for normal children. Jay Belsky, "Infant Daycare: A Cause for Concern? *Zero to Three,* vol. 6 (September 1986), pp. 1–7, has suggested that day care for normal children may have some deleterious effects. This is disputed by other scholars. See Tiffany Field, *Infancy* (Cambridge, Mass.: Harvard University Press, 1990), chap. 5. The issue cannot be regarded as resolved. In the low-birth-weight baby project, the improvements in IQ and infant behavior were greatest for the most disadvantaged children.

46. Edward Zigler and Nancy Hall, "The Implications of Early Intervention Efforts for the Primary Prevention of Juvenile Delinquency," and J. David Hawkins and others, "Delinquency Prevention through Parent Training: Results and Issues from Work in Progress," in Wilson and Loury, *From Children to Citizens,* pp. 154–85, and 186–204.

47. James S. Coleman, Thomas Hoffer, and Sally Kilgore, *High School Achievement: Public, Catholic, and Private Schools Compared* (New York: Basic Books, 1982).

48. For accounts in England, see Gertrude Himmelfarb, *Poverty and Compassion: The Moral Imagination of the Late Victorians* (New York: Alfred A. Knopf, 1991), especially chap. 13; for accounts in American, see Paul S. Boyer, *Urban Masses and Moral Order in America, 1820–1920* (Cambridge, Mass.: Harvard University Press, 1978).

49. Mercer Sullivan, "Crime and the Social Fabric," in John Hull Mollenkopf and Manuel Castells, eds., *Dual City: Restructuring New York* (New York: Russell Sage Foundation, 1991), pp. 225–44.

50. The preceding two paragraphs were taken from James Q. Wilson, "Human Nature and Social Progress," a Bradley Lecture delivered to the American Enterprise Institute, May 9, 1991.

51. The proposal is made in Magnet, *The Dream and the Nightmare*, pp. 141–42.

52. James Q. Wilson, *On Character* (Washington: AEI Press, 1991), chap. 3.

53. David Popenoe, *Disturbing the Nest: Family Change and Decline in Modern Societies* (New York: Aldine de Gruyter, 1988).

54. Arthur S. Kraus and Abraham M. Lilienfeld, "Some Epidemiologic Aspects of the High Mortality Rate in the Young Widowed Group," *Journal of Chronic Diseases*, vol. 10 (1959), pp. 207–17; Walter R. Gove, "Sex, Marital Status, and Mortality," *American Journal of Sociology*, vol. 79 (July 1973), pp. 45–67; Alicia Rand, "Transitional Life Events and Desistance from Delinquency and Crime," in Marvin E. Wolfgang, Terence P. Thornberry, and Robert M. Figlio, eds., *From Boy to Man, From Delinquency to Crime* (Chicago: University of Chicago Press, 1987), pp. 134–62; Peter Reuter and others, *Money from Crime: A Study of the Economics of Drug Dealing in Washington, D.C.* (Santa Monica, Calif.: Rand Corporation, 1990). I am indebted to Professor David Courtwright of the University of North Florida for directing my attention to some of these references.

55. Nicholas Eberstadt, "America's Infant-Mortality Puzzle," *Public Interest*, no. 105 (Fall 1991), pp. 37–38.

# 11

# The Urban Church: Faith, Outreach, and the Inner-City Poor

*John J. DiIulio Jr.*

Under what, if any, conditions can the life prospects of today's black inner-city poor be improved, and how, if at all, can we foster those conditions? I argue that supporting black churches and other faith-based grassroots organizations performing youth and community outreach functions in poor inner-city neighborhoods is a necessary and vital (but insufficient) condition for repairing the social fabric and restoring economic vitality in truly disadvantaged urban black neighborhoods. This is especially true, I maintain, when it comes to those clergy, volunteers, and persons of faith at the street level who are doing the most to monitor, mentor, and minister to the daily needs of inner-city black children. Such persons strive to help these children, from innocent toddlers to pregnant teenagers and young males on probation, to avoid violence, achieve literacy, access jobs, and otherwise reach adulthood physically, educationally, and economically whole.

As I have cautioned elsewhere, religious institutions alone cannot cure America's social and civic ills, including the social problems that disproportionately afflict the black inner-city poor. It remains to be seen how, if at all, local faith-based efforts can be taken to scale in ways that predictably, reliably, and cost-effectively cut crime, reduce poverty, or yield other desirable social consequences.[1] Still, overlooking, unduly discounting or simply failing to support the outreach efforts of black churches and other inner-city faith communities is the single biggest mistake that can be made by anyone who cares about those who call the inner cities home.

Fortunately, it is a mistake that is becoming somewhat less common, even in elite intellectual and policy circles, both left and right. "Now both [left and the right] are beginning to form an unlikely alliance founded on the idea that the only way to rescue [inner-city] kids from the seductions of the drugs and gang cultures is with another, more powerful set of values," according to a June 1998 *Newsweek* cover story. "And the only institution with the spiritual message and the physical presence to offer those traditional values, these strange bedfellows have concluded, is the church."[2]

This hopeful conclusion rests upon a constellation of ideas and findings: the relationship between religiosity and volunteerism in contemporary America; religious faith as a factor in ameliorating social problems; adult supports and structured activities for at-risk urban youth; the tradition of black churches as engines of youth and community outreach; surveys of the extent of church-anchored outreach in black urban neighborhoods; and the need for an action-oriented dialogue about race that focuses on black-white religious racial reconciliation and the needs of the black inner-city poor.

## BLACK INNER-CITY POVERTY

It is incontestable that black Americans have progressed economically over the last half-century.[3] Even analysts who emphasize the persistence of black poverty and black-white income gaps acknowledge that "there have been significant improvements since 1940 in the absolute and relative positions of blacks,"[4] that black Americans represent a trillion-dollar-plus annual market larger than that of "most countries in the world,"[5] and that "the majority of working-class and middle-class black families have made some important gains."[6] Moreover, black economic progress has clearly been accompanied by residential desegregation and substantial improvements in race relations. According to surveys by the Gallup Organization, white racial prejudice has steeply declined in the past several decades. Most blacks do not live in mostly or all black neighborhoods. And comparably matched groups of highly educated, higher income whites and blacks are equally satisfied with major aspects of their own everyday lives.[7]

While blacks remain substantially less likely than whites to perceive equality of treatment in housing, education, and other areas, and substantially more likely than whites to favor affirmative action,[8] recent research by Carol Swain indicates that "whites and blacks are not separated by unbridgeable gaps." For example, whites and blacks "show surprising agreement on the allocation of educational opportunities in zero-sum situations where only one person can win," and harbor "similar ideas about fairness and justice in college admissions."[9]

But as I have argued elsewhere, unless we propose to do nothing more than continue idle academic or ideological debates, the triumph of overall black economic progress and the narrowing of black-white differences on social issues neither can nor should obscure the tragedy of black poverty and joblessness.[10] In 1978, William Julius Wilson published his analysis of "the declining significance of race," followed in 1987 by his treatise on the inner city's "underclass" and in 1996 by his study of inner-city joblessness.[11] Wilson's research reminds us that working-class and low-income blacks get hit especially hard when economic booms go bust. Black Americans made substantial economic progress in the 1960s, but each post-1970 recession exacted a disproportionate toll on blacks regardless of family structure. Robert B. Hill has estimated that the four recessions between 1970 and 1985 led to a tripling in the jobless rates among blacks in two-parent families as well as among blacks in mother-only households.[12] As the national economy improved in the late 1980s, black men and women still had unemployment rates more than double those of whites. Even amidst the boom years of the 1990s, over 40 percent of black children, concentrated heavily in central city neighborhoods, continued to live in below-the-poverty-line households. According to a recent study by Scott J. South and Kyle D. Crowder, despite unprecedented residential mobility, blacks remain substantially less likely than whites to escape high-poverty neighborhoods and considerably more likely to move into them.[13]

Millions of black children, through absolutely no fault of their own, remain economically disadvantaged in neighborhoods where jobs are few and drugs, crime, and failed public schools are common. No one, at least no one who has actually spent time in such neighborhoods as North Central Philadelphia or South Central Los Angeles can fail to acknowledge the plight of these children. Thus, while the glass of black socioeconomic progress has become indisputably full for millions of middle- and upper middle-class blacks, it has remained more than half-empty for those remaining in black inner-city neighborhoods.

## BLACK INNER-CITY CRIME

Just as some conservatives seem disposed to trivialize or deny the reality of inner-city black poverty, some liberals seem determined to minimize or deny the reality of black inner-city crime, and to insist that high rates of black-on-black violence and black incarceration are mainly or solely a function of low incomes and racist policies rather than such risk factors as fatherlessness and child abuse. As growing numbers of black church leaders and others seem disposed to argue, however, while poverty and racism are undoubtedly among the so-called "root causes" of black inner-city crime, they are hardly its sole determinants, and they alone cannot begin to explain differences in crime rates and incarceration rates between blacks and whites, differences in these rates among blacks , or the 1985 to 1995 epidemic of black male youth violence.

In the mid-1990s blacks were roughly 12 percent of the total U.S. residential population. According to the Uniform Crime Reports of the Federal

Bureau of Investigation, blacks committed about 40 percent of all weapons violations, 42 percent of all rapes, 54 percent of all murders, 59 percent of all robberies, and 42 percent of all violent crimes.[14] According to James Alan Fox, black males ages 14 to 24 were slightly over 1 percent of the total U.S. residential population but 17 percent of the homicide victims and 30 percent of the murderers.[15]

It has been widely and accurately reported that in the mid-1990s about a third of blacks males in their twenties were under correctional supervision on any given day (in prison, in jail, on probation, or on parole).[16] In 1997, the U.S. Bureau of Justice Statistics calculated that a black male has a 28.5 percent lifetime likelihood of going to prison compared to a 4.4 percent lifetime likelihood of imprisonment for white males.[17]

In 1996, about 28.5 percent of black households, versus 13.7 percent of white households, were below the official poverty line ($16,036 for a family of four). The former figure was the lowest proportion of blacks living below the poverty line since the U.S. Census Bureau began keeping such statistics in 1955. A socially and morally unacceptable 4 in 10 black children lived in below-the-poverty-line homes in the mid-1990s. Still, since the mid-1970s rates of childhood poverty among blacks, and many other indices of black economic distress, even in many inner city neighborhoods, remained unchanged or improved[18] while rates of black youth crime and delinquency remained high or soared higher.

Despite much conventional wisdom to the contrary, most prisoners, black and white, were gainfully employed at some point prior to their most recent conviction or incarceration, while many had legitimate jobs during the period that they did the crime or crimes that resulted in their most recent trouble with the law.[19] If anything, therefore, the worsening of black inner-city crime during years of relative and absolute gains in material well-being is an acute case of what UCLA's James Q. Wilson once described as the paradox of "crime amidst plenty."[20]

As Glenn Loury has reasoned, the "simple fact of poverty is surely not an adequate explanation" for the "extraordinary disparity" in black and white crime rates.[21]

By the same token, racial discrimination is not an adequate explanation for the extraordinary disparity in black and white incarceration rates. According to a 1998 report prepared by the Council of Economic Advisors for the President's Initiative on Race, "Research suggests that most or all of the differences in the likelihood of conviction and imprisonment can be explained" by factors other than racial discrimination, "such as severity of crime or prior record of the offender."[22]

Even if one believes that racism and poverty are the twin determinants of black crime and incarceration rates, it still makes sense to ponder risk factors along with root causes. Among the social risk factors that go the longest way toward accounting not only for the difference between black and white rates of crime and incarceration, but for the differences in these rates among blacks, are those that relate to the densities of loving, capable, responsible adults in the daily lives of children and young adults. Two such interrelated risk factors are the absence of fathers and child abuse.

In 1993, 68.7 percent of births to black mothers, versus 23.6 percent of births to white mothers, were out of wedlock. In 1994, 96 percent of black teen births, versus 67 percent of white teen births, were out of wedlock. In 1996, 53 percent of black children, versus 19 percent of white children, lived in mother-only homes.

Robin Karr-Morse and Meredith Wiley observe that research on "the roles of African American and Hispanic fathers in their children's development has been sparse. But the data that do exist on African-American men are particularly troubling. . . . Where fathers have never married the mothers, 57 percent consistently visit their children in the first two years. But by the time the children are 7.5 years old, fewer than 25 percent of fathers are consistently visiting their children. . . . The lack of a father's presence has a direct impact on the child."[23]

Indeed it does. As indicated by a 1993 analysis by June O'Neill and Anne Hill, the likelihood that a young male will commit crime doubles if he is raised without a father and triples if he lives in a neighborhood with a high concentration of mother-only homes, such that blacks males raised in public housing in mother-only welfare-dependent homes are about twice as likely to commit crime as otherwise comparable black males raised with a father but also on welfare and in public housing.[24] Likewise, as reported in a 1998 study by Cynthia Harper and Sara McLanahan, even after controlling for race, income, and other socioeconomic variables, fatherless boys are twice as likely as boys living in two-parent homes to be incarcerated, and each year spent in a fatherless home raises a boy's odds of being imprisoned by about 5 percent.[25]

With regard to race, the criminogenic influence of fatherlessness can manifest itself in many ways, the most direct and obvious of which is captured in the classic 1965 statement of the problem by Daniel Patrick Moynihan: "A community that allows a large number of young men to grow up in broken families, dominated by women, never acquiring any stable relationship to male authority . . . asks for and gets chaos."

Boys without loving, law-abiding fathers to actively monitor and mentor them on a daily basis are more likely to act out at home and in school, run wild on the streets, and get into trouble with the law. But, if much of the relevant post-1985 empirical research is any guide, boys without such fathers are also more likely to be severely maltreated at home by one or both of their biological parents, or by a biological mother's boyfriend, in ways that increase their incidence of future crime and delinquency.

There is growing evidence of a child abuse-fatherlessness-crime nexus. To cite just a few examples, the results of a major longitudinal study as reported by the national Institute of Justice in 1992 indicate that abuse of children increases their chances of future delinquency and crime by about 40 percent.[26] A 1992 study by Leslie Margolin indicates that in mother-only homes the mother's live-in boyfriends provide almost no nonparental child care but are responsible for nearly two-thirds of all nonparental child abuse.[27] In one 1995 study, Carolyn Smith analyzed data indicating that only 3.2 percent of children raised by both parents, versus 18.6 percent of those raised by cohabitating partners and other adults, are abused,[28] and in a second 1995 study, she noted that child abuse "has long been associated with problematic outcomes for children" including criminality.[29] Or, in the 1995 words of Mark Fleisher, the country's leading urban street crime ethnographer, an "abundance of scholarly evidence shows that anti-social and delinquent tendencies emerge early in the lives of neglected, abused, and unloved youngsters, often by age nine."[30]

I agree with University of Southern California's Susan Estrich when she writes that "the only way truly to address racism in the criminal justice system is to cut the crime rate among blacks—to try to inoculate the children even as we punish many of their fathers and brothers. It is what we would do if it were our white sons facing their future." It is not racist to lock up violent and habitual criminals. "But planning prisons for preschoolers is" racist.[31]

The good news is that many clergy and religious volunteers, both black and white, concur that we must aggressively reach all socially at-risk preschoolers with loving, caring adults, reconnect responsible young fathers on probation and behind bars with their children and families, and, as I have argued elsewhere, "build churches, not jails."[32]

## RELIGIOSITY AND VOLUNTEERS

How we approach black inner-city poverty and crime is bound to be affected by religious ideals, influences, and institutions. From Alexis de Tocqueville to the latest social science findings, it has been abundantly clear that Americans are a religious people. "The United States," observes George Gallup Jr., "is one of the most devout nations of the entire industrialized world, in terms of religious beliefs and practices."[33] Belief in God remains the norm in America, with levels of belief ranging between 94 percent and 99 percent over the past five decades.

Black Americans are in many ways the most religious people in America. Some 82 percent of blacks (versus 67 percent of whites) are church members; 82 percent of blacks (versus 55 percent of whites) say that religion is "very important in their life"; and 86 percent of blacks (versus 60 percent of whites) believe that religion "can answer all or most of today's problems."[34]

All reports of the death of organized religion and religious sentiment in America have been greatly exaggerated. Since the end of the Second World War, we have witnessed what Roger Finke and Rodney Clark aptly described as the "churching of America," resulting by the mid-1990s in a nation with an estimated half a million churches, temples, and mosques, 2,000 or more religious denominations, and an unknown number of independent churches.[35] In 1995 Gallup's Religion Index, an on-going measurement of eight key religious beliefs and practices of the American public, hit a ten-year high.[36]

Laws have grown more faith-friendly. For example, the federal government's latest welfare reform overhaul measure, the Personal Responsibility and Work Opportunity Reconciliation Act of 1996, contains section 104, the so-called Charitable Choice provision encouraging states to utilize "faith-based organizations in serving the poor and needy," requiring that religious organizations be permitted to receive contracts, vouchers, and other government funding on the same basis as any other nongovernmental provider, and protecting "the religious integrity and character of faith-based organizations that are willing to accept government funds."[37] Charitable Choice covers the major federal anti-poverty and social welfare programs (Temporary Assistance to Needy Families, Medicaid, Supplemental Security Income, Food Stamps) and Congress could expand it to juvenile justice programs and other policy domains. Many states, most notably Texas, have moved aggressively to reorient their anti-poverty programs around Charitable Choice and kindred state laws favoring church-state cooperation.[38]

Philanthropy, too, has been gradually tilting toward religion. For example, in 1996 three foundations with long-standing programs in religion, The Lilly Endowment, The Pew Charitable Trusts, and The James Irvine Foundation, made record religion grants of $60 million, $13 million, and $7.7 million, respectively. In 1997, the Robert Wood Johnson Foundation made its 800th $25,000 grant to its "Faith in Action" program, which mobilizes interfaith networks of religious volunteers to serve some 200,000 elderly and disabled Americans. The program's director describes it as "the first mega program undertaken" by the foundation, and "the largest project" in the foundation's history.[39]

It is hardly surprising that networks of interfaith volunteers are the backbone of such a program. As Andrew Greely has aptly summarized the evidence, research has consistently shown that both "frequency of church attendance and membership in church organizations correlate strongly with voluntary service. People who attend services once a week or more are approximately twice as likely to volunteer as those who attend rarely if ever."[40] Greely also observes religious organizations and "relationships related to their religion" appear to be the major forces in mobilizing volunteers in America. Even a third of purely secular volunteers (persons who did not volunteer for specifically religious activities) also relate their service "to the influence of a relationship based in their religion."[41] Likewise, as George Gallup Jr. has reported, summarizing the results of various major surveys, "Churches and other religious bodies are the major supporters of voluntary services for neighborhoods and communities. Members of a church or synagogue . . . tend to be much more involved in charitable activity, particularly through organized groups. Almost half of the church members did unpaid volunteer work in a given year, compared to only a third of non-members. . . . Religion would appear to have an early impact upon volunteers and charitable giving. . . . Among the 76 percent of teens who reported that they were members of religious institutions, 62 percent were also volunteers, and 56 percent were charitable contributors. By contrast, among those who reported no religious affiliation, far fewer were either volunteers (44 percent) or contributors (25 percent)."[42]

## FAITH FACTOR FINDINGS

But is there any scientific evidence to show that religious do-gooding does any good, or to justify the faith of most black Americans that religion can "answer all or most of today's problems"? Over the last several years, journalists seem to have become more interested in this question, often crediting the ministry with working cooperatively with police and probation officials, working one-on-one with the city's most severely at-risk youngsters, and thereby helping to engineer a dramatic drop in youth crime and the virtual elimination of gun-related youth homicides. Two months before the *Newsweek* cover story, featuring Boston's Reverend Eugene Rivers, *Time* featured "In the Line of Fire," the tale of Brother Bill, a Catholic lay worker who "repeatedly walks into gunfire to stop the shooting—and love the unloved."[43] Two years earlier, the cover of *U.S. News & World Report* asked "Can Churches Cure America's Social Ills?," and the story answered largely in the affirmative.[44]

While such "faith factor" journalism is out ahead of the empirical research on religion and social action, it is hardly pure hype. As UCLA's James Q. Wilson has succinctly summarized the small but not insignificant body of credible evidence to date, "Religion, independent of social class, reduces deviance."[45] David Larson pioneered inquiry into the influence of the "faith factor" on public health outcomes, research that led to new training programs at Harvard and three dozen other medical schools.[46] In more recent work with criminologist Byron Johnson, Larson has reviewed some four hundred juvenile delinquency studies published between 1980 and 1997. They found that the better the study design and measurement methodology, the greater the likelihood the research will find statistically significant and beneficial results associated with "the faith factor."[47] The more scientific the study, the more optimistic are its findings about the extent to which "religion reduces deviance."[48] A 1997 study by Larson and Johnson found that prisoners who participated in Bible studies behind bars were only a third as likely to be rearrested a year after being released than otherwise comparable prisoners who did not participate in Bible studies before being paroled.[49]

In another major review of the relevant research literature David Evans and his associates confirmed that "the religiosity and crime relationship for adults is neither spurious nor contingent. . . . (R)eligion, as indicated by religious activities, had direct personal effects on adult criminality as measured by a broad range of criminal acts. Further, "the relationship held even with the introduction of secular controls."[50] In other words, "religion matters" in reducing adult crime.

Beyond crime and delinquency, in a sprightly 1996 synopsis of various faith factor research, Patrick Fagan of the Heritage Foundation summarized studies suggesting that religion enhances family stability (the family that prays together is indeed more likely to stay together), improves health, reduces adolescent sexual activities and teenage pregnancies, cuts alcohol and drug abuse, and reinforces other measures of "social stability."[51]

But in relation to black inner-city poverty and related social ills, perhaps the single most illustrative line of "religion reduces deviance" research begins with a 1985 study by Harvard economist Richard Freeman, runs through the work of Larson, and continues through the community development, mentoring, and "faith factor" research of analysts at Public/Private Ventures (P/PV), a Philadelphia-based national nonprofit youth policy research organization.

In 1985, Freeman reported that church-going, independent of other factors, made young black males from high-poverty neighborhoods substantially more likely to "escape" poverty, crime, and other social ills.[52] In their reanalysis and extension of Freeman's work, Larson and Johnson mine national longitudinal data on urban black youth and find that, using a more multidimensional measure of religious commitment than church-going, religion is indeed a powerful predictor of "escaping" poverty, crime, and other social ills, more powerful even than such variables as peer influences.[53] Like Freeman, Larson and Johnson conjecture that the potential of church-going and other religious influences to improve the life prospects of poor black urban youth is in part a function of how church-going and other "faith factors" influence how young people spend their time, the extent of their engagement in positive structured activities, and the degree to which they are supported by responsible adults.

## SUPPORT FOR YOUTH

This conjecture is borne out in part by an important 1998 P/PV analysis, based on original survey and field research, of how predominantly minority low-income urban youth spend their time in the "moderately poor" neighborhoods of three cities (Austin, Texas; Savannah, Georgia; and St. Petersburg, Florida).[54]

As P/PV researchers Cynthia L. Sipe and Patricia Ma observe, much has "been written on adolescents' use of their discretionary time and the lack of positive activities to fill that time. Many youth fall prey to antisocial activities in good part because positive activities and safe places are not available at crucial times" and during "so-called gap periods" (after school, weekends, summers).[55] Sipe and Ma analyze data on how three different cohorts of youth (12-to-14-year-olds, 15-to-17-year-olds, and 18-to-20-year-olds) spent their after-school time across the neighborhoods of three cities.

First, the bad news. A majority of youth in each cohort, neighborhood, and city spent most of their after-school time just "hanging out," on "unstructured leisure," or on things other than homework, chores, jobs, and so on.[56] Overall, "a disturbingly high share" (from 15 to 25 percent) of youth were "not engaged in any positive structured activities," had "no or very few adults in their lives," and were "not working."[57]

Now, however, the good news. Across all groups and cities, most youth who did receive adult support and guidance (whether at home, in school, or via community organizations) and did participate in positive structured activities were significantly more likely than their "disconnected" peers to succeed: "Youth who are engaged in more activities, have more leadership experiences and more adult support also tend to have higher self-efficacy, better grades and be less involved in risk activity," including but not limited to less "delinquency and gang involvement."[58]

Finally, the good news about religion. P/PV's youth study was undertaken as part of a larger, six-city, "resident-driven" project launched in 1993 and known as Community Change for Youth Development (CCYD).[59] Those who designed CCYD, including P/PV president Gary Walker, had expected to find that public schools and programs like Boys Clubs and Girls Clubs, Police Athletic League, Ys and Big Brothers, Big Sisters provided substantial and beneficial "support for youth" in these disadvantaged communities. They were not entirely disappointed. But they also found something that they did not expect or set out to find, namely, churches and faith-based programs serving as after-school "safe havens" and playing a major "support for youth" role (recreation, mentoring, child care, meals, and more) in these neighborhoods.

For example, in the predominantly Latino Austin study site, twenty-four churches sponsored various programs for the community, and over half of the youth participated in local religious services. In the Savannah study site, fifty-two churches dwarfed schools both in sheer numbers and in terms of outreach programs and activities for neighborhood youth, 97 percent of them black. And the surprising strength of churches in the St. Petersburg study site was ratified, as it were, by the fact that P/PV held its 1998 CCYD conference there and featured none other than Boston's Reverend Rivers as the keynote speaker. Indeed, from 1996 to 1998, P/PV's CCYD experience, and a fresh look at the implications of its own research on mentoring, led the organization to develop a new research program on religion and at-risk youth.

For years, P/PV had led in the production and dissemination of evaluation research on mentoring programs.[60] To date, the single most widely publicized P/PV study of mentoring was its 1995 evaluation of the Big Brothers, Big Sisters of America program. P/PV researchers Joseph P. Tierney and Jean Baldwin Grossman reported that youth (most of them low-income minority youth) who were matched with a mentor reaped significant benefits, compared with their counterparts who remained on agency waiting lists.[61] The Littles were 46 percent less likely to initiate drug use and 27 percent less likely to initiate alcohol use. They were about a third less likely to hit someone. They skipped school half as many days as wait-listed youth. They also liked school more, got slightly better grades, and formed more positive relationships with their parents and peers. These effects held for both boys and girls across all races. The study received lots of positive public notice, elicited bipartisan endorsements from national leaders, and was invoked repeatedly at the 1996 presidential "volunteer summit" in Philadelphia led by Colin Powell.

There were, however, at least two clouds in the study's silver linings. The study was possible only because thousands of eligible children remained on waiting lists. Worse, even if there were adult volunteers aplenty, the inner-city youth who needed responsible nonparental adult support and guidance in their lives would be least likely to get it. The simple reason is that Big Brothers, Big Sisters and most other effective mentoring programs that reach at-risk urban youth presuppose a youth who already has at least one parent, legal guardian, or other responsible adult in his or her life, an adult who is caring and functional enough to sign them up, follow through on interviews and phone calls, fill out forms, and so forth.

Many low-income minority youth lack even that much social capital. Recall the CCYD's youth study's disturbing finding that anywhere from 15 to 25 percent of minority youth in "moderately poor" neighborhoods were completely or totally "disconnected." There is every reason to suppose that the unsupported fraction runs even higher in the poorest inner-city neighborhoods, places that contribute disproportionately to such grim social statistics as the following: each year since 1993 there have been roughly one million substantiated cases of child abuse and neglect drawn; about 1.5 million persons age 18 or younger have one or both parents in prison or jail; more than 70 percent of all black births are out of wedlock; by age 8, three-quarters of nonmarital black children have no regular contact with their biological fathers; and sadly so on.

"Most private, nonprofit mentoring programs," comments P/PV's Walker, a twenty-five-year veteran of the field, "like most social policy-driven youth development programs, simply don't reach or support the most severely at-risk inner-city youth."[62]

## BLACK CHURCH OUTREACH TRADITION ALIVE

The black church's uniquely powerful community outreach tradition is grounded in eight major historically black Christian churches: African Methodist Episcopal; African Methodist Episcopal Zion; Christian Methodist Episcopal; Church of God in Christ; National Baptist Convention of America; National Baptist Convention, USA; National Missionary Baptist Convention; and the Progressive National Baptist Convention. There are also scores of independent or quasi-independent black churches or church networks, and at least nine certified religious training programs operated by accredited seminaries that are directed toward ministry in black churches and black faith communities. Together, the eight major black denominations alone encompass some 65,000 churches and about 20 million members.

Unfortunately, until quite recently, that outreach tradition and what it portends for social action against inner-city ills has been largely ignored by a strange bedfellows assortment of academics and intellectual elites. Until the 1990s, for example, the richly religious lives of black Americans and the black church outreach tradition were given short shrift by both historians and social scientists, and not just by white historians and social scientists. In the *National Journal of Sociology*, Andrew Billingsley, a dean of black family studies, noted that the subject was largely ignored even by leading black scholars who were keenly aware of "the social significance of the black church," including many who "were actually members of a black church."[63]

For example, James Blackwell's 1975 book *The Black Community*, considered by Billingsley and several other experts to be "the best study" of its kind since Du Bois's 1899 classic *The Philadelphia Negro*, devoted not a single chapter to the black church; and Billingsley's own 1968 book *Black Families In White America*, written as a rebuttal to the 1965 Moynihan Report, "devoted less than two pages to discussing the relevance of the black church as a support system for African-American families."[64] Billingsley speculates that black intellectuals ignore black churches in part out of a false fidelity to the canons of objective scholarship.

A refined and empirically well-grounded perspective on variations in the extent of black church outreach is provided by sociologist Harold Dean Trulear, an ordained black minister who did outreach work in New Jersey, taught for eight years at the New York Theological Seminary, has conducted extensive research on black clergy training, and is presently Vice President for research on religion and at-risk youth at P/PV.

"When it comes to youth and community outreach in the inner city," Trulear cautions, "not all black urban churches are created equal. . . . Naturally, it's in part a function of high resident membership. Inner-city churches with high resident membership cater more to high-risk neighborhood youth than . . . black churches with inner-city addresses but increasingly or predominantly suburbanized or commuting congregations. . . . (The high resident membership black churches) tend to cluster by size and evangelical orientation . . . It's the small-and medium-sized churches . . . (especially) the so-called . . . blessing stations and specialized youth chapels with their charismatic leader and their small, dedicated staff of adult volunteers (that) . . . do a disproportionate amount of the up close and personal outreach work with the worst-off inner-city youth."[65]

Today, a number of intellectual and policy leaders are reclaiming the black church tradition. In a 1997 essay, Boston University economists Glenn Loury and Linda Datcher Loury argue persuasively that a "spirit of self-help, rooted in a deep-seated sense of self respect, was widely embraced among blacks of all ideological persuasions well into this century."[66] They rebut the view that "economic factors ultimately drive" behavioral problems "involving sexuality, marriage, childbearing, and parenting," and, in turn, challenge the notion that merely fiddling with economic incentives via policy changes can change behavior for the good. Rather, they argue, voluntary associations, "as exemplified by religious institutions," can be valuable allies in the battle against social pathology.[67] From a less academic, more practice-driven perspective, Robert L. Woodson Sr., president of the National Center for Neighborhood Enterprise in Washington, D.C., reclaims the black church outreach tradition in his 1998 book on how "today's community healers are reviving our streets and neighborhoods."[68]

## SURVEYS OF CHURCH-BASED OUTREACH

How common are black-led outreach ministries? What, if any, systematic evidence suggests that the extent of youth and community outreach by black churches is nontrivial? As Harold Dean Trulear has observed, "Simply stated, there has yet to be a survey of the blessing stations and youth chapels that do most of the actual work with the worst-off kids in black inner-city neighborhoods."[69] But the pathbreaking research of scholars such as Eric C. Lincoln and Lawrence H. Mamiya, combined with recent systematic research by Trulear and others, should persuade even a dedicated skeptic to take black church-based outreach seriously.

In a recent study, P/PV's Jeremy White and Mary de Marcellus report on the results of their intensive six-month field exploration of youth-serving ministries in the District.[70] They interviewed leaders and volunteers in a total of 129 of the city's faith-based ministries, including on-site visits to 79 churches, faith-based nonprofit organizations, and schools, virtually all of them led by blacks and serving predominantly black populations. Based on this research, they concluded that "there is a critical mass of faith-based organizations in Washington, D.C. that work directly and intensively with at-risk youth."[71] The programs fell into six major categories: after-school or tutoring programs; evangelization; gang violence prevention; youth groups; and mentoring.[72] Interestingly, however, only 7 percent of the programs they studied focused exclusively on evangelization for children in the form of youth church, Bible study, or street preaching.

While the language and motivations of most of the ministers and volunteers they studied were plainly spiritual and religious, none of the programs studied by White and de Marcellus required youth to belong to a particular church, profess any particular religious beliefs, or agree to eventual "churching" as a condition for receiving services, entering church buildings, or otherwise benefitting from the programs. Likewise, almost none of the programs, even those that furnished children with material goods such as clothes or books, charged a fee. As one outreach minister phrased it: "The cost of real love is no charge."[73]

The results of a survey of "faith-based service providers in the nation's capital" were published in 1998 by the Urban Institute.[74] The survey found that 95 percent of the congregations performed outreach services. The 226 religious congregations (out of 1,100 surveyed) that responded (67 of them in the District, the rest in Maryland or Virginia) provided a total of over 1,000 community services to over 250,000 individuals in 1996. The services included food, clothing, and financial assistance. The survey was limited to religious congregations. Local faith-based nonprofits were not surveyed.

In the mid-1990s a six-city survey of how over 100 randomly selected urban churches (and four synagogues) constructed in 1940 or earlier serve their communities was undertaken by Ram A. Cnnan of the University of Pennsylvania. The study was commissioned and published by Partners for Sacred Places, a Philadelphia-based national nonprofit organization dedicated to the care and good use of older religious properties.[75] Congregations were surveyed in Philadelphia, New York, Chicago, Indianapolis, Mobile, (Alabama) and the Bay Area (Oakland and San Francisco). Each church surveyed participated in a series of in-depth interviews.

Among the Cnnan-Partners survey's key findings were the following: 93 percent of the churches opened their doors to the larger community; on average, each church provided over 5,300 hours of volunteer support to its community programs (the equivalent of two-and-a-half full-time volunteers stationed year-round at the church); on average, each church provided about $140,000 a year in community programs, or about 16 times what it received from program beneficiaries; on average, each church supported four major programs, and provided informal and impromptu services as well; and poor children who were not the sons or daughters of church members or otherwise affiliated with the church benefitted from church-supported programs more than any other single group.

The best known and still the most comprehensive survey focusing exclusively on black churches was published in 1990 by Lincoln and Mamiya.[76] In their book *The Black Church in the African-American Experience,* they reported on the results of surveys encompassing nearly 1,900 ministers and over 2,100 churches. Some 71 percent of black clergy reported that their churches engaged in community outreach programs including day care, job search, substance abuse prevention, food and clothing distribution, and many others.[77] Black urban churches, they found, were generally more engaged in outreach than rural ones. While many urban churches also engaged in quasi-political activities and organizing, few received government money, most clergy expressed concerns about receiving government money, and only about 8 percent of all the churches surveyed received any federal government funds.[78]

A number of site-specific and regional surveys of black churches followed the publication of Lincoln and Mamiya's book. So far, all of them have been broadly consistent with the Lincoln-Mamiya survey results on black church outreach. To cite just two examples, a survey of 150 black churches in Atlanta, Naomi Ward and her colleagues found that 131 of the churches were "actively engaged in extending themselves into the community."[79] Likewise, a survey of 635 Northern black churches found that two-thirds of the churches engaged in a wide range of "family-oriented community outreach programs," including mentoring, drug abuse prevention, teenage pregnancy prevention, and other outreach efforts "directed at children and youth."[80]

The raw data from the Lincoln-Mamiya surveys were reanalyzed in the course of a 1997 study of black theological education certificate programs (Bible institutes, denominational training programs, and seminary non-degree programs). The study was directed by Trulear in collaboration with Tony Carnes and commissioned by the Ford Foundation.[81] Trulear and Carnes reported no problems with the Lincoln-Mamiya data. Rather, they compared certain of the Lincoln-Mamiya survey results to data gathered in their own survey 724 students representing 28 theological certificate programs that focused on serving black students. Again, the findings were quite consistent with those of the Lincoln-Mamiya study. For example, three-quarters of those surveyed by Trulear and Carnes reported that their church encouraged them "to be involved in my local community," more than half said relevance to "my community's needs" was of major importance to them in choosing a theological certificate program, and about half were already involved in certain types of charitable community work.[82]

## RELIGIOUS RACIAL RECONCILIATION AND THE POOR

If black church outreach is so potent, why do inner-city poverty, crime, and other problems remain so severe? That is a fair question, but it can easily be turned around: How much worse would things be in Boston and Jamaica Queens, Philadelphia and Los Angeles, and other cities were it not for the largely unsung efforts of faith-based youth and community outreach efforts? How much more would government or other charitable organizations need to expend, and how many volunteers would suddenly need to be mobilized, in the absence of church-anchored outreach? The only defensible answers are "much worse" and "lots," respectively.

Citizens who for whatever reasons are nervous about religion or enhanced church-state partnerships should focus on the consistent finding that faith-based outreach efforts benefit poor unchurched neighborhood children most of all. If these churches are so willing to support and reach out to "the least of these," surely they deserve the human and financial support of the rest us—corporations, foundations, and, where appropriate, government agencies.

The oldest racial divide in America has been, and continues to be, between blacks and whites. To be more specific, the divide is between black Christians and white Christians. Or, to be dangerously specific, it is between white and black Protestants who found themselves (or whose fathers and grandmothers found themselves) on opposite sides of the civil rights divide and, before that, Jim Crow. But I sense a thaw in relations between black and white Christians in recent years. Everywhere, it seems, new flowers of religious racial reconciliation and cooperation are starting to bud. Consider Prison Fellowship Ministry, including its Neighbors Who Care program and its new initiative on Children, Youth, and Families, designed to help provide outreach to the sons and daughters of incarcerated adults. Or consider how the Catholic Church has struggled with success to provide excellent but affordable education to non-Catholic low-income inner-city minority children, and, as His Eminence Cardinal Bernard Law of Boston has done vis-à-vis the outreach ministry of Reverend Rivers and other local black Protestant clergy, supported black faith-based outreach efforts in other ways.

With Andrew Greely, I do not believe that churches or charity can or "should replace public support for those in distress."[83] But especially as regards social action against the problems of the black inner-city poor, I would also agree with him that it is long past time to recognize that there are in America many more clergy and "religiously motivated volunteers than there are activists engaged in the culture wars," or, I might add, in debates about multiculturalism, political correctness, or other fashionable topics of elite ideological dispute.[84]

I also agree with Father Richard John Neuhaus of *First Things* when he characterizes one of my earlier writings on black poverty as advancing the view that "religion is the key to anything good happening among the black poor" (well, at least the key to most good things that are happening among them). And I confess to being doubly in agreement with Father Neuhaus when he writes that, rather than turn our heads and harden our hearts to the plight of the black inner-city poor, rather than merely exposing "liberal fatuities about remedying the 'root causes' of poverty and crime . . . there must be another way. Just believing that is a prelude to doing something. The something in question is centered in religion that is both motive and means, and extends to public policy tasks that should claim the attention of all Americans."[85] Say amen.

## NOTES

1. For example, see John J. DiIulio Jr., "The Lord's Work: The Church and Civil Society," in E.J. Dionne, Jr., ed., *Community Works: The Revival of Civil Society in America* (Washington, D.C.: Brookings Institution Press, 1998), chapter 7.

2. John Leland, "Savior of the Streets,"*Newsweek*, June 1, 1998, p. 22.

3. Stephan Thernstrom and Abigail Thernstrom, *America in Black and White: One Nation, Indivisible* (New York: Simon and Schuster, 1997).

4. National Research Council, *A Common Destiny: Blacks and American Society* (Washington, D.C.: National Academy Press, 1989), p. 274.

5. Marcus Alexis and Geraldine R. Henderson, "The Economic Base of African-American Communities: A Study of Consumption Patterns," in *National Urban League, The State of Black America 1994* (New York: National Urban League, Inc., January 1994), p. 81.

6. Robert B. Hill et al., *Research on the African-American Family: A Holistic Perspective* (Westport, Conn.: Auburn House, 1993), p. 2.

7. The Gallup Organization, *Black/White Relations in the United States 1997* (Princeton, N.J.: The Gallup Organization, June 1997).

8. Gallup Organization, *Black/White Relations.*

9. Carol M. Swain and Bernard Silverman, "Where Blacks and Whites Agree," *Public Affairs Report, University of California, Berkeley,* 39, no. 4, 1998, pp. 8–9.

10. John J. DiIulio , Jr., "State of Grace," *National Review,* December 22, 1997, pp. 62–66.

11. William Julius Wilson, *The Declining Significance of Race* (Chicago: University of Chicago Press, 1978); *The Truly Disadvantaged: The Inner City, the Underclass, and Public Policy* (Chicago: University of Chicago Press, 1987); *When Work Disappears: The World of the New Urban Poor* (New York: Knopf, September 1996).

12. Robert B. Hill, "The Black Middle Class: Past, Present, and Future," in *National Urban League, The State of Black America 1986* (New York: National Urban League, Inc., 1986), pp. 43–64.

13. Scott J. South and Kyle D. Crowder, "Escaping Distressed Neighborhoods: Individual, Community, and Metropolitan Influences," *American Journal of Sociology,* 102, no. 4, January 1997, pp. 1040–84.

14. *Sourcebook of Criminal Justice Statistics* (Washington, D.C.: Bureau of Justice Statistics, 1997), p. 384.

15. James Alan Fox, *Trends in Juvenile Violence* (Washington, D.C.: Bureau of Justice Statistics, March 1996), p. 1.

16. "A Shocking Look at Blacks and Crime," *U.S. News & World Report,* October 16, 1995, p. 53.

17. *Lifetime Likelihood of Going to State or Federal Prison* (Washington, D.C.: Bureau of Justice Statistics, March 1997), p. 1.

18. Stephan Thernstrom and Abigail Thernstrom, *America in Black and White: One Nation, Indivisible* (New York: Simon and Schuster, 1997), and Thomas D. Boston and Catherine L. Ross, *The Inner City: Urban Poverty and Economic Development* (New Brunswick: Transaction, 1997).

19. John DiIulio, Anne Piehl, and Bert Useem, *Profiles of Prisoners in Three States: A Research Report for the Council on Crime in America* (New York: Center for Civic Innovation, forthcoming)

20. James Q. Wilson, *Thinking About Crime,* rev. ed. (New York: Basic Books, 1983), p. 13.

21. Glenn Loury, "Victims and Predators," *Times Literary Supplement,* September 25, 1995.

22. *Changing America* (Washington, D.C.: Council of Economic Advisers, September 1999), p. 51.

23. Robin Karr-Morse and Meredith S. Wiley, *Ghosts From the Nursery: Tracing the Roots of Violence* (New York: Atlantic Monthly Press, 1997), pp. 230–31.

24. June O'Neill and Anne M. Hill, "Underclass Behaviors in the United States, City University of New York, Baruch College, 1993," as summarized in Wade F. Horn, *Father Facts,* third edition (Gaithersburg, Md.: The National Fatherhood Initiative, 1998), p. 61.

25. Cynthia C. Harper and Sara McLanahan, "Father Absence and Youth Incarceration," paper presented at the annual meeting of the American Sociological Association, August 1998.

26. *Cycle of Violence* (Washington, D.C.: National Institute of Justice, 1992).

27. Leslie Margolin, "Child Abuse By Mothers' Boyfriends," *Child Abuse and Neglect*, 1992, pp. 541–51.

28. Carolyn Smith and Terrance Thornberry, "The Relationship Between Childhood Maltreatment and Adolescent Involvement in Delinquency," *Criminology,* 1993, pp. 451–79.

29. Carolyn Smith et al., "Resilient Youth: Identifying Factors That prevent High-Risk Youth From Engaging in Delinquency and Drug Use," *Current Perspectives on Aging and the Life Cycle*, 1995, p. 221

30. Mark S. Fleisher, *Beggars and Thieves: Lives of Urban Street Criminals* (Madison, Wis.: University of Wisconsin Press, 1995), p. 262.

31. Susan Estrich, *Getting Away With Murder* (Cambridge, Mass.: Harvard University press, 1998), p. 92.

32. TK. Senate testimony

33. George Gallup, Jr., *Emerging Trends, Princeton Religion Research Center,* 18, no. 3, March 1996, p. 5. Also see Richard Morin, "Keeping the Faith: A Survey Shows the United States Has the Most Churchgoing People in the Developed World," *The Washington Post Weekly Edition,* January 12, 1998, p. 37.

34. George Gallup, Jr., "Religion in America: Will the Vitality of Churches Be the Surprise of the Next Century?," *The Public Perspective,* October/November 1995, p. 4.

35. Roger Finke and Rodney Stark, *The Churching of America* (New Brunswick, N.J.: Rutgers University Press, 1992).

36. Gallup, *Emerging Trends,* p. 1.

37. Center for Public Justice, *A Guide to Charitable Choice* (Washington, D.C.: Center for Public Justice, 1997). Also see Carl H. Esbeck, "A Constitutional Case for Governmental Cooperation with Faith-Based Social Service Providers," *Emory Law*

*Journal*, 46, no. 1, Winter 1997, pp. 1–83, and Stanley W. Carlson-Thies and James W. Skillen, eds., *Welfare in America: Christian Perspectives on a Policy in Crisis* (Grand Rapids, Mich.: Eerdmans, 1996).

38. For example, see Governor's Advisory Task Force on Faith-Based Community Service Groups, *Faith in Action: A New Vision for Church-State Cooperation in Texas* (State of Texas, December 1996).

39. Mike Jackson, "Faith in Action Supporting Volunteering with 800 Grantees," *Advances: The Robert Wood Johnson Foundation Quarterly Newsletter*, Issue 1, 1998, p. 10.

40. Andrew Greely, "The Other Civic America: Religion and Social Capital," *The American Prospect*, no. 32, May-June 1997, p. 70.

41. Greely, "The Other Civic America," 72.

42. Gallup, "Religion in America," p. 2.

43. Ron Stodghill II, "In the Line of Fire," *Time*, April 20, 1998, pp. 34–37.

44. Joseph P. Shapiro, "Can Churches Save America," *US News & World Report*, September 9, 1996, pp. 46–53.

45. James Q. Wilson, "Two Nations," paper delivered at Francis Boyer Lecture, American Enterprise Institute, December 4, 1997, p. 10.

46. For example, see David B. Larson et al., *Scientific Research on Spirituality and Health* (Radnor, Pa.: John M. Templeton Foundation, October 1, 1997).

47. David B. Larson and Byron Johnson, "Systematic Review of Delinquency Research," preliminary draft, 1998, and personal correspondence with Larson, September 1, 1998.

48. David B. Larson and Byron Johnson, *Religion: The Forgotten Factor in Cutting Youth Crime and Saving At-Risk Urban Youth*, a report issued by The Center for Civic Innovation and The Jeremiah Project, The Manhattan Institute (New York, New York, November 13, 1998).

49. David B. Larson et al., "Religious Programs, Institutional Adjustment, and Recidivism Among Former Inmates in Prison Fellowship Programs," *Justice Quarterly*, 14, no. 1, March 1997, pp. 145–66.

50. T. David Evans et al., "Religion and Crime Reexamined: The Impact of Religion, Secular Controls, and Social Ecology on Adult Criminality," *Criminology*, 33, no. 2, 1995, pp. 211–12.

51. Patrick Fagan, "Why Religion Matters: The Impact of Religious Practice on Social Stability," *Heritage Foundation Backgrounded*, no. 164, January 25, 1996.

52. Richard B. Freeman, "Who Escapes? The Relation of Church-Going and Other Background Factors to the Socio-Economic Performance of Black Male Youths From Inner-City Poverty Tracts," Working Paper, no. 1656, National Bureau of Economic Research, Cambridge, Mass., 1985.

53. David B. Larson and Byron Johnson, "Who Escapes? Revisited," final draft, 1998, and personal correspondence with Larson, September 1, 1998; David B. Larson and Byron Johnson, *Religion: The Forgotten Factor in Cutting Youth Crime and Saving At-Risk Urban Youth*, a report issued by The Center for Civic Innovation and The Jeremiah Project, The Manhattan Institute (New York, New York, November 13, 1998).

54. Cynthia L. Sipe and Patricia Ma, *Support for Youth: A Profile of Three Communities* (Philadelphia, Pa.: Public/Private Ventures, Spring 1998), p. 31.

55. Sipe and Ma, *Support for Youth*, p. 31.

56. Sipe and Ma, *Support for Youth.* The one exception is the 18-to-20-year-olds of St. Petersburg, who spent only about a third of their after-school time in this way.

57. Sipe and Ma, *Support for Youth,* p. ii.
58. Sipe and Ma, *Support for Youth,* pp. 3, 81.
59. Michelle A. Gambone, *Launching a Resident-Driven Initiative: Community Change for Youth Development (CCYD) from Site Selection to Early Implementation* (Philadelphia, Pa.: Public/Private Ventures, 1997).
60. Cynthia L. Sipe, *Mentoring: A Synthesis of P/PV's Research: 1988–1995* (Philadelphia, Pa.: Public/Private Ventures, 1996).
61. Joseph P. Tierney and Jean Baldwin Grossman, *Making a Difference: An Impact Study of Big Brothers/Big Sisters* (Philadelphia, Pa.: Public/Private Ventures, 1995).
62. Gary Walker, Interview with the author, June 1998.
63. Andrew Billingsley, "The Social Relevance of the Contemporary Black Church," *National Journal of Sociology,* 8, numbers 1 and 2, Summer/Winter 1994, p. 3.
64. Billingsley, "The Social Relevance."
65. Interview with the author, June 1998.
66. Glenn Loury and Linda Datcher-Loury, "Not By Bread Alone," *The Brookings Review,* 15, no. 1, Winter 1997, p. 13.
67. Loury and Datcher-Loury, "Not By Bread Alone," p. 13.
68. Robert L. Woodson Sr., *The Triumphs of Joseph: How Today's Community Healers Are Reviving Our Streets and Neighborhoods* (New York: The Free Press, 1998).
69. Interview with the author, June 1998.
70. Jeremy White and Mary de Marcellus, *Faith-Based Outreach to At-Risk Youth in Washington, D.C.,* a report issued by The Center for Civic Innovation and The Jeremiah Project, The Manhattan Institute (New York, New York, November 13, 1998).
71. White and de Marcellus, *Faith-Based Outreach,* p. 4.
72. White and de Marcellus, *Faith-Based Outreach,* p. 6.
73. White and de Marcellus, *Faith-Based Outreach,* p. 1.
74. Tobi Jennifer Printz, *Faith-Based Service Providers in the Nation's Capital: Can They Do More?* (Washington, D.C.: The Urban Institute, April 1998).
75. Diane Cohen and A. Robert Jaeger, *Sacred Places At Risk* (Philadelphia, Pa.: Partners for Sacred Places, 1998).
76. Lincoln and Mamiya, *The Black Church.*
77. Lincoln and Mamiya, *The Black Church,* p. 151.
78. Lincoln and Mamiya, *The Black Church,* p. 15.
79. Naomi Ward et al., "Black Churches in Atlanta Reach Out to the Community," *National Journal of Sociology,* 8, numbers 1 and 2, Summer/Winter 1994, p. 59.
80. Roger H. Rubin et al., "The Black Church and Adolescent Sexuality," *National Journal of Sociology,* 8, numbers 1 and 2, Summer/Winter 1994, pp. 131, 138.
81. Harold Dean Trulear and Tony Carnes, *A Study of the Social Service Dimension of Theological Education Certificate Programs: The 1997 Theological Certificate Program Survey,* submitted to the Ford Foundation, November 1, 1997.
82. Trulear and Carnes, *Study of the Social Service Dimension,* pp. 34, 40–41.
83. Greely, "The Other Civic America," p. 73.
84. Greely, "The Other Civic America."
85. Richard John Neuhaus, "The Public Square: A Continuing Survey of Religion and Public Life," *First Things,* no. 81, March 1998, pp. 63–65.

# Part Four

# Civil Society: Civic Trust, Social Authority

# 12

# The Lost City: The Case for Social Authority

*Alan Ehrenhalt*

In 1975, after a long but singularly uneventful career in Illinois politics, a round-faced Chicago tavern owner named John G. Fary was rewarded with a promotion to Congress. On the night of his election, at age sixty-four, he announced his agenda for everyone to hear. "I will go to Washington to help represent Mayor Daley," he declared. "For twenty-one years, I represented the mayor in the legislature, and he was always right."

Richard J. Daley died the next year, but Fary soon discovered the same qualities of infallibility in Tip O'Neill, the U.S. House Speaker under whom he served. Over four congressional terms, he never cast a single vote against the Speaker's position on any issue of significance. From the leadership's point of view, he was an automatic yes.

And that, in a sense, was his undoing. Faced with a difficult primary challenge from an aggressive Chicago alderman, Fary had little to talk about other than his legendary willingness to do whatever he was told. The Chicago newspapers made sport of him. "Fary's lackluster record," one of them said, "forfeits his claim to a House seat." He was beaten badly and sent home to his tavern on the Southwest Side to ponder the troubling changes in modern political life.

It was not an easy thing for him to understand. The one principle John Fary had represented for more than thirty years in politics—obedience—had come into obvious disrepute. The legislator who simply followed the rules as they came down to him invited open ridicule as a mindless hack.

No quality is less attractive in American politics these days than obedience—not foolishness or deceit or even blatant corruption. There is no one we are more scornful of than the officeholder who refuses to make choices for himself. There are bumper stickers all over Washington that say, in big block capital letters, QUESTION AUTHORITY. There are none that say, LISTEN TO THE BOSS.

John Fary made a career out of listening to the boss. Of course, he didn't have much alternative. In the Chicago politics of the 1950s, you could either be part of the machine, and entertain a realistic hope of holding office, or be against it, and have virtually no hope at all. Fary actually began as something of an upstart. In 1951, he ran in the Twelfth Ward as a challenger to the Swinarski family, which more or less dominated ward politics in alliance with other machine lieutenants. After that unsuccessful experience, however, Fary made his accommodations to the system; he had no other choice.[1]

If Fary ever chafed at the rules of his constricted political world, he never did so in public. He seemed content voting with the leadership, gratified to be part of an ordered political system, content working behind the bar at his tavern when he was not practicing politics in Springfield or Washington. He didn't appear to give much thought to the possibilities of doing it any other way. When he achieved passage of the one notable legislative initiative of his long career, a state law legalizing bingo, he celebrated by inventing a new drink called "Bingo Bourbon"[2] and serving it to his customers on the house. In the years when John Fary was building a political career out of loyalty on the South Side of Chicago, Ernie Banks was making his baseball career on the North Side. From the day he joined the Chicago Cubs in the fall of 1953, Banks was special: skinny and not very powerful-looking, he swung with his wrists and propelled line drives out of Wrigley Field with a speed that sometimes seemed hard to believe.

The 1950s were a time of glory for Ernie Banks—forty home runs year after year, two Most Valuable Player awards in a row, gushing praise on the sports page—and yet in other ways, his rewards were meager. He played on a string of terrible Cubs teams, so he never came close to appearing in a World Series, and because the fans didn't buy many tickets, the Cubs weren't very generous about salaries. Compared to mediocre ballplayers today, Banks was woefully underpaid, even in the real-dollar terms of his time. In 1959, the year he recorded his second straight MVP season, the Cubs paid him $45,000.

But Banks never considered leaving the Cubs and going to another team. He couldn't, because he was not a free agent. The Cubs owned him, and according to the baseball rules of the 1950s, his only options were to accept the contract they offered him or leave baseball altogether. Like John Fary, he really didn't have any choice.

If Banks spent any time worrying about his limited choices, it didn't show. The Cubs were his team; they had lifted him out of the weedy fields of the Negro leagues, and he belonged with them. After a few years in Chicago, he became famous not only for his home runs but for his loyalty and enthusiasm. He loved to tell reporters about the "friendly confines" of Wrigley Field. Warming up before a doubleheader on a bright summer day, he would say two games weren't enough. "Let's play three!" Banks would exult.

What John Fary was to the present-day politician, Ernie Banks was to the present-day ballplayer. You can compare him, for example, to Rickey Henderson, who in the last fifteen years has stolen more bases than anyone in the history of the game. Henderson will be in the Hall of Fame some day, as Ernie Banks already is. Unlike Banks, however, he has been paid fabulous salaries, and the free agency system has allowed him to jump from team to team in search of money and World Series appearances. And yet he has never seemed content with his situation. Everywhere he has played, he has expressed his frustrations at his contract, at the team management, at the fans, and even, sometimes, at his own play. The market has made Rickey Henderson free, and it has made him rich. It just has not made him happy.

The differences between Ernie Banks and Rickey Henderson are, of course, partly a matter of temperament. Some people are content by nature, and some are restless. In another sense, though, they are a metaphor for the changes in American life over the past forty years. Today we live in a time of profuse choice, with all the opportunity and disillusionment that it brings. Ernie Banks and John Fary lived in a world where choice was much more limited—where those in authority made decisions that the free market now throws open to endless individual reexamination.

This observation applies not only to baseball and politics but to all of the important personal relationships in life. In an average year of the 1950s, the number of divorces in the United States was about ten per one thousand marriages—barely a third of what it was to become by 1980.[3] This was not because divorce was impossible to obtain—although it was difficult in a few states—or because it made anyone an outcast in the community. It was because divorce was simply not on the menu of options for most people, no matter how difficult or stressful life might become. The couples of the 1950s got married on the assumption that it was their job to make things work the best way they could. Like Ernie Banks and John Fary, they played the hand they were dealt, and refrained from agonizing over what might have been.

People just stayed married in the 1950s, to their spouses, to their political machines, to their baseball teams. Corporations also stayed married—to the communities they grew up with. Any one of a thousand examples could illustrate that point, but one will do: the story of the Lennox Corporation and its hometown, Marshalltown, Iowa.

In 1895, David Lennox invented a new kind of steel furnace and set up a business in Marshalltown. As the years went by, his company prospered as a manufacturer of boilers and, later, air conditioners. The Lennox Corporation became a solid source of respectable factory jobs that enabled generations of blue-collar families to enjoy the comforts of middle-class life. Its managers helped with countless local fairs, fund drives, and school building campaigns.

Lennox probably could have improved its profit margins in the 1950s by moving to a place where labor was cheaper, but its loyalty was to Marshalltown. Eventually, though, company officials did investigate other locations.

In the late 1970s Lennox moved its corporate headquarters to Dallas, arguing that a small town in central Iowa was inconvenient for the air travel needs of its executives. The factory stayed where it was.

In 1993, Lennox grew even more restless and announced that it might have to close the Marshalltown plant altogether, not because the company was losing money, or facing any sort of crisis, but just because the time had come to seek out the best opportunities. The fact that Marshalltown's very survival might depend on Lennox was of no consequence. "Strictly a business decision," the company vice president said. In the end, Marshalltown managed to keep Lennox—with what amounted to a bribe of $20 million in subsidies paid out by a local government that badly needed the money to a profitable corporation that really didn't.

If one marker that sets off America today from America a generation ago is our attitude toward choice, then another is our attitude toward physical space.[4]

To be a young homeowner in a suburb like Elmhurst in the 1950s was to participate in a communal enterprise that only the most determined loner could escape: barbecues, coffee klatches, volleyball games, baby-sitting co-ops and constant bartering of household goods, child rearing by the nearest parents who happened to be around, neighbors wandering through the door at any hour without knocking—all these were the devices by which young adults who had been set down in a wilderness of tract homes made a community. It was a life lived in public.

To live in a bungalow in St. Nick's parish was to live in a place where the walls of one's house did not constitute boundaries, where social life was conducted on the front stoop and in the alley, and where, even inside the house, four or five children in a three-bedroom home made privacy a rare commodity. Television was coming to such neighborhoods in the 1950s, but air-conditioning had not yet arrived, and summer evenings were one long community festival, involving just about everybody on the block and brought to an end only by darkness and the need to go to sleep.

And in the kitchenette and small-apartment world of Bronzeville, privacy was little more than a mirage. Sharing kitchens and bathrooms, sleeping on fire escapes to avoid the heat, residents performed on a public stage that recalls the swirling slum confusion of eighteenth-century London or Paris. To live in a kitchenette at Forty-third and Indiana in the 1950s was to do everything in public—to dance, drink, and even make love with somebody watching. It was an unrelentingly public world. As Cayton and Drake wrote in *Black Metropolis:* "In the black ghetto, privacy is one of the rarest of the good things of life."

The people who lived in these communities, moreover, went out of their way to make their lives more public still by joining clubs and organizations of every sort. The ranch-house suburb was a jumble of bridge clubs, book clubs, square-dancing societies—groups that men as well as women joined willingly, if sometimes grumpily, and to which they devoted large chunks of whatever free time they had. The parishioners of St. Nick's lived their lives not only through the church but through its subsidiary organizations, the Holy Name Society, the Altar and Rosary—engines of mass neighborhood participation that brought five hundred or more residents of a single neighborhood to pancake breakfasts at seven o'clock on a weekday morning. The more ambitious black residents of the South Side, many of them trapped in substandard housing and menial service jobs, compensated by creating a wealth of social clubs that helped at suppers and formal dances, generated endless coverage in the local black newspaper, and added dignity to neighborhood life that was not achievable any other way. They were joiners par excellence.

In the intervening years, the balance between public and private has changed in American life. Television and air-conditioning brought people inside, off the porches. The two-income family of today has little time for clubs or organized social activity. The departure of the black middle class from the South Side has obliterated the respectable social world that existed there in the 1950s; it has left behind a world in which privacy is still difficult to come by, but in which the only semblance of organized social life revolves around the pathology of drugs, gangs, and violence.

One should not go too far in romanticizing this more public urban life of the 1950s. It was hard at all levels on those who did not want to belong—who wanted to retreat inside the home at the end of the day, to skip the bridge club or the church social affair, who had more than enough fellowship in the course of the working routine. It was a world that offered few places to hide, in a very literal sense. Community was achieved, for many people, at a cost of intrusion and lack of privacy that nearly all of us would instantly regard as too high today.

In many ways, the hyperindividualism that characterizes the baby-boom generation is a reaction to the close quarters in which its members grew up during the 1950s. In the schools, hordes of children gridlocked the corridors and the infamous one-way staircases. The average elementary school class size in America in the 1950s was thirty-three, well above the "ideal" size of twenty-five to thirty. The number did not drop until the 1960s were well along.

Life at home produced the same sorts of memories, whether it was a matter of five children sleeping in two tiny bungalow bedrooms or of living in an open-plan suburban house in which walls hardly seemed to exist. Wherever they grew up, the children of the 1950s usually did so without a great deal of privacy.

The worship of privacy is, like the worship of choice and the fear of authority, rooted so deeply in our end-of-century value system that it has been virtually immune to serious debate, let alone reconsideration. But it is time to reconsider it nonetheless, and to confront the possibility that all of these self-evident contemporary "truths" are doing far more harm than good as they persist in the closing years of the century.

In the Chicago of 1957, most people believed, as many of us have ceased to believe, there were natural limits to life. They understood, whether they lived in a bungalow, tenement, or suburb, that choice and privacy were restricted commodities, and that authority existed, in large part, to manage the job of restricting them. Most people were prepared to live with this bargain most of the time. And they believed in one other important idea that has been lost in the decades since: they believed in the existence of sin. The Chicago of the 1950s was a time and place in which ordinary people lived with good and evil, right and wrong, sins and sinners, in a way that is almost incomprehensible to most of us on the other side of the 1960s moral deluge.

If it is true to say of 1950s America that it was a world of limited choices, it is also fair to call it a world of lasting relationships. This was as true of commerce as it was of sports and politics, and it was nearly as true of the smallest commercial transactions as it was of the big ones.

When John Fary was not busy at politics, he was the proprietor of the 3600 Club, at the corner of Thirty-sixth and South Damen Avenue, in the Back of the Yards neighborhood of Chicago, where his father had run a tavern before him. Fary lived in an apartment above the bar, and operated the place himself most of the time.

There was a saloon like Fary's on virtually every block of his neighborhood during most of the years of his life. Each saloon was a sort of community center, a place where stockyards workers, factory workers, cops, and city patronage employees repaired at the end of the day to rest and to recycle their earnings back through the neighborhood.

When it came to picking a saloon to patronize, these people actually had quite a bit of choice. Just within walking distance there were a dozen possibilities. Fary's own brother operated a similar establishment a couple of blocks away. But once a customer chose his bar, because he liked the smell of it or liked the people he found there, it was his. The market was not a factor. He didn't switch to another tavern because he heard that Hamm's was available on tap for five cents less. The residents of this neighborhood weren't hard-nosed consumers in the current sense. They had a different view of what was important in life.

It takes only the briefest of excursions back into the daily routine of an imaginary family in John Fary's neighborhood, circa 1957, to demonstrate that theirs was indeed a different sort of life altogether.

From the meal that started off the morning, in which the selection of cereals was tiny and the bread was always white, to the recreation in the evening, provided by a TV that received four stations, most of them carrying a western or a quiz show at any given moment, this family lived in a world where choice was highly limited and authority meant something it does not mean anymore. It was a world for which Wonder Bread and black-and-white TV are appropriate symbols. It was not necessary to make room for Pop-Tarts or toaster strudel, the Nashville Network or CNN.

If the breadwinner in this family drove to work in the morning, he almost certainly did it without the benefit of radio traffic commentators advising him on the best way to get there. One of the Chicago radio stations actually did institute a traffic alert feature in 1957, with a police officer hovering above the city in a helicopter, but most of the people who heard it were bewildered about what to do with the information. Wherever they were going, they had very few routes to choose from: the option of selecting the least congested freeway did not exist for most of them because the freeways themselves did not exist yet. They chose a city street and stayed on it until they reached their destination. If it was slow, it was slow.

Nor did this breadwinner have many choices, whether he worked in a factory or an office, about when to start the workday, when to take a break, or when to go to lunch. Those decisions, too, were out of the realm of choice for most employees in 1957, determined instead by the dictate of management or by the equally forceful strictures of habit. How to arrange the hours on the job was one of the many questions that the ordinary workers of the 1950s, white-collar and blue-collar alike, did not spend much time agonizing over.

The wife of this breadwinner, if she did not have a job herself, was likely to devote a substantial portion of her day to shopping, banking, and the other routines of household economic management. Like her husband, she faced relatively few personal decisions about where and how to do her daily activities. The chances are she took care of her finances at a place in the neighborhood, where she could deposit money, cash checks, and, at the end of the quarter, enjoy the satisfaction of recording a regular savings dividend. She knew the teller personally—the teller had been with the bank as long as she had, if not longer. But it was also likely that she knew the manager, and perhaps the owner. Once she opened an account, there was no need to reexamine the issue, no reason to check on what the competing bank further down Archer Avenue was offering for her money. They all offered about the same thing anyway.

Shopping, in the same way, was based on associations that were, if not permanent, then at least stable for long periods of time. The grocer was a man with whom the family had a relationship; even if his store was a small "supermarket," shoppers tended to personalize it: "I'm going down to Sam's for a minute," women told their children when they left in the afternoon to pick up a cartful of groceries. Because of fair trade laws and other economic regulations, the neighborhood grocery of 1957 was in fact reasonably competitive in price with the new mega-groceries in the suburbs, but price was not the important issue. Day-to-day commerce was based on relationships—on habit, not on choice.

If this Chicagoan had young children, there is a good chance she also spent part of her day on some school-related activity, volunteering around the building or attending a meeting of the PTA. When it came to schools, her family likely faced one important decision: public or Catholic. Once that decision was made, there were few others remaining. The idea of selecting the best possible school environment for one's children would have seemed foreign to these people; one lived within the boundaries of a district or a parish, and that determined where the children went to school. If St. Cecilia's or Thomas Edison wasn't quite as good as its counterpart a mile away (fairly improbable, given the uniformity of the product)—well, that was life.

It should not be necessary to belabor the question of how all these rituals have changed in the decades since then. Our daily lives today are monuments to selection, and to making for ourselves decisions that someone above us used to make in our behalf. We breakfast on choice (sometimes on products literally named for it); take any of several alternative but equally frustrating routes to work; shop in stores whose clerks do not know us; bank in banks where we need to show identification after twenty years, because the teller has been there two weeks; come home to a television set offering so many choices that the newspaper can't devise a grid to show them all.

In the past generation, we have moved whole areas of life, large and small, out of the realm of permanence and authority and into the realm of change and choice. We have gained the psychological freedom to ask ourselves at any moment not only whether we are eating the right cereal but whether we are in the right neighborhood, the right job, the right relationship.

This is, of course, in large measure a function of technology. Birth-control pills created new social and sexual options for women; instantaneous communication by computer made possible all the global options of the footloose corporation. And it is in part a function of simple affluence. Choices multiply in tandem with the dollars we have to invest in them.

But our love affair with choice has not been driven solely by machines, and it has not been driven solely by money. The Baby Boom generation was seduced by the idea of choice in and of itself.

Most of us continue to celebrate the explosion of choice and personal freedom in our time. There are few among us who are willing to say it is a bad bargain, or who mourn for the rigidities and constrictions of American life in the 1950s.

A remarkable number of us, however, do seem to mourn for something about that time. We talk nostalgically of the loyalties and lasting relationships that characterized those days: of the old neighborhoods with mom-and-pop storekeepers who knew us by name; of not having to lock the house at night because no one would think of entering it; of knowing that there would be a neighbor home, whatever the time of day or night, to help us out or take us in if we happened to be in trouble.

There is a longing, among millions of Americans now reaching middle age, for a sense of community that they believe existed during their childhoods and does not exist now. That is why there is a modern movement called communitarianism that has attracted many adherents and much attention. "I want to live in a place again where I can walk down any street without being afraid," Hillary Rodham Clinton said shortly after becoming first lady. "I want to be able to take my daughter to a park at any time of day or night in the summer and remember what I used to be able to do when I was a little kid." Those sorts of feelings, and a nostalgia for the benefits of old-fashioned community life at the neighborhood level, are only growing stronger as a new century dawns.[5]

The very word community has found a place, however fuzzy and imprecise, all over the ideological spectrum of the present decade. On the far left it is a code word for a more egalitarian society in which the oppressed of all colors are included and made the beneficiaries of a more generous social welfare system that commits far more than the current amount to education, public health, and the eradication of poverty. On the far right it signifies an emphasis on individual self-discipline that would replace the welfare state with a private rebirth of personal responsibility. In the middle it seems to reflect a much simpler yearning for safety, stability, and a network of reliable relationships. Despite these differing perceptions, though, the general idea of community has been all over the pages of popular journalism and political discourse in the first half of the 1990s.

Authority is something else again. It evokes no similar feelings of nostalgia. Few would dispute that it has eroded over the last generation. Walk into a large public high school in a typical middle-class suburb today, and you will see a principal who must spend huge portions of his or her day having to cajole recalcitrant students, teachers, and staff into accepting direction that, a generation ago, they would have accepted unquestioningly just because the principal was the principal and they were subordinates.

Or consider the mainstream Protestant church. We haven't yet reached the point where parishioners curse their minister in the same way high school students curse their teachers, but if it is even a faintly liberal congregation, there is a good chance that the minister has lost his title: he is no longer "Dr." but "Jim," or "Bob," or whatever his friends like to call him. Putting the minister on a level with his parishioners is one small step in the larger unraveling of authority.

Authority and community have in fact unraveled together, but few mourn the passing of authority. To most Americans in the baby-boom generation, it will always be a word with sinister connotations, calling forth a rush of uncomfortable memories about the schools, churches, and families in which they grew up. Rebellion against those memories constituted the defining event of their generational lives. Wherever on the political spectrum this generation has landed, it has brought its suspicion of authority with it. "Authority," says P. J. O'Rourke, speaking for his baby-boom cohort loud and clear, "has always attracted the lowest elements in the human race."[6]

The suspicion of authority and the enshrinement of personal choice are everywhere in the American society of the 1990s. They extend beyond the routines of our individual lives in to the debates we conduct on topics as diverse as school reform and corporate management.

Of all the millions of words devoted in the past decade to the subject of educational change, hardly any have suggested improving the schools by putting the rod back in the teacher's hand, or returning to a curriculum of required memorization and classroom drill. The center of the discussion is the concept of school choice: the right of families to decide for themselves which schools their children will attend. Many things may be said for and against the concept of school choice, but one point is clear enough—in education, as in virtually every other social enterprise, individual choice is the antithesis of authority. It is a replacement for it.

Similarly, one can comb the shelves of a bookstore crowded with volumes on corporate management without coming across one that defends the old-fashioned pyramid in which orders come down from the chief executive, military-style, and descend intact to the lower reaches of the organization. There are corporations that still operate that way, but they are regarded as dinosaurs. Corporate hierarchies are out of fashion. The literature is all about constructing management out of webs rather than pyramids, about decentralizing the decision process, empowering people at all levels of the organization. The phrase "command and control" is the obscenity of present-day management writing.

Five years ago, few Americans were familiar with the command economy. Now, virtually all of us know what it means. It is the definition of a society that fails because it attempts to make economic decisions by hierarchy rather than by the free choice of its individual citizens. It is the most broadly agreed-upon reason for the abject failure of communism around the world. The communist implosion both reinforced and seemed to validate baby boomers' generational suspicions about hierarchy and authority in all their manifestations, foreign and domestic, the American CEOs and school principals of the 1950s almost as much as the dictators who made life miserable in authoritarian countries around the world.

Not surprisingly, what has happened in education and economics has also happened in the precincts of political thought. There has in fact been a discussion about authority among political philosophers in the past two decades, and its tone tells us something. It has been a debate in which scholars who profess to find at least some value in the concept have struggled to defend themselves against libertarian critics who question whether there is any such thing as legitimate authority at all, even for duly constituted democratic governments.

America is full of people willing to remind us at every opportunity that the 1950s are not coming back. Ozzie and Harriet are dead, they like to say, offering an instant refutation to just about anyone who ventures to point out something good about the social arrangements of a generation ago—conventional families, traditional neighborhoods, more stable patterns of work, school, politics, religion. All of these belong, it is said, to a world that no longer exists and cannot be retrieved. We have moved on.

And of course they are right. If retrieving the values of the 1950s means recreating a world of men in fedora hats returning home at the end of the day to women beaming at them with apron and carpet sweeper, then the idea is indeed foolish. It was an exaggeration even in 1957.

But the real questions raised by our journey back to the 1950s are much more complicated, and they have nothing to do with "Ozzie and Harriet" or "Leave It to Beaver." They are questions like these: Can we impose some controls on the chaos of individual choice that we have created in the decades since then? Can we develop a majority culture strong enough to tell children that there are inappropriate ways to behave in a high school corridor and that there are programs that eight-year-olds should not be free to watch on television? Is there a way to relearn the simple truth that there is sin in the world and that part of our job in life is to resist its temptations?

The quickest way of dealing with these questions is to say that the genie is out of the bottle and there is no way to put it back. Once people free themselves from rules and regulations, and taste the temptations of choice, they will never return to a more ordered world. Once they have been told they do not have to stay married—to their spouses, communities, careers, or any of the commitments that used to be made for life—they will be on the loose forever. Once the global economy convinces corporations that there is no need for the personal and community loyalties they once practiced, those loyalties are a dead letter. So we will be told many times in the years to come.

But is it true? Is the only sequel to social disorder further disorder? There are other scenarios, if we do not mind making a leap to look for them.

There is no doubt that nostalgia plays strange tricks on us. It plays them in our individual lives, filtering out the complexities of childhood and adolescence, so that we see them as uncomplicated even if they were not always very happy. Perhaps, it can be argued, our societal memory works the same way: we filter out the complexity so that life always appears to have been simple and then to have come apart in the last generation.

After all, the desire to escape from rigid authority and stifling communities is what this country has always been about. It is the force that brought millions of people here from Europe and drove them west across the continent, leaving behind extended families, close-knit villages, and clearer sets of social rules. Perhaps those who talk about the decline of community and authority have merely been noticing some of the downside of the American experience, and disguising those feelings in the mistaken notion that the country's values were somehow different a generation earlier.

One can argue quite plausibly that the modern history of Western civilization is itself a history of eroding community and authority, reaching back to the Reformation, if not further; that the West has spent the last five hundred years moving inexorably away from the values of tribe and hierarchy and village life and toward individualism and the market. Perhaps all we have done since the 1950s is play out the process one generation further.

It is a tempting proposition, and carries with it the potential to trump virtually all the arguments one can make about the losses of the past generation. It is a means of minimizing not just the eclipse of familiar social institutions but the transience of personal relationships and the decline of the notions of character and virtue. Relax, we are told. It is normal to worry about the quickening pace of society, the erosion of old standards, the depersonalization of everyday life. The task for the years ahead is not to nurse the memories of the old days; it is to prepare for the changed world of the twenty-first century.

The argument is seductive, but ultimately it does not work. It collapses in the face of all the tangible changes of the past forty years that we cannot live through a day without encountering.

Nostalgic illusion does not explain the disappearance of lasting relationships between merchant and customer in the commercial life of a neighborhood or suburb. It does not explain the willingness of profitable corporations to leave the communities that nurtured them in an aimless quest for a higher stock price. Those are genuine changes and genuine losses. What explains them is our worship of choice. It is true that in the 1950s, traditionalists were already lamenting that the corner grocery store was not what it had been a generation earlier. But that does not argue against the magnitude of what has transpired between the 1950s and the present, or suggest that it is somehow irrational to point out that some of the most important foundations of a stable neighborhood life are now gone.

Nor does nostalgia account for the public high schools where, in the 1950s, the principal passed out ropes to boys who failed to wear belts each day, but where today the most offensive displays of speech, dress, and conduct are now regarded as individual liberties and protected from discipline. Only a wave of individualism and disrespect for authority is powerful enough to explain that. There is no denying that the parents and teachers of the 1950s were already fearful of juvenile delinquency and youthful disrespect. But the realities of the 1990s dwarf those concerns, not because of any nostalgic illusions, but because the problem itself has expanded in geometric terms.

Memory may play tricks on all of us, but the flight from authority and the enshrinement of individualism and choice in the last forty years do not represent lapses of memory, personal or societal. They represent losses that it is altogether rational to mourn.

The America of the 1990s may be a welter of confused values, but on one point we speak with unmistakable clarity: we have become emancipated from social authority as we used to know it.

We don't want the 1950s back. What we want is to edit them. We want to keep the safe streets, the friendly grocers, and the milk and cookies, while blotting out the political bosses, the tyrannical headmasters, the inflexible rules, and the lectures on 100 percent Americanism and the sinfulness of dissent. But there is no easy way to have an orderly world without somebody making the rules by which order is preserved. Every dream we have about re-creating community in the absence of authority will turn out to be a pipe dream in the end.

This is a lesson that people who call themselves conservatives sometimes seem determined not to learn. There are many on the right who, while devoting themselves unquestioningly to the ideology of the free market, individual rights, and personal choice, manage to betray their longing for old-fashioned community and a world of lasting relationships. In the 1980s, Ronald Reagan was one of them. His 1984 reelection campaign, built around a series of "Morning in America" television commercials featuring stage-set small-town Main Streets of the sort Reagan strolled down in his youth and in Hollywood movies, was a small token of communitarian rhetoric in the midst of a decade of unraveling economic and moral standards. But when people tell us markets and unlimited choice are good for communities and traditional values, the burden of proof is on them, not on us.

It is the disruptiveness of the market that has taken away the neighborhood savings and loan, with its familiar veteran tellers, and set down in its place a branch of Citibank where no one has worked a month and where the oldest depositor has to slide his driver's license under the window. It is market power that has replaced the locally owned newspaper, in most of the cities in America, with a paper whose owner is a corporate executive far away and whose publisher is a middle manager stopping in town for a couple of years on his way to a higher position at headquarters. Once the pressures of the global market persuaded the Lennox Corporation that it had the moral freedom of choice to make air conditioners wherever in the world it wanted, the bonds that had tied it to a small town in Iowa for nearly a century were breakable.

In its defense, one can say that the global market onslaught of the last two decades was technologically inevitable, or more positively, that it is the best guarantor of individual freedom, and that individual freedom is the most important value for us to preserve. Or one can say that the market puts more dollars in the ordinary citizen's pocket, and that after all, the bottom line should be the bottom line. But in the end there is no escaping the reality that the market is a force for disruption of existing relationships. To argue that markets are the true friend of community is an inversion of common sense. And to idealize markets and call oneself a conservative is to distort reality.

To worship choice and community together is to misunderstand what community is all about. Community means not subjecting every action in life to the burden of choice, but rather accepting the familiar and reaping the psychological benefits of having one less calculation to make in the course of the day. It is about being Ernie Banks and playing for the Chicago Cubs for twenty years; or being John Fary and sticking with the Daley machine for life; or being one of John Fary's customers and sticking with his tavern at Thirty-sixth and South Damen year in and year out. It is being the Lennox Corporation and knowing that Marshalltown, Iowa, will always be your home.

It would similarly be a pleasure to allow one's children to watch television or listen to the radio without having to worry that they will be seeing or hearing obscenity, but here, too, the market has assumed a role that used to be occupied by authority.

Consider television in the 1950s. No doubt there would have been considerable viewer demand for a pornographic version of *Some Like It Hot,* or perhaps a version of *20,000 Leagues Under the Sea* in which Kirk Douglas was eaten alive in CinemaScope by the giant squid. Those things were absent from television in the 1950s not because no one would have watched them, but because there were sanctions against their being shown. There was someone in a position of authority—in this case, a censor—who stepped in to overrule the market and declare that some things are too lurid, too violent, or too profane for a mass audience to see.

It is in the absence of such authority that five-year-olds can conveniently watch MTV or listen to Howard Stern, and twelve-year-olds can buy rap albums that glorify gangsterism, murder, and rape. It is a matter of free choice. Obscenity and violence sell, and we do not feel comfortable ordering anyone, even children, not to choose them. We are unwilling as yet to pay the price that decency in public entertainment will require. But if children are not to gorge themselves on violent entertainment, then it is an inconvenient fact that someone besides the children themselves must occupy a position of authority.

Some readers will no doubt object that I am portraying the 1950s as a premodern, precapitalist Eden. I am not that naive. Nobody who spends any time studying the period—nobody who lived through it—can entertain for long the notion that it was a time in which people were insulated from market forces. The 1950s were the decade of tail fins, mass-produced suburban subdivisions, and the corruption of television quiz shows by greedy sponsors. The market was immensely powerful; it was the enemy that an entire generation of postwar social critics took aim against.

In the 1950s, however, a whole array of social institutions still stood outside the grip of the market and provided ordinary people with a cushion against it. In the last generation, as Alan Wolfe and others have eloquently pointed out, that cushion has disappeared. The difference between the 1950s and the 1990s is to a large extent the difference between a society in which market forces challenged traditional values and a society in which they have triumphed over them.

And the decisiveness of that triumph is written in the values that the baby-boom generation has carried with them from youth on into middle age: the belief in individual choice and the suspicion of any authority that might interfere with it.

Of course, there will be quite a few people to whom none of this makes any sense, people who believe that individual choice is the most important standard, period; that no society can ever get enough of it; that the problem in the last generation is not that we have abandoned authority but that there are still a few vestiges of it yet to be eradicated. Many of these people call themselves libertarians, and arguing with them is complicated by the fact that they are nearly always intelligent, interesting, and personally decent.

Libertarian ideas are seductive and would be nearly impossible to challenge if one thing were true—if we lived in a world full of P. J. O'Rourkes, all of us bright and articulate and individualistic, and wanting nothing more than the freedom to try all the choices and experiments that life has to offer, to express our individuality in an endless series of new and creative ways.

But this belief is the libertarian fallacy: the idea that the world is full of repressed libertarians, waiting to be freed from the bondage of rules and authority. Perhaps, if this were true, life would be more interesting. But what the libertarians failed to notice, as they squirmed awkwardly though childhood in what seemed to them the straitjacket of school and family and church, is that most people are not like them. Most people want a chart to follow and are not happy when they don't have one, or when they learned one as children and later see people all around them ignoring it. While the legitimacy of any particular set of rules is a subject that philosophers will always debate, it nonetheless remains true, and in the end more important, that the uncharted life, the life of unrestricted choice and eroded authority, is one most ordinary people do not enjoy leading.

There is no point in pretending that the 1950s were a happy time for everyone in America. For many, the price of the limited life was impossibly high. To have been an independent-minded alderman in the Daley machine, a professional baseball player treated unfairly by his team, a suburban housewife who yearned for a professional career, a black high school student dreaming of possibilities that were closed to him, a gay man or woman forced to conduct a charade in public—to have been any of these things in the 1950s was to live a life that was difficult at best, and tragic at worst. That is why so many of us still respond to the memory of those indignities by saying that nothing in the world could justify them.

It is a powerful indictment, but it is also a selective one. While it is often said that history is written by the winners, the truth is that the cultural images that come down to us as history are written, in large part, by the dissenters—by those whose strong feelings against life in a particular generation motivate them to become the novelists, playwrights, and social critics of the next, drawing inspiration from the injustices and hypocrisies of the time in which they grew up. We have learned much of what we know about family life in America in the 1950s from women who chafed under its restrictions, either as young, college-educated housewives who found it unfulfilling or as teenage girls secretly appalled by the prom-and-cheerleader social milieu. Much of the image of American Catholic life in those years comes from the work of former Catholics who considered the church they grew up in not only authoritarian but destructive of their free choices and creative instincts. The social critics of the past two decades have forced on our attention the inconsistencies and absurdities of life a generation ago: the pious skirt-chasing husbands, the martini-sneaking ministers, the sadistic gym teachers.

I am not arguing with the accuracy of any of those individual memories. But our collective indignation makes little room for the millions of people who took the rules seriously and tried to live up to them, within the profound limits of human weakness. They are still around, the true believers of the 1950s, in small towns and suburbs and big-city neighborhoods all over the country, reading the papers, watching television, and wondering in old age what has happened to America in the last thirty years. If you visit middle-class American suburbs today, and talk to the elderly women who have lived out their adult years in these places, they do not tell you how constricted and demeaning their lives in the 1950s were. They tell you those were the best years they can remember. And if you visit a working-class Catholic parish in a big city, and ask the older parishioners what they think of the church in the days before Vatican II, they don't tell you that it was tyrannical or that it destroyed their individuality. They tell you they wish they could have it back. For them, the erosion of both community and authority in the last generation is not a matter of intellectual debate. It is something they can feel in their bones, and the feeling makes them shiver.

## NOTES

1. *Career of John G. Fary: Congressional Quarterly Weekly Report,* April 3, 1982, p. 779; *Governing Magazine,* August 1992, p. 6.

2. "Bingo Bourbon": obituary of John G. Fary, *Chicago Tribune,* June 8, 1984.

3. *Divorce Rate Statistics: U.S. Department of Commerce, Bureau of the Census, Statistical Abstract of the United States* (Government Printing Office, 1958 and 1994), p. 72 (1958) and p. 104 (1994).

4. Lennox Corporation and Marshalltown, Iowa: *Governing Magazine,* July 1993, p. 9.

5. Hillary Rodham Clinton on being able to "walk down any street": quoted in profile by Michael Kelly, *New York Times Magazine,* May 23, 1993.

6. P. J. O'Rourke on authority: P. J. O'Rourke, *A Parliament of Whores* (New York: Vintage, 1992), p. 233.

# 13

# Trust: The Social Virtues and the Creation of Prosperity

*Francis Fukuyama*

The early 1990s saw a flood of writing about the information revolution and the transformation that will be brought to everyone's doorstep as a result of the information superhighway. One of the most consistent and widely heralded themes of information age futurologists is that this technological revolution will spell the end of hierarchy of all sorts—political, economic, and social. As the story goes, information is power, and those at the top of traditional hierarchies maintained their dominance by controlling access to information. Modern communications technologies—telephones, fax machines, copiers, cassettes, VCRs, and the centrally important networked personal computer—have broken this stranglehold on information. The result, according to information age gurus from Alvin and Heidi Toffler and George Gilder to Vice President Al Gore and House Speaker Newt Gingrich, will be a devolution of power downward to the people and a liberation of everyone from the constraints of the centralized, tyrannical organizations in which they once worked.[1]

Information technology has indeed contributed to many of the decentralizing and democratizing tendencies of the past generation. It has been widely remarked that the electronic media have contributed to the fall of tyrannical regimes, including the Marcos dictatorship in the Philippines and communist rule in East Germany and the former Soviet Union.[2] But information age theorists argue that technology is deadly to all forms of hierarchy, including the giant corporations that employ the vast majority of American workers. The dislodging of IBM from its once-legendary dominance of the computer industry by upstarts like Sun Microsystems and Compaq during the 1980s is often presented as a morality play, where small, flexible, innovative entrepreneurship challenges large, centralized, bureaucratized tradition and is handsomely rewarded. A variety of authors have argued that as a result of the telecommunications revolution, all of us will someday be working in small, networked "virtual" corporations. That is, firms will ruthlessly downsize until they have stripped out all activities but their "core competence," contracting out through glass telephone lines to other small firms for everything from supplies and raw materials to accounting and marketing services.[3] Some argue that networks of small organizations, rather than large hierarchies or chaotic markets, will be the wave of the future, all driven by the relentless advance of electronic technology. Spontaneous community, not chaos and anarchy, will emerge only if society is freed from the centralized authority of large organizations, from the federal government to IBM and AT&T. With technologically powered communications, good information will drive out bad information, the honest and industrious will shun the fraudulent and parasitic, and people will come together voluntarily for beneficial common purposes.[4]

Clearly broad changes will be brought about by the information revolution, but the age of large, hierarchical organizations is far from over. Many information age futurologists overgeneralize from the computer industry, whose fast-changing technology does in fact tend to reward small and flexible firms. But many other areas of economic life, from building airliners and automobiles to fabricating silicon wafers, require ever-increasing amounts of capital, technology, and people to master. Even within the communications industry, fiber optic transmission favors a single, giant long-distance company, and it is no accident that by 1995 AT&T had grown back to the size it was in 1984, when 85 percent of the firm was divested into local telephone companies.[5] Information technology will help some small firms do large tasks better but will not eliminate the need for scale.

More important, when the information age's most enthusiastic apostles celebrate the breakdown of hierarchy and authority, they neglect one critical factor: trust, and the shared ethical norms that underlie it. Communities depend on mutual trust and will not arise spontaneously without it. Hierarchies are necessary because not all people within a community can be relied upon to live by tacit ethical rules alone. A small number may be actively asocial, seeking to undermine or exploit the group through fraud or simple mischievousness. A much larger number will tend to be free riders, willing to benefit from membership in the group while contributing as little as possible to the common cause. Hierarchies are necessary because all people cannot be trusted at all times to live by internalized ethical rules and do their fair share. They must ultimately be coerced by explicit rules and sanctions in the event they do not live up to them. This is true in the economy as well as in society more broadly: large corporations have their origins in the fact that it is very costly to contract out for goods or services with people one does not know well or trust. Consequently, firms found it more economical to bring outside contractors into their own organization, where they could be supervised directly.

Trust does not reside in integrated circuits or fiber optic cables. Although it involves an exchange of information, trust is not reducible to information. A "virtual" firm can have abundant information coming though network wires about its suppliers and contractors. But if they are all crooks or frauds, dealing with them will remain a costly process involving complex contracts and time-consuming enforcement. Without trust, there will be a strong incentive to bring these activities in-house and restore the old hierarchies.

Thus, it is far from clear that the information revolution makes large, hierarchical organizations obsolete or that spontaneous community will emerge once hierarchy has been undermined. Since community depends on trust, and trust in turn is culturally determined, it follows that spontaneous community will emerge in differing degrees in different cultures. The ability of companies to move from large hierarchies to flexible networks of smaller firms will depend, in other words, on the degree of trust and social capital present in the broader society. A high-trust society like Japan created networks well before the information revolution got into high gear; a low-trust society may never be able to take advantage of the efficiencies that information technology offers.

Trust is the expectation that arises within a community of regular, honest, and cooperative behavior, based on commonly shared norms, on the part of other members of that community.[6] Those norms can be about deep "value" questions like the nature of God or justice, but they also encompass secular norms like professional standards and codes of behavior. That is, we trust a doctor not to do us deliberate injury because we expect him or her to live by the Hippocratic oath and the standards of the medical profession.

Social capital is a capability that arises from the prevalence of trust in a society or in certain parts of it. It can be embodied in the smallest and most basic social group, the family, as well as the largest of all groups, the nation, and in all the other groups in between. Social capital differs from other forms of human capital insofar as it is usually created and transmitted through cultural mechanisms like religion, tradition, or historical habit. Economists typically argue that the formation of social groups can be explained as the result of voluntary contract between individuals who have made the rational calculation that cooperation is in their long-term self-interest. By this account, trust is not necessary for cooperation: enlightened self-interest, together with legal mechanisms like contracts, can compensate for an absence of trust and allow strangers jointly to create an organization that will work for a common purpose. Groups can be formed at any time based on self-interest, and group formation is not culture-dependent.

But while contract and self-interest are important sources of association, the most effective organizations are based on communities of shared ethical values. These communities do not require extensive contract and legal regulation of their relations because prior moral consensus gives members of the group a basis for mutual trust.

The social capital needed to create this kind of moral community cannot be acquired, as in the case of other forms of human capital, through a rational investment decision. That is, an individual can decide to "invest" in conventional human capital like a college education, or training to become a machinist or computer programmer, simply by going to the appropriate school. Acquisition of social capital, by contrast, requires habituation to the moral norms of a community and, in its context, the acquisition of virtues like loyalty, honesty, and dependability. The group, moreover, has to adopt common norms as a whole before trust can become generalized among its members. In other words, social capital cannot be acquired simply by individuals acting on their own. It is based on the prevalence of social, rather than individual virtues. The proclivity for sociability is much harder to acquire than other forms of human capital, but because it is based on ethical habit, it is also harder to modify or destroy.

Another term that I will use widely is *spontaneous sociability*, which constitutes a subset of social capital. In any modern society, organizations are being constantly created, destroyed, and modified. The most useful kind of social capital is often not the ability to work under the authority of a traditional community or group, but the capacity to form new associations and to cooperate within the terms of reference they establish. This type of group, spawned by industrial society's complex division of labor and yet based on shared values rather than contract, falls under the general rubric of what Durkheim labeled "organic solidarity."[7] Spontaneous sociability, moreover, refers to that wide range of intermediate communities distinct from the family or those deliberately established by governments. Governments often have to step in to promote community when there is a deficit of spontaneous sociability. But state intervention poses distinct risks, since it can all too easily undermine the spontaneous communities established in civil society.

Social capital has major consequences for the nature of the industrial economy that society will be able to create. If people who have to work together in an enterprise trust one another because they are all operating according to a common set of ethical norms, doing business costs less. Such a society will be better able to innovate organizationally, since the high degree of trust will permit a wide variety of social relationships to emerge. Hence highly sociable Americans pioneered the development of the modern corporation in the late nineteenth and early twentieth centuries, just as the Japanese have explored the possibilities of network organizations in the twentieth.

By contrast, people who do not trust one another will end up cooperating only under a system of formal rules and regulations, which have to be negotiated, agreed to, litigated, and enforced, sometimes by coercive means. This legal apparatus, serving as a substitute for trust, entails what economists call "transaction costs." Widespread distrust in a society, in other words, imposes a kind of tax on all forms of economic activity, a tax that high-trust societies do not have to pay.

Social capital is not distributed uniformly among societies. Some show a markedly greater proclivity for association than others, and the preferred forms of association differ. In some, family and kinship constitute the primary form of association; in others, voluntary associations are much stronger and serve to draw people out of their families. In the United States, for example, religious conversion often induced people to leave their families to follow the call of a new religious sect, or at least enjoined on them new duties that were in competition with duty to their families. In China, by contrast, Buddhist priests were less often successful, and frequently castigated, for seducing children away from their families. The same society may acquire social capital over time, or lose it. France at the end of the Middle Ages had a dense network of civil associations, but the French capacity for spontaneous sociability was effectively destroyed beginning in the sixteenth and seventeenth centuries by a victorious centralizing monarchy.

Conventional wisdom maintains that Germany and Japan are group-oriented societies. Traditionally prizing obedience to authority, they both practice what Lester Thurow labels "communitarian capitalism."[8] Much of the literature of the past decade or so on competitiveness makes a similar assumption: Japan is a "group-oriented" society; the United States lies at the other extreme as the epitome of an individualistic society, in which people do not readily work together or support one another. According to the Japanologist Ronald Dore, all societies can be located somewhere along a continuum that stretches from the individualistic Anglo-Saxon Countries like the United States and Britain at one extreme to the group-oriented Japan at the other.[9]

This dichotomy, however, represents a great distortion of the way social capital is distributed around the globe, and it represents as well a profound misunderstanding of Japan and, particularly, the United States. There are indeed truly individualistic societies with little capacity for association. In such a society, both families and voluntary associations are weak; it often happens that the strongest organizations are criminal gangs. Russia and certain other former communist countries come to mind, as well as inner-city neighborhoods in the United States.

At a higher level of sociability than contemporary Russia are familistic societies, in which the primary (and often only) avenue to sociability is family and broader forms of kinship, like clans or tribes. Familistic societies frequently have weak voluntary associations because unrelated people have no basis for trusting one another. Chinese societies like Taiwan, Hong Kong, and the People's Republic of China itself are examples; the essence of Chines Confucianism is the elevation of family bonds above all other social loyalties. But France and parts of Italy also share this characteristic. Although familism is not as pronounced in either society as in China, there is a deficit of trust among people not related to one another, and therefore weakness in voluntary community.

In contrast to familistic societies are ones with a high degree of generalized social trust and, consequently, a strong propensity for spontaneous sociability. Japan and Germany do indeed fall into this category. But from the time of its founding, the United States has never been the individualistic society that most Americans believe it to be; rather, it has always possessed a rich network of voluntary associations and community structures to which individuals have subordinated their narrow interests. It is true that Americans have been traditionally much more antistatist when compared to Germans or Japanese, but strong community can emerge in the absence of a strong state.

Social capital and the proclivity for spontaneous sociability have important economic consequences. If we look at the size of the largest firms in a series of national economies (excluding those that are owned and/or heavily subsidized by the state, or else by foreign multinationals), we notice some interesting results.[10] In Europe and North American, private sector firms in the United States and Germany are significantly larger than those in Italy and France. In Asia, the contrast is even sharper between Japan and Korea, on the one hand, which have large firms and highly concentrated industries, and Taiwan and Hong Kong, on the other, whose firms tend to be much smaller.

One might think at first that the ability to spawn large-scale firms is related simply to the absolute size of a nation's economy. For obvious reasons, Andorra and Liechtenstein are not likely to be seedbeds for giant multinationals on the scale of Shell or General Motors. On the other hand, there is no necessary correlation between absolute gross domestic product and large corporations for much of the industrialized world. Three of Europe's smaller economies—Holland, Sweden, and Switzerland—are host to gigantic private corporations; by most measures, Holland is the most industrially concentrated nation in the world. In Asia, the economies of Taiwan and South Korea have been roughly comparable in size over the past generation, yet Korea's firms are much larger than those of Taiwan.

Although there are other factors accounting for firm size, including tax policy, antitrust, and other forms of regulatory law, there is a relationship between high-trust societies with plentiful social capital—Germany, Japan, and the United States—and the ability to create large, private business organizations.[11] These three societies were the first—both on an absolute time scale and relative to their own development histories—to develop large, modern, professionally managed hierarchical corporations. The economies of relatively low-trust societies like Taiwan, Hong Kong, France, and Italy, by contrast, have traditionally been populated by family businesses. In these countries, the reluctance of nonkin to trust one another delayed and in some cases prevented the emergence of modern, professionally managed corporations.

If a low-trust, familistic society wants to have large-scale businesses, the state must step in to help create them through subsidies, guidance, or even outright ownership. The result will be a saddle-shaped distribution of enterprises, with a large number of relatively small family firms at one end of the scale, a small number of large state-owned enterprises at the other, and relatively little in between. State sponsorship has enabled countries like France to develop large-scale, capital-intensive industrial sectors, but at a cost: state-owned companies are inevitably less efficient and well managed than their private sector counterparts.

The prevalence of trust does not simply facilitate the growth of large-scale organizations. If large hierarchies are able to evolve into networks of smaller companies through modern information technology, trust will help in this transition as well. Societies well supplied with social capital will be able to adopt new organizational forms more readily than those with less, as technology and markets change.

At least at an early stage of economic development, firm size and scale do not appear to have serious consequences for a society's ability to grow and prosper. Although the absence of trust in a society may encourage small enterprises and imposes a tax on economic activity, these deficiencies may be more than compensated for by advantages that small companies often have over larger ones. They are easier to establish, more flexible, and adjust more quickly to changing markets than large corporations. And in fact, countries with relatively small firms on average—Italy within the European Community, for example, and Taiwan and Hong Kong in Asia—have grown faster in recent years than their neighbors with large firms.

But firm size does affect the sectors of the global economy that a nation can participate in and may in the long run affect overall competitiveness. Small firms are associated with relatively labor-intensive goods destined for segmented, fast-changing markets, such as apparel, textiles, plastics, electronics components, and furniture. Large firms are required to master complicated manufacturing processes requiring large amounts of capital, such as aerospace, semiconductors, and automobiles. They are also necessary to create the marketing organizations that stand behind brand names, and it is no accident that the world's best-known brand names—Kodak, Ford, Siemens, AEG, Mitsubishi, Hitachi—come from countries that are also good at creating large organizations. By contrast, it is much harder to think of brand names from small-scale Chinese firms.

In classical liberal trade theory, the global division of labor is determined by comparative advantage, usually measured by different nations' relative endowments of capital, labor, and natural resources. The evidence suggests that social capital needs to be factored into a nation's resource endowment. The implications of differing endowments of social capital are potentially enormous for the global division of labor. The nature of Chinese Confucianism, for example, may mean that China may never be able to duplicate Japan's development path and will continue to participate in very different economic sectors.

How much the inability to create large organizations will matter for economic growth in the future will depend on unknowable factors, like future directions in technology and markets. But under certain circumstances, this constraint may prove to be a significant one that will harm the long-term growth potential of countries like China and Italy.

There are, moreover, other benefits to a strong propensity for spontaneous sociability, some of them not economic. A high-trust society can organize its workplace on a more flexible and group-oriented basis, with more responsibility delegated to lower levels of the organization. Low-trust societies, by contrast, must fence in and isolate their workers with a series of bureaucratic rules. Workers usually find their workplaces more satisfying if they are treated like adults who can be trusted to contribute to their community rather than like small cogs in a large industrial machine designed by someone else. The Toyota lean manufacturing system, which is a systemization of a communally organized workplace, has led to enormous productivity improvements as well, indicating that community and efficiency can go together. The lesson is that modern capitalism, shaped by technology, does not dictate a single form of industrial organization that everyone must follow. Managers have considerable latitude in organizing their businesses to take account of the sociable side of the human personality. There is no necessary trade-off, in other words, between community and efficiency; those who pay attention to community may indeed become the most efficient of all.

## NOTES

1. See, for example, Alvin Toffler and Heidi Toffler, *War and Anti-War: Survival at the Dawn of the 21st Century* (Boston: Little, Brown, 1993); Peter W. Huber, *Orwell's Revenge: The 1984 Palimpsest* (New York: Free Press, 1994).

2. Scott Shane, *Dismantling Utopia: How Information Ended the Soviet Union* (Chicago: Ivan Dee, 1994); Gladys D. Ganley, "Power to the People via Personal Electronic Media," *Washington Quarterly* (Spring 1991): 5–22.

3. William H. Davidow and Michael S. Malone, *The Virtual Corporation: Structuring and Revitalizing the Corporation for the 21st Century* (New York: HarperCollins, 1992).

4. Huber, *Orwell's Revenge*, pp. 177–81, 193.

5. This argument is made by Peter Huber himself. See Peter W. Huber, Michael K. Kellogg, and John Thorne, *The Geodesic Network II: 1993 Report on Competition in the Telephone Industry* (Washington, D.C.: Geodesic Co., 1992), chap. 3.

6. It is not sufficient that members of the community expect regular behavior. There are many societies in which there is the expectation that other people will reg-

ularly cheat their fellows; behavior is regular but dishonest, and leads to a deficit of trust.

7. Emile Durkheim, *The Division of Labor in Society* (New York: Macmillan, 1933), pp. 181–82. On the insufficiency of contract to produce organic solidarity, see p. 183.

8. Lester Thurow, *Head to Head: The Coming Economic Battle among Japan, Europe, and America* (New York: Warner Books, 1993), p. 32.

9. See, for example, Ronald P. Dore, *British Factory, Japanese Factory* (London: Allen and Unwin, 1973), pp. 375–76; James Fallows, *More Like Us: Making America Great Again* (Boston: Houghton Mifflin, 1989), p. 48; Seymour Martin Lipset, "Pacific Divide: American Exceptionalism—Japanese Uniqueness," in *Power Shifts and Value Changes in the Post Cold War World,* Proceedings of the Joint Symposium of the International Sociological Association's Research Committees: Comparative Sociology and Sociology of Organizations (Japan: Kibi International University, Institute of International Relations of Sophia University, and Social Science Research Institute of International Christian University, 1992), pp. 41–84.

10. The following list contains the revenues (in US$ millions) of the ten, twenty, and forty largest private, nonforeign companies in eight economies:

| | *Top Ten* | *Top Twenty* | *Top Forty* |
|---|---|---|---|
| United States | 755,202 | 1,144,477 | 1,580,411 |
| Japan | 551,227 | 826,049 | 1,224,294 |
| Germany | 414,332 | 629,520 | 869,326 |
| France | 233,350 | 366,547 | 544,919 |
| Italy | 137,918 | 178,669 | 259,595 |
| Korea | 61,229 | 86,460 | 107,889 |
| Hong Kong | 24,725 | 30,633 | 35,515 |
| Taiwan | 10,705 | N.A. | N.A. |

Sources: *Hoover's Handbook of American Business 1994* (Austin, Tex.: The Reference Press, 1994); *Moody's International Company Data, May 1994;* Korea Trade Center of Los Angeles; *Germany's Top 300, 1993/94 Edition* (Austin, Tex.: The Reference Press, 1994).

This table is based on data from the 100 largest companies in each of the eight listed economies, excluding firms that are publicly owned or are subsidiaries of foreign multinationals. There is some ambiguity about the ownership of certain firms; they may be only partially publicly or foreign owned, or true ownership is hidden through holding companies or cross-shareholding.

A number of problems are associated with comparative measurements of the size of large companies in different economies. It is possible to measure the size of firms by revenues, value-added (i.e., pretax earnings), employment, or total market capitalization. Value-added is perhaps the best all-around measure of a company's size in any particular year, though market capitalization would measure expectations of future earnings. Revenues as a measure do not take into account profit margins and future expectations; they are used here because of the difficult of obtaining firm-level earnings data and capitalization data on all of the countries and companies. This table does not present concentration ratios because they tend to be somewhat misleading as to the relative scale of corporations in our company. A concentration ratio for a single sector of an economy is calculated by measuring the total value-added, employment, or market capitalization for the top X number of firms (where X is, typically, three to ten firms for individual sectors), and dividing this total by the value-added, employment, or market capitalization for that sector. Hence a three-firm concentration ratio for the U.S. steel industry will show how much of total U.S. steel output is produced by the three largest producers. This ratio is commonly used as a measure of monopoly or oligopoly in a particular sector. This kind of analysis can be extended to national economies as well, by expanding the concentration ratios to the top ten, twenty, or more largest firms in the economy as a whole.

One might be tempted to think that the concentration ratio is a better measure than the absolute size of a nation's largest companies, since it is easy to imagine that there is some relationship between a country's gross domestic product, population, and the size of firms it is able to support. On the other hand, a number of small European countries have been hosts to extremely large corporations. Switzerland, Sweden, and Holland all have ten-firm concentration ratios higher than the United States, Japan, or Germany. Past a certain minimum population, as well as a certain level of overall economic development, the correlation between an economy's absolute size and its ability to produce large companies would appear to be weak.

Nor is average size of firms in a national economy a good measure of the ability to generate large companies. In addition to hosting extremely large corporations, Japan's economy has produced a very large number of very small firms. Based simply on average firm size, one would be led to conclude that Japanese companies were smaller than their Taiwanese counterparts. The data in the table above on Japan exclude the revenues of the first six general trading companies, since in my view they for the most part represent not new net sales but what in the United States would be accounted as intracompany transfers.

11. To take just one example, there are many fewer large banks in the American economy than in, say, the Japanese or Italian ones. This has entirely to do with the American law on interstate banking; with this law's abolition in 1994, the size of American banks is likely to grow substantially.

# Part Five

# Civil Society and the Democratic State

# 14

# Democracy's Discontent: The Procedural Republic

*Michael J. Sandel*

Times of trouble prompt us to recall the ideals by which we live. But in America today, this is not an easy thing to do. At a time when democratic ideals seem ascendant abroad, there is reason to wonder whether we have lost possession of them at home. Our public life is rife with discontent. Americans do not believe they have much say in how they are governed and do not trust government to do the right thing.[1] Despite the achievements of American life in the last half-century—victory in World War II, unprecedented affluence, greater social justice for women and minorities, the end of the Cold War—our politics is beset with anxiety and frustration.

The political parties, meanwhile, are unable to make sense of our condition. The main topics of national debate—the proper scope of the welfare state, the extent of rights and entitlements, the proper degree of government regulation—take their shape from the arguments of an earlier day. These are not unimportant topics; but they do not reach the two concerns that lie at the heart of democracy's discontent. One is the fear that, individually and collectively, we are losing control of the forces that govern our lives. The other is the sense that, from family to neighborhood to nation, the moral fabric of community is unraveling around us. These two fears—for the loss of self-government and the erosion of community—together define the anxiety of the age. It is an anxiety that the prevailing political agenda has failed to answer or even address.

Why is American politics ill equipped to allay the discontent that now engulfs it? The answer lies beyond the political arguments of our day, in the public philosophy that animates them. By public philosophy, I mean the political theory implicit in our practice, the assumptions about citizenship and freedom that inform our public life. The inability of contemporary American politics to speak convincingly about self-government and community has something to do with the public philosophy by which we live.

A public philosophy is an elusive thing, for it is constantly before our eyes. It forms the often unreflective background to our political discourse and pursuits. In ordinary times, the public philosophy can easily escape the notice of those who live by it. But anxious times compel a certain clarity. They force first principles to the surface and offer an occasion for critical reflection.

## LIBERAL AND REPUBLICAN FREEDOM

The political philosophy by which we live is a certain version of liberal political theory. Its central idea is that government should be neutral toward the moral and religious views its citizens espouse. Since people disagree about the best way to live, government should not affirm in law any particular vision of the good life. Instead, it should provide a framework of rights that respects persons as free and independent selves, capable of choosing their own values and ends.[2] Since this liberalism asserts the priority of fair procedures over particular ends, the public life it informs might be called the procedural republic.[3]

In describing the prevailing political philosophy as a version of liberal political theory, it is important to distinguish two different meanings of liberalism. In the common parlance of American politics, liberalism is the opposite of conservatism; it is the outlook of those who favor a more generous welfare state and a greater measure of social and economic equality.[4] In the history of political theory, however, liberalism has a different, broader meaning. In this historical sense, liberalism describes a tradition of thought that emphasizes toleration and respect for individual rights and that runs from John Locke, Immanuel Kant, and John Stuart Mill to John Rawls. The public philosophy of contemporary American politics is a version of this liberal tradition of thought, and most of our debates proceed within its terms.

The idea that freedom consists in our capacity to choose our ends finds prominent expression in our politics and law. Its province is not limited to those known as liberals rather than conservatives in American politics; it can be found across the political spectrum. Republicans sometimes argue, for example, that taxing the rich to pay for welfare programs is a form of coerced charity that violates people's freedom to choose what to do with their own money. Democrats sometimes argue that government should assure all citizens a decent level of income, housing, and health, on the grounds that those who are crushed by economic necessity are not truly free to exercise choice in other domains. Although the two sides disagree about how government should act to respect individual choice, both assume that freedom consists in the capacity of persons to choose their values and ends.

So familiar is this vision of freedom that it seems a permanent feature of the American political and constitutional tradition. But Americans have not always understood freedom in this way. As a reigning public philosophy, the version of liberalism that informs our present debates is a recent arrival, a development of the last forty or fifty years. Its distinctive character can best be seen by contrast with a rival public philosophy that it gradually displaced. This rival public philosophy is a version of republican political theory.

Central to republican theory is the idea that liberty depends on sharing in self-government. This idea is not by itself inconsistent with liberal freedom. Participating in politics can be one among the ways in which people choose to pursue their ends. According to republican political theory, however, sharing in self-rule involves something more. It means deliberating with fellow citizens about the common good and helping to shape the destiny of the political community. But to deliberate well about the common good requires more than the capacity to choose one's ends and to respect others' rights to do the same. It requires a knowledge of public affairs and also a sense of belonging, a concern for the whole, a moral bond with the community whose fate is at stake. To share in self-rule therefore requires that citizens possess, or come to acquire, certain qualities of character, or civic virtues. But this means that republican politics cannot be neutral toward the values and ends its citizens espouse. The republican conception of freedom, unlike the liberal conception, requires a formative politics, a politics that cultivates in citizens the qualities of character self-government requires.

Both the liberal and republican conceptions of freedom have been present throughout our political experience, but in shifting measure and relative importance. Broadly speaking, republicanism predominated earlier in American history, liberalism later. In recent decades, the civic or formative aspect of our politics has largely given way to the liberalism that conceives persons as free and independent selves, unencumbered by moral or civic ties they have not chosen.

This shift sheds light on our present political predicament. For despite its appeal, the liberal vision of freedom lacks the civic resources to sustain self-government. This defect ill-equips it to address the sense of disempowerment that afflicts our public life. The public philosophy by which we live cannot secure the liberty it promises, because it cannot inspire the sense of community and civic engagement that liberty requires.

## REPUBLICAN FREEDOM: DIFFICULTIES AND DANGERS

Any attempt to revitalize the civic strand of freedom must confront two sobering objections. The first doubts it is possible to revive republican ideals; the second doubts it is desirable. The first objection holds that, given the scale and complexity of the modern world, it is unrealistic to aspire to self-government as the republican tradition conceives it. From Aristotle's polis to Jefferson's agrarian ideal, the civic conception of freedom found its home in small bounded places, largely self-sufficient, inhabited by people whose conditions of life afforded the leisure, learning, and commonality to deliberate well about public concerns. But we do not live that way today. To the contrary, we live in a highly mobile continental society, teeming with diversity. Moreover, even this vast society is not self-sufficient but is situated in a global economy whose frenzied flow of money and goods, information and images, pays little heed to nations, much less neighborhoods. How, under conditions such as these, could the civic strand of freedom possibly take hold?

In fact, this objection continues, the republican strand of American politics, for all its persistence, has often spoken in a voice tinged with nostalgia. Even as Jefferson valorized the yeoman farmer, America was becoming a manufacturing nation. And so it was with the artisan republicans of Jackson's day, the apostles of free labor in Lincoln's time, the producer-citizens of the Knights of Labor, and the shopkeepers and pharmacists Brandeis defended against the curse of bigness. In each of these cases—or so one might argue—republican ideals found their expression at the last moment, too late to offer feasible alternatives, just in time to offer an elegy for a lost cause. If the republican tradition is irredeemably nostalgic, then whatever its capacity to illuminate the defects of liberal politics, it offers little that could lead us to a richer civic life.

The second objection argues that even were it possible to recover republican ideals, to do so would not be desirable. That the civic strand of our tradition has given way in recent decades to a liberal public philosophy is not necessarily cause for regret. All things considered, it may represent a change for the better. Critics of the republican tradition might even concede that the procedural republic comes with a certain loss of community and self-government, and still insist that this is a price worth paying for the toleration and individual choice the procedural republic makes possible.

Underlying this objection are two related worries about republican political theory as traditionally conceived. The first is that it is exclusive; the second is that it is coercive. Both worries flow from the special demands of republican citizenship. If sharing in self-rule requires the capacity to deliberate well about the common good, then citizens must possess certain excellences—of character, judgment, and concern for the whole. But this implies that citizenship cannot be indiscriminately bestowed. It must be restricted to those who either possess the relevant virtues or can come to acquire them.

Some republican theorists have assumed that the capacity for civic virtue corresponds to fixed categories of birth or condition. Aristotle, for example, considered women, slaves, and resident aliens unworthy of citizenship because their nature or roles deprived them of the relevant excellences. Similar arguments were offered in nineteenth-century America by defenders of property qualifications for voting, southern defenders of slavery, and nativist opponents of citizenship for immigrants.[5] All linked republican notions of citizenship to the further assumption that some group or other—the propertyless, or African-Americans, or Catholic immigrants—were, by nature or condition or conviction, incapable of the virtues good citizenship requires.

But the assumption that the capacity for virtue is incorrigible, tied to roles or identities fixed in advance, is not intrinsic to republican political theory, and not all republicans have embraced it. Some have argued that good citizens are made, not found, and have rested their hopes on the formative project of republican politics. This is especially true of the democratic versions of republican thought that arose with the Enlightenment. When the incorrigibility thesis gives way, so does the tendency of republican politics to sanction exclusion.

As the tendency to exclusion recedes, however, the danger of coercion looms larger. Of the two pathologies to which republican politics is prone, modern democracies are more likely to suffer the second. For given the demands of republican citizenship, the more expansive the bounds of membership, the more demanding the task of cultivating virtue. In Aristotle's polis, the formative task was to cultivate virtue among a small group of people who shared a common life and a natural bent for citizenship. When republican thought turns democratic, however, and when the natural bent of persons to be citizens can no longer be assumed, the formative project becomes more daunting. The task of forging a common citizenship among a vast and disparate people invites more strenuous forms of soulcraft. This raises the stakes for republican politics and heightens the risk of coercion.

This peril can be glimpsed in Rousseau's account of the formative undertaking necessary to a democratic republic. The task of the founder, or great legislator, he writes, is no less than "to change human nature, to transform each individual . . . into a part of a larger whole from which this individual receives, in a sense, his life and his being." The legislator "must deny man his own forces" in order to make him reliant on the community as a whole. The more each person's individual will is "dead and obliterated," the more likely he is to embrace the general will. "Thus if each citizen is nothing and can do nothing except in concert with all the others . . . one can say that the legislation has achieved the highest possible point of perfection."[6]

The coercive face of soulcraft is by no means unknown among American republicans. For example, Benjamin Rush, a signer of the Declaration of Independence, wanted "to convert men into republican machines" to teach each citizen "that he does not belong to himself, but that he is public property."[7] But civic education need not take so harsh a form. In practice, successful republican soulcraft involves a gentler kind of tutelage. For example, the political economy of citizenship that informed nineteenth-century American life sought to cultivate not only commonality but also the independence and judgment to deliberate well about the common good. It worked not by coercion but by a complex mix of persuasion and habituation, what Tocqueville called "the slow and quiet action of society upon itself."[8]

What separates Rousseau's republican exertions from the civic practices described by Tocqueville are the dispersed, differentiated character of American public life in Tocqueville's day and the indirect modes of character formation this differentiation allowed. Unable to abide disharmony, Rousseau's republican ideal seeks to collapse the distance between persons so that citizens stand in a kind of speechless transparence, or immediate presence to one another. Where the general will prevails, the citizens "consider themselves to be a single body," and there is no need for political argument. "The first to propose [a new law] merely says what everybody else has already felt; and there is no question of intrigues or eloquence" to secure its passage. Given the unitary character of the general will, deliberation at its best issues in silent unanimity: "The more harmony reigns in the assemblies, that is to say, the closer opinions come to unanimity, the more dominant too is the general will. But long debates, dissensions, and tumult betoken the ascendance of private interests and the decline of the state." Since the common good does not admit of competing interpretations, disagreement signals corruption, a falling away from the common good.[9]

It is this assumption—that the common good is unitary and uncontestable—not the formative ambition as such, that inclines Rousseau's politics to coercion. It is, moreover, an assumption that republican politics can do without. As America's experience with the political economy of citizenship suggests, the civic conception of freedom does not render disagreement unnecessary. It offers a way of conducting political argument, not transcending it.

Unlike Rousseau's unitary vision, the republican politics Tocqueville describes is more clamorous than consensual. It does not despise differentiation. Instead of collapsing the space between persons, it fills this space with public institutions that gather people together in various capacities that both separate and relate them.[10] These institutions include the townships, schools, religions, and virtue-sustaining occupations that form the "character of mind" and "habits of the heart" a democratic republic requires. Whatever their more particular purposes, these agencies of civic education inculcate the habit of attending to public things. And yet given their multiplicity, they prevent public life from dissolving into an undifferentiated whole.[11]

So the civic strand of freedom is not necessarily exclusive or coercive. It can sometimes find democratic, pluralistic expression. To this extent, the liberal's objection to republican political theory is misplaced. But the liberal worry does contain an insight that cannot be dismissed: Republican politics is risky politics, a politics without guarantees. And the risks it entails inhere in the formative project. To accord the political community a stake in the character of its citizens is to concede the possibility that bad communities may form bad characters. Dispersed power and multiple sites of civic formation may reduce these dangers but cannot remove them. This is the truth in the liberal's complaint about republican politics.

## THE ATTEMPT TO AVOID THE FORMATIVE PROJECT

What to make of this complaint depends on the alternatives. If there were a way to secure freedom without attending to the character of citizens, or to define rights without affirming a conception of the good life, then the liberal objection to the formative project might be decisive. But is there such a way? Liberal political theory claims that there is. The voluntarist conception of freedom promises to lay to rest, once and for all, the risks of republican politics. If liberty can be detached from the exercise of self-government and conceived instead as the capacity of persons to choose their own ends, then the difficult task of forming civic virtue can finally be dispensed with. Or at least it can be narrowed to the seemingly simpler task of cultivating toleration and respect for others.

On the voluntarist conception of freedom, statecraft no longer needs soulcraft, except in a limited domain. Tying freedom to respect for the rights of freely choosing selves would dampen old disputes about how to form the habits of self-rule. It would spare politics the ancient quarrels about the nature of the good life. Once freedom is detached from the formative project, "the problem of setting up a state can be solved even by a nation of devils," in Kant's memorable words. "For such a task does not involve the moral improvement of man."[12]

But the liberal attempt to detach freedom from the formative project confronts problems of its own, problems that can be seen in both the theory and the practice of the procedural republic. The philosophical difficulty lies in the liberal conception of citizens as freely choosing, independent selves, unencumbered by moral of civic ties antecedent to choice. This vision cannot account for a wide range or moral and political obligations that we commonly recognize, such as obligation of loyalty or solidarity. By insisting that we are bound only by ends and roles we choose for themselves, it denies that we can ever be claimed by ends we have not chosen—ends given by nature or God, for example, or by our identities as members of families, peoples, cultures, or traditions.

Some liberals concede we may be bound by obligations such as these, but insist they apply to private life alone and have no bearing on politics. But this raises a further difficulty. Why insist on separating our identity as citizens from our identity as persons more broadly conceived? Why should political deliberation not reflect our best understanding of the highest human ends? Don't arguments about justice and rights unavoidably draw on particular conceptions of the good life, whether we admit it or not?

The problems in the theory of procedural liberalism show up in the practice it inspires. Over the past half-century, American politics has come to embody the version of liberalism that renounces the formative ambition and insists government should be neutral toward competing conceptions of the good life. Rather than tie liberty to self-government and the virtues that sustain it, the procedural republic seeks a framework of rights, neutral among ends, within which individuals can choose and pursue their own ends.

But the discontent that besets American public life today illustrates the inadequacy of this solution. A politics that brackets morality and religion too completely soon generates its own disenchantment. Where political discourse lacks moral resonance, the yearning for a public life of larger meaning finds undesirable expression. Groups like the Moral Majority seek to clothe the naked public square with narrow, intolerant moralisms. Fundamentalists rush in where liberals fear to tread. The disenchantment also assumes more secular forms. Absent a political agenda that addresses the moral dimension of public questions, attention becomes riveted on the private vices of public officials. Political discourse becomes increasingly preoccupied with the scandalous, the sensational, and the confessional as purveyed by tabloids, talk shows, and eventually the mainstream media as well. It cannot be said that the public philosophy of contemporary liberalism is wholly responsible for these tendencies. But its vision of political discourse is too spare to contain the moral energies of democratic life. It creates a moral void that opens the way for intolerance and other misguided moralisms.

A political agenda lacking substantive moral discourse is one symptom of the public philosophy of the procedural republic. Another is the loss of mastery. The triumph of the voluntarist conception of freedom has coincided with a growing sense of disempowerment. Despite the expansion of rights in recent decades, Americans find to their frustration that they are losing control of the forces that govern their lives. This has partly to do with the insecurity of jobs in the global economy, but it also reflects the self-image by which we live. The liberal self-image and the actual organization of modern social and economic life are sharply at odds. Even as we think and act as freely choosing, independent selves, we confront a world governed by impersonal structures of power that defy our understanding and control. The voluntarist conception of freedom leaves us ill equipped to contend with this condition. Liberated though we may be from the burden of identities we have not chosen, entitled though we may be to the range of rights assured by the welfare state, we find ourselves overwhelmed as we turn to face the world on our own resources.

The inability of the reigning political agenda to address the erosion of self-government and community reflects the impoverished conceptions of citizenship and freedom implicit in our public life. The procedural republic that has unfolded over the past half-century can now be seen as an epic experiment in the claims of liberal as against republican political thought. Our present predicament lends weight to the republican claim that liberty cannot be detached from self-government and the virtues that sustain it, that the formative project cannot be dispensed with after all. The procedural republic, it turns out, cannot secure the liberty it promises because it cannot inspire the moral and civic engagement self-government requires.

If the public philosophy of contemporary liberalism fails to answer democracy's discontent, it remains to ask how a renewed attention to republican themes might better equip us to contend with our condition. How would a political agenda informed by the civic strand of freedom differ from the one that now prevails? Is self-government in the republican sense even possible under modern conditions? If so, what economic and political arrangements would it require, and what qualities of character would be necessary to sustain them?

How American politics might recover its civic voice is not wholly a speculative matter. Although the public philosophy of the procedural republic predominates in our time, it has not extinguished the civic understanding of freedom. Around the edges of our political discourse and practice, hints of the formative project can still be glimpsed. As the reigning political agenda lost energy in the 1980s and 1990s, these residual civic impulses quickened. Americans of various ideological persuasions groped to articulate a politics that reached beyond the terms of the procedural republic and spoke to the anxieties of the time.

These gropings, however partial and inchoate, gesture nonetheless toward the kind of political debate that would accord greater attention to republican themes. These expressions of Americans' persisting civic aspirations have taken two forms; one emphasizes the moral, the other the economic prerequisites of self-government. The first is the attempt, coming largely but not wholly from the right, to revive virtue, character formation, and moral judgment as considerations in public policy and political discourse. The second involves a range of efforts, coming mostly though not entirely from the left, to contend with economic forces that disempower communities and threaten to erode the social fabric of democratic life.

## THE RECRUDESCENCE OF VIRTUE

From the 1930s to the 1980s, conservatives criticized the welfare state in the name of the voluntarist conception of freedom. However desirable old-age pensions or school lunches or aid to the poor might be, argued conservatives such as Milton Friedman and Barry Goldwater, it was a violation of liberty to use state power to coerce taxpayers to support these causes against their will. By the mid-1980s, however, the conservative argument began to change. Increasingly, conservatives focused their criticism on the moral and civic consequences of federal social policy. For a time, debate over public policy had proceeded without reference to the formative project, reflecting the conviction that government should be neutral among competing conceptions of the good life. But now social commentators observed "a deepening concern for the development of character in the citizenry," and a "growing awareness that a variety of public problems can only be understood—and perhaps addressed—if they are seen as arising out of a defect in character formation."[13]

Nowhere was the recrudescence of virtue more pronounced than in debates about welfare. Welfare policy was a failure, many now argued, not because it coerced taxpayers but because it bred dependence among recipients and rewarded immoral and irresponsible behavior.[14] In the 1960s and 1970s it was widely held that public assistance programs should not impose any particular moral judgment about family arrangements or sexual behavior but simply enable recipients to choose their values for themselves. In 1965 Daniel Patrick Moynihan, then assistant secretary of Labor under Lyndon Johnson, wrote a report citing the alarming rate of out-of-wedlock births among blacks and calling for a national effort to enhance "the stability of the Negro American family."[15] Much of the protest that greeted the report attacked its judgmental aspect.[16] "My major criticism of the report is that it assumes that middle class American values are the correct ones for everyone in America," said Floyd McKissick, director of the Congress on Racial Equality (CORE). "Just because Moynihan believes in the middle class values doesn't mean that they are the best for everyone in America." Even sympathetic commentators averred that "it would have been well to reduce the discussion of illegitimacy" because of "its inevitable overtones of immorality."[17]

Three decades later, the terms of debate had changed. Welfare reform efforts of the 1980s and 1990s reflected a departure from the "nonjudgmental" approach of earlier years, a "new willingness to discuss sensitive, value-laden issues," and a greater effort to "reorder the personal lives of the poor."[18] Advocates of a civic conception of social policy argued that work requirements were essential, not for the sake of saving money but for the sake of including welfare recipients in the common obligations of citizenship.[19] As Moynihan, now a senior U.S. senator, declared, "you're talking here about what is the central task of any society: to produce citizens."[20]

For civic conservatives of the 1980s and 1990s, a renewed concern for the formative project extended beyond welfare to education, crime, and other aspects of public policy. William J. Bennett, secretary of Education and drug czar in the Reagan and Bush administrations, noted "a seismic shift" in American political discourse of the 1990s: "A set of issues once thought beyond the purview of politics—the social issues, the moral issues, the family issues—is now suddenly driving the public debate." Bennett applauded this shift and called for "public policies that once again make the connection between our deepest beliefs and our legislative agenda."[21]

The notion that public life should express the moral convictions and shape the moral character of citizens might seem at odds with the conservative's instinct for smaller, less intrusive government. But Bennett insisted that these conservative purposes were compatible. Statecraft could be soulcraft without big government, provided that families, schools, and churches served as the primary agents of character formation. Bennett blamed big government for weakening these instruments of moral and civic education. Government should be limited, he argued, "not only, or even primarily, for fiscal reasons, but because the 'nanny state' has eroded self-reliance and encouraged dependency, crowding out the character-forming institutions and enfeebling us as citizens."[22]

Beyond the baleful effects of big government, civic conservatives alleged that the public philosophy of contemporary liberalism was itself a source of moral decline. The notion that government must be neutral among competing moral and religious visions had taken a corrosive toll on American public life. It had made for a "naked public square," inhospitable to religion and empty of moral purposes larger than the pursuit of individual rights and entitlements.[23] In the area of education, the contagion of "value neutrality" had led schools to abandon their traditional role as "incubators of civic and personal virtue." The flight from public moral judgment had abetted the epidemic of drug use, a scourge that proved the folly of thinking that government "can be neutral regarding human character and personal responsibility."[24]

The abiding shame of American life, the urban ghetto, also attested to the poverty of a public life bereft of authoritative moral judgment, civic conservatives maintained. Glenn Loury, a prominent black intellectual, lamented the fact that American political discourse "fail[s] to engage questions of personal morality," of "character and values. . . . The public debate gives only muted voice to the judgment that it is wrong to be sexually promiscuous, to be indolent and undisciplined, to be disrespectful of legitimate authority, or to be unreliable, untruthful, or unfaithful." Given government's abdication of moral instruction, Americans must look to other sources of moral teaching, such as families and churches. "Until these institutions are restored, the behavioral problems of the ghetto will remain."[25] Absent an appeal to spiritual and religious precepts, Loury saw little hope of teaching ghetto youths to abstain from sex, drugs, and violence: "successful efforts at reconstruction in ghetto communities invariably reveal a religious institution, or set of devout believers, at the center of the effort."[26]

Liberals came more reluctantly to the revolt against the procedural republic. By the 1990s, however, Americans' discontent with their moral and civic condition was too pervasive to ignore. Bill Clinton was elected to the presidency in 1992 as a "New Democrat," stressing responsibility as well as rights. What set him apart from Democrats such as Michael Dukakis, Walter Mondale, and Jimmy Carter had less to do with his stand on particular issues than with his ability, at least at moments, to transcend the terms of the procedural republic. Speaking in the Memphis church where Martin Luther King Jr. had preached before his assassination, President Clinton ventured onto moral and spiritual terrain that liberals of recent times had sought to avoid. Restoring work to the life of the inner city was essential, he explained, not only for the income it brings but also for its character-forming effects, for the discipline, structure, and pride that work confers on family life. He also acknowledged that even the best efforts government might make to deal with crime, drugs, violence, and the breakdown of the family would achieve little without changes people must make "from the inside out," changes that reach "the values, the spirit, the soul."[27]

On other occasions Clinton continued to trespass on value-laden territory once occupied by conservatives and the religious right. "Our problems go way beyond the reach of the government," he declared in his 1994 State of the Union Address. "They are rooted in the loss of values, in the disappearance of work, and the breakdown of our families and communities."[28] Among the sources of family breakdown was the soaring number of children born outside of marriage. Clinton allowed that former vice president Dan Quayle had been right when he maintained that having children out of wedlock was wrong and that government should act to discourage it.[29]

Other members of Clinton's administration, however, continued to display the nonjudgmental reflex characteristic of contemporary liberalism. Surgeon General Joycelyn Elders refused to condemn out-of-wedlock birth, stating: "Everyone has different moral standards. You can't impose your standards on someone else." Donna Shalala, secretary of Health and Human Services, was unable to suppress the old reflex even as she endorsed her president's position. "I don't like to put this in moral terms," she conceded, "but I do believe that having children out of wedlock is just wrong."[30]

Other Democrats of the 1990s joined the call to restore moral and religious discourse to public life and to repair the character-forming agencies of civil society. The political agenda of recent decades, mainly concerned with adjudicating the roles of market and government, did not address the loss of community and the erosion of civic life. U.S. Senator Bill Bradley called for a politics that focused more on the institutions of civil society. Neither the market nor government was "equipped to solve America's central problems, which are the deterioration of our civil society and the need to revitalize our democratic process." Politics should be concerned, he urged, with restoring "churches, schools, fraternities, community centers, labor unions, synagogues, sports leagues, PTAs, libraries, and barber shops" as "civic spaces," sites of deliberation about the common good. The "distinctive moral language of civil society"—the language of community, family, citizenship, and mutual obligation—should play a more prominent role "in our public onversation."[31]

## REVIVING THE POLITICAL ECONOMY OF CITIZENSHIP

Those in the 1990s who spoke of virtue and soulcraft emphasized the moral and cultural prerequisites of self-government. Others emphasized the economic prerequisites. They worried, as many civic conservatives did not, about the way the modern economy disempowered communities and eroded the social fabric essential to democracy. Their search for economic arrangements conducive to community and self-government went beyond familiar arguments about prosperity and fairness and recalled the terms of debate that informed the political economy of citizenship.

### The Civic Case against Inequality

One gesture toward a political economy of citizenship could be seen in a growing concern with the civic consequences of economic inequality. By the 1990s the gap between rich and poor was approaching levels unknown in American society since the 1920s. The sharpest increase in inequality unfolded from the late 1970s to the 1990s. From 1950 to 1978, rich and poor alike had shared in the gains from economic growth; real family income doubled for lower-, middle-, and upper-income Americans, confirming the economist's maxim that a rising tide lifts all boats. From 1979 to 1993, however, this maxim ceased to hold. Almost all of the increase in household incomes during this period went to the richest fifth of the population. Most Americans lost ground.[32] The distribution of wealth also showed increasing inequality. In 1992 the richest 1 percent of the population owned 42 percent of total private wealth, up from 34 percent a decade earlier, and more than twice the concentration of wealth in Britain.[33]

Some blamed the rising inequality on Reagan-era tax policy, which lowered income taxes for the wealthy while increasing taxes—including Social Security, state, and local taxes—that fall more heavily on lower- and middle-income taxpayers. Others pointed to an increasingly competitive global economy that rewarded highly educated workers but eroded the wages of low-skill laborers.[34] Whatever the explanation, the growing gap between rich and poor occasioned a new set of arguments about why inequality matters and what should be done about it. Some of these arguments went beyond the terms of the procedural republic and revived the civic strand of economic argument.

One argument against wide disparities of income and wealth, familiar in American politics of recent decades, is based on fairness or distributive justice. This argument, consistent with the public philosophy of contemporary liberalism, reflects the voluntarist conception of freedom. According to this view, a just society provides a framework of rights, neutral among ends, within which individuals are free to choose and pursue their own conceptions of the good life. This notion of justice requires that government do more than maximize the general welfare by promoting economic growth. It also requires that government assure each person a measure of social and economic security sufficient to the meaningful exercise of choice. Absent fair social and economic conditions, persons cannot truly be free to choose and pursue their own values and ends. In this way, the liberal's emphasis on fairness and distributive justice reflects the voluntarist conception of freedom.

But fairness to freely choosing, independent selves is not the only reason to worry about inequalities of income and wealth. A second reason draws not on the liberal but on the republican conception of freedom. The republican tradition teaches that severe inequality undermines freedom by corrupting the character of both rich and poor and destroying the commonality necessary to self-government. Aristotle held that persons of moderate means make the best citizens. The rich, distracted by luxury and prone to ambition, are unwilling to obey, while the poor, shackled by necessity and prone to envy, are ill suited to rule. A society of extremes lacks the "spirit of friendship" self-government requires: "Community depends on friendship; and when there is enmity instead of friendship, men will not even share the same path." Rousseau argued, on similar grounds, that "no citizen should be so rich as to be capable of buying another citizen, and none so poor that he is forced to sell himself." Although absolute equality is impossible, a democratic state should "[t]olerate neither rich men nor beggars," for these two estates "are equally fatal to the common good."[35]

As the gap between America's rich and poor deepened in the 1980s and 1990s, the civic case against inequality found at least tentative expression. Robert B. Reich, secretary of Labor in the Clinton administration, argued that the imperatives of technological change and global competition required greater federal spending on job training and education. The decline of the middle class could be reversed if American workers acquired the skills the new economy prized.[36] In a book he wrote shortly before taking office, however, Reich acknowledged a serious obstacle to this solution. A national commitment to invest more in the education and training of American workers presupposed a national sense of mutual responsibility that could no longer be assumed. As rich and poor grew further apart, their sense of shared fate diminished, and with it the willingness of the rich to invest, through higher taxes, in the skills of their fellow citizens.[37]

More than a matter of money, the new inequality gives rise, Reich observed, to increasingly separate ways of life. Affluent professionals gradually secede from public life into "homogeneous enclaves" where they have little contact with those less fortunate than themselves. "As public parks and playgrounds deteriorate, there is a proliferation of private health clubs, golf clubs, tennis clubs, skating clubs," accessible only to paying members. As the children of the prosperous enroll in private schools or in relatively homogeneous suburban schools, urban public schools are left to the poor. By 1990, for example, 45 percent of children in New York City public schools were on welfare. As municipal services decline in urban areas, residents and businesses in upscale districts manage to insulate themselves from the effects by assessing themselves surtaxes to provide private garbage collection, street cleaning, and police protection unavailable to the city as a whole. More and more, the affluent evacuate public spaces, retreating to privatized communities defined largely by income level, or by the zip code direct-mail marketers use to target likely customers. As one such marketer proclaims, "Tell me someone's zip code and I can predict what they eat, drink, and drive—even think."[38]

Reich's concern with the erosion of national community had mostly to do with the obstacle this posed for worthy federal spending. For him, as for advocates of national community such as Mario Cuomo, community was important not for the sake of forming citizens equipped for self-rule but rather for the sake of inspiring the ethic of sharing a more generous welfare state required. In this respect it fit within the terms of the reigning political agenda.

But Reich's account of the communal consequences of inequality highlights a defect in American life that also bears on the prospect of self-government. The secession of the affluent from the public sphere not only weakens the social fabric that supports the welfare state; it also erodes civic virtue more broadly conceived. The republican tradition long viewed the public realm not only as a place of common provision but also as a setting for civic education. The public character of the common school, for example, consisted not only in its financing but also in its teaching; ideally at least, it was a place where children of all classes would mix and learn the habits of democratic citizenship. Even municipal parks and playgrounds were once seen not only as places of recreation but also as sites for the promotion of civic identity, neighborliness, and community.[39]

As affluent Americans increasingly buy their way out of reliance on public services, the formative, civic resources of American life diminish. The deterioration of urban public schools is perhaps the most conspicuous and damaging instance of this trend. Another is the growing reliance on private security services, one of the fastest-growing occupational categories of the 1980s. So great was the demand for security personnel in shopping malls, airports, retail stores, and residential communities that by 1990 the number of private security guards nationwide exceeded the number of public police officers.[40] "The nation, in effect, is putting less emphasis on controlling crime for everyone—the job of publicly employed police officers—and more emphasis on private police officers who carve out secure zones for those who pay for such protection."[41] Even children's recreation is subject to these privatizing forces. Far from the spirit of the playground movement of the Progressive era is the new franchise business of "pay-per-use" playgrounds. For $4.95 per hour per child, parents can now take their children to private playcenters, often in shopping malls. "Playgrounds are dirty," one pay-for-play proprietor explains. "We're indoors; we're padded; parents can feel their child is safe."[42]

Civic conservatives have not, for the most part, acknowledged that market forces, under conditions of inequality, erode those aspects of community life that bring rich and poor together in public places and pursuits. Many liberals, largely concerned with distributive justice, have also missed the civic consequences of growing inequality. A politics attentive to the civic strand of freedom might try "to restrict the sphere of life in which money matters" and shore up the public spaces that gather people together in common experiences and form the habits of citizenship. Such a politics would worry less about the distribution of income as such, and more "about rebuilding, preserving, and strengthening community institutions in which income is irrelevant, about preventing their corruption by the forces of the market." It would encourage "class-mixing institutions" like public schools, libraries, parks, community centers, public transportation, and national service. Although such policies might also be favored by welfare-state liberals, the emphasis and justification would differ. A more civic-minded liberalism would seek communal provision less for the sake of distributive justice than for the sake of affirming the membership and forming the civic identity of rich and poor alike.[43]

## Community Development Corporations

Some gestures toward a political economy of citizenship can be seen in the shifting terms of political discourse. Others can be glimpsed in pockets of political activism that defy the trend toward civic disengagement and try to contend with economic forces that disempower communities and undermine civic life. One range of examples is offered by community development corporations (CDCs). Begun in the mid-1960s as an alternative to large-scale government programs of urban renewal, CDCs are nonprofit corporations designed to give low-income communities a voice in shaping their economic destinies. Among the first and best-known was the Bedford-Stuyvesant Restoration Corporation of Brooklyn, initiated by Robert Kennedy as a means of economic revitalization and also as "an experiment in self-government." Governed by boards of local residents and business leaders, CDCs promote the economic development of the neighborhoods they serve by funding housing projects, new businesses, job training, and other social services.[44] When, in the 1980s, the Reagan administration cut their major sources of federal supports, CDCs survived by relying more heavily on private investment, foundation funding, and financing from community banks. By the 1990s the thousand-plus CDCs in operation had achieved some success in reviving depressed communities. Whether, as some hoped, CDCs might be a vehicle for more self-reliant local and regional economies and greater democratic control, remained to be seen.[45]

## Sprawlbusters

Another recent example of the political economy of citizenship recalls the long-forgotten anti-chain store movement of the 1930s. Then, opponents of national chains such as Sears Roebuck and A&P argued that the proliferation of chain stores undermined self-government by destroying local businesses and replacing independent shopkeepers with hirelings and clerks. In the 1990s, opponents of Wal-Mart and other discount superstores voiced similar concerns. As of 1994 Wal-Mart, with 2,400 stores and annual sales of $80 billion, was the largest retailer in the country.[46] So pervasive were its massive, boxlike structures and vast parking lots at highway interchanges across the land that, in the words of *Time* magazine, it was "redesigning the social structure of rural and small-town Americans more than any other force besides nature."[47] As Americans flocked to buy brand-name merchandise at discount prices, many downtown merchants were forced out of business. Critics complained not only of the ugly sprawl and environmental blight the superstores wrought, but also of the damage they did to the civic landscape.[48] "In older town centers, retail was the glue that connected a myriad of public places—government offices, parks, schools, libraries, and so forth. The intermingling of retail and community facilities created a setting for repetitive chance encounters with friends and neighbors that built and strengthened community bonds." The arrival of megastores accessible only by automobile destroyed these settings and "contributed to the atrophy of community and neighborhood activites."[49] The damage was compounded when Wal-Mart entered a community, destroyed local businesses, and then moved out in search of higher profits elsewhere. Residents were left with vacant sprawl, a downtown of shuttered stores, and a heightened sense of being victims of forces beyond their control.[50]

When, in the 1990s, Wal-Mart sought to expand beyond its base in the South and Midwest, it met resistance from community activists who opposed the zoning changes the big-box stores require. In Greenfield, Massachusetts, local voters, turning out in record numbers, narrowly defeated a 1993 referendum that would have permitted Wal-Mart to enter the New England town.[51] Veterans of the successful Greenfield campaign joined Wal-Mart opponents in other communities across the country in a coalition of "Sprawlbusters," sharing tactics and experiences. By the mid-1990s these activists were engaging Wal-Mart and other retail giants in over a hundred local battles against megastore development. Like the antichain activists of old, they argued for the priority of civic values over consumer values. As one activist declared, "I'd rather have a viable community than a cheap pair of underwear."[52]

## The New Urbanism

Another contemporary movement that expresses civic aspirations recalls the town planning efforts of the Progressive era. A growing number of urban planners, architects, citizens' groups, and regional planning agencies are exploring ways to build communities more hospitable to a vibrant civic life. Advocates of the New Urbanism, as the movement is called, seek to reverse the pattern of suburban development that has unfolded since the end of World War II. Prompted by the automobile, government highway subsidies, and Americans' desire to retreat to a private life at a safe distance from urban centers, the spread of suburbs carried with it mounting costs: long commutes for working people, isolation for children and elderly persons who cannot drive, traffic congestion and air pollution, the segregation of neighborhoods by class, race, and generation, the sense of placelessness bred by homogeneous chain stores, office parks, and subdivisions.[53]

The New Urbanists worry that suburban arrangements leave little room for the public settings in which people of different ages, incomes, and races encounter one another in the course of their daily lives. "By isolating people in houses and cars and by segregating households into homogeneous enclaves, the late twentieth century suburban metropolis has done little to replace the urban vitality it so aggressively displaced, and little to foster desperately needed civic responsibility in our increasingly diverse society." Some view the rise of the suburb as reflecting and furthering the depreciation of American life: "Our faith in government and the fundamental sense of commonality at the center of any vital democracy is seeping away in suburbs designed more for cars than people, more for market segments than communities." The ultimate expression of this tendency is the growing number of gated communities, walled-off enclaves of private parks, roads, police, and schools, open only to residents.[54]

The New Urbanists build communities that offer some of the virtues of traditional towns. They place housing, parks, and schools within walking distance of shops, civic services, jobs, and public transportation, not only for convenience but also to encourage the encounters that promote a common life. "Without the pedestrian, a community's common ground—its parks, sidewalks, squares, and plazas—become useless obstructions to the car." Instead of the arterials and highways that speed cars in and out of suburbs, the New Urbanists favor gridlike street patterns that promote pedestrian and bicycle traffic, tame car traffic with frequent stops, and knit neighborhoods and communities together on a human scale. Another tenet of the New Urbanism that highlights its civic aspirations is to design neighborhoods around central public spaces and accord primacy to town halls, libraries, schools, and other civic buildings. "We must return meaning and stature to the physical expression of our public life. From streets and parks to plazas, village squares, and commercial centers, the Commons defines the meeting ground of a neighborhood and its local identity." By the 1990s, dozens of developments inspired by the New Urbanism had been built or planned across the country, from the town of Seaside on Florida's panhandle to Laguna West in Sacramento County, California.[55]

## Community Organizing

One of the most promising expressions of the civic strand of freedom can be found in the work of the Industrial Areas Foundation (IAF), a network of community-based organizations that teaches residents of poor communities how to engage in effective political activity. The IAF traces its origins to Saul Alinsky, the well-known community organizer of the 1940s and 1950s, who brought his aggressive style of organizing to the slums behind the stockyards of Chicago. Alinksy stressed the importance of building on local "pockets of power" such as unions, religious groups, ethnic and civic groups, small business associations, and political organizations. In recent decades, however, most traditional bases of civic activity in inner cities have eroded, leaving religious congregations the only vital institutions in many communities. As a result, Alinsky's successors in the IAF have organized primarily around congregations, especially Catholic and Protestant churches.[56]

The most influential modern IAF organization is Communities Organized for Public Service (COPS), a citizens' group founded in 1974 in the impoverished Hispanic neighborhoods of San Antonio. Its base in Catholic parishes provides not only a stable source of funds, participants, and leaders but also a shared moral language as a starting point for political discourse.[57] The leaders COPS identifies and trains are not established political figures or activists but those accustomed to working in community-sustaining institutions like school PTAs and church councils. Often they are women "whose lives by and large have been wrapped up in their parishes and their children. What COPS has been able to do is to give them a public life and a public visibility, to educate, to provide the tools whereby they can participate in the political process."[58]

By equipping its members to deliberate about community needs and to engage in political activity, COPS brought a billion dollars' worth of improvements for roads, schools, sewers, parks, and other infrastructure to long-neglected neighborhoods of San Antonio. Together with a network of affiliated organizations throughout Texas, it helped pass statewide legislation reforming public education, health care, and farm safety. By 1994 the IAF had spawned some forty grassroots organizations in seventeen states. Like civic conservatives, IAF leaders stressed the importance of mediating institutions such as families, neighborhoods, and churches, and the character-forming role such institutions can play. For the IAF, however, these structures were points of departure for political activity, ways of linking the moral resources of community life to the exercise of freedom in the republican sense.[59]

As these disparate expressions of the republican tradition suggest, the case for reviving the civic strand of freedom is not that it would make for a more consensual politics. There is no reason to suppose that a politics organized around republican themes would command a greater measure of agreement than does our present politics. As the reigning political agenda invites disagreement about the meaning of neutrality, rights, and truly voluntary choice, a political agenda informed by civic concerns would invite disagreement about the meaning of virtue and the forms of self-government that are possible in our time. Some would emphasize the moral and religious dimensions of civic virtue, while others would emphasize the ways in which economic arrangements and structures of power hinder or promote the exercise of self-rule. The political divisions arising in response to these issues would probably differ from those that govern the debate over the welfare state. But political divisions there would surely be. A successful revival of republican politics would not resolve our political disputes; at best, it would invigorate political debate by grappling more directly with the obstacles to self-government in our time.

## GLOBAL POLITICS AND PARTICULAR IDENTITIES

But suppose the civic aspirations that roil our present politics did find fuller voice and succeeded in reorienting the terms of political discourse. What then? What is the prospect that a revitalized politics could actually alleviate the loss of mastery and the erosion of community that lie at the heart of democracy's discontent? Politics is an unpredictable activity, so it is difficult to say with certainty. But even a politics that engaged rather than avoided substantive moral discourse, that attended to the civic consequences of economic inequality, that strengthened the mediating institutions of civil society—even such a politics would confront a daunting obstacle. This obstacle consists in the formidable scale on which modern economic life is organized and the difficulty of constituting the democratic political authority necessary to govern it.

This difficulty actually involves two related challenges. One is to devise political institutions capable of governing the global economy. The other is to cultivate the civic identities necessary to sustain those institutions, to supply them with the moral authority they require. It is not obvious that both these challenges can be met.

In a world where capital and goods, information and images, pollution and people, flow across national boundaries with unprecedented ease, politics must assume transnational, even global forms, if only to keep up. Otherwise, economic power will go unchecked by democratically sanctioned political power. Nation-states, traditionally the vehicles of self-government, will find themselves increasingly unable to bring their citizens' judgments and values to bear on the economic forces that govern their destinies. The disempowering of the nation-state in relation to the global economy may be one source of the discontent that afflicts not only American politics but other democracies around the world.

If the global character of the economy suggests the need for transnational forms of governance, however, it remains to be seen whether such political units can inspire the identification and allegiance—the moral and civic culture—on which democratic authority ultimately depends. In fact there is reason to doubt that they can. Except in extraordinary moments, such as war, even nation-states find it difficult to inspire the sense of community and civic engagement self-government requires. Political associations more expansive than nations, and with fewer cultural traditions and historical memories to draw upon, may find the task of cultivating commonality more difficult still.

Even the European Community, one of the most successful experiments in supranational governance, has so far failed to cultivate a common European identity sufficient to support its mechanisms of economic and political integregation. Advocates of further European integration worry about the "democratic deficit" that arises when expert commissioners and civil servants rather than elected representatives conduct most of the Community's business. Such an "attenuated political scene," Shirley Williams observes, misses "the anger, the passion, the commitment, and the partisanship that constitute the lifeblood of politics." It makes for a "businessman's Europe," not a "citizens' Europe." Czech President Vaclav Havel emphasizes the absence of shared moral purpose: "Europe today lacks an ethos. . . .There is no real identification in Europe with the meaning and purpose of integration." He calls upon pan-European institutions "to cultivate the values from which the spirit and ethos of European integration might grow."[60]

In certain ways, the challenge to self-government in the global community resembles the predicament American politics faced in the early decades of the twentieth century. Then as now, there was a gap, or lack of fit, between the scale of economic life and the terms in which people conceived their identities, a gap that many experienced as disorienting and disempowering. Americans long accustomed to taking their bearings from small communities suddenly found themselves confronting an economy that was national in scope. Political institutions lagged behind, inadequate to life in a continental society. Then as now, new forms of commerce and communication spilled across familiar political boundaries and created networks of interdependence among people in distant places. But the new interdependence did not carry with it a new sense of community. As Jane Addams observed, "the mere mechanical fact of interdependence amounts to nothing."[61]

Addams' insight is no less apt today. What railroads, telegraph wires, and national markets were to her time, satellite hookups, CNN, cyberspace, and global markets are to ours—instruments that link people in distant places without necessarily making them neighbors or fellow citizens or participants in a common venture. Converting networks of communication and interdependence into a public life worth affirming is a moral and political matter, not a technological one.

Given the similarity between their predicament and ours, it is instructive to recall the solution they pursued. Confronted with an economy that threatened to defy democratic control, Progressives such as Theodore Roosevelt and Herbert Croly and their New Deal successors sought to increase the powers of the national government. If democracy were to survive, they concluded, the concentration of economic power would have to be met by a similar concentration of political power. But this task involved more than the centralization of government; it also required the nationalization of politics. The primary form of political community had to be recast on a national scale. Only in this way could they hope to ease the gap between the scale of social and economic life and the terms in which people conceived their identities. Only a strong sense of national community could morally and politically underwrite the extended involvements of a modern industrial order. The "nationalizing of American political, economic, and social life," Croly wrote, was "an essentially formative and enlightening political transformation." America would become more of a democracy only as it became "more of a nation. . . in ideas, in institutions, and in spirit."[62]

It is tempting to think that the logic of their solution can be extended to our time. If the way to deal with a national economy was to strengthen the national government and cultivate a sense of national citizenship, perhaps the way to deal with a global economy is to strengthen global governance and to cultivate a corresponding sense of global, or cosmopolitan citizenship.

Internationally minded reformers have already begun to articulate this impulse. In 1995 the Commission on Global Governance, a group of twenty-eight public officials from around the world, published a report stressing the need to strengthen international institutions. Global interdependence was growing, they observed, driven by powerful technological and economic forces. But the world's political structures had not kept pace. The Commission called for a new international institution to deal with economic and environmental issues, a "people's assembly" that might ultimately be elected by the people of the world, a scheme of international taxation to finance activities of global goverance, and greater authority for the world court. Mindful of the need to cultivate an ethic adequate to its project, the Commission also called for efforts to "foster global citizenship," to inspire "broad acceptance of a global civic ethic," to transform "a global neighborhood based on economic exchange and improved communications into a universal moral community."[63]

Other commentators of the 1990s saw in international environmental, human rights, and women's movements the emergence of a "global civil society" that might serve as a counterweight to the power of global markets and media. According to political scientist Richard Falk, such movements hold promise for a new "global citizenship. . . premised upon global or species solidarity." "This spirit of global citizenship is almost completely deterritorialized," he observes. It has nothing to do with loyalty to a particular political community, whether city or state, but aspires instead to the ideal of "one-world community." Philosopher Martha Nussbaum argues, in a similar spirit, for a civic education that cultivates cosmopolitan citizenship. Since national identity is "a morally irrelevant characteristic," students should be taught that their "primary allegiance is to the community of human beings in the entire world."[64]

The cosmopolitan ideal rightly emphasizes the humanity we share and directs our attention to the moral consequences that flow from it. It offers a corrective to the narrow, sometimes murderous chauvinism into which ethnic and national identities can descend. It reminds wealthy nations that their obligations to humanity do not end at the water's edge. It may even suggest reasons to care for the planet that go beyond its use to us. All this makes the cosmopolitan ideal an attractive ethic, especially now that the global aspect of political life requires forms of allegiance that go beyond nations.

Despite these merits, however, the cosmopolitan ideal is flawed, both as a moral ideal and as a public philosophy for self-government in our time. The notion that universal identities must always take precedence over particular ones has a long and varied history. Kant tied morality to respect for persons as rational beings independent of their particular characteristics, and Marx identified the highest solidarity as that of man with his species-being. Perhaps the clearest statement of the cosmopolitan ethic as a moral ideal is the one offered by the Enlightenment philosopher Montesquieu: "If I knew something useful to me, but prejudicial to my family, I would reject it from my soul. If I knew something useful to my family but not to my country, I would try to forget it. If I knew something useful to my country, but prejudicial to Europe, or useful to Europe but prejudicial to humankind, I would regard it as a crime. . . . [For] I am a man before I am a Frenchman, or rather . . . I am necessarily a man, while I am a Frenchman only by chance."[65]

If our encompassing loyalties should always take precedence over more local ones, then the distinction between friends and strangers should ideally be overcome. Our special concern for the welfare of friends would be a kind of prejudice, a measure of our distance from universal human concern. Montesquieu does not shrink from this conclusion. "A truly virtuous man would come to the aid of the most distant stranger as quickly as to his own friend," he writes. "If men were perfectly virtuous, they wouldn't have friends."[66]

It is difficult to imagine a world in which persons were so virtuous that they had no friends, only a universal disposition to friendliness. The problem is not simply that such a world would be difficult to bring about but that it would be difficult to recognize as a human world. The love of humanity is a noble sentiment, but most of the time we live our lives by smaller solidarities. This may reflect certain limits to the bounds of moral sympathy. More important, it reflects the fact that we learn to love humanity not in general but through its particular expressions.

J.G. Herder, the German Romantic philosopher, was among the first to affirm differences of language, culture, and national identity as distinctive expressions of our humanity. He was scornful of the cosmopolitan citizen whose devotion to humankind is wholly abstract: "The savage who loves himself, his wife and child, with quiet joy, and in his modest way works for the good of his tribe" is "a truer being than that shadow of a man, the refined citizen of the world, who, enraptured with the love of all his fellow-shadows, loves but a chimera." In practice, Herder writes, it is the savage in his poor hut who welcomes the stranger. "The inundated heart of the idle cosmopolite, on the other hand, offers shelter to nobody." Charles Dickens also caught the folly of the unsituated cosmopolitan in his description of Mrs. Jellyby, the character in Bleak House who woefully neglects her children while pursuing charitable causes overseas. She was a woman "with handsome eyes," Dickens writes, "though they had a curious habit of seeming to look a long way off. As if . . . they could see nothing nearer than Africa."[67]

To affirm as morally relevant the particular communities that locate us in the world, from neighborhoods to nations, is not to claim that we owe nothing to persons as persons, as fellow human beings. At their best, local solidarities gesture beyond themselves toward broader horizons of moral concern, including the horizon of our common humanity. The cosmopolitan ethic is wrong, not for asserting that we have certain obligations to humanity as a whole but rather for insisting that the more universal communities we inhabit must always take precedence over more particular ones.

Most of us find ourselves claimed, at one point or another, by a wide range of different communities, some overlapping, others contending. When obligations conflict, there is no way of deciding in advance, once and for all, which should prevail. Deciding which of one's identities is properly engaged—as parent or professional, follower of a faith or partisan of a cause, citizen of one's country or citizen of the world—is a matter of moral reflection and political deliberation that will vary according to the issue at stake. The best deliberation will attend to the content of the claims, their relative moral weight, and their role in the narratives by which the participants make sense of their lives. Montesquieu to the contrary, such claims cannot simply be ranked according to the size or scope of the community that gives rise to them. No general principle of much practical use can rank obligations in advance, and yet some responses to moral and political dilemmas are better—more admirable or worthy or fitting—than others. Unless this were so, there would be no point, and no burden, in deliberation itself.

The moral defect of the cosmopolitan ethic is related to its political defect. For even as the global economy demands more universal forms of political identity, the pull of the particular reasserts itself. Even as nations accede to new institutions of global governance, they confront rising demands from ethnic, religious, and linguistic groups for various forms of political recognition and self-determination. These demands are prompted in part by the dissolution of the empires that once contained them, such as the Soviet Union. But the growing aspiration for the public expression of communal identities may also reflect a yearning for political identities that can situate people in a world increasingly governed by vast and distant forces.

For a time, the nation-state promised to answer this yearning, to provide the link between identity and self-rule. In theory at least, each state was a more or less self-sufficient political and economic unit that gave expression to the collective identity of a people defined by a common history, language, or tradition. The nation-state laid claim to the allegiance of its citizens on the ground that its exercise of sovereignty expressed their collective identity.

In the contemporary world, however, this claim is losing its force. National sovereignty is eroded from above by the mobility of capital, goods, and information across national boundaries, the integration of world financial markets, the transnational character of industrial production. At the same time, national sovereignty is challenged from below by the resurgent aspirations of subnational groups for autonomy and self-rule. As their effective sovereignty fades, nations gradually lose their hold on the allegiance of their citizens. Beset by the integrating tendencies of the global economy and the fragmenting tendencies of group identities, nation-states are increasingly unable to link identity and self-rule. Even the most powerful states cannot escape the imperatives of the global economy; even the smallest are too heterogeneous to give full expression to the communal identity of any one ethnic or national or religious group without oppressing others who live in their midst.

Given the limits of cosmopolitan politics, the attempt to save democracy by globalizing citizenship, as Progressives once sought to save democracy by nationalizing citizenship, is unlikely to succeed. The analogy between the globalizing impulse of our time and the nationalizing project of theirs holds to this extent: We cannot hope to govern the global economy without transnational political institutions, and we cannot expect to sustain such institutions without cultivating more expansive civic identities. This is the moment of truth in the cosmopolitan vision. Human rights conventions, global environmental accords, and world bodies governing trade, finance, and economic development are among the undertakings that will depend for public support on inspiring a greater sense of engagement in a shared global destiny.

But the cosmopolitan vision is wrong to suggest that we can restore self-government simply by pushing sovereignty and citizenship upward. The hope for self-government lies not in relocating sovereignty but in dispersing it. The most promising alternative to the sovereign state is not a one-world community based on the solidarity of humankind, but a multiplicity of communities and political bodies—some more, some less extensive than nations—among which sovereignty is diffused. The nation-state need not fade away, only cede its claim as sole repository of sovereign power and primary object of political allegiance. Different forms of political association would govern different spheres of life and engage different aspects of our identities. Only a regime that disperses sovereignty both upward and downward can combine the power required to rival global market forces with the differentiation required of a public life that hopes to inspire the reflective allegiance of its citizens.

In some places, dispersing sovereignty may entail according greater cultural and political autonomy to subnational communities—such as Catalans and Kurds, Scots and Quebecois—even while strengthening and democratizing transnational structures, such as the European Union. Or it may involve modes of devolution and subsidiarity along geographic rather than ethnic and cultural lines. Arrangements such as these may ease the strife that arises when state sovereignty is an all-or-nothing affair, absolute and indivisible, the only meaningful form of self-determination.

In the United States, which never was a nation-state in the European sense, proliferating sites of political engagement may take a different form. America was born of the conviction that sovereignty need not reside in a single place. From the start, the Constitution divided power among branches and levels of government. Over time, however, we too have pushed sovereignty and citizenship upward, in the direction of the nation.

The nationalizing of American political life occurred largely in response to industrial capitalism. The consolidation of economic power called forth the consolidation of political power. Present-day conservatives who rail against big government often ignore this fact. They wrongly assume that rolling back the power of the national government would liberate individuals to pursue their own ends instead of leaving them at the mercy of economic forces beyond their control.

Conservative complaints about big government find popular resonance, but not for the reasons conservatives articulate. The American welfare state is politically vulnerable because it does not rest on a sense of national community adequate to its purpose. The nationalizing project that unfolded from the Progressive era to the New Deal to the Great Society succeeded only in part. It managed to create a strong national government but failed to cultivate a shared national identity. As the welfare state developed, it drew less on an ethic of social solidarity and mutual obligation and more on an ethic of fair procedures and individual rights. But the liberalism of the procedural republic proved an inadequate substitute for the strong sense of citizenship the welfare state requires.

If the nation cannot summon more than a minimal commonality, it is unlikely that the global community can do better, at least on its own. A more promising basis for a democratic politics that reaches beyond nations is a revitalized civic life nourished in the more particular communities we inhabit. In the age of NAFTA, the politics of neighborhood matters more, not less. People will not pledge allegiance to vast and distant entities, whatever their importance, unless those institutions are somehow connected to political arrangements that reflect the identity of the participants.

This is no reason to consider the unrealized possibilities implicit in American federalism. We commonly think of federalism as a constitutional doctrine that, once dormant, has recently been revived by conservatives who would shift power from the federal government to the states. But federalism is more than a theory of intergovernmental relations. It also stands for a political vision that offers an alternative to the sovereign state and the univocal political identities such states require. It suggests that self-government works best when sovereignty is dispersed and citizenship formed across multiple sites of civic engagement. This aspect of federalism informs the pluralist version of republican politics. It supplies the differentiation that separates Tocqueville's republicanism from Rousseau's, that saves the formative project from slipping into coercion.

Rousseau conceived political community as an undifferentiated whole and so insisted that citizens conform to the general will. Tocqueville stressed the republican benefits of political bodies intermediate between the individual and the state, such as townships. "The native of New England is attached to his township because it is independent and free," he wrote. "He takes a part in every occurrence in the place; he practices the art of government in the small sphere within his reach; he accustoms himself to those forms without which liberty can only advance by revolutions; he imbibes their spirit; he acquires a taste for order, comprehends the balance of powers, and collects clear practical notions on the nature of his duties and the extent of his rights." Practicing self-government in small spheres, Tocqueville observed, impels citizens to larger spheres of political activity as well.[68]

Jefferson spoke for a similar vision when he worried, late in life, that the Constitution did not make adequate provision for the cultivation of civic virtue. Even the states, and for that matter the counties, were too distant to engage the civic energies and affection of the people. In order "to nourish and perpetuate" the republican spirit, Jefferson proposed dividing the counties into wards, local self-governing units that would permit direct political participation. By "making every citizen an acting member of the government," the ward system would "attach him by his strongest feelings to the independence of his country, and its republican constitution." The "division and subdivision of duties" among federal, state, county, and ward republics was not only a way of avoiding the abuse of power. It was also, for Jefferson, a way of cementing the whole by giving each citizen a part in public affairs.[69]

Jefferson's ward system was never adopted, and the New England township Tocqueville admired has faded in power and civic significance. But the political insight underlying their federalism remains revelant today. This is the insight that proliferating sites of civic activity and political power can serve self-government by cultivating virtue, equipping citizens for self-rule, and generating loyalties to larger political wholes. If local government and municipal institutions are no longer adequate arenas for republican citizenship, we must seek such public spaces as may be found amidst the institutions of civil society—in schools and workplaces, churches and synagogues, trade unions and social movements.

Public spaces such as these were indispensable to the finest expression of republican politics in our time, the civil rights movement of the 1950s to mid-1960s. In retrospect, the republican character of the civil rights movement is easily obscured. It unfolded at just the time when the procedural republic was taking form. Partly as a result, Americans learned the lessons of the movement through the lens of contemporary liberalism: Civil rights was about nondiscrimination and equality before the law, about vindicating individual rights against the prejudices of local communities, about respecting persons as persons, regardless of their race, religion, or other particular characteristics.

But this is not the whole story. To assimilate the civil rights movement to the liberalism of the procedural republic is to miss its most important lessons for our time. More than a means to equal rights, the movement itself was a moment of empowerment, an instance of the civic strand of freedom. The laws that desegregated public facilities and secured voting rights for blacks served freedom in the voluntarist sense—the freedom to choose and pursue one's purposes and ends. But the struggle to win these rights displayed a higher, republican freedom—the freedom that consists in acting collectively to shape the public world.[70]

Beyond the legal reforms it sought, the civil rights movement undertook a formative project; it aimed at the moral and civic "transformation of a whole people." As Martin Luther King Jr. explained, "When legal contests were the sole form of activity, the ordinary Negro was involved as a passive spectator. His interest was stirred, but his energies were unemployed. Mass marches transformed the common man into the star performer. . . . The Negro was no longer a subject of change; he was the active organ of change."[71]

The formative aspect of republican politics requires public spaces that gather citizens together, enable them to interpret their condition, and cultivate solidarity and civic engagement. For the civil rights movement, these public spaces were provided by the black churches of the South. They were the sites of the mass meetings, the civic education, the prayer and song, that equipped blacks to join in the boycotts and the marches of the movement.[72]

We commonly think of the civil rights movement as finding its fruition in the civil rights and voting rights laws passed by Congress. But the nation would never have acted without a movement whose roots lay in more particular identities and places. Moreover, the movement offered a vision of republican citizenship that went beyond the right to vote. Even after the Voting Rights Act was won, King hoped for a public life that might realize the intimations of republican freedom present in the civil rights movement at its best: "How shall we turn the ghettos into a vast school? How shall we make every street corner a forum . . . every houseworker and every laborer a demonstrator, a voter, a canvasser and a student? The dignity their jobs may deny them is waiting for them in political and social action."[73]

## BEYOND SOVEREIGN STATES AND SOVEREIGN SELVES

The global media and markets that shape our lives beckon us to a world beyond boundaries and belonging. But the civic resources we need to master these forces, or at least to contend with them, are still to be found in the places and stories, memories and meanings, incidents and identities, that situate us in the world and give our lives their moral particularity.

The public philosophy by which we live bids us to bracket these attachments, to set them aside for political purposes, to conduct our political debates without reference to them. But a procedural republic that banishes moral and religious argument from political discourse makes for an impoverished civic life. It also fails to answer the aspiration for self-government; its image of citizens as free and independent selves, unencumbered by moral or civic ties they have not chosen, cannot sustain the public spirit that equips us for self-rule.

Since the days of Aristotle's polis, the republican tradition has viewed self-government as an activity rooted in a particular place, carried out by citizens loyal to that place and the way of life it embodies. Self-government today, however, requires a politics that plays itself out in a multiplicity of settings, from neighborhoods to nations to the world as a whole. Such a politics requires citizens who can think and act as multiply situated selves. The civic virtue distinctive to our time is the capacity to negotiate our way among the sometimes overlapping, sometimes conflicting obligations that claim us, and to live with the tension to which multiple loyalties give rise. This capacity is difficult to sustain, for it is easier to live with the plurality between persons than within them.

The republican tradition reminds us that to every virtue there corresponds a characteristic form of corruption or decay. Where civic virtue consists in holding together the complex identities of modern selves, it is vulnerable to corruption of two kinds. The first is the tendency to fundamentalism, the response of those who cannot abide the ambiguity associated with divided sovereignty and multiply encumbered selves. To the extent that contemporary politics puts sovereign states and sovereign selves in question, it is likely to provoke reactions from those who would banish ambiguity, shore up borders, harden the distinction between insiders and outsiders, and promise a politics to "take back our culture and take back our country," to "restore our sovereignty" with a vengeance.[74]

The second corruption to which multiply encumbered citizens are prone is the drift to formless, protean, storyless selves, unable to weave the various strands of their identity into a coherent whole. Political community depends on the narratives by which people make sense of their condition and interpret the common life they share; at its best, political deliberation is not only about competing policies but also about competing interpretations of the character of a community, of its purposes and ends. A politics that proliferates the sources and sites of citizenship complicates the interpretive project. At a time when the narrative resources of civic life are already strained—as the sound-bites, factoids, and disconnected images of our media-saturated culture attest—it becomes increasingly difficult to tell the tales that order our lives. There is a growing danger that, individually and collectively, we will find ourselves slipping into a fragmented, storyless condition. The loss of the capacity for narrative would amount to the ultimate disempowering of the human subject, for without narrative there is no continuity between present and past, and therefore no responsibility, and therefore no possibility of acting together to govern ourselves.

Since human beings are storytelling beings, we are bound to rebel against the drift to storylessness. But there is no guarantee that the rebellions will take salutary form. Some, in their hunger for story, will be drawn to the vacant, vicarious fare of confessional talk shows, celebrity scandals, and sensational trials. Others will seek refuge in fundamentalism. The hope of our times rests instead with those who can summon the conviction and restraint to make sense of our condition and repair the civic life on which democracy depends.

## NOTES

1. Only 20 percent of Americans believe they can trust the government in Washington to do what is right most of the time; *Gallup Poll Monthly*, February 1994, p.

12. Three-fourths say they are dissatisfied with the way the political process is working; *Gallup Poll Monthly,* September 1992. A similar percentage believe that government is run by a few big interests rather than for the benefit of all; Alan F. Kay et al., "Steps for Democracy," *Americans Talk Issues,* March 25, 1994, p. 9.

2. See John Rawls, *A Theory of Justice* (Cambridge, Mass.: Harvard University Press, 1971); Ronald Dworkin, "Liberalism," in Stuart Hampshire, ed., *Public and Private Morality* (Cambridge: Cambridge University Press, 1978), pp. 114–43; idem, *Taking Rights Seriously* (Cambridge, Mass.: Harvard University Press, 1977); Robert Nozick, *Anarchy, State, and Utopia* (New York: Basic Books, 1977); Bruce Ackerman, *Social Justice in the Liberal State* (New Haven: Yale University Press, 1980).

3. The term "procedural republic" was suggested to me by Judith N. Shklar.

4. On the meaning of "liberal" as used in contemporary American politics, see Ronald D. Rotunda, *The Politics of Language* (Iowa City: Iowa University Press, 1986).

5. On republican arguments for and against freehold suffrage, see the debates in the Virginia Convention of 1829–30, in Merrill D. Peterson, ed., *Democracy, Liberty, and Property* (Indianapolis: Bobbs-Merrill, 1966), pp. 377–408; also Chilton Williamson, *American Suffrage: From Property to Democracy,* 1760–1860 (Princeton: Princeton University Press, 1960). On defenders of slavery, see James Henry Hammond, "'Mud-Sill' Speech" (1858), and Josiah Nott, "Types of Mankind" (1854), in Eric L. McKitrick, ed., *Slavery Defended: The Views of the Old South* (Englewood Cliffs, N.J.: Prentice-Hall, 1963), pp. 121–138; also Kenneth S. Greenberg, *Masters and Statesmen: The Political Culture of American Slavery* (Baltimore: Johns Hopkins University Press, 1985), pp. 3–22, 85–106. On opposition to citizenship for immigrants, see Tyler Anbinder, *Nativism and Slavery: The Northern Know Nothings and the Politics of the 1850s* (New York: Oxford University Press, 1992), pp. 118–26.

6. Jean-Jacques Rousseau, *On the Social Contract* (1762), trans. and ed. Donald A. Cress, book 2, chap. 7 (Indianapolis: Hackett, 1983), p. 39.

7. Benjamin Rush, *A Plan for the Establishment of Public Schools and the Diffusion of Knowledge in Pennsylvania* (1786), in Frederick Rudolph, ed., *Essays on Education in the Early Republic* (Cambridge, Mass.: Harvard University Press, 1965), pp. 9, 17, 14.

8. Alexis de Tocqueville, *Democracy in America* (1835), trans. Henry Reeve, ed. Phillips Bradley (New York: Alfred A. Knopf, 1945), vol. 1, p. 416.

9. Rousseau, *On the Social Contract,* book 4, chaps. 1–2, pp. 79–81. See also book 2, chap. 3, p. 32: "If, when a sufficiently informed populace deliberates, the citizens were to have no communication among themselves, the general will would always result."

10. Hannah Arendt's account of the public realm also emphasizes this feature: "What makes mass society so difficult to bear is not the number of people involved, or at least not primarily, but the fact that the world between them has lost its power to gather them together, to relate and to separate them"; *The Human Condition* (Chicago: University of Chicago Press, 1958), pp. 52–53.

11. Tocqueville, *Democracy in America,* vol. 1, chap. 17, p. 299; see generally chap. 5, pp. 66–68, and chap. 17, pp. 299–325. The idea that freedom requires a common life that is nonetheless differentiated or articulated by particular, identity-forming agencies of civil society is central to G. W. F. Hegel, *Philosophy of Right* (1821), trans. T. M. Knox (London: Oxford University Press, 1952).

12. Immanuel Kant, "Perpetual Peace" (1795), in *Kant's Political Writings,* ed. Hans Reiss (Cambridge: Cambridge University Press, 1970), pp. 112–13.

13. James Q. Wilson, "The Rediscovery of Character: Private Virtue and Public Policy," *The Public Interest,* Fall 1985, p. 3. See also idem, *On Character* (Washington, D.C.: American Enterprise Institute Press, 1995).

14. This new line of argument is recounted and defended in Lawrence M. Mead, *Beyond Entitlement: The Social Obligations of Citizenship* (New York: Free Press, 1986); and idem, *The New Politics of Poverty* (New York: Basic Books, 1992).

15. Daniel P. Moynihan, *The Negro Family: The Case for National Action* (Washington, D.C.: Office of Policy Planning and Research, U.S. Department of Labor, March 1965), reprinted in Lee Rainwater and William L. Yancey, eds., *The Moynihan Report and the Politics of Controversy* (Cambridge, Mass.: MIT Press, 1967), pp. 39–124; quotation on p. 94.

16. Moynihan emphasized that the national interest in family structure extended to the civic consequences of family life, not to its moral character as such: "The object should be to strengthen the Negro family so as to enable it to raise and support its members as other families do. After that, how this group of Americans chooses to run its affairs, take advantage of its opportunities, or fail to do so, is none of the nation's business"; ibid., pp. 93–94.

17. Floyd McKissick, quoted in ibid., p. 200; the sympathetic commentators are Rainwater and Yancey, p. 162. See also William J. Bennett, "Reflections on the Moynihan Report Thirty Years Later," *American Enterprise,* 6 (January/February 1995), 30.

18. Nathan Glazer, "The Social Policy of the Reagan Administration: A Review," *The Public Interest,* Spring 1984, pp. 87–88; Robert D. Reischauer, "Welfare Reform: Will Consensus Be Enough?" *Brookings Review,* 5 (Summer 1987), 6; Mead, *The New Politics of Poverty,* pp. 22–23.

19. Mead, *Beyond Entitlement,* pp. 13–14.

20. Moynihan quoted in "Daniel Patrick Moynihan: Making Welfare Work," *Congressional Quarterly Weekly Report,* 45 (March 21, 1987), 507.

21. Bennett, "Reflections on the Moynihan Report," p. 32; idem, "Revolt Against God," *Policy Review,* no. 67 (Winter 1994), 23.

22. Idem, *The De-Valuing of America* (New York: Simon & Schuster, 1992), p. 37; idem, "What to Do about the Children," *Commentary,* March 1995, pp. 24–25.

23. See Richard John Neuhaus, *The Naked Public Square: Religion and Democracy in America* (Grand Rapids, Mich.: William B. Eerdmans, 1984).

24. Bennett, *The De-Valuing of America,* pp. 58, 121.

25. Glenn C. Loury, "Beyond Victimhood," *Times Literary Supplement,* June 10, 1994.

26. Idem, "God and the Ghetto," *Wall Street Journal,* February 25, 1993.

27. President William J. Clinton, "Remarks to the Convocation of the Church of God in Christ in Memphis," November 13, 1993, *Weekly Compilation of Presidential Documents,* vol. 29, November 22, 1993 (Washington, D.C.: Government Printing Office, 1993), pp. 2360–62.

28. Clinton, "Address before a Joint Session of the Congress on the State of the Union," January 25, 1994, ibid., vol. 30.

29. Joe Klein, "The Out-of-Wedlock Question," *Newsweek,* December 13, 1993, p. 37.

30. Joycelyn Elders and Donna Shalala, quoted ibid. See also Gertrude Himmelfarb, *The De-Moralization of Society* (New York: Alfred A. Knopf, 1995), pp. 240–41.

31. Senator Bill Bradley, National Press Club, Washington, D.C., February 9, 1995.

32. The $826 billion figure is in constant 1993 dollars. From 1950 to 1978, real family income growth by quintile, from the lowest to the highest, was 138 percent, 98 percent, 106 percent, 111 percent, and 99 percent respectively. Comparable figures for 1979 to 1993 were 17 percent, 8 percent, 3 percent, 5 percent, and 18 percent. Department of Labor figures presented with remarks by Labor Secretary Robert B. Reich, National Press Club, Washington, D.C., January 5, 1995.

33. David R. Francis, "New Figures Show Wider Gap between Rich and Poor," *Christian Science Monitor,* April 21, 1995, p. 1, citing a study by economist Edward N. Wolff; and Keith Bradsher, "Gap in Wealth in U.S. Called Widest in West," *New York Times,* April 17, 1995, pp. A1, D4, also citing Wolff. See also Edward N. Wolff, *Top Heavy* (New York: Twentieth Century Fund Press, 1995); and Kevin Phillips, *Boiling Point: Republicans, Democrats, and the Decline of Middle-Class Prosperity* (New York: Random House, 1993), p. xix, citing economic historian Claudia Goldin.

34. These and other factors are discussed in Robert B. Reich, *The Work of Nations* (New York: Alfred A. Knopf, 1991), pp. 202–224; Phillips, *Boiling Point,* pp. 32–57, 85–128; and idem, *The Politics of Rich and Poor* (New York: Random House, 1990), pp. 52–153.

35. Aristotle, *The Politics,* trans. and ed. Ernest Barker, book 4, chap. 11 (1295b) (London: Oxford University Press, 1946), pp. 180–82; Rousseau, *On the Social Contract,* book 2, chap. 11, pp. 46–47.

36. Robert B. Reich, "The Revolt of the Anxious Class," Democratic Leadership Council, Washington, D.C., November 22, 1994; idem, "The Choice Ahead," National Press Club, Washington, D.C., January 5, 1995.

37. Idem, *The Work of Nations,* pp. 249–315.

38. Ibid., pp. 268–277.

39. On the formative role of parks and playgrounds in the Progressive era, see Paul Boyer, *Urban Masses and Moral Order in America, 1820–1920* (Cambridge, Mass.: Harvard University Press, 1978), pp. 233–51.

40. Reich, *The Work of Nations,* p. 269.

41. Louis Uchitelle, "Sharp Rise of Private Guard Jobs," *New York Times,* October 14, 1989, p. 33.

42. Elizabeth Rudolph, *Time,* November 4, 1991, p. 86. See also Mickey Kaus, *The End of Equality* (New York: Basic Books, 1992), p. 56.

43. Kaus, *The End of Equality,* pp. 18, 21–22, 96–100. A political theory based on restricting the sphere in which money matters is advanced by Michael Walzer, *Spheres of Justice* (New York: Basic Books, 1983). On class-mixing places, see Ray Oldenburg, *The Great Good Place* (New York: Paragon House, 1989).

44. See Neal R. Peirce and Carol F. Steinbach, *Corrective Capitalism: The Rise of America's Community Development Corporations* (New York: Ford Foundation, 1987); Mitchell Sviridoff, "The Seeds of Urban Revival," *The Public Interest,* Winter 1994, pp. 82–103; Robert Zdenek, "Community Development Corporations," in Severyn T. Bruyn and James Meehan, eds., *Beyond the Market and the State* (Philadelphia: Temple University Press, 1987), pp. 112–30.

45. Those who relate CDCs to democratic political economy include James Meehan, "Working toward Local Self-Reliance," in Bruyn and Meehan, *Beyond the Market and the State,* pp. 131–151; Richard Schramm, "Local, Regional, and National Strategies,"

ibid., pp. 152–170; and Charles Derber, "Coming Glued: Communitarianism to the Rescue," *Tikkun,* 8 (July–August 1993), 95–99.

46. David Clark Scott, "Ready or Not, Here Comes Wal-Mart," *Christian Science Monitor,* September 29, 1994, p. 8.

47. Hugh Sidey, "The Two Sides of the Sam Walton Legacy," *Time,* April 20, 1992, pp. 50–52.

48. See Constance E. Beaumont, *How Superstore Sprawl Can Harm Communities* (Washington, D.C.: National Trust for Historic Preservation, 1994); Jon Bowermaster, "When Wal-Mart Comes to Town," *New York Times Magazine,* April 2, 1989; Alan Ehrenhalt, "Up Against the Wal-Mart," *Governing,* September 1992, pp. 6–7.

49. Alex Achimore, "Putting the Community Back into Community Retail," *Urban Land,* August 1993, p. 34, quoted in Beaumont, *Superstore Sprawl,* p. 11.

50. See Steve Bishop, "Death of a Town," *Dallas Morning News,* January 26, 1992, p. 4J; Lisa Belkin, "Wal-Mart Is Closing, and Texas Towns Reels," *New York Times,* December 14, 1990; Peter T. Kilborn, "When Wal-Mart Pulls Out, What's Left?" *New York Times,* March 5, 1995, pp. F1, F6.

51. Caroline L. Cole, "Greenfield Rejects Offer by Wal-Mart," *Boston Globe,* October 20, 1993, p. 45; "In Two Towns, Main Street Fights Off Wal-Mart," *New York Times,* October 21, 1993, p. A16; Sophronia Scott Gregory, "They're Up Against the Wal," *Time,* November 1, 1993, p. 56.

52. Al Norman, quoted in Andrew Friedman, "Citizens Fight Wal-Mart Sprawl," *Neighborhood Works,* October/November 1994, p. 10. See Chris Reidy, "Crusade, of the 'Sprawl-buster,'" *Boston Globe,* July 7, 1994, p. 37; Joseph Pereira and Bob Ortega, "Once Easily Turned Away by Local Foes, Wal-Mart Gets Tough in New England," *Wall Street Journal,* September 7, 1994, p. B1; Jonathan Walters, "National 'Sprawl Busters' Coalition Emerges," *Historic Preservation News,* December 1994/January 1995, pp. 10–12; Jonathan Walters, "Taming the Mega-Store Monster," *Governing,* January 1995, pp. 27–33.

53. The primary texts of the New Urbanism are Peter Katz, ed., *The New Urbanism: Toward an Architecture of Community* (New York: McGraw-Hill, 1994); and Peter Calthorpe, *The Next American Metropolis: Ecology, Community, and the American Dream* (New York: Princeton Architectural Press, 1993). I am grateful to Gerald Frug for bringing these works to my attention. The movement is also described in "The New Urbanism Takes Hold," *Utne Reader,* May/June 1994, pp. 28–30.

54. Todd W. Bressi, "Planning the American Dream," in Katz, *The New Urbanism,* p. xxx; Peter Calthorpe, "The Region," ibid., p. xi. On gated communities, see Calthorpe, *The Next American Metropolis,* p. 37; and Timothy Egan, "Many Seek Security in Private Communities," *New York Times,* September 3, 1995, pp. 1, 22.

55. Quotations are from Calthorpe, *The Next American Metropolis,* pp. 17, 23; see also Bressi, "Planning the American Dream," p. xxxii; and Andres Duany and Elizabeth Plater-Zyberk, "The Neighborhood, the District and the Corridor," in Katz, *The New Urbanism,* pp. xvii–xx. For descriptions and photographs of Seaside and Laguna West, see ibid., pp. 2–29.

56. Harry C. Boyte, *Common Wealth: A Return to Citizen Politics* (New York: Free Press, 1989), pp. 49–61, 81–86; Ernesto Cortes, Jr., "Reweaving the Fabric: The Iron Rule and the IAF Strategy for Power and Politics," in Henry G. Cisneros, ed., *Interwoven Destinies: Cities and the Nation* (New York: W. W. Norton, 1993), p. 303.

57. Boyte, *CommonWealth,* pp. 87–99; Mark R. Warren, "Social Capital and Community Empowerment: Religion and Political Organization in the Texas Industrial Areas Foundation" (Ph.D. diss., Harvard University, 1995), chap. 2; Geoffrey Rips, "A Democratic Conversation," *Texas Observer,* November 22, 1990, pp. 4–5; Mary Beth Rogers, "Gospel Values and Secular Politics," ibid., pp. 6–8.

58. COPS organizer Christine Stephens, quoted in Boyte, *CommonWealth,* p. 90.

59. Peter Applebome, "Changing Texas Politics at Its Roots," *New York Times,* May 31, 1988; Laurie Goodstein, "Harnessing the Force of Faith," *Washington Post,* February 6, 1994, pp. B1, B4; Boyte, *CommonWealth,* pp. 90–94, 191.

60. Shirley Williams, "Sovereignty and Accountability in the European Community," in Robert O. Keohane and Stanley Hoffman, eds., *The New European Community* (Boulder: Westview Press, 1991), pp. 155–176; Vaclav Havel, address to the General Assembly of the Council on Europe, Vienna, October 9, 1993, trans. Paul Wilson, *New York Review of Books,* 40 (November 18, 1993), p. 3.

61. Jane Addams, *Democracy and Social Ethics* (New York: Macmillan, 1907), pp. 210–11.

62. Herbert Croly, *The Promise of American Life* (1909; reprint, Indianapolis: Bobbs-Merrill, 1965), pp. 271–73.

63. *Our Global Neighborhood: The Report of the Commission on Global Governance* (New York: Oxford University Press, 1995), pp. 154, 257, 303–4, 5, 46–49, 336.

64. Richard Falk, "The Making of Global Citizenship," in Jeremy Brecher, John Brown Childs, and Jill Cutler, eds., *Global Visions: Beyond the New World Order* (Boston: South End Press, 1993), pp. 39–50; Martha Nussbaum, "Patriotism and Cosmopolitanism," *Boston Review,* October/November 1994, p. 3.

65. Montesquieu, *Mes pensées,* in *Oeuvres completes,* ed. Roger Chaillois (Paris: Gallimard, 1949), nos. 10, 11, pp. 980–81.

66. Ibid., no. 604, pp. 1129–30.

67. Johann Gottfried Herder, *Ideas for a Philosophy of the History of Mankind* (1791), in *J. G. Herder on Social and Political Culture,* trans. and ed. F. M. Bernard (Cambridge: Cambridge University Press, 1969), p. 309; Charles Dickens, *Bleak House* (1853) (Oxford: Oxford University Press, 1987), chap. 4, p. 36.

68. Tocqueville, *Democracy in America,* vol. 1, chap. 5, p. 68.

69. Thomas Jefferson to Samuel Kercheval, July 12, 1816, in *Jefferson Writings,* ed. Merrill D. Peterson (New York: Library of America, 1984), pp. 1399–1400.

70. See Richard H. King, *Civil Rights and the Idea of Freedom* (New York: Oxford University Press, 1992).

71. Martin Luther King Jr., *Where Do We Go from Here: Chaos or Community?* (1967), reprinted in *A Testament of Hope: The Essential Writings and Speeches of Martin Luther King Jr.,* ed. James M. Washington (New York: HarperCollins, 1986), pp. 566–67.

72. See Aldon D. Morris, *The Origins of the Civil Rights Movement* (New York: Free Press, 1984).

73. King, *Where Do We Go from Here?* p. 611.

74. The quoted phrases are from Patrick J. Buchanan, speech to Republican National Convention, August 12, 1992, and from Buchanan as quoted in Richard L. Berke, "A Conservative Sure His Time Has Come," *New York Times,* May 30, 1995, p. A1.

# 15

# Rights Talk: The Impoverishment of Political Discourse

*Mary Ann Glendon*

If history teaches us anything, it is that freedom cannot be taken for granted. There are conditions that are more, or less, favorable to liberty and self-government. Those conditions, as the American Founders knew, involve the character and competence of citizens and public servants. A democratic republic needs an adequate supply of citizens who are skilled in the arts of deliberation, compromise, consensus-building, and reason-giving. And, if liberty is not to degenerate into license, most citizens must be willing to exercise their freedoms responsibly and to respect the rights of their neighbors. Character and competence, however, do not emerge on command. They require social and political settings where the qualities and skills that make for good citizenship and statesmanship can be developed and transmitted from one generation to the next. In other words, the world's democratic experiments depend upon a cultural ecology.

Americans, blessed with abundance of natural and human resources, all too easily forget that their "new nation, conceived in liberty" was and remains a bold experiment. The American Founders knowingly defied the wisdom of classical political philosophers who held that a republic could not be sustained in a large territory with a heterogeneous population. The framers of our Constitution believed that they had solved that problem with an ingenious design for government. They acknowledged, however, that their ambitious project would impose exceptional demands on citizens and statesmen. Madison, in *Federalist* 55, put it plainly: "As there is a degree of depravity in mankind which requires a certain degree of circumspection and distrust, so there are other qualities in human nature which justify a certain portion of esteem and confidence. Republican government presupposes the existence of these qualities in a higher degree than any other form." Admitting that no one could foresee whether these traits would remain in good supply as the country grew, Madison expressed confidence that "the present genius" and "political character" of the American people were equal to the challenge.

In the early years of the republic, the sources of character, competence and citizenship must have appeared self-sustaining or nearly so. The social settings that constitute our principal seedbeds of civic virtue and schools for citizenship—families, churches, townships, and a myriad of small associations—were seemingly permanent, like gravity on whose continued existence we rely to keep us grounded, steady, and attached to our surroundings. Most men, women and children lived on family farms or were engaged in running a family business (both involving intense cooperation among the participants). The township form of government afforded numerous opportunities for participatory activity—from selectman to fence-viewer to attendance at town meetings. The social environment, like the natural environment, was simply there. In both respects, we seemed endowed with inexhaustible riches.

On the European continent, things were different. The French Revolutionaries, in their zeal to abolish the intermediate groups of the old regime that stood between citizen and state, inadvertently guaranteed that "civil society," as something quite distinct from the state, would become a major subject of political discourse. The men of 1789 deliberately targeted feudal statuses, the Church, craft guilds, and many aspects of family organization as oppressive to individuals and as competitors with the state for the loyalty of citizens. They were succeeded by Napoleon who, in his drive to unify the country under a strong central administration, deprived communal and regional governments of most of their power. Though his famous Napoleonic Code reversed radical changes in family law such as the provision for unilateral divorce, its dramatic reforms of inheritance law continued the revolutionary program of breaking up large family estates. Part of the legacy of the French Revolution was thus a debate about civil society that continued throughout the nineteenth century in continental Europe. Tocqueville, Durkheim, Hegel, Marx, and others wrote at length about what the relations were or should be among individuals, the institutions of civil society, and the state.

In France, where state and society had been placed most sharply in confrontation, Alexis de Tocqueville speculated about what might ensue if social institutions, once regarded as too powerful, became too weak. He pointed out that, with the growth of centralized states, the very same groups that had once seemed to stifle individual development and to obstruct national consolidation, might turn out to be essential bulwarks of personal freedom and checks on government. He was concerned that growing individualism ("a word unknown to our ancestors"), plus excessive preoccupation with material comfort, would render people susceptible to insidious new forms of tyranny. It seemed to him that as the bonds of family, religion, and craft fraternities were loosened, people would be much more disposed to think exclusively of their own interests, and to be indifferent to the public good.[1]

Americans, he thought, had an especially good chance of forestalling such a fate. He was impressed by the townships and other settings where citizens could accumulate "clear, practical ideas about the nature of their duties and the extent of their rights."[2] "Local institutions are to liberty," he wrote, "what primary schools are to science; they put it within the people's reach; they teach people to appreciate its peaceful enjoyment and accustom them to make use of it. Without local institutions a nation may give itself a free government, but it has not got the spirit of liberty."[3] The stakes were high, he pointed out, for if democratic nations should fail "in imparting to all citizens those ideas and sentiments which first prepare them for freedom and then allow them to enjoy it, there will be no independence left for anybody."[4] In a country which permits its fonts of public virtues to run dry, he observed, there would be "subjects" but no "citizens."[5]

It took over a century for such insights to be widely appreciated on this side of the Atlantic. Anglo-American political thought traditionally has focused on the individual, the market and the state, providing neither a vocabulary nor an adequate conceptual apparatus for dealing with the social systems that compose civil society.[6] Civil society studies came into their own in the United States only as urbanization, bureaucracy, geographic mobility, mass culture, and centralization of political power brought men and women into ever more unmediated relationships with distant agencies and officials.

For a time, it had seemed as though Americans could have it all—ever-enlarging spheres of liberty and equality, plus freedom from want—with everything sustained by habits and beliefs that held appetites in check. We had shown that a republic could not only exist, but flourish, in an extended territory with a diverse population. Our territory expanded further, our population became ever more heterogeneous, and we became bolder. We dared to increase the civic demands we placed on ourselves. The social legislation of the 1930s established a collective responsibility for the welfare of the poorest and most vulnerable among us (a commitment which asks citizens on the one hand to accept a certain responsibility for others in need, and on the other hand to assume as much responsibility as possible for their own needs and the needs of their immediate dependents). After World War II, we raised the ante again when the country set out in earnest to eradicate all forms of unjust discrimination, making tolerance a more important civic virtue than ever. Meanwhile, however, the institutions upon which Americans have traditionally relied to foster the necessary habits and beliefs were coming under unprecedented stress.

Ironically, just as we have begun to appreciate the importance of the social conditions that promote competence and character, "society" with its little communities of memory and mutual aid, its relationships that cannot be captured in purely economic terms, appears to be in considerable disarray.

Consider the family. Tocqueville took for granted that women, presiding over "orderly and peaceful homes" would continue to be the main teachers of children. The family home would be a dependable setting where human beings would learn how to respect others and to moderate their own tendencies toward greed and selfishness. Habits acquired in the home would provide the foundation for developing further skills of communal living in other sites such as schools and workplaces. Neither the Founders nor Tocqueville could have foreseen how profoundly family life would be unsettled by potent ideas of equality and individual self-determination that were slowly spreading through the body politic—or by the sudden sexual revolution that took even professional demographers by surprise.

Beginning in the 1960s, divorce rates, births outside marriage, and the labor force participation of mothers of pre-school children rose steeply. At about the same time, there were signs of disturbance in schools, neighborhoods, churches, local governments, and workplace associations—institutions that traditionally depended on families for support, and that in turn served as important resources for families, especially in times of stress. That was no coincidence. Families, in order to function effectively, need to be composed of individuals capable of commitment and to be supported by external communities of various sorts. But communities themselves need members schooled in cooperation and civility—and they rely on families to produce such men and women. Trouble in one system spells trouble in the others.

The close interdependence of families and other character-forming institutions has been vividly demonstrated by a path-breaking, long-term study begun in the early 1950s by a team of researchers headed by Dr. Emmy Werner.[7] Dr. Werner's group undertook to closely follow the development—from prenatal history to adulthood—of the entire group of children born in 1955 in a moderate-sized American community. The team selected the Hawaiian island of Kauai, with a population of about 45,000, as the location for the study. The inhabitants were willing to cooperate, and the multiracial population afforded the opportunity to take a variety of cultural differences in child-rearing practices into account. Health, educational, and social services on Kauai were comparable to those in communities of similar size on the mainland United States.

Nearly a third of the 698 children born on Kauai in 1955 were classified at some point as in a "high risk" category; that is, they were exposed to four or more such drawbacks as physical disability, family discord, chronic poverty, and parents who were alcoholic, undereducated, or mentally disturbed. (Kauai was similar in this respect, too, to mainland communities.) As time passed, the researchers were struck by the fact that many of the children they had identified as subject to severe disadvantages were able to lead personally satisfying and socially productive lives as adults. Remarkably, one out of three of these seriously disadvantaged children "went on to develop healthy personalities, stable careers and strong interpersonal relations."

Intrigued by that finding, Dr. Werner and her team tried to discover what had enabled the "survivor" children to overcome severe adversity. Their investigation confirmed the importance of a family's social ecology. In the course of monitoring the development of these boys and girls, the researchers were able to identify certain "protective factors" that helped the children to survive and thrive despite early adverse conditions. These factors fall into three broad groups. The first, relating to the intelligence and other personal characteristics of the child, is largely beyond anyone's control. (Some fortunate children apparently possess, even in infancy, engaging temperamental qualities that enable them to elicit positive responses from others and to recruit substitute parents if necessary.) The second group of factors, not surprisingly, affirmed conventional wisdom that children benefit from having a stable, interactive, intact household; from having at least one caretaker (not necessarily a parent) with whom they can establish a close bond; and from having structure and rules in their milieu.

The third group of protective factors, being more susceptible to external influences, should be of most interest to ecologically minded policymakers. The Kauai study found that various support systems outside the family often made all the difference in the life of an at-risk youngster. School, for example, played a crucial role in the lives of many of the survivor-children who saw it as a "home away from home, a refuge from a disordered household." Several youngsters also found role models, mentors, confidants, and opportunities for friendship in church groups, the YMCA or YWCA, 4-H, Boy and Girl Scouts, athletic groups, and the like. As Dr. Werner put it, "With the help of these support networks, the resilient children developed a sense of meaning in their lives and a belief that they could control their fate." Active participation in a church (especially one providing intense activity, acceptance, and a sense of mission) was often a "critical turning point" in a child's life.[8]

Interestingly, neither formal social service agencies nor mental health professionals were found to have played a significant role in enabling the children to cope with adversity.[9] In adulthood, too, most of the "survivor" individuals, in times of need, turned to informal sources of support and to other family members, rather than to the helping professions. This led Dr. Werner (herself a psychologist) to suggest that, "In many situations it might make better sense and be less costly as well to strengthen such available informal ties to kin and community than it would to introduce additional layers of bureaucracy into delivery of services." Family sociologist David Popenoe independently reached the same conclusion: "To improve the conditions for childrearing in America today, nothing may be more important than trying to protect and cultivate those natural, tribal- or village-like communities that still remain—communities which have families as their basic building blocks, and in which a mix of people through free association and sets of relational networks maintain a common life."[10] There is "no evidence," Popenoe maintains, "that realistic social alternatives exist for the traditional 'tribal' structures of family and community."

The significance of the Kauai study was increased by a fortuitous accident of timing. The 1955 cohort, we now know, were pioneers in uncharted territory. The children born that year entered adolescence just at the beginning of the period of sudden demographic change that swept the entire industrialized world. The major shifts in birth rates, marriage rates, and divorce rates that began in the mid-1960s caught population experts everywhere by surprise. In 1985, looking back over the cross-national data, French demographer Louis Roussel observed, "What we have seen between 1965 and the present, among the billion or so people who inhabit the industrialized nations, is . . . a general upheaval across the whole set of demographic indicators, a phenomenon rare in the history of populations. In barely twenty years, the birth rate and the marriage rate have tumbled, while divorces and illegitimate births have increased rapidly. All these changes have been substantial, with increases or decreases of more than fifty percent. They have also been sudden, since the process of change has only lasted about fifteen years. And they have been general, because all industrialized countries have been affected beginning around 1965."[11]

When the winds of change began to blow, families on Kauai experienced the same stresses as American families generally. The children in the Kauai study were born just in time to experience not only the great social upheavals, but the ambitious Great Society programs, of the 1960s. Unfortunately, it was just in this period that traditional ways of handling distress within families, neighborhoods, and churches began to break down. As an insightful "Talk of the Town" essay in *The New Yorker* put it, the country experienced a "fraying of the net of connections between people at many critical intersections. . . . Each fraying connection accelerates the others. A break in one connection, such as attachment to a stable community, puts pressure on other connections: marriage, the relationship between parents and children, religious affiliation, a feeling of connection with the past—even citizenship, that sense of membership in a large community which grows best when it is grounded in membership in a small one."[12]

Today, the risk factors identified by Dr. Werner's group affect an even larger proportion of American children, while the protective factors that had promoted the welfare of a significant minority of high-risk children born in the 1950s are less and less securely in place. Whereas in 1960, fewer than 10 percent of American children lived in a single-parent home, that figure rose to nearly one-quarter by the end of the 1980s. At present, over half of all American children are spending at least part of their childhood in a one-parent household. The overwhelming majority of these homes are headed by women, and their economic circumstances are notoriously precarious. Nearly half of all female-headed families with children under six live in poverty.

Under current conditions, then, families and their individual members need help from external support systems like those identified in the Kauai study more than ever. Even intact and functioning families need help to keep going, not to mention the special needs of members of families that are broken or faltering. But the schools, churches, youth groups, and so on, that once provided such help are in trouble too. They not only served as reinforcements for, but depended on, families, neighborhoods, and each other for personnel and reinforcement. What lends further poignancy to the present dilemma is that—as with the natural environment—many threats to the social environment are the by-products of genuine advances. The loosening of social bonds has been associated with a great expansion of individual freedom to realize one's own hopes, dreams, and ambitions. Several of the changes that have adversely affected the care-taking and socializing capacity of families are associated with improvements in the educational and economic position of women. At the same time, many religious groups and other voluntary associations are still struggling to cope with the loss of the unpaid labor of women that they took for granted for so long.

Whatever else may be said for good or ill about these new conditions, they have impaired society's capacity for fostering the habits and practices that make for good citizenship. Nathan Glazer has pointed out that there are compelling arguments both for "a radical and egalitarian individualism, and for the defense of complex institutions and social bonds. . . . But if the first side wins out, as it is doing, the hope that social policy will assist in creating more harmonious social relations, better working social institutions, broadly accepted as the decent and right way to order society, cannot be realized."[13]

The alarm has been sounded many times—across the entire political spectrum—about the personal, social and economic consequences of the rise in the proportion of the nation's children who are at risk. Conservatives and liberals alike have deplored the fact that most of such children will be unable to develop their full potential. They have duly noted the ominous implications for the quality of the work force, the fate of the social security system, America's competitive position in the world economy, and the incidence of crime and delinquency. Surprisingly little attention has been paid, however, to the *political* implications—the likely effect upon our democratic experiment of the simultaneous weakening of child-raising families and their surrounding and supporting institutions.

The first questions that Tocqueville would have posed have been too long ignored: Just where do you think citizens acquire the capacity to care for the common good? Where does a boy or girl learn to view others with respect and concern, rather than to regard them as objects, means, or obstacles? What is it that causes individual men and women to keep their promises, to limit consumption, to stick with a family member in sickness and health, to spend time with their children, to answer their country's call for service, to reach out to the unfortunate, to moderate their own demands on loved ones, neighbors, and the polity?

The handwriting is on the wall. Consider the disquieting findings of a 1989 survey of the political attitudes of young Americans, aged 18 to 24, conducted by People for the American Way. The group found to its dismay that a sense of the importance of civic participation was almost entirely lacking among the respondents: "Young people have learned only half of America's story. Consistent with the priority they place on personal happiness, young people reveal notions of America's unique character that emphasize freedom and license almost to the complete exclusion of service or participation. Although they clearly appreciate the democratic freedoms that in their view, make theirs the 'best country in the world to live in,' they fail to perceive a need to reciprocate by exercising the duties and responsibilities of good citizenship."[14] When asked to describe what makes a "good citizen," only 12 percent of the young people surveyed mentioned voting. Fewer than a quarter said that they considered it important to help their community to be a better place. Remarkably, when asked what makes America special, only seven percent mentioned that the United States was a democracy.

People for the American Way offered no theory about why young people seemed so lacking in a sense of civic responsibility. In fact, one might be tempted to surmise that the attitudes revealed by their findings were simply a function of immaturity. The current generation might be no more or less self-centered or politically apathetic than their parents once were. That interpretation, however, was rendered implausible by a *Times-Mirror* study that searched back through 50 years of public opinion data to compare young people in 1990 with Americans of the past.[15] That inquiry revealed that the 1990 cohort knew less, cared less, voted less, and was less critical of its leaders and institutions than young people had been at any time over the preceding five decades. Furthermore, although younger members of the public in the past had been at least as well informed as older people, the study found that was no longer the case. Without purporting to provide an explanation of why this might be so, the *Times-Mirror* group speculated that the "decline of the family" might have played a role, along with "television" and the "lack of mobilizing issues."

Even if the political implications of the crisis in civil society began to be taken more seriously, it is far from clear what specific measures should follow. It does seem plain that we need a more "ecological" approach to public policy.[16] Apparently, the strong state, the free economy, and a vital civil society are all indispensable to one another, but at the same time constitute potential threats to individual citizens and to each other. A serious weakness in any one of them puts the entire democratic enterprise in jeopardy, yet so does too much encroachment by any one on the legitimate spheres of the others. The tension among state, market and civil society thus seems permanent and necessary. The challenge is to maintain the sort of equilibrium that retains their benefits and restrains their destructive potential. Now that the structures of civil society have become so weak in relation to the market and the state, the problem is to determine how law and policy might help to revitalize, or at least to avoid further harm to these fragile institutions. That daunting task is hampered by a legal and conceptual apparatus which is too narrowly focused on the individual, market actors, and governments.

The fact is that we do not know very much about how to support, or reinforce, or even how to avoid damage to the ongoing, mutually conditioning systems that both undergird and buffer the free market and the democratic state. We know even less about the dynamics of social environments than we do about natural environments. Thus, an ecological approach to public policy would have to proceed modestly, preferring local experiments and small-scale pilots to broad, standardized, top-down programs. For starters, regulatory techniques need to be re-imagined, for the ham-fisted, top-down regulation favored by many liberals is not the only alternative to the hands-off laissez-faire approach advocated by many conservatives. Regulation could, alternatively, empower the intermediate institutions of civil society, e.g., by promoting self-organization and private-ordering (as did the labor legislation of the 1930s) or by helping parents to regain control over the education of their children (as in school choice plans). Where social services such as education, health care and child care are concerned, it may well be the case that smaller seedbed institutions (religious groups, workplace associations) can deliver them better, more economically and more humanely than state-run bureaucracies.[17] Reawakened interest in federalism and in the principle of subsidiarity (assigning social tasks to the smallest social unit that can perform them adequately) are encouraging signs.

Where family policy is concerned, the principle of "do no harm" will often be the best guide. Government could at least endeavor to avoid undermining the social structures on which families rely. At a minimum, we should be attentive to the ways in which governmental or employer policies may inadvertently be discouraging, impeding, or even penalizing those who are responsibly trying to carry out family roles. Certainly, we should not have to apologize for defining our society as one that relies heavily on families to socialize its young citizens, and that encourages, aids and rewards persons who perform family obligations.

As in the case of natural ecological systems, the possibility exists that disintegration of family life, and the fraying of other social networks, have progressed beyond repair. Perhaps American society already is producing too many individuals who are incapable of responsible parenthood, or of sustaining personal relationships, or of participating in civic life. As Michael Walzer has warned, Americans have a special history of mobility—geographic, social, political, and marital. "There is no one out there," he says, except Americans—"separated, rights-bearing, voluntarily associating, freely speaking, liberal" Americans.[18] Can such a people, one wonders, re-acquire a taste for stability and self-restraint?

Is it possible for a society as free and open as ours to avoid undermining its own cultural foundations? The Founders believed that good government could be established—and maintained—by reflection and choice. The wager they made over two hundred years ago is still open. Paradoxically, it seems that liberal democracy may be inherently destructive of the very qualities and institutions it needs in order to survive. The corrective for that problem may lie in another paradox: liberalism, for its own sake, may need to refrain from imposing its own image on all the institutions of civil society. Democratic experiments may depend, in fact, on preserving here and there within the liberal polity certain institutions, like the family, that are not necessarily democratic, egalitarian, or liberal, and whose highest loyalty is not to the state.

Skeptics might protest: What can hold together a polity containing a wide array of small institutions that thrive on different virtues from those that animate the regime itself? And what would assure that the seedbeds would be conducive to the flowering of civic virtue rather than weeds of civil strife? The answers to such questions—or at least the path to better rather than worse judgments—must ultimately be sought, not only in the seedbeds, but in the seed: the human person, uniquely individual, yet inescapably social; a creature of unruly passions who nevertheless possesses a certain ability to transcend and even to transform those passions; a knower and a chooser who constitutes himself, for better or worse, through his knowing and his choosing.

Thus the starting point for the infant study of the ecology of freedom must be the human person in all his imperfection and with all his potency. Character and competence arise, if at all, first, through the capacity of men and women, individually and collectively, to reflect upon their existence, to deliberate, and to make judgments concerning the good life and how to live it. Civic virtues, like any other virtues, are acquired only through habitual practice. Those practices will either be sustained or undermined by the settings in which we live, work and raise our children. Those settings in turn can be affected to some degree by norms and institutions of human design. Human beings, having shown themselves capable of creating norms and institutions, can be supposed to be capable of reshaping norms and institutions. Now, as in ancient times, all depends on how we employ the qualities for which Sophocles praised the human race in the famous "Ode to Man" chorus of Antigone: "mastery of the art of speech, and of wind-swift thought, and the skill of living together in neighborliness." It cannot be an accident that the word chosen by the poet to describe our species means—in addition to "clever"—"fearful" and "terrible."[19]

## NOTES

Learned Hand Professor of Law, Harvard University. This essay is adapted from Mary Ann Glendon, *Rights Talk: The Impoverishment of Political Discourse* (New York: Free Press, 1991), Chapter 5 ("The Missing Dimension of Sociality") and from "Forgotten Questions" in *Seedbeds of Virtue: Sources of Competence, Character & Citizenship in American Society*, Mary Ann Glendon and David Blankenhorn, eds. (New York: Madison Books, 1995), 1–15.

1. Alexis de Tocqueville, *The Old Regime and the French Revolution*, trans. Stuart Gilbert (New York: Doubleday Anchor, 1955), xiii.
2. Alexis de Tocqueville, *Democracy in America,* trans. George Lawrence, ed. J. P. Mayer (Garden City, N.Y.: Doubleday Anchor, 1969), I, 70.
3. Tocqueville, *The Old Regime*, 63.
4. Tocqueville, *The Old Regime*, 315.
5. Tocqueville, *The Old Regime*, 93–94
6. Scholars in many fields, especially those with a sociological orientation, make this point. See, especially, Alan Wolfe, *Whose Keeper? Social Science and Moral Obligation* (Berkeley: University of California Press, 1989). See also Robert Bellah et al., *Habits of the Heart: Individualism and Commitment in American Life* (Berkeley: University of California Press, 1985); Amitai Etzioni, *An Immodest Agenda* (New York: McGraw-Hill, 1983); Nathan Glazer, *The Limits of Social Policy* (Cambridge: Harvard University Press, 1988).
7. Emmy E. Werner, "Children of the Garden Island," *Scientific American,* April 1989, 106–11. See also, Emmy E. Werner and Ruth S. Smith, *Vulnerable but Invincible: A Longitudinal Study of Resilient Children and Youth* (New York: McGraw-Hill, 1982); Emmy E. Werner, "High-Risk Children in Young Adulthood: A Longitudinal Study from Birth to 32 Years," 59 (1) *American Journal of Orthopsychiatry* 72 (1989). All quotations in the text are from the *Scientific American* article, except where otherwise indicated.
8. Spencer Rich, "Troubled Children Assessed" (interview with Dr. Emmy Werner), *Washington Post,* 17 April 1990.
9. At the end of the second decade of the study, the researchers found that only a small proportion of the resilient children had had contacts with social service agencies, and these contacts were typically related to obtaining temporary financial assistance. None of the resilient children had sought or obtained any help from mental health professionals. Werner and Smith, *Vulnerable but Invincible,* 96–97.
10. David Popenoe, "The Roots of Declining Social Virtue: Family, Community, and the Need for a 'Natural Communities Policy'," in *Seedbeds of Virtue: Sources of Competence and Character in American Society,* Glendon and Blankenhorn, eds., 94
11. Louis Roussel, "Démographie: deux décennies de mutations dans les pays industrialisés," in *Family, State, and Individual Economic Security,* ed. M.-T. Meulders-Klein and J. Eekelaar (Brussels: Story Scientia, 1988), I, 27–28.
12. "The Talk of the Town," *New Yorker,* 30 August 1976, 22.
13. Glazer, *The Limits of Social Policy,* 155.
14. People for the American Way, *Democracy's Next Generation* (Washington, D.C.: People for the American Way, 1989), 27.

15. Michael Oreskes, "Profiles of Today's Youth: They Couldn't Care Less," *New York Times,* 28 June 1990, A1, D21.

16. Like many others, I have found ecology a useful concept in dealing with contemporary social phenomena. See, Bellah et al., *Habits of the Heart,* 283 ("social ecology"); Urie Bronfenbrenner, *The Ecology of Human Development* (Cambridge: Harvard University Press, 1979); Clifford Geertz, *The Interpretation of Cultures* (New York: Basic Books, 1973), 3 ("cultural ecology"); Mary Ann Glendon, *The Transformation of Family Law* (Chicago: University of Chicago Press, 1989), 306 ("family ecology") and *Rights Talk* (New York: Free Press, 1991), chapter 5; Alan Wolfe, *Whose Keeper?*, 256.

17. Peter L. Berger and Richard John Neuhaus, *To Empower People: From State to Civil Society* (Washington, D.C.: American Enterprise Institute, 1996).

18. Michael Walzer, "The Communitarian Critique of Liberalism," 18 *Political Theory* 6, 11–12 (1990). According to Stephan Thernstrom, transiency was a part of the American way of life at least since the beginning of the nineteenth century. In what was "not a frontier phenomenon, or a big-city phenomenon, but a national phenomenon," people came and went from villages, towns, and cities at "a rapid and surprisingly uniform rate." *The Other Bostonians: Poverty and Progress in the American Metropolis 1880–1970* (Cambridge: Harvard University Press, 1973), 227.

19. Richard M. Weaver, *The Ethics of Rhetoric* (Chicago: Regnery, 1953), 119.

# 16

# The Progressive Assault of Civic Community

*William A. Schambra*

Given the mounting flood of news articles, television programs, political addresses, academic seminars, and national commissions devoted to the contemporary condition of civil society, one might think its prospects are bright indeed. Certainly the entire discussion has come a long way from the time and place I first encountered it, as a young research assistant at the American Enterprise Institute (AEI) in the late 1970s. There, almost lost amid the swarms of prominent economists and political scientists, a handful of scholars had begun to explore the possibility of meeting human needs not through government, and not through the market, but rather through what they called "mediating structures"—family, neighborhood, church, ethnic and voluntary association, and other social institutions that mediated between the individual and the state.

Although AEI was considered a conservative think tank, it was by no means obvious that this was a peculiarly conservative idea. To be sure, Robert Nisbet, who had alerted us to the centrality of "intermediate associations" for human well-being in his landmark *The Quest for Community*, was clearly of the right.[1] But that was not so clear with sociologist Peter Berger and antiwar cleric Richard John Neuhaus, whose *To Empower People* had been the first serious exploration of the utility of mediating structures for delivering public services.[2] And former George McGovern speechwriter Michael Novak clearly hoped at the time that mediating structures would become the vehicle for a revitalized *left*—one that would, as he put it in *The Rise of the Unmeltable Ethnics,* "turn toward the organic networks of communal life . . . family, ethnic group, and voluntary association in primary groups."[3]

Ideological classification of this tiny band of scholars was additionally complicated by the fact that they professed equally a profound skepticism about conservatism's romance with the marketplace and rugged individualism, on the one hand, and about liberalism's infatuation with the state, on the other. Neither ideological position, they insisted, took adequately into account the small, humble civic institutions in between state and individual institutions through which the American people had traditionally lived their daily lives and directed their own affairs, sharing benefits and burdens, constructing and passing on to their children their moral and spiritual values, and enjoying a sense of belonging, purpose, and meaning. Indeed, insofar as most of our political energies were drawn either upward to the state or downward to the individual, they feared for the future of that fragile but vital middle zone of our national life.

What I first encountered in the 1970s as a clunky, arcane sociological term has today bedecked itself in the far more glamorous garb of "civil society" and found its way onto the covers of major news magazines. Even U.S. senators are celebrating the virtues of that realm between state and individual, where, as Bill Bradley put it so eloquently, "Americans make their homes, sustain their marriages, raise their families, hang out with their friends, meet their neighbors, educate their children, worship their god."[4]

Yet it is difficult for partisans of mediating structures simply to take pleasure in all this attention, for, as is usually the case, to be big news, it has to be bad news. Civil society's prospects are, apparently, not so bright after all. The headlines tell us that American citizens today are massively alienated from their public institutions, refusing even to vote, much less to involve themselves actively in public affairs. They are so absorbed in enjoying and defending their individual rights that they have turned their backs altogether on any sense of civic or moral responsibility. People are no longer engaging themselves in civic associations but instead are "bowling alone."[5]

We are now in the midst of a furious debate among social scientists about the magnitude of this decline in our civic vitality, or indeed about whether in fact there has been a decline at all. Wherever one finally comes down on this empirical question, though, there can be no dispute that our civic institutions face an uphill struggle for survival against a number of powerful intellectual and social trends today. And the prime suspects among potential civic corrosives are pretty much the same ones discussed by that small band at AEI back in the 1970s—namely, the marketplace, on the one hand, and the state, on the other.

In this chapter I shall consider first the relationship between the marketplace and civil society, noting that there is indeed friction between the two realms, but arguing that this friction or tension, fully intended by the architects of our national political life, has been by and large healthy and invigorating. The relationship between state and civil society, on the other hand, has not been so healthy. That is because the state has, over the course of the twentieth century, attempted to arrogate unto itself the community-building functions once considered the exclusive province of civil society. A substantial federal government is, by itself, not incompatible with civic health, as the Founders understood. But a federal government that sets out explicitly to build a great national community by absorbing the authority and function of all lesser communities is another matter altogether.

## CIVIL SOCIETY AND THE MARKETPLACE

Contemporary liberals enjoy chiding conservatives about their failure to acknowledge any tension between civil society and the marketplace, with its attendant characteristics of individualism and materialism. To be sure, the purely libertarian strand of conservatism may not concern itself much about this friction. The same, however, cannot be said about Robert Nisbet conservatives.

"Unfortunately, it has been the fate of [civic] institutions and relationships to suffer almost continuous attrition during the capitalist age," Nisbet noted in *Quest.*[6] The marketplace produces and celebrates a materialistic individualism that inevitably distracts the citizen from his civic obligations and erodes the authority of family, church, and neighborhood, he warned. Capitalism's tendency to produce a "sand heap of disconnected particles of humanity,"[7] or "enlarging masses of socially 'free,' insecure individuals,"[8] left citizens easy prey to the state's embrace, he cautioned, and so it was "absurd to suppose that the rhetoric of nineteenth-century individualism will offset present tendencies in the direction of the absolute political community."[9] Here is one conservative with no illusions about the tension between civil society and the marketplace.

The important thing about this tension in the American context, however, is that it was very much part of the design of our nation's Founders. Believing that the only legitimate government was one that secured the individual's "unalienable rights" to "life, liberty, and the pursuit of happiness" outlined in the Declaration of Independence, James Madison, Alexander Hamilton, and other leading Federalists were reluctant to leave such rights to the tender mercies of the small, homogeneous states of the time, in which popular majorities easily formed behind schemes of oppression and abuse of minority rights.

The Founders' answer to this dilemma, as Martin Diamond taught, was to establish through the Constitution the world's first large, modem, commercial republic.[10] Here, the marketplace could be counted on to give rise to an endless variety of occupations and economic interests (*Federalist* 10's famous "multiplicity of interests"), thus making far more difficult successful collusion in schemes of oppression.

Commerce requires large markets, and large markets require "a great extent of territory"—sufficiently great that its orderly administration demanded an energetic national government. This national government would serve as a sentinel of individual rights against potentially abusive local majorities, intervening forcibly when necessary, but more generally accomplishing this purpose through the upbuilding of a vigorous, continent-wide commercial infrastructure, which would diversify and fragment potentially oppressive local majorities.[11]

The Founders understood full well that commerce brought with it strong and not altogether attractive tendencies toward self-interested individualism and materialism, which would in turn diminish the authority of traditional, local civic communities. But for the Federalists, commerce's vice was also its chief virtue. Small communities powerfully animated by cohesive ideological or religious sentiments, they had learned from history, were precisely those most likely to be violators of the individual rights whose protection was the first object of government. By "multiplying the means of gratification" and "promoting the introduction and circulation of the precious metals, those darling objects of human avarice and enterprise," as Hamilton put it in *Federalist* 12, government would ensure that the lives of its citizens were animated more by the relatively peaceful and subdued self-interested pursuit of material prosperity than by the sort of religious or philosophical zeal that had traditionally been fatal to human rights.[12] Did the Founders understand that there would be a tension between civic virtues or civil society and the marketplace? Absolutely—and they made the most of it.

America might long ago have been dissolved into Nisbet's "sand heap of disconnected particles of humanity" had the commercial republic been the sole impulse behind the American founding. Happily, though, another critical element was contributed by the Anti-Federalists—public figures such as Richard Henry Lee, Patrick Henry, Mercy Warren, and Melancton Smith, who, as Herbert Storing suggests, are "entitled to be counted among the Founders."[13]

These political theorists were by no means persuaded that a large, commercial republic was desirable, or even possible. Taking their cue from Montesquieu's *Spirit of the Laws,* they insisted that republicanism was possible only with public-spirited or virtuous citizens, who would willingly put aside matters of self-interest for the sake of the public good. They must be imbued with the "love of the laws and of our country" and "exhibit a constant preference of public to private interest."[14] Such a rigorous standard of civic virtue, however, could only be maintained in a small, intense community, in which citizens readily sensed their oneness with each other, and where public affairs were immediately accessible and understandable. For binding together such intense communities, the Anti-Federalists insisted, nothing was more important than rigorous moral or religious codes: "without the prevalence of Christian piety and morals, the best republican Constitution can never save us from slavery and ruin," one wrote.[15]

All of these critical republican features, the Anti-Federalists understood, would be radically compromised by the large commercial regime. A large, distant federal government would be too remote and alien for people to involve themselves in its affairs. Commerce would corrupt civic virtue and distract people from dutiful commitment to the public business. "As people become more luxurious, they become more incapacitated of governing themselves," noted one.[16] And commerce diminished the strong moral and religious bonds that were critical for the virtuous republican community. Mercy Warren feared that Americans might be destined for the disastrous path taken by the Europeans: "Bent on gratification, at the expense of every moral tie, they have broken down the barriers of religion, and the spirit of infidelity is nourished at the fount."[17]

Clearly, the sort of small, virtuous republic championed by the Anti-Federalists was inconceivable on the continental scale of the Federalists' plans, and so they pressed hard at the Constitutional Convention for mitigation of the radically nationalist scheme proposed originally by Madison, John Randolph, and others. As a result of their efforts, we were bequeathed a strong national Constitution that nonetheless imposed many decentralizing limitations on the reach of the national government, thereby leaving the management of the critical, everyday affairs of civic life to the states, localities, and civil associations.

Insofar as America has enjoyed a vital and active civil society for much of its history, we probably owe it less to well-known statesmen such as Madison or Hamilton than to the far more obscure Anti-Federalists. Although our civic institutions have always been a far cry from the rigorously virtuous republics they envisioned (the Federalists enjoyed reminding them that even at the time of the Founding, such virtuous republics were nonexistent), the barriers against nationalist centralization that they managed to build into the Constitution secured enclaves within which local civil and public associations flourished, nurturing at least attenuated versions of the qualities so important to the Anti-Federalists, including civic virtue, public-spiritedness, religious faith, and intense involvement in and devotion to community.

No one understood better than Alexis de Tocqueville the complex coexistence of Federalist large-republicanism and Anti-Federalist small-republicanism in American life, from which emanates the ongoing tension between the market and civil society. According to Tocqueville, Americans had "forcibly reconciled" those "two theoretically irreconcilable systems."[18] There was no name for the government that resulted—it was a kind of "incomplete national government,"[19] which combined the "various advantages of large and small size for nations."[20]

America was destined to be prosperous, Tocqueville understood, because it was a large, commercial republic, giving "free scope to the unguided strength and common sense of individuals."[21] This led to some by-now familiar problems: it is "always an effort" for the commerce minded to "tear themselves away from their private affairs and pay attention to those of the community," thus permitting the public business to languish or to gravitate into the hands of a distant and potentially oppressive state.[22] Furthermore, commerce's "love of comfort" threatens to erode the moral and spiritual capacities of individuals; its aims are "petty," but "the soul clings to them; it dwells on them every day . . . in the end they shut out the rest of the world and sometimes come between the soul and God."[23]

But Americans had found ways to counter these tendencies, Tocqueville suggested, through their traditions of local self-government and civic association—traditions preserved constitutionally by the rearguard skirmishing of the Anti-Federalist small-republicans. American lawgivers had wisely "given each part of the land its own political life so that there would be an infinite number of occasions for the citizens to act together and so that every day they should feel they depended on one another."[24] Within "each part's" political life, citizens were bound closely to one another by strong families, tightly knit neighborhoods, active voluntary and fraternal groups, and vigorous churches. Through these small, local, human-scale associations, Americans not only achieved a sense of belonging and connectedness, but they also involved themselves directly in solving the most important human problems. As Nisbet noted, echoing Tocqueville, "the social problems of birth and death, courtship and marriage, employment and unemployment, infirmity and old age were met, however inadequately at times, through the associated means of these social groups."[25]

Thanks to the small-republican impulse, Tocqueville understood, citizens were thus fully engaged in creating their own public life and in solving their own social problems, and so were unlikely to succumb to the temptation merely to immerse themselves in the self-interested pursuit of material gain. Moreover, their ability to construct, within each locality, a coherent and powerful moral and spiritual community—a community reinforced by the mutually supportive teachings of churches, schools, associations, and neighborhoods—made unlikely the spiritual and moral decline threatened by an untrammeled marketplace.

For Tocqueville, the "forcible reconciliation" of "two theoretically irreconcilable systems" was absolutely central to the survival of America. When he inquired into the "main causes tending to maintain a democratic republic in the United States," he listed first the "federal form . . . which allows the Union to enjoy the power of a great republic and the security of a small one."[26]

The two systems or principles would always be in tension, according to Tocqueville, each threatening to consume or overwhelm the other. In his own time, for instance, he feared that the states and localities were inordinately powerful and posed a challenge to the union. The real danger, however, he foresaw for the future, when a centralizing national government might threaten to swallow up the local institutions so important for civic life.[27] But for all its messiness and occasional tilts toward the excess of one principle over the other, Tocqueville understood, America had found a realistic way to extract the best of the two principles while minimizing their vices, in the event giving us a polity that preserved both liberty and community.

As we look back today at our history, a century and a half after Tocqueville's American tour, can we not agree with him that the tension between the local civic life preserved by the Constitution's small-republican features and the national market created by its large-republican features has been, by and large, healthy and invigorating, each element moderating the worst aspects of the other? Not according to a significant strand of America's literary tradition, of course, which would have us believe that America's ethnic and religious communities are hopelessly and unprecedentedly narrow-minded, stultifying, moralistic, and oppressive. But any fair-minded analysis would have to conclude that American associative life, for all its occasional excess, is vastly more tolerant and open than the village life of traditional societies.

For that, we must thank the national commercial republic, whose penetrating networks of trade and finance permit no local community to seal itself off completely from the moderate habits and values of the outside commercial world. Commerce compels shopkeepers to befriend "outsiders" who might become customers, tempers ideological and religious zeal with the awareness that one has to go to work in the morning, and gives rise to huge, diverse urban centers, to which embittered writers may flee and where they may write (commercially successful) novels about the oppressiveness of Main Street. Those who warn darkly that "civic renewal" will instead reduce America to a distinctly uncivil, balkanesque collection of bitterly warring ethnic and religious factions forget that *our* civil society has been thoroughly tamed and subdued by the commercial regime within which it is embedded and by whose sober, stolid values it is permeated.

Likewise, for all the jeremiads about the terminal civic and moral decline of the American republic, surely our churches, neighborhoods, and civic associations have over time managed to temper and moderate the harshest aspects of the marketplace's self-interest and materialism. Generation after generation, Americans have been taught that there are obligations beyond mere personal gain and the pursuit of wealth—obligations to family, community, and faith—and have behaved accordingly. When, as is often the case, they organize themselves to protect their families and communities against the harshest and most disintegrative aspects of the marketplace, we celebrate their display of courage and public-spiritedness. It is no accident that one of America's most beloved movies, *It's a Wonderful Life,* should relate the tale of a communitarian Bedford Falls refusing to dissolve itself into the self-interested commercial riot of Potterville.

But is it not the case, as some scholars suggest today, that the market has assumed such an unprecedentedly virulent, global form that it threatens to destroy civic community once and for all? That is possible, of course, but a certain skepticism creeps in when we consider all the *preceding* unprecedentedly disruptive forms the market is alleged to have taken over the past two centuries. Indeed, Thomas Bender points out in *Community and Social Change in America* that the "technology destroys community" theme is an old and familiar canard in scholarship's account of the American experience.

After surveying American historical texts, Bender wryly observes that if they "are placed in serial order, they offer a picture of community breakdown repeating itself in the 1650s, 1690s, 1740s, 1780s, 1820s, 1850s, 1880s, and 1920s," each work treating the change in its particular era as "*the* great change in which the scales were decisively tipped in favor of modernity."[28]

We are entitled to wonder with Bender, "How many times can community collapse in America?"[29] And we are entitled to share his conclusion that, for all the historical variations in the relationship between community and marketplace (or, in his terms, Gerneinschaft and Gesellschaft), "American social history refutes the notion of community collapse."[30] Today, as in Tocqueville's time, we may conclude with Bender, it is possible to enjoy a "humane urban life" built upon "a complex balance of gemeinschaft and gesellschaft that is itself grounded upon appreciation of both of these patterns of social relations."[31]

The interplay between the large commercial republic and the small, civically virtuous republic, like all human contrivances, has not always and everywhere worked well. Individual lives *have* been stunted by oppressive local communities. Families and communities *have* been ripped asunder by commerce. And the system has experienced larger episodes of profound and tragic breakdown. James Madison had hoped that the spread of national commercial institutions and values into the southern states would open up and moderate insulated local custom, putting an end to the slavery at the heart of those "virtuous" small republics. Instead, the insularity, as well as the power, of the slaveholding states grew, until they mounted an armed challenge against the principle of national union.

Even after a bloody civil war, the tightly knit "small republics" of the South persisted in the massive violation of the rights of minorities, necessitating an ongoing effort by the national government to vindicate those rights. The tremendous moral authority of the struggle for civil rights, however, derived precisely from its ability to appeal to the Founders' unfulfilled promise of protection for "certain unalienable rights," and the Federalists' national government has been a potent, if not always steadfast or successful, instrument of enforcement. Furthermore, the spread of modem business and market values into what has come to be known as the "New South" may yet, albeit belatedly, vindicate Madison's hopes for the ameliorative effects of commerce on that region.

Nonetheless, in light of this history, it is small wonder that discussion of the virtues of local government and civic institutions should send up storm signals within the African American community. That is why it is necessary to remind ourselves constantly that the small-republican impulse must always be checked by the large-republican impulse and that, as the Federalists planned, the national government must be prepared, even in decentralizing times, to protect the rights of minorities against overbearing local majorities.

Without claiming more than is appropriate for any human device in this broken and imperfect world, the interplay between Federalism's national commercial republic and Anti-Federalism's small, virtuous republic has given us a healthy and vigorous, if not always coherent or tidy, national political life. Within the clash of "irreconcilable systems," we have managed to sustain a remarkable degree of material prosperity and individual freedom, on the one hand, and civic vitality and moral community, on the other. Yes, there is a tension between civil society and the marketplace—and it has been good for the Republic.

## CIVIL SOCIETY, THE STATE, AND THE GREAT NATIONAL COMMUNITY

The same, however, cannot be said for the relationship between state and civil society, at least as it has evolved in the course of the twentieth century. Whereas the state and the community-building impulse were held in balance during our early political history, at the beginning of this century, an attempt was made to resolve the tension and bring the two harmoniously together. This "fateful combination of widespread quest for community . . . and the apparatus of political power that has become so vast in contemporary democratic societies" is, as Nisbet suggested, "the single most impressive fact in the twentieth century."[32] It has certainly had ominous implications for American civil society.

This effort to marry the two impulses originated with American progressive liberalism at the turn of the century. Whereas the crisis of the Civil War had come about because the small-republican impulse had become too powerful, the Progressives understood themselves to be dealing with the opposite problem: national trends after the late 1800s were threatening to overwhelm the small-republican impulse.

The decentralized, self-governing, civically vital way of life within America's "island communities" (as Robert Wiebe aptly describes them) was doomed, according to theorists such as Herbert Croly, Walter Lippmann, Richard Ely, Charles Horton Cooley, Edward Alsworth Ross, Robert Park, and John Dewey, and public figures such as Theodore Roosevelt. In their view, the irresistible forces of modernity were beginning to sweep away the boundaries that historically had contained and preserved our island communities. Modern means of transportation and communication—the railroad, telegraph, telephone, and high-speed press—had breached the small town's borders, ending its isolation and opening it up to the influences of the larger world. Technology had given rise to vast corporate giants whose operations reached far beyond the jurisdiction of any single state or city. Great cities had sprung up, populated by aggregates of isolated, disconnected individuals, rather than by tightly knit neighbors. Immigration added millions more people from threateningly alien cultures to these already forbidding metropolises. Political control all too often passed out of the hands of town meetings, into the grasp of what were described as corrupt, boss-driven political machines. Citizenly duty seemed to have been lost in the stampede for wealth, a stampede that was legitimated by new doctrines of emancipated individualism.

In short, the forces of modernity had precipitated a crisis of community and civil society in America: the small town and its civic virtues had been shattered. As Lippmann described it, modernity had forever and permanently "upset the old life of the prairies [and] destroyed village loyalties."[33] Although it was pointless, in the Progressives' view, to try to preserve or restore the civic and moral ethos of the small town (that had been the failed Populist response), it was now possible to move to a new and higher form of community: the great, national community.

The essential instrument of this new and higher form would be a far more powerful and active national government than had theretofore characterized our political system. In Croly's famous formulation, the Jeffersonian values of "community of feeling and . . . ease of communication" could now be established within the nation as a whole, using the Hamiltonian instrument of a vigorous central government.[34] Or, as Tocqueville might have understood it, the sense of community once thought possible by the Anti-Federalists only within the small republic would now be reestablished on a national scale, through the energetic government established by the Federalists.

The central government, for instance, could tame through regulatory measures those great and disruptive concentrations of private wealth, the corporations, thereby turning them into "express economic agents of the whole community," as Croly put it.[35] The government would also become "expressly responsible for an improved distribution of wealth" and would begin to alleviate, through the progressive income tax and social welfare programs, the inequalities of wealth that might imperil the sense of national oneness.[36] A vigorous program of "Americanization" would serve to integrate diverse immigrant populations into a single, coherent people. "Scientific management" and other new developments in the social sciences held out the promise that enlightened, bureaucratic administration could order and direct toward public purposes the chaotic popular masses. (As sociologist Charles

Horton Cooley put it, the era demanded "a comprehensive 'scientific management' of mankind, to the end of better personal opportunity and social function in every possible line.")[37]

Behind these specific developments and programs, however, lay a larger moral purpose: the creation of a genuine national community that could evoke from the American people a self-denying devotion to the "national idea," a far-flung community of millions in which citizens nonetheless would be linked tightly by bonds of compassion, fellow-feeling, and neighborliness. In Croly's words, there would be a "subordination of the individual to the demand of a dominant and constructive national purpose."[38] A citizen would begin to "think first of the State and next of himself,"[39] and "individuals of all kinds [would] find their most edifying individual opportunities in serving their country."[40] Indeed, America would come to be bound together by a "religion of human brotherhood," which "[could] be realized only through the loving-kindness which individuals feel . . . particularly toward their fellow-countrymen."[41]

The catalyst of the national community, the articulator of the "national purpose," in the Progressive view, was to be the president—the galvanizing, unifying voice of all the American people. The president's is the "only national voice in affairs," Woodrow Wilson argued.[42] He alone could unite and inspire the people by combining their many views into one, coherent whole: "The voices of the nation unite in his understanding in a single meaning and reveal to him a single vision, so that he can speak . . . the common meaning of the common voice."[43] From the "bully pulpit" of the executive office, the president would summon from the American people the self-sacrifice, publicspiritedness, and compassion that the national community required.

This vision of national community reached its apotheosis in World War I. Suddenly, the Progressives discovered the awesome capacity of war to nurture public-spiritedness and national oneness, and to legitimate the accretion of power to the central state. Dewey would speak appreciatively afterward of the "social possibilities of war."[44] Lippmann noted approvingly that "the war has given Americans a new instinct for order, purpose, and discipline" and served to "draw Americans out of their local, group, and ethnic loyalties into a greater American citizenship."[45] Richard Ely insisted that "after the War we must 'carry on' and gather the fruits of the splendid accumulation of energy which has been engendered during the War . . . from top to bottom cultivating that social cement of mutual loyalty which makes working together a joy."[46] Liberalism would never forget the wonderfully unified national selflessness of 1917–1918. Henceforth, in times of peace, it would search diligently for the "moral equivalent of war," a kind of war that would energize the national community without the actual spilling of blood.

What would all these developments mean for the humble, local institutions of civil society? Clearly, the new philosophy of national community suggested dramatic changes in the way everyday civic life was to be conducted and experienced. Whereas before the public business had been well within the grasp of the average citizen, easily comprehended and managed by everyday folk wisdom and common sense, now public affairs had allegedly been so complicated by modernity that the average citizen could no longer hope to understand or manage them. Among the more promising "social possibilities of war" foreseen by Dewey, however, was that the public would now come to realize the centrality of the expert for the management of its affairs. The "one phase of Prussianism, borrowed under the stress of war from the enemy, which is likely permanently to remain, is systematic utilization of the scientific expert," Dewey remarked. Indeed, this "social mobilization of science is likely in the end to effect such changes in the practice of government—and finally in its theory—as to initiate a new type of democracy."[47]

In this new democracy, Dewey believed, broad public education in the social sciences would teach citizens, in Timothy Kaufman-Osborn's formulation, "the radical insufficiency of the maxims of everyday conduct," as well as that "the roots of most problematic situations do not lie within the jurisdiction of the locality and hence that their commonsense analyses of those situations are unreliable."[48] The good citizen now accepted his "inescapable dependence upon those trained in the expert methods of the social sciences" and graciously deferred to the experts who alone knew how to manage the complexity of modern public life.[49] As city management advocate Henry Bruere put it, "citizens of larger cities must frankly recognize the need for professional service in behalf of citizen interests. . . . Even efficient private citizens will evidence their efficiency by supporting constructive efforts for governmental betterment."[50]

For the Progressive elites, "governmental betterment" meant reforms in governing systems that all but assured deference to the new professionals by structurally elevating public affairs out of the average citizen's reach. Historian Samuel P. Hays points out that decentralized, localized ward and precinct systems of representation, which had "enabled local and particularistic interests to dominate" and had assured that elected officials "spoke for . . . those aspects of community life which mattered most" to the average citizen, now gave way to at-large, citywide systems of voting and representation, which handed over governance to corporate and professional elites possessed of an enlarged, scientific, rational view of governance.[51]

As Hays suggests, structural revisions such as the short ballot, initiative, referendum, recall, and city manager system that familiarly present themselves as prodemocratic, antimachine reforms, might in fact be better understood as methods to subvert and undermine the smaller civic associations through which common citizens had previously expressed themselves, so that the enlightened elites might rule. In Hays's formulation, the earlier, decentralized system "involved wide latitude for the expression of grass-roots impulses and their involvement in the political process." The Progressive vision, by contrast, "grew out of the rationalization of life which came with science and technology, in which decisions arose from expert analysis and flowed from fewer and smaller centers outward to the rest of society."[52] As E. A. Ross bluntly put it, "removing control farther away from the ordinary citizen and taxpayer is tantamount to giving the intelligent, farsighted, and publicspirited element in society a longer lever to work with."[53]

The triumph of Progressive structural reform would mean, in essence, that citizen involvement in public affairs was reduced from active, intense, face-to-face problem solving on a daily basis, to passively casting a lonely, solitary ballot once in a great while, for a handful of offices. ("Probably no voter should be called upon to vote for more than three men in a year, even as a maximum," suggested Richard Ely.)[54] That ballot would be aggregated with vast numbers of other solitary votes into a mandate for an elite corps of professional experts, who would now conduct the real business of public life.

Clearly, this new reliance on rational, scientific principles and institutions to create a national community prompted serious doubts about religion, traditional morality, and their local civic manifestations, which tended to be fragmenting, parochial, and divisive. E. A. Ross complained that America had been peculiarly plagued by "thousands of local groups sewed up in separatist dogmas and dead to most of the feelings which thrill the rest of society." The remedy was the "widest possible diffusion of secular knowledge" among the many, which "narrows the power of the fanatic or the false prophet to gain a following," plus university training for the few, which "rears up a type of leader who will draw men together with unifying thoughts, instead of dividing them, as does the sectfounder, with his private imaginings and personal notions."[55] James Nuechterlein notes that the Progressives at the *New Republic* were particularly contemptuous of the Roman Catholic Church, considering it "the champion of obscurantism and the enemy of modem intellectual progress. It committed the great sin of 'looking for truths in the past' and stood stubbornly 'against most efforts to advance scientific knowledge.'"[56]

Indeed, many of the Progressives understood the new social sciences and their seeming capacity to reorder society into a coherent and orderly whole to be a secular evolution from or substitute for religion, a realization of the Kingdom on Earth—to recall Croly's formulation, a "religion of human brotherhood." Sociologist Albion Small considered his discipline "a science . . . of God's image," "the holiest sacrament open to men," teaching that "we live, move and have our being as members one of another" (rather than as children of "our heavenly Father," as taught by discredited conventional Christianity).[57] John Bascom argued that "a theology which seeks the regeneration of society in ignorance of social laws is doomed to failure," while a government that grasped such laws was "a surrogate for the churches and voluntary societies."[58] Progressives generally shared Bascom's view that traditional, local civic institutions—as he put it, "rambling, halting voluntaryism"—based on traditional moral principles could only obstruct and delay the creation of a new, sleek, streamlined, rational centralized order.[59]

Was it in fact true that, at the dawn of this century, a crisis on the order of the Civil War had arrived in America because, as sociologist Robert Park put it, "the old forms of social control represented by the family, the neighborhood, and the local community [had] been undermined and greatly diminished" by irresistible modern forces?[60] This is, of course, one of the many precedents of today's claim of an unprecedented crisis of community advanced by some contemporary scholars. Given the strong links between the Progressive movement and the organization of the American historical profession, it is perhaps not surprising that today we should be left with the impression that the Progressive era was the *real* crisis of American community. Nonetheless, we are well armed against such claims by Bender's critique of the "crisis of community" industry in American scholarship, and so we should treat this interpretation of the era with considerable skepticism.

It is surely clear, however, that the Progressives seized on one of the periodic imbalances in the interplay between Federalist and Anti-Federalist impulses to advance a political order they considered a vast improvement over the old civil society's "rambling, halting voluntaryism." As Robert Nisbet argued, Progressivism's desire to create a national community through bureaucratization, rationalization, centralization, and the centripetal moral impulse of the national idea bespoke an active hostility to civil society's intermediate associations, which Progressives worked to destroy by shifting function and authority upward to the national state and its elite corps of experts. American civil society was not so much dead as in need of euthanasia, in the Progressives' view, to clear the way for a vastly superior order that overcame the tension between and brought harmoniously together the Anti-Federalist small-republican impulse with the Federalist large-republican impulse within the great national community.

The implications of the Progressive program for civil society and genuine self-government were not lost on prescient observers at the time. Presidential candidate Woodrow Wilson sounded the alarm: "What I fear . . . is a government of experts," he noted in his 1912 Labor Day address in Buffalo.

> God forbid that in a democratic country we should resign the task and give the government over to experts. What are we if we are to be [scientifically] taken care of by a small number of gentlemen who are the only men who understand the job? Because if we don't understand the job, then we are not a free people.[61]

Wilson's campaign for a decentralist alternative to an expert-led national community left us what Fred Siegel and Will Marshall describe as "liberalism's lost tradition."[62] Before his first term had ended, though, Wilson would himself succumb to the charms of the Progressive project and the "social possibilities of war." After a hiatus in the 1920s, this project would be brought to political power by Franklin D. Roosevelt's New Deal, and then pursued relentlessly throughout the rest of the century by a succession of powerful, energetic, progressive liberal presidents.

## THE REIGN OF PROGRESSIVE COMMUNITY

Indeed, every great liberal president of the twentieth century following Wilson made the cultivation of the national community the central goal of his administration, expanding the power and reach of the national govemment and calling on Americans to put aside self-interest and local allegiances on behalf of the national idea (often invoking the moral equivalent of war). The explosion of govemment power during the New Deal, for instance, proceeded behind FDR's call in his first inaugural address for Americans to "move as a trained and loyal army willing to sacrifice for the good of a common discipline." We must be "ready and willing to submit our lives and property to such discipline," he insisted, and pledge that "larger purposes will bind upon us all as a sacred obligation with a unity of duty hitherto evoked only in times of armed strife."[63]

Samuel Beer notes that, for all the debate about the intentions and impact of the New Deal, nonetheless "in creating among Americans the expectation that the federal government could and should deal with the great economic questions and that the nation could and should bear the consequent burdens, the achievement of the New Deal was close to revolutionary." (Beer brings an insider's perspective: as a young speechwriter for FDR, he notes, "I vividly recall our preoccupation with persuading people to look to Washington for the solution of problems.")[64]

Within the Roosevelt administration, the most coherent expression of this centralizing tendency was the drive for national planning. (The drive's slogan, "We planned in war, why not in peace?" harked back to the glorious centralizing years of World War I.) Nurturing a sense of national oneness, as much as a return to prosperity, was the planners' highest ambition. As *New Republic* editor George Soule put it in the final sentences of his 1932 paean *A Planned Society,* "[I]nstead of being baffled and burdened by . . . social forces, we shall be at work, through society, mastering our life and creating it as a whole. We shall have a warm and active bond with our fellows."[65]

Roosevelt was quite lucid about his intention to bring to a national scale America's traditionally localized sense of civic community. To his neighbors at Hyde Park, he explained that the "drastic changes in the methods and forms of the functions of govemment" followed from the fact that "we have been extending to our national life the old principle of the local community." All Americans, he affirmed, must now think of themselves as neighbors: "The many are the neighbors. In a national sense, the many, the neighbors, are the people of the United States as a whole."[66] Roosevelt adviser Rexford Tugwell suggested that this homely metaphor captured perfectly the "general direction" of the New Deal, beneath its "multifarious and confusing" details: "It is a march renewed, as a nation, to land marks which in our earlier pioneer neighborhoods stood always plain. Common neighborliness. Common decency. In a recent talk to his neighbors at Hyde Park, the President made that plain."[67]

Looking back almost wistfully from the early 1960s at the Depression years, Harry Girvetz noted that Americans had indeed been "imbued with a spirit of mutuality [and] a sense of common purpose" and had "discovered a sense of community and developed the kind of social conscience that produced the New Deal." So far had we tumbled from this sense of national community by the 1960s, however, that Girvetz would suggest "we need a moral equivalent to depression."[68]

Henry Luce and the editors of *Life* magazine shared Girvetz's alarm, and so in 1960 they asked a series of major public figures to propose ways to restore America's flagging sense of mission and togetherness. Published as a volume with the title *The National Purpose* (the subtitle—this is *1960*—was "America in Crisis: An Urgent Summons"), the perspectives were typified by Clinton Rossiter's view that America must develop a "profound, inspiring, benevolent sense of mission." But, he continued:

> if we choose greatness . . . we choose effort—the kind of national effort that transcends the ordinary lives of men and commits them to the pursuit of a common purpose, that persuades them to sacrifice private indulgences to the public interest, that sends them on a search for leaders who call forth strengths rather than pander to weakness.[69]

As if responding to the call for such an inspiring, unifying leader, John F. Kennedy stepped forward and issued his stirring summons to America to put aside self-interest on behalf of national purpose: "Ask not what your country can do for you—ask what you can do for your country." Concrete accomplishments aside, Kennedy promised to make us feel as a nation that we were together, united, "moving again." "These are times that appeal to every citizen's sense of sacrifice and self-discipline," he announced during the campaign of 1960. "They call out to every citizen to weigh his rights and comforts against the common good." The presidency, according to Kennedy, "must be the center of moral leadership—a 'bully pulpit' . . . for only the President represents the national interest." He must be "willing and able to summon his national constituency to its finest hour . . . to demand of them the sacrifices that would be necessary."[70]

Liberalism's national community project reached its modern zenith, however, in Lyndon Johnson's Great Society (it would have been more accurately named the Great Community). Again, there was the familiar explosion of federal government activity, justified by an equally familiar rhetoric: "I see a day ahead with a united nation, divided neither by class nor by section nor by color, knowing no South or North, no East or West, but just one great America, free of malice and free of hate, and loving thy neighbor as thyself."[71] America, Johnson insisted, must "turn unity of interest into unity of purpose, and unity of goals into unity in the Great Society."[72]

At the heart of the Great Society, Johnson believed, was the presidency, whose task was to forge among the American people a sense of national community. "As I conceive it," he noted, "a President's first role and first responsibility is to help perfect the unity of the people."[73] It was "one of the great tasks of political leadership to make our people aware . . . that they share a fundamental unity of interest and purpose and belief."[74] Thus, he pledged his presidency to "[keeping] us pulling together, keeping our ranks closed, keeping us loving our brother and our fellow man."[75]

Johnson hoped to perfect American unity in part by launching an allout war on poverty, calling citizens to a passionate, unified effort behind this great national crusade. "We will not win the war against poverty until the conscience of the entire nation is aroused," he insisted.[76] The effort to eradicate poverty would erect a "standard of service [that] will decrease the isolation of men from each other and will increase the deep feeling of community and concern that are the sinews of a large and great democracy's strength."[77] Naturally, the metaphor of a *war* on poverty was chosen quite deliberately: war "evokes cooperation [and a] sense of brotherhood and unity." The "military image" of the war on poverty would "rally the nation" and "sound a call to arms which will stir people . . . to lend their talents to a massive effort to eradicate the evil."[78]

Hidden beneath this summons to a passionate embrace of national community, however, another Great Society trend was running in a dramatically different direction. The "professionalization of reform," Daniel Patrick Moynihan noted in 1965, was quietly taking political initiative out of the uncertain hands of the public and passing it instead into "the hands of the administrators and the professional organizations of doctors, teachers, social workers, therapists, counselors and so forth." Because huge numbers of professionals "were involved in various aspects of social welfare and reform," he noted, "they would tend to have their way." Beyond that, though, "as professionals in a professionalizing society, they are increasingly *entitled* to have their way. That is how the system works." An elite corps of professionals organized into vast, gleaming bureaucracies would now run a burgeoning array of programs without undue interference from citizens or "clients" because "professionals *profess.* They profess to know better than others the nature of certain matters, and to know better than their clients what ails them or their affairs."

Unhappily, Moynihan conceded, the price of this professionalization was apt to be a "decline in the moral exhilaration of public affairs." (So much for "stirring the conscience of the nation" or creating a "deep feeling of community and concern.") Just when the civil rights movement had "at long last provided the youth of America with a moral equivalent of war," professionalization would mean "this kind of passion could seep out of the life of the nation."[79] But this was a small price to pay, in Moynihan's view, as we began to tackle social problems that seemed to require technical professional expertise more than moral exhilaration or popular passion.

The Progressive vision, of course, had always sought to conceal its icy reliance on apolitical, scientific expertise beneath the legitimating cloak of a fiery political summons to national community. But would Americans so readily acquiesce in leadership by experts were the cloak to begin to slip away? The Great Society would raise this question more forcefully than any other version of this century's progressive project. Had Moynihan been listening carefully to the era's rumblings among the "youth of America" and elsewhere, he might have been less sanguine about our willingness to acknowledge that professionals are "entitled to have their way" in public policy simply because they "profess to know better than others." Indeed, he might have been shocked at the "passion" this casual and self-serving assumption of the Great Society elites was about to provoke and introduce into the life of the nation.

Before we turn to the Great Society's difficulties, however, it might be useful to reflect for a moment on the progressive project's impact on the vitality of American civil society over the course of this century—that is, to return explicitly to the question of the relationship between state and civil society. About the adamant hostility of the progressive elites toward small, civic institutions and their "rambling, halting voluntaryism," there can be little doubt. While extolling the glories of the centralized, rationalized, secular national community, those elites have, for some eighty years, relentlessly hammered civic institutions for being notoriously and hopelessly backward, partial, parochial, reactionary, and riddled with irrational myths and prejudices. Such backwaters of reaction stubbornly cling to obscure and retrograde notions of traditional morality and religious faith, rather than bowing sensibly to the authority of scientifically credentialed professionals and experts, who alone can exploit the potential of modernity. It is no surprise that Progressivism should have worked steadily throughout this century to transfer authority and function away from civic institutions into the hands of bureaucratic, secular elites.

To be sure, a quick head count suggests that this century has seen no shortage of new civic associations. Theda Skocpol triumphantly points to this as proof—in the face of the unremitting hostility of the progressive elites—that state and civil society are perfectly compatible.[80] But a hasty look at *quantity* cannot begin to measure the dramatically diminished *quality* of civic association and membership over this century. Where once, as Nisbet put it, "the social problems of birth and death, courtship and marriage, employment and unemployment, infirmity and old age were met . . . through the associated means of these social groups," these tasks have today largely been transferred into the hands of centralized bureaucracies. Responding to this trend, many of our largest civic associations now seem designed chiefly to lobby for favors from those bureaucracies, maintaining "grassroots" membership lists chiefly to increase clout in Washington. Indeed, many civic groups have themselves become bureaucratic, secular, and expert-driven as they have evolved into statefunded "service delivery vehicles"—in the meantime, relegating citizens (now mere "volunteers," annoyingly underfoot) to trivial supportive and symbolic roles.[81]

Clearly, taking out a membership in this sort of civic association is a far cry from the immediate, everyday involvement in public affairs that civic groups once made possible. Occasionally signing a mass-produced form letter to a legislator or stuffing envelopes for a fund drive are radically diminished versions of the citizenship that once meant direct engagement in making and carrying out public decisions about the most significant human matters. Our progressive elites would have no problem with the new, "civic lite" associations. Humble petitions to the authorities and sentimental volunteerism pose no challenge to the "entitlement" of experts to run our affairs.

"Civic lite" is nicely illustrated by the PTA, which typifies, Skocpol accurately argues, many of the large civic associations launched earlier this century. Did the impulse for the PTA well up from parents and neighborhoods, demanding more say in the education of their children? Precisely the opposite: it was launched in 1897 by two inside-the-future-Beltway Progressives who were determined to bring the new, enlightened, expertdriven science of "child culture" to benighted parents. The PTA must always "begin its activities from the school as a center," Julian Butterworth noted in *The Parent-Teacher Association and Its Work* (1929), because "here the most progressive educational thinking in the community is apt to be taking place. Sooner or later the school is likely to expose the limitations of out-of-school experiences [read: reactionary parental influences]." Should parents even be allowed to make *suggestions* about running the schools? "The obvious danger . . . is that parents may go too far," Butterworth cautioned. "They may insist their point of view be adopted, when the professional officers with their greater insight may realize that it is neither feasible nor sound. . . . Decision concerning the suggestions is a technical job that should be left to the teachers and supervisors."[82]

In short, far from posing any challenge to the growing power of the progressive elites, the PTA and other such organizations were shrewdly organized by the elites themselves to project their expertise and authority into the remotest schoolhouse, town hall, and parlor. Indeed, properly structured and manipulated, "civic lite" associations could themselves be useful in eroding parochial loyalties and building up instead allegiance to the national community. Writing in the midst of the gloriously unifying days of World War I, Richard Ely observed that "our Councils of Defense, our Red Cross Societies and other patriotic organizations are a magnificent beginning of that cooperation which embraces the entire nation. . . . They are bringing us together and organizing America as a nation."[83] Once Ely and his friends have been permitted to tamper with and recalibrate the gauge of civic vitality, Skocpol should have no problem demonstrating the compatibility of state and civil society.

Given the manifest intentions of the progressive elites, it should not be surprising that their state has, over this century, posed a threat to genuine civic vitality far more formidable than the market. The market, after all, understands itself to be altogether different from and in tension with civic community. The progressive state, by contrast, claims to be able to perform civil society's critical communitybuilding function *better than civil society itself,* and so feels entitled to absorb the authority and functions of its institutions. It promises to deliver a vastly superior version of community—no longer confined to contemptible ethnic and religious backwaters, but rather now spread over a grand, national stage, coherently coordinated by credentialed, social scientific professionals.

The problem with a vision that seeks to conceal the rule of a dispassionate, bureaucratic, scientific elite beneath a passionate summons to national community—all the while denigrating the traditional sources of community—would come to light in the course of the 1960s and 1970s.

## THE DECLINE OF THE NATIONAL COMMUNITY IDEA

If a central theme runs through the diverse currents of dissatisfaction and unrest that marked the 1960s, it would have to be the loss of faith in the idea of national community that lay behind progressive liberalism, and a radical disenchantment with the elites whose rule it had once legitimated. As Theodore White noted in his account of the presidential election of 1968, the period was dominated by a "general sense of breakdown of control of old instruments, . . . breakdown of leadership uncertain of its purposes and unclear in its language, breakdown, above all, of ideas and dreams that once made America a community."[84]

Instead—and in spite of six decades of progressive warfare against "parochial" civil institutions—there appeared once again a yearning for the intimate, face-to-face, participatory community to be found in small groups, family, neighborhood, church, and ethnic and voluntary association. The Anti-Federalist small-republican impulse apparently had not, after all, been subsumed into and satisfied by the Federalist state.

The New Left, for instance, insisted that the Great Society was, in spite of its claims, radically anticommunitarian, characterized by (in the Port Huron Statement's formulation) "loneliness, estrangement, [and] isolation."[85] This was inevitable in a society governed by what they now described as a massive, distant, alienating bureaucracy, linked closely with giant business concerns in that unholy alliance the New Left came to call "corporate liberalism." Federal social programs were not expressions of national community but rather cynical devices for "regulating the poor," as Francis Fox Piven and Richard Cloward put it.[86]

As an alternative, the New Left offered "participatory democracy." A society organized according to that principle would devolve major political and economic decision making to small, tightly knit local groups, within which people would "share in the social decisions determining the quality and direction of their lives."[87] Wini Breines observes of the New Left that "a basic if rarely articulated purpose of the movement was to create communities of equality, direct democracy and solidarity. In bold contrast to the values of competition, individualism, and efficiency, the movement yearned for and occasionally achieved the community it sought."[88] As Greg Calvert of the Students for a Democratic Society (SDS) put it, "while fighting to destroy the power of the loveless anti-community, we would ourselves create the community of love—the Beloved Community."[89]

The rejection of the national community and the impulse toward smaller, more intimate communities also characterized the Black Power movement of the 1960s and 1970s, and the subsequent flowering of similar movements centered on ethnic identity and community control that it inspired. According to Stokely Carmichael and Charles Hamilton in *Black Power*, blacks should begin to "recognize the need to assert their own definitions, to reclaim their history, their culture; to create their own sense of community and togetherness." Local social institutions such as the schools and police should not be run by white liberals downtown but by blacks in the neighborhood: "We must begin to think of the black community as a base of organization to control institutions in that community." With the celebration of black culture and morality in their own schools and other public places, a "growing sense of community" at the neighborhood level would be further encouraged.[90]

So powerful were these new doctrines that Senator Robert Kennedy seized on them for his electoral challenge to Johnson's Great Society. He argued in *To Seek a Newer World* that the nation's slums could be transformed only through "new community institutions that local residents control, and through which they can express their wishes." He called for a "decentralization of some municipal functions and some aspects of government into smaller units, no matter what the race or economic status of the governed." This would, he noted, move us "toward [Jefferson's] vision of participating democracy," an objective that had otherwise become "increasingly difficult in the face of the giant organizations and massive bureaucracies of the age."[91]

Perhaps the most politically potent expression of dissatisfaction with the national community in the 1960s and 1970s, however, came from the opposite end of the political spectrum—from lower-middle-class, bluecollar neighborhoods, usually connected to the older industrial cities of the North and East, usually heavily ethnic (of Southern and Eastern European origin), Democratic, and Catholic. As they saw it, the national government seemed to have launched a massive assault—through cold, bureaucratic edict or equally cold judicial fiat—against the traditional prerogatives of locality and neighborhood to define and preserve their own ways of life. Suddenly, they could neither pray in their local schools, nor indeed count on sending their own children to the local school because of compulsory busing, nor ban from their community forms of expression or sexual conduct that they considered offensive, nor define the conditions under which abortion might be proper, nor even enforce the most rudimentary forms of civil order under the police power.

The most spectacular expression of this discontent came, of course, from George Wallace, who insisted that people were "fed up with strutting pseudo-intellectuals lording over them . . . telling them they have not got sense enough to run their own schools and hospitals and domestic institutions." Consequently, Wallace explained, there had been a "backlash against the theoreticians and bureaucrats in national government who are trying to solve problems that ought to be solved at the local level." His answer to this was "States' Rights and local government and territorial democracy."[92]

Describing the deeper impulses behind the white ethnic revolt, Michael Novak in *The Rise of the Unmeltable Ethnics* suggested that ethnics had historically been the primary victims of progressive liberalism's effort to eradicate particularist allegiances on behalf of one vast homogenized, rationalized, bureaucratized national community. Now they had made a dramatic and forceful "turn toward the organic networks of communal life . . . family, ethnic groups, and voluntary associations in primary groups."[93]

## THE POLITICAL ECLIPSE OF NATIONAL COMMUNITY

Beneath the variety of intellectual currents of revolt during the 1960s lay this central truth: progressive liberalism's intention to eradicate "parochial" loyalties and allegiances on behalf of the great national community had failed miserably. That failure became ever more conspicuous during the 1970s and 1980s, when the nation's political landscape reshaped itself to accommodate this truth, along with the groups that had been roused to an angry political revolt over the assault on their "organic networks."

Indeed, after 1964, *no one* would again win the presidency by boasting about building a Great Society, a great national community, in America. No one would again call proudly and forthrightly for a shift of power to Washington and away from the local organic networks. Indeed, every president from 1968 to the present has placed at the center of his agenda the *denunciation* of centralized, bureaucratic government, along with promises to slash its size and power and to reinvigorate states, small communities, and civil society's intermediate associations.

Thus, President Richard Nixon complained that "a third of a century of centralizing power and responsibility in Washington has produced a bureaucratic monstrosity, cumbersome, unresponsive, ineffective." He proposed a New Federalism in which "power, funds, and responsibility will flow from Washington to the State and to the people," through block grants and revenue sharing.[94] During the presidential campaign of 1972—even after he had presided over four years of dramatically *expanding* government programs—Nixon would nonetheless insist that the "central question" of that election was "Do we want to turn more power over to bureaucrats in Washington. . ., or do we want to return more power to the people and to their State and local governments, so that people can decide what is best for themselves?"[95] Similarly, President Gerald Ford characterized his programs as an effort to "return power from the banks of the Potomac to the people in their communities."[96]

During this period, Republican presidential hegemony would be interrupted but once, by an "outsider" Democrat who insisted that the Republicans had, rhetoric notwithstanding, permitted the federal government to become too large and inefficient. What was needed, Jimmy Carter insisted, was an engineer's savvy to trim it down to size. Thus, his schemes for government reorganization, zero-based budgeting, and sunset provisions were aimed at proving government could "serve basic needs without proliferating wasteful, bloated bureaucracies." Cultivating his image as a man steeped in the moral and religious traditions of a small southern town, Carter promised a new emphasis on local community: "the only way we will ever put the government back in its place is to restore the families and neighborhoods to their proper places," because they can "succeed in solving problems where governments will always fail."[97] Neighborhood activist Father Geno Baroni was brought into the government to establish an agenda for the reinvigoration of local community.

Carter, of course, eventually drifted away from his pledge to reduce government and restore the prerogatives of families and neighborhoods. Faced by shrinking popularity, he resorted to what almost amounts to a self-caricature of liberalism's "moral equivalent" ploy. In his now infamous "malaise" speech, Carter declared, "We are the generation that will win the war on the energy problem and in that process rebuild the unity and confidence of America" (as if shivering in an underheated home, remembering to turn out the lights, or sitting in endless queues at gas stations would somehow restore our faith in the central government and sense of national oneness).[98]

Americans were not particularly pleased to be told that they suffered from "malaise," nor were they up for a "war" that simply masked yet another expansion of federal power, in this case the nationalization of energy supplies. Thus was Carter replaced by this century's most consistent and eloquent critic of federal power and spokesman for reinvigoration of local community. Ronald Reagan promised an end to the state of affairs in which "thousands of towns and neighborhoods have seen their peace disturbed by bureaucrats and social planners through busing, questionable education programs, and attacks on family unity." He called instead for "an end to giantism, for a return to the human scale . . . the scale of the local fraternal lodge, the church organization, the block club, the farm bureau," and he pursued it through budget reductions, block grants, a program of private sector initiatives, and a (new) New Federalism.[99] His successor George Bush, in turn, followed Reagan in explicitly rejecting liberalism's project of national community, proclaiming instead a vision of "a nation of communities, of thousands of ethnic, religious, social, business, labor union, neighborhood, regional, and other organizations, all of them varied, voluntary, and unique," which would stand as a "thousand points of light" in America's struggle to solve social problems.[100]

Republican ascendancy in the 1990s was terminated when President Bush not only failed to reduce government but actually acquiesced in its expansion through significant tax hikes. His victorious opponent—like Carter, draping himself in the traditional values of a small, southern town, albeit called Hope rather than Plains—swore that he had gotten the message about his party's traditional allegiance to big government.

Proclaiming himself a "New Democrat" by way of shorthand for this political epiphany, Bill Clinton pledged to end welfare as we know it, get tough on crime, and "reinvent" government. He raised questions about reliance on big government and suggested a return to "organic networks." As he noted, "our problems go way beyond the reach of government. They're rooted in the loss of values, in the disappearance of work and the breakdown of families and communities." Problems will be solved, he continued, only when "all of us are willing to join churches and other good citizens . . . who are saving kids, adopting schools, making streets safer."[101] After an early, politically disastrous feint to the left with a centralizing, bureaucratic plan for health care reform, Clinton won reelection when he remembered that "the world of today has moved away from big centralized bureaucracies and top-down solutions; so has your federal government."[102]

All of these quadrennial political promises to the contrary notwithstanding, of course, the power and authority of the federal bureaucratic apparatus continued to grow throughout these years. The point, however, is that such growth came increasingly to be treated as aberrant and illegitimate—the product of "uncontrollable entitlements," "gridlocked" government, "iron triangles," or bureaucratic inertia—even by the presidents under whom such growth continued. After 1968, they seldom affirmed in Lyndon Johnson's ringing tones the centrality of the federal government in American life, or suggested that its purpose was to pull us together into a cohesive, national community.

What explains an erosion of the idea of national community so severe that even the Democratic party itself now hesitates to speak up for it? In part, it must be noted, the moral momentum of national community is extremely difficult to sustain. The project strains to create artificially, at the level of the entire nation, a sense of mutuality and oneness that appears readily and naturally only at the level of the family or local civic community. This transfer may be possible in times of crisis, when the threat to the nation is sufficiently obvious that people do, indeed, feel obliged to pull together as one. The United States has experienced its share of such crises since the turn of the century—the Great Depression, World War II, the cold war—and liberalism has used them to maximum effect, to construct an ever more powerful central government. When real crises are not available, liberal presidents must turn instead to moral equivalents, reviving the language and symbolism associated with periods of national cohesion. A war on poverty, however (to say nothing of a "war on the energy problem"), is but a pallid substitute for the real thing. Today, with the end of a long and exhausting cold war, Americans seem distinctly unwilling to rally around the "national idea."

With the moral foundations of the liberal project thus eroding, its programmatic superstructure—a massive, centralized federal government—is left in a peculiarly exposed and precarious position. No longer understood to be the instrument of high national purpose, the federal government comes to be seen instead as a distant, alienating, bureaucratic monstrosity. To put it in the context of Moynihan's "professionalization of reform," once the aura of moral legitimacy lent by the spirit of national community has dropped away from the federal apparatus, citizens awaken to the fact that public life has been removed from their grasp and transferred into the hands of distant elites who presume they are "entitled to have their way" due to their professional expertise. Moynihan may have thought that the American people would quietly acquiesce in this arrangement, forgoing the "moral exhilaration of public affairs." But our politics since the 1960s has shown that, once the central logic of progressive liberalism is thus laid bare before us, we reject it resoundingly, and insist that public affairs be given back to us because *we,* not the experts, "know better."

Thus we arrive at the contemporary condition of public opinion captured so well in James Davison Hunter and Carl Bowman's exhaustive survey of

American political culture, *The State of Disunion.* The American people, they find, are radically dissatisfied with their national institutions and governing elites, believing them to be "out of touch," "incompetent," "unconcerned with values and morality," "irreligious," and generally evidencing an "imperious disregard for the concerns of ordinary citizens."[103] (The elites, it should be noted, return the favor, being generally "dubious about, if not dismissive toward, traditional middle-class morality," uncomfortable with religion, and "most likely to reject bourgeois family life.")[104] Only the institutions closer to home—states, local communities, and churches—are held in high regard, Hunter and Bowman remark, and so there is strong public sentiment for shifting authority away from the national government, back to the localities. "Tocqueville observed that democracy works best when it is local," they conclude, and so "democratic processes and the institutions that sustain them also have greater legitimacy as they become local."[105]

The Anti-Federalists, of course, would not have been surprised by any of these developments. Once we had begun to experience the yearning genuinely to be in charge of our own affairs again, the small-republicans could have told us, naturally we would return to the idea of community that finds expression in small, participatory groups such as family, neighborhood, and ethnic and voluntary associations—in short, we would turn again to civil society. As the Anti-Federalists had insisted two centuries ago, genuine self-government and a communitarian sense of belonging and purpose are possible only within such small, tightly knit groups, not spread over a vast continent. Progressivism's attempt to use the Federalists' central government to re-create at the national level the Anti-Federalists' small republic, they could have told us, was destined to fail.

The final assessment of the relationship between state and civil society will not, of course, be rendered by theorists speculating about their philosophical compatibility or by social scientists tallying the number of civic organizations with headquarters in Washington. That assessment will be made by the American people themselves, reacting to the specific form the relationship has tangibly taken within the political practice of this century. Given the political trends of the past thirty years and down to the present, the assessment seems to be in—and it is not favorable to the state. The progressive state has not, apparently, delivered on its promise to create a form of community superior to those contemptible backwaters of reaction, local civic institutions. To secure genuine community and self-government, evidently we still need civil society.

## THE FUTURE OF CIVIL SOCIETY

As we consider the prospects for civil society's future, it is easy to share the pessimism so widespread among social and political commentators today. For the first sixty years of this century, the progressive project sought with some success to delegitimate our civic institutions and transfer their functions upward to centralized, credentialed bureaucracies. Those they did not destroy, they corrupted, seducing many of them into taking on the centralized, rationalistic, bureaucratic trappings of corporations and governments.

Over the succeeding thirty years, the American people have evinced a strong desire to reverse this process and bring authority back to the civic institutions closest to home. Nonetheless, most of the governing authority remains in the hands of the central institutions that, as Hunter and Bowman suggest, enjoy the least legitimacy, while the far more legitimate local civic institutions remain dramatically less powerful. For thirty years, our national political leadership has acknowledged this problem and promised to do something about it. But so far, and with some notable exceptions, very little by way of actual return of governing authority to civic institutions has in fact been accomplished.

Whenever these sorts of reflections lead me to the brink of despair, I recall some of the extraordinary individuals with whom I have had the privilege to work in Milwaukee's inner-city neighborhoods: Bill Lock, who turned a shuttered factory given to his church into a thriving small business incubator; Gerald Saffold, who brings former gang members and drug addicts into his "Unity in the Community" Choir, filling an abandoned VFW hall with gospel music; Brother Bob Smith, whose Messmer High School imparts both character and competence to innercity teens; Cordelia Taylor, who established a community-based elder care facility in her former home and is now turning the entire block into a senior village; Deborah Darden, who helps AFDC mothers in a public housing project restore a strong spiritual atmosphere for their children.

While scholars and experts in well-appointed conference rooms fret and tussle over the fate of civil society, these Milwaukeeans are actually *rebuilding* civil society—and under circumstances the experts would say are absolutely prohibitive. Major businesses have long since left their neighborhoods; they have watched government programs come and go without leaving a trace; and they are still waiting for their invitation to join the latest coalition or collaboration or alliance formed by the big, downtown nonprofits. Yet in the midst of what we might see as desolation—long after all the experts have thrown up their hands and fled—these grassroots leaders are rebuilding strong families, vigorous neighborhoods, and powerful churches and voluntary associations.

Here, under the least hospitable circumstances imaginable, civil society is being reborn, one block, one neighborhood at a time. Tocqueville would have had no problem recognizing the common ingredient of success running through these diverse efforts: each is designed to turn passive clients or victims into genuine citizens, through a rigorous call to personal responsibility, self-discipline, civicmindedness, and faith. The Anti-Federalists would have acknowledged that these are precisely the sorts of small, faith-based, virtue-cultivating civic communities that are essential to the survival of democracy, and that they had worked so hard to protect. Robert Nisbet would have seen that, far from being pleasant little voluntary societies gathered "merely to be together," these groups are literally saving lives and souls on a daily basis, and so are squarely in the old tradition of civic associations engaging themselves with the most urgent problems of human life. Finally, Robert Woodson would remind us that these remarkable undertakings in Milwaukee are by no means isolated instances but can be found in various forms throughout the inner-city neighborhoods of this nation—wherever citizens have given up on the hollow promises of the progressive state and have turned instead to the untapped resources of their own neighborhoods.[106]

When the problem of civic revival seems hopelessly abstract or complicated or daunting, perhaps the place to start is with this simple question: What can we do to help these grassroots initiatives flourish and spread? For their leaders are the true experts on civil society. They are civic trauma specialists, able to breathe life back into civic institutions that had long since been left for dead.

Here, an agenda readily presents itself. Much of it has to do with removing the obstacles thrown up against such upstart local challenges by the jealous bureaucracies left behind by the failed progressive project. We can dismantle the credentialing regimes that serve chiefly to protect the prerogatives of those who "profess to know better"; strike down laws and regulations that impede start-up businesses, schools, and community initiatives; and lower the barriers against the involvement of faith-based organizations in meeting human needs. Beyond that, we can connect such groups to sources of finance through broader organizations such as community development corporations and help them rebuild order and security in the neighborhood through community-oriented policing. We can begin to convert public assistance to vouchers, so that citizens may escape the hulking prisons of the educational and social bureaucracies and instead engage themselves with their own community institutions, which still cultivate the competence and character they know to be the paths out of poverty.

Around this sort of decentralist, community-building agenda, it might be possible to rally significant elements of both conservatism and liberalism. Among conservatives, for instance, the "mediating structures" approach has grown considerably in influence since its humble beginnings at AEI. As Peggy Noonan cast about for ideas for George Bush's acceptance speech in 1988, for instance, she happened upon an account of the "mediating structures" concept, and concluded, "it was all there, I read and thought, This is Bush; this is what he means." Prosaic "mediating structures" was soon transmuted into a poetic presidential vision of "a nation of communities," composed of a "thousand points of light."[107]

More important, though, is the substantial clout brought to the concept today by the growing influence of the so-called "religious right." While their pronouncements are invariably misunderstood to mean that they wish to establish a rigorously Christian version of the national community—and while they are occasionally prone to utterances that fuel this misunderstanding—in fact they wish only to defend their small, local, virtuous "republics" against progressivism's corrosive secular ethos and its aggressive national agents. Their ongoing insurgency brings enormous political heft to the small-republican impulse within conservative circles.

The small-republican conservatives will have to contend internally, of course, with the perennial skepticism of the libertarians. When *National Review* editor Frank Meyer first encountered Nisbet's defense of intermediate associations, he wondered why we would want to exchange the "all-powerful totalitarian state" for the "subtler, quieter tyranny of 'customarily' imposed community."[108] Echoing this view, David Brooks at the *Weekly Standard* professes to be "taken aback" by conservative enthusiasm for "orderly, coherent, authoritative moral communities."[109] All of which is simply to say that within the conservative camp will be played out once again the old tension between the Federalist impulse toward commerce, individualism, and secularism and the Anti-Federalist impulse toward community, civic virtue, and faith.

The truly heartening news is that within contemporary liberalism, there is a growing skepticism of the progressive project of national community and a turn toward the "organic networks of community life" that Novak had once hoped might become the foundation for a revitalized left. Michael Sandel acknowledges that the "nationalizing project that unfolded from the Progressive Era to the New Deal to the Great Society" has become "politically vulnerable because it does not rest on a sense of national community adequate to its purpose." In the future, he continues, "a more promising basis for a democratic politics . . . is a revitalized civic life nourished in the more particular communities we inhabit."[110] Harking back to Woodrow Wilson's "lost liberal tradition" of decentralization, a small but influential group of communitarians and "New Democrats" now pledges to work to "revitalize economic self-reliance and self-government by returning power from large institutions to people . . . and from the national government to more accessible and accountable institutions, whether they be local government agencies or community organizations."[111]

Their version of the Anti-Federalist impulse will have to contend internally with the towering, bureaucratic empires of "service providers" left behind by the old progressive project, which still retain enormous power even as they have lost legitimacy after the decline of the idea of national community. (They simply refuse to believe that the American people will not someday rally again to the "one big idea" that, Mario Cuomo maintains, is "the heart of the matter"—that "this nation is at its best only when we see ourselves, all of us, as one farnily.")[112] All of which is to say that within the liberal camp will be played out a relatively new tension between Roosevelt's statist doctrine of centralized, bureaucratic national community and Wilson's preference for decentralized, localist community.

As should be evident, these political developments leave room for some very interesting new alignments, as increasingly influential elements of both left and right now acknowledge the urgent need to protect the middle range of human existence against the tendency of our politics to gravitate either upward to the state or downward to the individual. Within that middle range, Bill Lock, Cordelia Taylor, Brother Bob Smith, and thousands of other grassroots leaders around the country are working every day to re-create civil society—not because they are sentimental and kind-hearted volunteers, but because they know that unless they heed God's call to them, lives and souls will be lost, and revitalized civic institutions are the only tools they have found that make a difference. If we can look beyond old alliances and antagonisms and keep ourselves focused on supplying the civic trauma specialists with the material, political, and spiritual support they need, then the prospects for the future of American civil society will indeed be bright.

## NOTES

1. Robert A. Nisbet, *The Quest for Community* (Oxford: Oxford University Press, 1971).
2. Peter Berger and Richard John Neuhaus, *To Empower People: The Role of Mediating Structures in Public Policy* (Washington, D.C.: American Enterprise Institute, 1977).
3. Michael Novak, *The Rise of the Unmeltable Ethnics: Politics and Culture in the Seventies* (New York: Macmillan, 1972), 273.
4. Senator Bill Bradley, "America's Challenge: Revitalizing our National Community," address to the National Press Club, 9 February 1995, 2.
5. Robert D. Putnam, "Bowling Alone: America's Declining Social Capital," *Journal of Democracy* 6 (January 1995): 65–78.
6. Nisbet, *The Quest for Community,* 238.
7. Nisbet, *The Quest for Community,* 241.
8. Nisbet, *The Quest for Community,* 245.
9. Nisbet, *The Quest for Community,* 245.
10. This account of the political theory of the Federalists is drawn from the teachings of Martin Diamond. See especially Martin Diamond, *As Far as Republican Principles Will Admit,* ed. William A. Schambra (Washington, D.C.: American Enterprise Institute, 1992).
11. Alexander Hamilton, James Madison, and John Jay, *The Federalist Papers,* ed. Jacob E. Cooke (Cleveland: World, 1961), 56–65.
12. Hamilton et al., *The Federalist Papers,* 73.
13. Herbert Storing, *What the Anti-Federalists Were For* (Chicago: University of

Chicago Press, 1981), 3. This account of the political theory of the Anti-Federalists relies heavily on Storing's teachings. An earlier version of this synthesis of Federalist and Anti-Federalist thought may be found in William A. Schambra, "The Roots of the American Public Philosophy," *Public Interest* 67 (1982): 36–48.

14. Baron de Montesquieu, *The Spirit of the Laws,* trans. Thomas Nugent (New York: Hafner, 1949), 34.

15. Charles Turner, quoted in Storing, *What the Anti-Federalists Were For,* 23.

16. Turner, quoted in Storing, *What the Anti-Federalists Were For,* 21.

17. Quoted in Storing, *What the Anti-Federalists Were For,* 22.

18. Alexis de Tocqueville, *Democracy in America,* trans. George Lawrence (Garden City, N.J.: Doubleday, 1969), 118.

19. Tocqueville, *Democracy in America,* 157.

20. Tocqueville, *Democracy in America,* 161.

21. Tocqueville, *Democracy in America,* 413.

22. Tocclueville, *Democracy in America,* 671.

23. Tocqueville, *Democracy in America,* 533.

24. Tocqueville, *Democracy in America,* 511.

25. Nisbet, *The Quest for Community,* 54.

26. Nisbet, *The Quest for Community,* 287.

27. Nisbet, *The Quest for Community,* 668–74.

28. Thomas Bender, *Community and Social Change in America* (Baltimore: Johns Hopkins University Press, 1978), 51.

29. Bender, *Community and Social Change,* 46.

30. Bender, *Community and Social Change,* 145.

31. Bender, *Community and Social Change,* 148.

32. Nisbet, *The Quest for Community,* vii.

33. Walter Lippmann, *Drift and Mastery* (Upper Saddle River, N.J.: Prentice Hall, 1961), 81.

34. Herbert Croly, *The Promise of American Life* (Cambridge, Mass.: Harvard University Press, 1965), 61–62.

35. Croly, *The Promise of American Life,* 372.

36. Croly, *The Promise of American Life,* 209.

37. Quoted in Jean B. Quandt, *From the Small Town to the Great Community: The Social Thought of Progressive Intellectuals* (New Brunswick, N.J.: Rutgers University Press, 1970), 139. Quandt's book is an underappreciated resource for understanding the role of the idea of community, and especially of the "great community," in the thought of the Progressives.

38. Croly, *The Promise of American Life,* 23.

39. Croly, *The Promise of American Life,* 418.

40. Croly, *The Promise of American Life,* 406.

41. Croly, *The Promise of American Life,* 453.

42. Woodrow Wilson, *Constitutional Government* (New York: Columbia University Press, 1908), 68.

43. Woodrow Wilson, *Papers,* ed. Arthur S. Link (Princeton, N.J.: Princeton University Press, 1978), XIX: 42.

44. John Dewey, *Character and Events: Popular Essays in Social and Political Philosophy,* ed. Joseph Ratner (New York: Holt, 1929), 11: 551.

45. Walter Lippmann, "Integrated America," *New Republic,* 19 February 1916, 62, 64.

46. Richard T. Ely, *The World War and Leadership in a Democracy* (New York: Macmillan, 1918), 151.

47. Dewey, *Character and Events,* 552–53.

48. Timothy Kaufman-Osborn, "John Dewey and the Liberal Science of Community," *Journal of Politics* 46 (1984): 1157.

49. Kaufman-Osborn, "John Dewey and the Liberal Science of Community," 1158.

50. Quoted in Samuel Haber, *Efficiency and Uplift: Scientific Management in the Progressive Era, 1890–1920* (Chicago: University of Chicago Press, 1964).

51. Samuel R Hays, "The Politics of Reform in Municipal Government in the Progressive Era," *Pacific Northwest Quarterly* 55 (October 1964): 161.

52. Hays, "The Politics of Reform," 169.

53. Edward Alsworth Ross, *Principles of Sociology* (New York: Century, 1920), 268.

54. Ely, *The World War and Leadership in a Democracy,* 94–95.

55. Ross, *Principles of Sociology,* 422.

56. James Nuechterlein, "The Dream of Scientific Liberalism: The *New Republic* and American Progressive Thought, 1914–1920," *Review of Politics* 42 (April 1980): 175.

57. Albion Small, *The Meaning of Social Science* (Chicago: University of Chicago Press, 1910), 277, 295.

58. Quoted in J. David Hoeveler, Jr., "The University and the Social Gospel: The Intellectual Origins of the 'Wisconsin Idea,'" *Wisconsin Magazine of History* 59 (Summer 1976): 288, 289.

59. Hoeveler, Jr., "The University and the Social Gospel," 292.

60. Robert E. Park and Ernest W. Burgess, *The City* (Chicago: University of Chicago Press, 1967), 107.

61. Woodrow Wilson, *A Crossroads of Freedom: The 1912 Campaign Speeches* (New Haven, Conn.: Yale University Press, 1956), 83.

62. Fred Siegel and Will Marshall, "Liberalism's Lost Tradition," *New Democrat* (September/October 1995): 8–13.

63. Franklin D. Roosevelt, *The Public Papers and Addresses of Franklin D. Roosevelt,* ed. Samuel I. Rosenman, 13 vols. (New York: Random House, 1938–1950), 2, 14. Perhaps the best account of the Roosevelt administration's reliance on the war metaphor to mobilize the population is to be found in William E. Leuchtenburg, "The New Deal and the Analogue of War," in *Change and Continuity in Twentieth Century America,* ed. John Braeman, Robert Bremner, and Evert Walters (Columbus: Ohio University Press, 1964), 81–143.

64. Samuel Beer, "In Search of a New Public Philosophy," in *The New American Political System,* ed. Anthony King (Washington, D.C.: American Enterprise Institute, 1978), 8. Perhaps because of his personal involvement in crafting the New Deal's rhetoric, Professor Beer is by far the most thoughtful analyst of its community-building aspects, which, as he notes, found their initial expression in the earlier writings of Herbert Croly. See especially "Liberalism and the National Idea," in *Left, Right and Center,* ed. Robert A. Goldwin (Chicago: Rand-McNally, 1967), and "The Idea of the Nation," *New Republic,* 19 and 26 April 1982, 23–29.

65. George Soule, *A Planned Society* (New York: Macmillan, 1932), 283.

66. Roosevelt, *The Public Papers and Addresses,* 11: 342.

67. Rexford Tugwell, *The Battle for Democracy* (New York: Columbia University Press, 1935), 72. Theda Skocpol concedes that the New Deal was characterized by at least a stab at the rhetoric of national community, when it called for action "in the name of values of neighborliness that would bring the whole nation together in response to the emergency." She concludes, however, that such rhetoric was half-hearted and quickly abandoned, and ultimately condemns the New Deal for failing "to legitimate new national welfare programs in communal terms" or to "offer a sustained vision of new state actions as expressions of *public* interests and the well-being of the national *community*" (emphasis hers). She also insists that such failures should not stop modern liberals from pushing for an "*expansion* of community, regional, and national planning and . . . an explicit legitimation for a *broader,* rather than narrower, public sphere in U.S. capitalism and American society" (emphasis hers). Writing in the early 1980s, she does not provide any clue about how such an expansion of government planning in the name of national community might fit in with a vigorous civil society. Theda Skocpol, "Legacies of New Deal Liberalism," *Dissent* (Winter 1983): 37, 38, 39, 42, 43.

68. Harry K. Girvetz, *The Evolution of Liberalism* (New York: Collier, 1963), 330–31.

69. In *The National Purpose,* ed. Henry R. Luce (New York: Holt, Rinehart, & Winston, 1960), 82.

70. John F. Kennedy, Speech to the National Press Club, January 1960.

71. *Public Papers of the Presidents of the United States: Lyndon B. Johnson, 1963–1964* (Washington, D.C.: Government Printing Office, 1965), 1371.

72. *Public Papers of the Presidents of the United States,* 797.

73. *Public Papers of the Presidents of the United States,* 943.

74. *Public Papers of the Presidents of the United States,* 729.

75. *Public Papers of the Presidents of the United States,* 450.

76. *Public Papers of the Presidents of the United States,* 628.

77. *Public Papers of the Presidents of the United States: Lyndon B. Johnson,* 1966, 435.

78. Lyndon B. Johnson, *The Vantage Point* (New York: Popular Library, 1971), 74.

79. Daniel P. Moynihan, "The Professionalization of Reform," *Public Interest* 1 (Fall 1965): 6–16.

80. Theda Skocpol, "The Tocqueville Problem: Civic Engagement in American Democracy," Presidential Address to the Annual Meeting of the Social Science History Association, New Orleans, 12 October 1996, unpublished manuscript.

81. See John McKnight, *The Careless Society: Community and Its Counterfeits* (New York: Basic Books, 1995).

82. Julian P. Butterworth, *The Parent-Teacher Association and Its Work* (New York: Macmillan, 1929), 48–49, 61–62.

83. Ely, *The World War and Leadership in a Democracy,* 106–7.

84. Theodore H. White, *The Making of the President 1968* (New York: Pocket Books, 1968), 518.

85. "Selections from the Port Huron Statement," in *How Democratic Is America? Responses to the New Left Challenge,* ed. Robert A. Goldwin (Chicago: Rand McNally, 1971), 6.

86. Frances Fox Piven and Richard A. Cloward, *Regulating the Poor* (New York: Pantheon Books, 1971).

87. *How Democratic Is America?* ed. Goldwin, 7.

88. Wini Breines, *Communiy and Organization in the New Left, 1962–1969: The Great Refusal* (New York: Praeger, 1982), 27.

89. Quoted in Breines, *Community and Organization in the New Left,* 48.

90. Stokely Carmichael and Charles V. Hamilton, *Black Power: The Politics of Liberation in America* (New York: Vintage Books, 1967), 53, 37, 39.

91. Robert E. Kennedy, *To Seek a Newer World* (New York: Bantam Books, 1968), 53, 54, 58. For an illuminating discussion of Senator Kennedy's largely unremarked Jeffersonianism, see Michael J. Sandel, "The Politics of Community: Robert E. Kennedy versus Ronald Reagan," *Responsive Community* 6 (Spring 1996): 1427. Sandel quotes Kennedy's observations to a rural Minnesota audience: "Bigness, loss of community, organizations, and society grown far past the human scale—these are the besetting sins of the twentieth century, which threaten to paralyze our capacity to act."

92. Quoted in John J. Synon, *George Wallace: Profile of a Presidential Candidate* (Kilmarnock, Va.: Ms, Inc., n.d.), 59, 77, 83.

93. Novak, *The Rise of the Unmeltable Ethnics,* 321.

94. *Public Papers of the Presidents of the United States: Richard Nixon, 1969* (Washington, D.C.: Government Printing Office, 1970), 637–38.

95. *Public Papers of the Presidents of the United States: Richard Nixon, 1972,* 997.

96. Quoted in Henry J. Schmandt et al., "CDBG: Continuity or Change?" *Publius* (Summer 1983): 7.

97. *The Presidential Campaign 1976,* 2 vols. (Washington, D.C.: Government Printing Office, 1978),1: 708–9, 714.

98. *Public Papers of the Presidents of the United States: Jimmy Carter, 1979* (Washington, D.C.: Government Printing Office, 1980), 1238.

99. Ronald Reagan, "Let the People Rule," Speech to the Executive Club of Chicago, 26 September 1975, manuscript.

100. Quoted in Peggy Noonan, *What I Saw at the Revolution* (New York: Random House, 1990), 311.

101. Bill Clinton, 1994 State of the Union Address. Alan Brinkley would observe of Clinton's speech that he was "trying to reclaim from the right a moral language that liberals have—in recent years, at least—largely abdicated. He was continuing the effort . . . to rescue liberalism from the symbolically barren, socially fragmented world it has inhabited for a generation, and to link it to a popular yearning for values and community." Brinkley, "At Last, Maybe a Vision," *New York Times,* 27 January 1994, 21.

102. Bill Clinton, "Commencement Address at Penn State University," 10 May 1996.

103. James Davison Hunter and Carl Bowman, *The State of Disunion: 1996 Survey of American Political Culture, Summary Report* (Ivy, Va.: In Medias Res Educational Foundation, 1996), 25–28.

104. Hunter and Bowman, *The State of Disunion,* 47–48.

105. Hunter and Bowman, *The State of Disunion,* 22.

106. Robert L. Woodson, *The Triumphs of Joseph: How Today's Community Healers Are Reviving Our Streets and Neighborhoods* (New York: Free Press, 1998).

107. Noonan, *What I Saw at the Revolution,* 311–12.

108. Frank S. Meyer, *In Defense of Freedom: A Conservative Credo* (Chicago: Regnery, 1962), 141.

109. David Brooks, "'Civil Society' and Its Discontents," *Weekly Standard*, 5 February 1996, 18.

110. Michael J. Sandel, "America's Search for a New Public Philosophy," *Atlantic Monthly* 277 (March 1996): 74.

111. "The New Progressive Declaration," in *Building the Bridge: 10 Big Ideas to Transform America*, ed. Will Marshall (Lanham, Md.: Rowman & Littlefield, 1997), 23–24.

112. Mario Cuomo, Address to the Democratic National Convention, 28 August 1996 (www.dnc96.org/day2/draftO8.html). For other contemporary arguments on behalf of the national community idea, see especially Alan Brinkley's contributions to Alan Brinkley, Nelson W Polsby, and Kathleen M. Sullivan, *New Federalist Papers* (New York: Norton, 1997). Brinkley urges us to remember that, in addition to the Tocquevillean tradition of local community, there is "also a larger vision of community that . . . transcends localism and parochialism. . . . The idea of national community is, in fact among the oldest and most powerful in our history" (95), Similarly, Nicholas Lemann suggests that America's racial divisions will not be healed without a return to that "larger vision": "It is during the times when there has been a strong sense of *national* community that [racial] problems have been addressed. . . . The ghettos, and race relations in general, are the one area in American domestic life where . . . the vocabulary of crisis and national responsibility is not in the least trumped up." Nicholas Lemann, *The Promised Land* (New York: Knopf, 1991), 352–53.

# 17

# Individualism, Liberalism, and Democratic Civic Society

*William A. Galston*

## TENSIONS WITHIN LIBERALISM

For two generations, scholarly inquiry has been dominated by the belief that the liberal polity does not require individual virtue. On the theoretical plane, liberalism has been understood by many as the articles of a peace treaty among individuals with diverse conceptions of the good but common interests in preservation and prosperity. On the level of basic institutions, the liberal constitution has been regarded as an artful contrivance of countervailing powers and counterbalancing passions. In the arena of liberal society, individual behavior has been analyzed through the prism, and public policy guided by the precepts, of neoclassical economics.

The conclusion that liberalism could be severed, in theory and in practice, from the concern for virtue was shared by scholars of widely divergent orientations. While Leo Strauss was on the whole sympathetic, and C. B. Macpherson hostile, to the liberal polity, they converged on an interpretation of Locke that stressed his effort to liberate individual acquisitiveness from traditional moral constraints.[1] Martin Diamond and Gordon Wood could agree on the essentials of the interest-based "new science of politics" that displaced civic republicanism and undergirded the Constitution.[2] The understanding of modern liberal society as an agglomeration of self-interested individuals and groups formed a common point of departure for defenders of pluralism (such as Robert Dahl in his 1950s incarnation) and critics, led by Theodore Lowi.[3]

Although the various analysts of liberalism were not in agreement on a specific conception of virtue, they were united in the belief that liberal theory and practice stood in tension with virtue however conceived. For Strauss and many of his followers, liberalism placed in jeopardy both the restraints on passion that should govern the daily life of the many and the striving for excellence that should guide the activities of the few. For J. G. A. Pocock and his allies, liberalism represented the evisceration of republican virtue, understood as the disposition to subordinate personal interests to the common good.[4] For Charles Taylor and his fellow communitarians, liberalism undercut the very possibility of community and thus the significance of the virtues, understood as the habits needed to sustain a common life.[5] To the extent that virtue could nonetheless be found in the actual practices of liberal society, it was to be understood, argued Irving Kristol and many others, as the residue of an older moral and religious tradition at odds with—and under relentless assault by—liberalism's most fundamental tendencies.[6]

The proposition that liberalism does not rest on virtue is not the arbitrary invention of contemporary scholarship. Albert Hirschman has traced the emergence in seventeenth- and eighteenth-century social thought of the thesis that republican government could best be secured, not through civic virtue, but rather through the liberation of the commercial-acquisitive "interests" of the middle class in opposition to the politically destructive "passions" of the aristocracy.[7] The most famous *Federalist* papers (nos. 10 and 51) contain memorable formulations of the need to counteract interest with interest and passion with passion. Immanuel Kant, who was at once the profoundest moral philosopher and the most devoted liberal theorist of his age, argued vigorously for the disjunction between individual virtue and republican government:

> The republican constitution is the only one entirely fitting to the rights of man. But it is the most difficult to establish and even harder to preserve, so that many say a republic would have to be a nation of angels, because men with their selfish inclinations are not capable of a constitution of such sublime form. But [this is an error: republican government] is only a question of a good organization of the state, whereby the powers of each selfish inclination are so arranged in opposition that one moderates or destroys the ruinous effect of the other. The consequence . . . is the same as if none of them existed, and man is forced to be a good citizen even if not a morally good person. The problem of organizing a state, however hard it may seem, can be solved even for a race of devils, if only they are intelligent.[8]

In spite of the considerable evidence for the proposition that the liberal-republican polity requires no more than the proper configuration of rational self-interest, this orthodoxy has in recent years come under attack from scholars who argue that liberal theory, institutions, and society embody—and depend upon—individual virtue. Judith Shklar has traced the emergence of liberalism to a revulsion against the cruelty of religious wars—that is, to a decision to replace military and moral repression with a "self-restraining tolerance" that is "morally more demanding than repression."[9] Rogers Smith has found in Locke a core conception of "rational liberty" on which a distinction between liberty and license and an account of individual excellence are based.[10] Summarizing a painstaking reexamination of the neglected *Thoughts Concerning Education*, Nathan Tarcov concludes: "Instead of a narrowly calculating selfishness, Locke teaches a set of moral virtues that make men able to respect themselves and be useful to one another both in private and in public life."[11] Ronald Terchek extends this thesis to Adam Smith and John Stuart Mill, whom he interprets as recommending "the cultivation of those habits which turned us toward the practice of virtue."[12] J. Budziszewski offers a general argument for the proposition that liberalism and the cultivation of the virtues can be logically compatible and even mutually supportive.[13] In Harvey Mansfield Jr.'s striking rereading of the *Federalist*, the automatic or mechanical view of our constitutional arrangements is replaced by a focus on well-ordered souls as the foundation of sustainable republican government: "Not only are the people expected to be virtuous but also those who run for office."[14] James Q. Wilson's survey of contemporary public policy dilemmas concludes that economic diagnoses and prescriptions, which treat individual dispositions as fixed and exogenously determined "tastes," are at best one-sided. The challenge of social policy is not just the manipulation of incentives but also the formation of character: "In almost every area of important public concern, we are seeking to induce persons to act virtuously. . . . In the long run, the public interest depends on private virtue."[15]

If this line of argument is correct, there is a tension at the heart of liberalism. The liberal state must by definition be broadly inclusive of diversity, yet it cannot be wholly indifferent to the character of its citizens. As Thomas Spragens has noted, "A citizenry without public spirit, without self-restraint, and without intelligence accords ill with the demands of effective self-governance."[16] To quote Judith Shklar once more, the alternative before us

> is not one between classical virtue and liberal self-indulgence. . . . Far from being an amoral free-for-all, liberalism is, in fact, extremely difficult and constraining, far too much so for those who cannot endure . . . the risks of freedom. The habits of freedom are developed, moreover, both in private and in public, and a liberal character can readily be imagined.[17]

The challenge, then, is to give an account of individual virtue that supports rather than undermines liberal institutions and the capacious tolerance that gives liberal society its special attraction.

The thesis that liberalism rests in some measure on virtue is not the palpable absurdity that the liberal polity requires an impeccably virtuous citizenry, a "nation of angels." Nor is it incompatible with the mechanical-institutional interpretation of liberalism, for clearly the artful arrangement of "auxiliary precautions" can go some distance toward compensating for the defect of better motives. Nor, finally, does this thesis maintain that the liberal polity should be understood as a tutelary community dedicated to the inculcation of individual virtue or excellence. The claim is more modest: that the operation of liberal institutions is affected in important ways by the character of citizens (and leaders), and that at some point, the attenuation of individual virtue will create pathologies with which liberal political contrivances, however technically perfect their design, simply cannot cope. To an extent difficult to measure but impossible to ignore, the viability of liberal society depends on its ability to engender a virtuous citizenry.

While this requirement is not unique to liberal societies, it poses special difficulties for them. The liberal way of life frees individuals from traditional restraints and allows them to pursue their own conceptions of happiness. To the extent that the liberal virtues are not simply consistent with individual self-interest, processes of forming and maintaining them will come into conflict with other powerful tendencies in liberal life. The liberal virtues are the traits of character liberalism needs, not necessarily the ones it has. Yet these virtues need not be imported from the outside, for they are immanent in liberal practice and theory. The tension between virtue and self-interest is a tension within liberalism, not between liberalism and other traditions.

## THE CLASSICAL CONCEPTION OF VIRTUE

The classical conception of the relation between virtue and politics was spelled out by Aristotle. Individual virtue (or excellence—the Greek *arete* will bear both meanings) is knowable through everyday experience, definable through philosophic inquiry, and is always and everywhere the same. For Aristotle, the virtues are not just Greek, but rather human, virtues. Political life must be seen as in large measure a means to the attainment of virtue, understood as an end in itself. Once the threshold conditions of physical and material security are met, the political community should structure its institutions and policies to promote virtue in its citizens, and its worth as a community depends on the extent to which it achieves that goal.

Aristotle was under no illusion that the communities of his day were actually organized in pursuit of virtue. Some, like Sparta, were devoted to military victory; others, to commercial prosperity; most had no single discernible goal. Each nonetheless had a largely tacit, operative conception of the virtuous individual as the good citizen whose character and conduct were most conducive to the preservation of the community and of its way of life. In this understanding, the relation of politics and virtue are reversed: virtue becomes the means, and the political community provides the end.

This reversal gave rise to the question explored by Aristotle in Book III of the *Politics:* Are the virtues of the good human being and of the good citizen identical or different? It turns out that they are nearly always different, a conclusion that generates a double dilemma. If a community is notably imperfect, the citizen who shapes himself in its image and devotes himself to its service will undergo a kind of moral deformation. Conversely, the virtues of the good human being *simpliciter* may not only not promote, but may actually impede, the activities of the particular community in which he happens to find himself.

Liberal theorists were not unaware of this dilemma, and they responded to it in two very different ways. Some, such as John Stuart Mill, retained a place for the Aristotelian conception of virtue as an intrinsic good but argued that the practice of virtue, so understood, would also be supportive of the liberal polity. In a liberal order, the same virtues are both ends and means: the good human being and the good citizen are identical.

The other liberal strategy was to cut the knot by denying the very existence of intrinsic virtue, that is, by reinterpreting virtue as purely instrumental to the nonmoral goods that constitute the true ends of liberal politics. Thus Hobbes says:

> All men agree on this, that peace is good, and therefore also [that] the way, or means, of peace, which . . . are justice, gratitude, modesty, equity, mercy, and the rest of the laws of nature, are good. . . . But the writers of moral philosophy, though they acknowledge the same virtues and vices, [do not see] wherein consisted their goodness; nor that they come to be praised as the means of peaceable, sociable, and comfortable living.[18]

During the past two decades, John Rawls has moved between the Hobbesian and Millian strategies. For Rawls, the ultimate justification—and overriding objective—of the liberal polity is the attainment of justice, viewed not as an individual virtue but as a social state of affairs. Rawls rejects "perfectionism"—the thesis that society should be so arranged as to maximize the achievement of individual virtue or excellence. Yet justice as a virtue predicated of individuals does occupy a place within his overall theory. Individuals are presumed to have a capacity for a sense of justice—that is, the ability to accept and to act upon the agreed-on principles of social justice, which in turn supply the substantive content of individual justice. As this conception is developed in *A Theory of Justice*, the engendering of just individuals is not the goal of liberal society but rather the means to the preservation of that society. That is why each member of a well-ordered liberal society wants the others to have a developed sense of justice. And more broadly, Rawls declares in a Hobbesian spirit, "a good person has the features of moral character that it is rational [i.e., instrumentally rational] for members of a well-ordered society to want in their associates."[19] In his more recent work, however, he has placed increased emphasis on the development and exercise of "moral personality" as an intrinsic good or end in itself. The very practices that help sustain a just society also express our nature as free and equal rational beings who have realized their innate capacity for justice.[20]

In the liberal tradition, then, we find traces of both sides of the Aristotelian conception—virtue as end and as means. It would be surprising, however, if on closer inspection the liberal canon of the virtues turned out to mirror the classical enumeration. Indeed, I shall argue (*pace* Hobbes) that it does not. The liberal virtues are not simply the classical virtues justified on a different basis. They are in important respects different virtues.

## LIBERAL VIRTUES AS MEANS

I begin by examining the liberal virtues understood instrumentally, as means to the preservation of liberal societies and institutions. To fix terms, let me characterize the liberal polity as a community possessing to a high degree the following features: popular-constitutional government; a diverse society with a wide range of individual opportunities and choices; a predominantly market economy; and a substantial, strongly protected sphere of privacy and individual rights. And to avoid misunderstanding, let me briefly characterize the status of the propositions I am about to advance.

1. The discussion of the instrumental virtues in this section is a catalog, not of logical entailments within liberal theory, but rather of empirical hypotheses concerning the relationship between social institutions and individual character. I offer a most fragmentary evidence in support of these hypotheses, an adequate test of which would require a far more systematic historical and comparative inquiry.
2. When I speak of certain virtues as instrumental to the preservation of liberal communities, I do not mean that every citizen must possess these virtues, but rather that most citizens must. The broad hypothesis is that as the proportion of nonvirtuous citizens increases significantly, the ability of liberal societies to function successfully will progressively diminish.
3. The fact (if it is a fact) that the instrumental virtues are socially functional does not mean that they are individually advantageous. To be sure, there is some overlap between these two objectives. The liberal virtues demand less self-discipline and sacrifice than do the virtues of classical antiquity, of civic republicanism, or of Christianity, and the practice of many of these social virtues will simultaneously make it easier for individuals to succeed within liberal communities. Still, these virtues are not reducible to self-interest, even self-interest "rightly understood." Thus, while the liberal virtues do not presuppose a specific moral psychology, they do at least imply the rejection of any comprehensive egoism.

## General Virtues

Some of the virtues needed to sustain the liberal state are requisites of every political community. From time to time, each community must call upon its members to risk their lives in its defense. Courage—the willingness to fight and even die on behalf of one's country—is thus very widely honored, even though there may be occasions on which the refusal to fight is fully justified. In addition, every community creates a complex structure of laws and regulations in the expectation that they will be accepted as legitimate, hence binding, without recourse to direct threats or sanctions. The net social value of a law is equal to the social benefits it engenders minus the social costs of enforcing it. As the individual propensity to obey the law diminishes, so does a society's ability to pursue collective goals through the law. Law-abidingness is therefore a core social virtue, in liberal communities and elsewhere. (This does not mean that disobedience is never justified, but only that a heavy burden of proof must be discharged by those who propose to violate the law.) Finally, every society is constituted by certain core principles and sustained by its members' active belief in them. Conversely, every society is weakened by the diminution of its members' belief in its legitimacy. Loyalty—the developed capacity to understand, to accept, and to act on the core principles of one's society—is thus a fundamental virtue. And it is particularly important in liberal communities, which tend to be organized around abstract principles rather than shared ethnicity, nationality, or history.

Beyond the virtues needed to sustain all political communities are virtues specific to liberal communities—those required by the liberal spheres of society, economy, and polity.

## Virtues of Liberal Society

A liberal society is characterized by two key features—individualism and diversity. To individualism corresponds the liberal virtue of independence—the disposition to care for and take responsibility for oneself, and to avoid becoming needlessly dependent on others. Human beings are not born independent, nor do they attain independence through biological maturation alone. A growing body of evidence suggests that in a liberal society the family is the critical arena in which independence and a host of other virtues must be engendered. The weakening of families is thus fraught with danger for liberal societies. In turn, strong families rest on specific virtues. Without fidelity, stable families cannot be maintained. Without a concern for children that extends well beyond the narrow boundaries of adult self-regard, parents will not effectively discharge their responsibility to help form secure, self-reliant young people. In short, the independence required for liberal social life rests on self-restraint and self-transcendence—the virtues of family solidarity. Let us turn now from individualism to diversity, the second defining feature of liberal society. The maintenance of social diversity requires the virtue of tolerance. This virtue is widely thought to rest on the relativistic belief that every personal choice, every "life-plan," is equally good, hence beyond rational scrutiny and criticism. Nothing could be further from the truth. Tolerance is fully compatible with the proposition that some ways of life can be known to be superior to others. It rests, rather, on the conviction that the pursuit of the better course should be (and in many cases can only be) the consequence of education or persuasion rather than coercion. Indeed, tolerance may be defined as the ability to make this conviction effective as a maxim of personal conduct.

## Virtues of the Liberal Economy

The liberal/market economy relies on two kinds of virtues—those required by different economic roles, and those required by liberal economic life taken as a whole. In a modern market economy, the basic roles are the entrepreneur and the organization-employee. The entrepreneurial virtues form a familiar litany—imagination, initiative, drive, determination. The organizational virtues are very different from (and in some respects the reverse of) the entrepreneurial. They include such traits as punctuality, reliability, civility toward coworkers, and a willingness to work within established frameworks and tasks. As economic units evolve, one of the great management challenges is to adjust the mix of entrepreneurial and organizational practices. Sometimes this takes the form of an organizational displacement (or routinization) of entrepreneurial charisma, as in the ouster of Steven Jobs as head of Apple Computer. Sometimes it requires just the opposite, as when a large, stodgy organization replaces a centralized structure with semiautonomous units and loosens individual task and role definitions in an effort to encourage more entrepreneurial practices on the part of its employees.

There are three generic (as distinct from role-specific) virtues required by modern market economies. The first is the work ethic, which combines the sense of obligation to support personal independence through gainful effort with the determination to do one's job thoroughly and well. The second is the achievement of a mean between ascetic self-denial and untrammeled self-indulgence—call it a capacity for moderate delay of gratification. For while market economies rely on the liberation and multiplication of consumer desires, they cannot prosper in the long run without a certain level of saving, which rests on the ability to subordinate immediate gratification to longer-run self-interest.

The third generic economic virtue is adaptability. Modern market economies are characterized by rapid, sweeping changes that reconfigure organizations and occupations. Patterns of lifelong employment within a single task or organization, common for much of this century, are being displaced. Most individuals will change jobs several times during their working lives, moving into new occupations, new organizations, and even new sectors of the economy. To be sure, collective political action can help regulate the pace of change, ameliorate its consequences, and share its costs. Still, domestic and international pressures combine to make the fact and basic direction of economic change irresistible. Thus, the disposition to accept new tasks as challenges rather than threats and the ability to avoid defining personal identity and worth in reference to specific, fixed occupations are essential attributes of individuals and economies able to cope successfully with the demands of change.[21]

## Virtues of Liberal Politics

Let us examine, finally, the sphere of politics, which calls for virtues of both citizens and leaders.

*Virtues of citizenship.* Some generic citizen virtues have already been identified: courage, law-abidingness, loyalty. In addition to these are the citizen virtues specific to the liberal polity. Because a liberal order rests on individual rights, the liberal citizen must have the capacity to discern, and the restraint to respect, the rights of others. (Invasion of the rights of others is the form of *pleonexia* specific to liberal political life.) Because liberalism incorporates representative government, the liberal citizen must have the capacity to discern the talent and character of candidates vying for office, and to evaluate the performance of individuals who have attained office. Liberalism also envisions popular government, responsive to the demands of its citizens. The greatest vices of popular governments are the propensity to gratify short-term desires at the expense of long-term interests and the inability to act on unpleasant truths about what must be done. To check these vices, liberal citizens must be moderate in their demands and self-disciplined enough to accept painful measures when they are necessary. From this standpoint, the willingness of liberal citizens to demand no more public services than their country can afford and to pay for all the benefits they demand is not just a technical economic issue, but a moral issue as well. Consistently unbalanced budgets—the systematic displacement of social costs to future generations—are signs of a citizenry unwilling to moderate its desires or to discharge its duties.

The liberal citizen is not the same as the civic-republican citizen. In a liberal polity, there is no duty to participate actively in politics, no requirement to place the public above the private and to systematically subordinate personal interest to the common good, no commitment to accept collective determination of personal choices. But neither is liberal citizenship simply the pursuit of self-interest, individually or in factional collusion with others of like mind. Liberal citizenship has its own distinctive restraints—virtues that circumscribe and check, without wholly nullifying, the prompting of self-aggrandizement.

*Virtues of leadership.* The need for virtue and excellence in political leaders is perhaps more immediately evident than is the corresponding requirement in the case of citizens. The Founders saw popular elections as the vehicle for discerning and selecting good leaders. Thomas Jefferson spoke for them when he wrote to John Adams:

> [T]here is a natural aristocracy among men. The grounds of this are virtue and talents. . . . The natural aristocracy I consider as the most precious gift of nature, for the instruction, trusts, and government of society. . . . May we not even say, that that form of government is the best, which provides the most effectively for a pure selection of these natural *aristoi* into the offices of government? . . . I think the best remedy is exactly that provided by all our constitutions, to leave to the citizens the free election and separation of the *aristoi* from the *pseudo-aristoi.*[22]

The leadership virtues specific to liberal polities include patience—the ability to accept, and work within, the constraints on action imposed by social diversity and constitutional institutions. Second, the liberal leader must have the capacity to forge a sense of common purpose against the centrifugal tendencies of an individualistic and fragmented society. Third, the liberal leader must be able to resist the temptation to earn popularity by pandering to immoderate public demands. Against desire the liberal leader must counterpose restraints; against the fantasy of the free lunch he must insist on the reality of the hard choice; against the lure of the immediate he must insist on the requirements of the long-term. Finally, while the liberal leader derives authority from popular consent, he cannot derive policy from public opinion. Rather, he must have the capacity to narrow—so far as public opinion permits—the gap between popular preference and wise action. The liberal leader who disregards public sentiment will quickly come to grief, but so will the leader who simply takes that sentiment as the pole-star of public policy. Through persuasion, the liberal leader tries to move the citizenry toward sound views. But the limits of persuasion must constitute the boundaries of public action, or else leadership becomes usurpation.

As the authors of the *Federalist* insisted, and as experience confirms, there are also specific virtues required for the successful conduct of the different offices in a liberal-constitutional order: optimism and energy in the executive, deliberative excellence and civility in the legislator, impartiality and interpretive skill in the judge.[23] And, as Jefferson suggested, the ultimate test of systems of election or appointment is their tendency to select officeholders with the appropriate virtues. For that reason, it is appropriate and necessary to inquire whether particular systems of selection (e.g., presidential nominating primaries) tend on balance to reward the kinds of personal traits that their corresponding offices require.

*General political virtues.* There are two other political virtues required of liberal citizens and leaders alike. While not all public policies need be made in the full light of day, liberal politics rests on a presumption of publicity—that is, on a commitment to resolve disputes through open discussion unless compelling reasons can be adduced for restricting or concealing the policy process. Thus, a general liberal political virtue is the disposition—and the developed capacity—to engage in public discourse. This includes the willingness to listen seriously to a range of views that, given the diversity of liberal societies, will include ideas the listener is bound to find strange and even obnoxious. The virtue of political discourse also includes the willingness to set forth one's own views intelligibly and candidly as the basis of a politics of persuasion rather than manipulation or coercion.

A second general political virtue is the disposition to narrow the gap (so far as is in one's power) between principles and practices in liberal society. For leaders, this means admitting and confronting social imperfections through a public appeal to collective convictions. For citizens it can mean either such a public appeal or quiet acts that reduce the reach of hypocrisy in one's immediate community. For both, it can lead to a tension between social transformation and law-abidingness, which can be resolved prudentially only with reference to the facts of specific cases. This is a tension rather than a contradiction between these two liberal virtues because the virtue of law-abidingness embodies, not the absolute priority of law, but rather a presumption in favor of the law that can be rebutted in a narrow range of instances.

## LIBERAL VIRTUES AS ENDS

The thrust of the argument thus far has been to specify the virtues instrumental to the preservation and operation of the liberal polity. Let us turn now from pondering liberal virtues as means to examining them as ends. The question is whether there is a conception of the virtuous or excellent individual linked intrinsically to liberal theory and seen as valuable, not instrumentally, but for its own sake.

It might be thought that the answer must be negative. After all, it is characteristic of both liberal societies and liberal theories to be open to a wide variety of life plans and to their corresponding excellences. Yet the liberal tradition is by no means silent on this question. Indeed, it suggests three conceptions of intrinsic individual excellence, overlapping yet distinct. The first is the Lockean conception of excellence as rational liberty or self-direction. As persuasively reconstructed by Rogers Smith, rational self-direction includes the capacity to form, pursue, and revise life plans in light of our personal commitments and circumstances. But it is a substantive, not merely instrumental standard:

> [I]f we value rational self-direction, we must always strive to maintain in ourselves, and to respect in others, these very capacities for deliberative self-guidance and self-control. Correspondingly, we must see the habitual exercise of these capacities as constituting morally worthy character and their enhancement as constituting morally praiseworthy action.[24]

The second noninstrumental liberal conception of individual excellence is the Kantian account of the capacity to act in accordance with the precepts of duty—that is, to make duty the effective principle of personal conduct and to resist the promptings of passion and interest insofar as they are incompatible with this principle. Judith Shklar has offered a fine sketch of Kant's morally excellent individual in action:

> At all times, he must respect humanity, the rational moral element in himself and in *all* other men. For his own sake, he must choose to avoid all self-destructive and gross behavior, and above all else, he must not lie. . . . To other men he owes no liberality or pity or *noblesse oblige* of any kind, because this might humiliate the recipients. What he does have to show them is a respect for their rights, decent manners, and an avoidance of calumny, pride, and malice . . . This is a thoroughly democratic liberal character, built to preserve his own self-respect and that of others, neither demanding nor enduring servility.[25]

The third liberal conception of individual excellence was adapted in different ways from romanticism by John Stuart Mill, Ralph Waldo Emerson, Henry David Thoreau, and Walt Whitman. It is the understanding of excellence as the full flowering of individuality. As Mill expounded this thesis, the excellence of individuality combines the Greek emphasis on the development, through activity, of human powers with the modern realization that the blend and balance of these powers will differ from individual to individual. Because liberal societies allow maximum scope for diversity, they are the most (though not perfectly) conducive to the development of individuality. And because liberal societies rest on individual freedom, they tend to foster the self-determination that is at the heart of true individuality. As Mill put it, "He who lets the world, or his own portion of it, choose his plan of life for him, has no need of any other faculty than the ape-like one of imitation. He who chooses his plan for himself, employs all his faculties."[26] Or, as George Kateb sums up the parallel argument within the Emersonian tradition,

> One must take responsibility for oneself—one's self must become a project, one must become the architect of one's soul. One's *dignity* resides in being, to some important degree, a person of one's own creating, making, choosing rather than in being merely a creature or a socially manufactured, conditioned, created thing.[27]

Can these three distinct, but recognizably liberal, conceptions of human excellence be made to cohere in a single unified view? Yes, to a point. They have a common core—a vision of individuals who in some manner take responsibility for their own lives. Each links excellence to a kind of activity. And all lead to a vindication of the dignity of every individual and to the practice of mutual respect. Beyond this common core, however, certain tensions become manifest. The exercise of Lockean rational liberty can lead to a wide range of deliberative outcomes, while Kantian duty usually prescribes a single course of conduct as generally binding. The pursuit of Emersonian individuality can tend toward a kind of poetic, even mystical self-transcendence at war with both the rationalism of Kantian morality and the prosaic, orderly self-discipline of Lockean liberty.[28]

It is possible, of course, to resolve these tensions by giving one conception pride of place and requiring the others to maintain consistency with the preferred standard. (This is the course that Rawls—like Kant—follows when he subordinates the rational pursuit of individual life-plans to the social requirements of moral right.) But it may be more advisable to accept a range of tension and indeterminacy—that is, to see the liberal polity at its best as a community that encourages all of these overlapping but distinct conceptions of individual excellence and provides an arena within which each may be realized, in part through struggle against the others.

## WAYS OF DEVELOPING LIBERAL VIRTUES

The health of liberal polities is intertwined in complex ways with the practice of liberal virtues. Now assuming that these virtues are not innate, by what means are they to be engendered? And are they adequately developed in our own liberal community? A full examination of these issues lies well beyond the scope of the present discussion. But let me briefly discuss three alternative hypotheses.

The optimistic hypothesis claims that daily life in the liberal polity is a powerful if tacit force for habituation to at least the minimal requirements of liberal virtue. The sorts of things regularly expected of us at home, in school, and on the job shape us in the manner required for the operation of liberal institutions. And while hardly models of moral perfection, citizens of modern liberal communities are at least adequately virtuous—and not demonstrably less so than were citizens in times past.

The neutral hypothesis maintains that tacit socialization is not enough; that authoritative institutions such as families, schools, churches, the legal system, political leaders, and the media must deliberately and cooperatively foster liberal virtues; that these institutions are not now performing this task adequately; but that there is no reason in principle why they cannot do so once they come more fully to understand their responsibility.

Finally, the pessimistic hypothesis—associated with such thinkers as

Daniel Bell—suggests that powerful strands of contemporary liberal culture tend to undermine liberal virtues, that in particular the various forms of liberal self-restraint have fallen victim to the imperatives of self-indulgence and self-expression.[29] From this perspective, the task of strengthening and renewing liberal virtues requires more than improving the formal institutions of moral and civic education. It requires as well a sustained effort to reverse corrosive tendencies fundamental to modern culture. Evidence can be adduced for each of these hypotheses. Optimists can point to the demonstrable fact that our polity has generated—or at least has not thwarted the generation of—the minimal conditions for its survival over the past two centuries. Neutralists can argue that key social indicators—crime, drugs, family stability, and others—are headed in alarming directions and that the impact of major forces of socialization—in particular, television and popular culture—is on balance negative. And pessimists can observe that with the important exception of organized religion, most sources of social authority have a diminished confidence in their ability to establish, inculcate, and enforce social norms of conduct and character.

In a perspective study of contemporary city government, Stephen Elkin has argued that the operation of urban political institutions has a pervasive, and predominantly negative, effect on the character of the citizenry. In order for a commercial republic to move toward the "commercial public interest," it needs at the heart of the liberal democratic citizen "a disposition to think of political choice as involving the giving of reasons." Public choice is to involve "justification, not just the aggregation of wants and interest."[30] Unfortunately, modern city governments systematically fail to foster this disposition, for three reasons. These governments are executive-centered and are therefore not geared to eliciting reasoned argument from individual citizens, or to listening attentively if it happens to be forthcoming. They induce citizens to relate to one another as interest-bearers and as bargainers rather than as participants in a shared process of justification. And finally, many urban citizens relate to one another as "clients" whose interests are defined and mediated by bureaucratic experts.[31] These negative consequences of urban public life cannot be reversed without systematic reform in the characteristic institutions and procedures of city governments.[32]

Richard Dagger also looks to the city as the locus of citizenship, and he is equally discouraged by what he finds. In his view, three features of contemporary urban life are particularly destructive. The sheer size of most cities militates against individual interest in its affairs and against the development of mutual trust. The fragmentation of governmental responsibility breeds "confusion, disorientation, and a sense of impotence." Rapid mobility loosens the ties that bind individuals to the community and erodes the disposition to participate and cooperate. Like Elkin, Dagger argues that the negative consequences for citizenship of the modern city cannot be reduced without systematic reforms that ameliorate their causes.[33]

George Kateb takes a more optimistic view. He argues that representative democracy has a tendency to foster the kinds of character traits that liberal societies particularly need: independence of spirit, the democratization of social life, and a "general tolerance of, and even affection for, diversity."[34] Overall, liberal democratic society is taught, or teaches itself, a fundamental lesson about the nature of all authority:

> a pervasive skepticism . . . ; a reluctance to defer; a conviction that those who wield authority must themselves be skeptical toward their roles and themselves and that necessary authority must be wielded in a way that inflicts minimum damage on the moral authority of all people . . . [and] a tendency to try to do without authority wherever possible or to disperse or disguise it, and thus to soften it.[35]

While not insensitive to the very real difficulties inherent in such dispositions, Kateb is willing to defend them, not just as instrumentally necessary for liberal democracies, but also as intrinsically preferable to the sets of disposition associated with alternative forms of political organization—in particular, direct democracy.[36]

Robert Lane has undertaken what is probably the most thorough and systematic effort to assemble and assess the empirical evidence concerning the effects of liberal democratic life on character formation. He begins by defining, and defending, a model of "mature and developed personality" that has five components: cognitive capacity; autonomy; sociocentrism—the ability to understand and recognize the thoughts and claims of others as well as oneself; identity—some combination of self-knowledge, self-acceptance, and self-respect; and identification with normal values, as a necessary bulwark against sociopathic behavior.[37] Lane then examines in detail the effects of capitalist markets and democratic politics on the development of such a personality. His conclusion is a nuanced blend of hope and concern:

> The market has taught us much, including cognitive complexity, self-reliance, and a version of justice where work or contribution to the economy is rewarded. Through its emphasis on transactions it has eroded some of the sources of sociocentrism. By its destruction of sources of humane values, its instrumentalism, it has made identity hard to achieve and its amoralism has made difficult the identification with moral values. Democracy, too, has made people think; it has offered a promise of fate control which it only partially fulfills. While it embodies a form of sociocentrism, it does not model morality for the public, although its form of justice allows for beneficence, the justice of need. And its complex diversity makes identity hard to achieve, but once achieved, all the more valuable.[38]

In a parallel analysis focusing exclusively on the capitalist market, Lane examines—and largely rejects—recent pessimism about its effects. Consumerism has not perceptibly eroded the work ethic; modern industry requires as much cooperation as competition; individuals continue to have confidence in their efficacy—that is, in some nonrandom relation between the effort, contribution, and skill they display and the rewards they receive; the capacity to innovate, and to take the initiative, is higher among workers in market economies than in command economies; and the ability to question authority by adopting a skeptical stance toward authoritarian morality remains high.[39]

These findings help us focus the debate between optimists, pessimists, and neutralists. It is surely important, as the optimists insist, to take a long view—to recall that America has survived social conflict and dislocation as severe as any we are now experiencing, and to recognize that our current civic culture retains many healthy elements that help sustain personal liberty while warding off public oppression. But it is at least as important to give sustained attention to the phenomena on which neutralists dwell: rising rates of drug use, crime, and family breakdown; inadequate levels of public education, public provision, and public involvement; greed and shortsightedness in public and private affairs; and the growing barbarization and tribalization of American life. Nor can we afford to ignore the pessimists' thesis that these problems are structural rather than accidental—for example, that media-driven patterns of consumption and self-involvement are steadily breaking down the habits of restraint and responsibility on which the liberal polity (like any other) inescapably depends. In *Federalist* 55, James Madison reminds us that,

> As there is a degree of depravity in mankind which requires a certain degree of circumspection and distrust, so there are other qualities in human nature which justify a certain portion of esteem and confidence. Republican government presupposes the existence of these qualities in a higher degree than any other form. Were the pictures which have been drawn by the political jealousy of some among us faithful likenesses of the human character, the inference would be that there is not sufficient virtue among us for self-government.

Madison speaks of "human nature." But he was under no illusion that the balance between depravity and estimable qualities that we actually observe in individuals is just given by nature. While we are endowed with certain capacities for virtue, we become virtuous only under certain circumstances—through appropriate upbringing, education, and experience. What is most striking about our constitution—a point Mary Ann Glendon has stressed—is its failure to provide for, or even to mention, these formative forces.[40] Our national political institutions presuppose the existence of certain kinds of individuals but do nothing to produce them.

There are, I think, three linked explanations for this odd hiatus. The first is that Madison and others saw American society—families, communities, and daily life—as fundamentally healthy, as productive of adequately virtuous citizens, and they assumed (or at least hoped) that these institutions would remain healthy of their own accord. Second, the federal, as opposed to purely national, design of our new political institutions was meant to leave nearly all social questions to states and local communities. Third, the rise of liberal democracy, in contradistinction to classical republicanism, meant an emerging (though constantly contested) demarcation between the public and private realms. The formation of character, including public character, was left to institutions such as families and religious communities which were to be significantly free from public direction.

In essence, in the American liberal democratic order, as opposed to totalitarian or even classical republican regimes, semiautonomous families play a key role in the formation of citizens. It follows directly that if families become less capable of performing that role, the well-being of the entire community is jeopardized. There is evidence that the family breakdown of recent decades is yielding just that result.

Among these liberal virtues is what I have called "independence"—the disposition to care for, and take responsibility for, oneself and to avoid becoming needlessly dependent on others. A growing body of evidence suggests that in a liberal democracy, the family is the critical arena in which independence is fostered. For example, after correcting for other variables such as educational attainment, the children of long-term welfare-dependent single parents are far more likely to become similarly dependent themselves.

Equally suggestive is the evidence concerning the difficulties that many young unwed mothers experience in raising their sons. The absence of fathers as models and co-disciplinarians contributes to the low self-esteem, anger, violence, and peer-bonding through gang lawlessness characteristic of many fatherless boys. The erosion of the two-parent family structure thus threatens to generate a growing subset of the population that cannot discharge the basic responsibilities of citizenship in a liberal democracy.

One key function of strong families in liberal democracies is the encouragement of civic character and competence in young people. A second, closely related, function is the linking of the young to the broader community. More than two centuries ago Edmund Burke suggested that the seeds of public concern are sown in the sense of connection we feel to our family and kin. A half century after the founding, Tocqueville's observations led him to conclude that America's families helped mute self-centered egoism and link individuals to their political institutions. Recent sociological studies confirm a strong correlation between family solidarity and the sense of obligation to a wider community and society. In this connection, among others, the decline of stable marriages is a worrisome sign for our polity. Various studies suggest, for example, that children of divorced parents experience greater than average difficulty in making commitments and forging bonds of trust with others. Taken in conjunction with the Burke/Tocqueville thesis, these observations generate the prediction that in the aggregate, today's young people would feel a lower sense of connection to the political community than did those of previous generations. A recent *Times Mirror* study is consistent with this prediction. As Glendon summarizes its principal finding, the current group "knows less, cares less, [and] votes less" than young people at any time during the past half century.[41]

Pondering these developments, along with many others tending in the same direction, we have at least as much food for concern as for celebration. It is fashionable, and all too easy, to denigrate this stance by pointing out that cultural pessimism is a pervasive theme of human history in nearly every community and in nearly every generation. But the fact remains that political communities can move, and throughout history have moved, from health to disrepair for reasons linked to moral and cultural decay. In the face of this, contemporary American liberals cannot afford to be complacent. We cannot simply chant the mantra of diversity and hope that fate will smile upon us. We must try as best we can to repair our tattered social fabric by attending more carefully to the moral requirements of liberal public life and by doing what is possible and proper to reinforce them.

## NOTES

1. Leo Strauss, *Natural Right and History* (Chicago: University of Chicago Press, 1953); C. B. Macpherson, *The Political Theory of Possessive Individualism* (London: Oxford University Press, 1962).
2. Martin Diamond, "Democracy and *The Federalist:* A Reconsideration of the Framers' Intent," *American Political Science Review* 53: 52–68; Gordon Wood, *The Creation of the American Republic, 1776–1787* (New York: Norton, 1969).
3. Robert Dahl, *A Preface to Democratic Theory* (Chicago: University of Chicago Press, 1956); Theodore Lowi, *The End of Liberalism* (New York: Norton, 1969).
4. J. G. A. Pocock, *The Machiavellian Moment* (Princeton: Princeton University Press, 1975); Quentin Skinner, "The Idea of Negative Liberty," in *Philosophy in History,* ed. Richard Rorty, J. B. Schneewind, and Quentin Skinner (Cambridge: Cambridge University Press, 1984).
5. Charles Taylor, "Atomism," in *Powers, Possessions, and Freedoms: Essays in Honor of C. B. Macpherson,* ed. Alkis Kontos (Toronto: University of Toronto Press, 1979); Alasdair MacIntyre, *After Virtue* (Notre Dame, Ind.: University of Notre Dame Press, 1981) and "Is Patriotism a Virtue?," *The Lindley Lecture* (University of Kansas: Department of Philosophy, 1984); Michael Sandel, *Liberalism and the Limits of Justice* (New York: Cambridge University Press, 1982) and the "The Procedural Republic and the Unencumbered Self," *Political Theory* 12 (1984): 81–96.
6. Irving Kristol, "The Adversary Cultures of the Intellectuals," in *The Moral Basis of Democratic Capitalism,* ed. Michael Novak (Washington, D.C.: American Enterprise Institute, 1980).

7. Albert Hirschman, *The Passions and the Interests* (Princeton: Princeton University Press, 1977).

8. Immanuel Kant, "Perpetual Peace," in *Kant on History,* ed. Lewis White Beck (Indianapolis: Bobbs-Merrill, 1963), 111–12.

9. Judith Shklar, *Ordinary Vices* (Cambridge, Mass.: Harvard University Press, 1984), 5.

10. Rogers Smith, *Liberalism and American Constitutional Law* (Cambridge, Mass.: Harvard University Press, 1985).

11. Nathan Tarcov, *Locke's Education for Liberty* (Chicago: University of Chicago Press, 1984); see also his "A 'Non-Lockean' Locke and the Character of Liberalism," in *Liberalism Reconsidered,* ed. Douglas Maclean and Claudia Mills (Totowa, N.J.: Rowman and Allanheld, 1983).

12. Ronald Terchek, "The Fruits of Success and the Crisis of Liberalism," in *Liberals on Liberalism,* ed. Alfonso Damico (Totowa, N.J.: Rowman and Littlefield, 1986), 18.

13. J. Budziszewski, *The Resurrection of Nature: Political Theory and the Human Character* (Ithaca, N.Y.: Cornell University Press, 1986).

14. Harvey Mansfield Jr., "Constitutional Government: the Soul of Modern Democracy," *The Public Interest* 86 (1987): 59.

15. James Q. Wilson, "The Rediscovery of Character: Private Virtue and Public Policy," *The Public Interest* 81 (1985): 15–16.

16. Thomas Spragens Jr. "Reconstructing Liberal Theory: Reason and Liberal Culture," in *Liberals on Liberalism,* ed. Damico, 43.

17. Shklar, *Ordinary Vices,* 5.

18. Thomas Hobbes, *Leviathan* (New York: Macmillan, 1962), 124.

19. John Rawls, *A Theory of Justice* (Cambridge, Mass.: Harvard University Press, 1971), 436–37.

20. See William A. Galston, *Liberal Purposes: Goods, Virtues, and Diversity in the Liberal State* (Cambridge: Cambridge University Press, 1991), ch. 6.

21. This virtue should be not confused with Robert Unger's much broader strictures against identifying personality with external structure. See *Liberal Purposes,* ch. 3.

22. Thomas Jefferson to John Adams, 28 October 1813, in *Free Government in the Making,* ed. Alpheus T. Mason (New York: Oxford University Press, 1965), 385.

23. For a parallel account, see Mansfield, "Constitutional Government," p. 60.

24. Smith, *Liberalism and American Constitutional Law,* 200.

25. Shklar, *Ordinary Vices,* 233.

26. John Stuart Mill, *On Liberty,* ed. David Spitz (New York: Norton, 1975), 56.

27. George Kateb, "Democratic Individuality and the Claims of Politics," *Political Theory* 12 (1984): 343.

28. See Nancy Rosenblum, *Another Liberalism: Romanticism and the Reconstruction of Liberal Thought* (Cambridge, Mass.: Harvard University Press, 1987), ch. 2.

29. Daniel Bell, *The Cultural Contradictions of Capitalism* (New York: Basic Books, 1976).

30. Stephen L. Elkin, *City and Regime in the American Republic* (Chicago: University of Chicago Press, 1987), 149.

31. Elkin, *City and Regime*, 159–64.

32. Elkin, *City and Regime*, ch. 9.

33. Richard Dagger, "Metropolis, Memory and Citizenship," *American Journal of Political Science* 25, 4 (November 1981): 715–37.

34. George Kateb, "The Moral Distinctiveness of Representative Democracy," *Ethics* 91, 3 (April 1981): 359–61.

35. Kateb, "The Moral Distinctiveness," 358.

36. Kateb, "The Moral Distinctiveness," 369–74.

37. Robert E. Lane, "Markets and Politics: The Human Project," *British Journal of Political Science* 11, 1 (January 1981): 3–6.

38. Lane, "Markets and Politics," 15.

39. Lane, "Capitalist Man, Socialist Man," *Philosophy, Politics and Society,* fifth series, ed. Peter Laslett and James Fishkin (New Haven: Yale University Press, 1979), 57–77.

40. Mary Ann Glendon, "Virtues, Families and Citizenship," in *The Meaning of the Family in a Free Society,* ed. W. Lawson Taitte (Dallas: University of Texas Press, 1991).

41. Glendon, "Virtues," 67.

# 18

# "American Exceptionalism" Revisited: The Role of Civil Society

*Daniel Bell*

The rise and fall of nations and empires is a mystery that has perennially fascinated philosophers and historians, tempting them to entertain grand visions of a ghostly demiurge that drives events, as with Hegel, or of some Wagnerian drama of challenge and response, of purification and heroism, as with Arnold Toynbee.

What accounts for the sudden gathering of energies that spur a people to surge mightily across oceans and continents and then lie spent—perhaps never to rise again, like the Near Eastern empire of the Assyrians, or like the Mongols, who by the fourteenth century had conquered China and spread their rule across Eurasia to the Danube, only to collapse? Histories of the West often begin with the rise and fall of Rome and, after a long hiatus, the shift of strength from the Mediterranean to the Atlantic littoral, with the sudden rise and falling away of the Dutch, Spanish and Portuguese empires, and, nearer our own time, the expansive spread and then contraction of Britain's global imperium.

An arabesque interpretation was given by the fourteenth-century Berber philosopher Ibn Khaldun, who in his beguiling work *The Muqadimmah* took Plato's cyclical account of the "fevered city" (with its self-destructive desire for luxury) and elaborated it into a philosophy of history: the rude but vigorous barbarians storm the older centers of civilization; their children consolidate their gains and build the great cities and palaces; then *their* children, soft and sybaritic, given over to perfumed arts and moral permissiveness, become unable to resist the new barbarians at the gates.

So simple an explanation is inherently suspect; its single-threaded story line makes it more fit for a Cecil B. DeMille extravaganza than for sound sociological analysis. Recognizing this, the contemporary French moralist and cynic E. M. Cioran has said: "It takes time to destroy an empire, but it only takes time." This observation may be true enough, but it hardly provides an explanation.

So the mystery remains, and historians and sociologists continue to seek, with their mundane instruments, to pluck out its heart. Brooks Adams, the brother of Henry Adams and also a historian of large ambition, exulted in 1900 that the United States was replacing Great Britain on the center stage of history. The reason was a shift not in military might, as in the past, but in the index of industrial production—in this instance, the production of steel—that was helping the United States to forge ahead of Britain as the mightiest nation on earth. For Brooks Adams, all this was fated, because access to and control of strategic metals and minerals, combined with energy and national will, were the bases of power. In *The New Empire* (1902), he skillfully showed how resource exhaustion creates fault lines in economic history—the tremors, one might say, of geology and geopolitics. (And, in an intriguing side glance, Adams observed Japan waiting in the wings for its own sun to rise.)

Although no single theory is altogether persuasive, there remains the striking fact that each nation, when it begins to gather its energies—military, political, and economic—to make a decisive entry onto the stage of history, does define itself in terms of its uniqueness. And later, as intimations of morality begin to be felt, there arises the question (and hope) of exemption from decline, of "exceptionalism." In this country there has always been a strong belief in American exceptionalism. From the start, Americans have believed that destiny has marked their country as different from all others—that the United States is, in Lincoln's marvelous phrase, "an almost chosen nation." American greatness seemed like a magnetic field that would shape the nation's contours from sea to sea, and the expansion across a vast continent seemed to confirm that manifest destiny. American strength after World War II, when the United States emerged as *the* paramount world power, seemed to define the "American century."

Yet as that century closed, there arose doubts as to whether America can maintain its greatness, whether the curtain may be falling on the main act of the American episode. So the question is being raised: How exceptional, really, is "American exceptionalism"?

## RISE AND FALL, UNIQUENESS, EXCEPTIONALISM

In all these speculations and debates, three different historical questions are intertwined, and I wish to sort them out.

The first and most spectacular question is the one with which I began—the puzzle of the rise and fall of empires, and its possible application to the United States today. About a decade and a half ago, the economic historian Charles

P. Kindleberger foresaw in a few years "an American climacteric" (the male equivalent of menopause), basing his prediction on the notion that the United States was losing the drive that had made it the economic and technological leader in field after field. And in the last year or two, a number of books have emphasized the theme of decline: Walter Russell Mead's *Mortal Splendor,* David P. Calleo's *Beyond American Hegemony,* and, with the warning that top-heavy military expenditures and low productive investment would reproduce in the United States the conditions that toppled France, Spain, and the United Kingdom, Paul Kennedy's *Rise and Fall of the Great Powers: Economic Change and Military Conflict from 1500 to 2000.*

There are many reasons to appreciate the suggestiveness of these works, and also many reasons to be skeptical of their tendentious theme. As Samuel P. Huntington has wryly remarked: "In 1988 the United States reached the zenith of its fifth wave of declinism since the 1950s." And, more combatively, Huntington declared: "With some exceptions, declinist writings do not elaborate testable propositions involving independent and dependent variables." True—but then, what statements about macrohistorical phenomena do? The inherent difficulty of the social sciences, as Seymour Martin Lipset once observed, is that there are too many variables and too few cases.

Indeed, there are often no clear time-frames indicating when to start the count, where to locate the midpoint of change, and where to mark the downturn to a conclusion. There have been various efforts, from Henry Adams to Derek de Solla Price, to create a "social physics" by plotting an S-curve based on initial exponential rates of change—e.g., the doubling rates of the number of scientific journals of population—and identifying the falling-off phase as the inverse of the early, exuberant period; unfortunately, the parameters simply cannot be stated accurately.

Evaluating the significance of national decline is also complicated by the possibility that nations are less and less the relevant units of analysis as different structures emerge in world society—an international and integrated set of markets for capital and investment, for instance. In culture, too, we see a growing syncretism in which mass communication and mass markets shape popular culture—especially the youth culture—and middle-brow culture everywhere. So if economic and social forces are weakening national boundaries, what do we mean by the "rise and fall" of nations or national empires?

The second, very different, kind of question is that of the uniqueness of each nation or culture. That wise Harvard psychologist, Henry A. Murray, once remarked that each of us is in some ways like everybody else and in some ways like nobody else. What is true of individuals is also true of nations. All societies face the problems of exercising authority, of organizing and allocating resources. Many societies are alike in being, say, democratic of free-market societies. And each society has an idiosyncratic history, shaped by topography and location, traditions and culture, and that less definable element of *esprit* or *moeurs* that makes its culture and people distinctive. That idiosyncratic contour—call it national style—is often the overriding feature that one must identify in order to understand the history, politics, or character of a country.

But uniqueness is not "exceptionalism." All nations are to some extent unique in one way or another. The idea of "exceptionalism," as it has been used to describe American history and institutions, assumes not only that the United States has been unlike other nations, but that it is exceptional in the sense of being *exemplary* ("a city upon a hill")—a light unto the nations, immune from the social ills and decadence that have beset all other republics in the past, a nation exempt from the "social laws" of development that all nations eventually follow. It is this idea of "exceptionalism" as a distinct historical theme, not "uniqueness" or "rise and fall," that I wish to pursue.

## SOMBART AND THE ABSENCE OF SOCIALISM

For intellectuals, and particularly for radicals—who see themselves as the standard-bearers of the intellectual class—the theme of American exceptionalism is interwoven with the question first raised by Werner Sombart in 1906: "Why is there no socialism in the United States?" In 1896 Sombart, then a professor at the University of Breslau, had published a small book, based on eight lectures, under the title *Socialism and the Social Movement in the Nineteenth Century.* In this context, "social movement" means simply *socialist* movement. If socialism was the necessary, evolutionary outcome of capitalist development, the socialist movement was also inevitably brought into being by capitalism, a product of the class divisions of society.

The book reviewed the ideas of various socialist thinkers, in particular Marx, and dealt as well with the history and spread of working-class movements in England, France, and Germany. As John Bates Clark, a professor of political economy at Columbia University,[1] wrote in his introduction to the American edition of 1898:

> The structure of the world industry is changing. Great establishments are exterminating small ones, and are forming federations with each other. Machinery is producing nearly every kind of goods, and there is no longer a place for such a middle class as was represented by the master workman, with his slowly learned handicraft and his modest shop. These facts construed in a certain way are the material of socialism. If we see in them the dawn of an era of state industry that shall sweep competition and competitors out of the field, we are evolutionary socialists.
>
> We may need a doctrinal basis for our view of evolution that is going on; and we may find it in the works of Marx and others. . . . Marxism, in practice, means realism and a reliance on evolution, however little the wilder utterances of Marx him-

> self may suggest that fact. Internationalism is also a trait of this modern movement. . . . It is a natural affiliation of men of all nations having common ends to gain.

Sombart's book was an immediate success. In five years, it went through four editions in Germany and was translated into eleven languages. In 1905, when a fifth edition appeared in Germany (to be translated into seventeen languages, including Japanese), the book was two and a half times longer, and included detailed historical material on the development of the "social movement" in Germany, France, and England, as well as cursory surveys of eleven other countries. Its general themes were summed up in the chapter and subject headings: "The tendency to uniformity," "The social movement cannot be stayed," "Its present form is necessary." The argument, repeated in the conclusion, is that "the social movement is inevitable," and "the movement has taken the only form possible."

Yet there was the puzzle of the United States. In 1905 Sombart (then a professor at the commercial school in Berlin) wrote a number of long essays in the *Archiv fur Sozialwissenschaft und Sozialpolitik* (one of whose editors was Max Weber) entirely devoted to the United States. These essays appeared in book form in German the following year, and began to be translated into English as *Why Is There No Socialism in the United States?*

It was a puzzle because Sombart assumed that there had to be a growing socialist movement in the United States, since "modern socialism follows as a necessary reaction to capitalism." And, of course,

> the United States is the country where the model of the Marxist theory of development is being the most precisely fulfilled, since the concentration of capital has reached the stage (as described in the famous penultimate chapter of *Capital*) at which the final cataclysm of the capitalist world is near at hand. [In 1905, no less.]

Why, then, was there no socialist movement in the United States, as in Europe? Why did socialism have so little appeal to the American worker? To answer his questions, Sombart (who had never visited the United States) drew heavily on the earlier work of Lord Bryce and on official statistics, and made some shrewd observations about the "capitalist mentality" of the American worker, the populist character of the electorate, the high standard of living, and the expectations of social mobility; he tried to show, to put it crassly, how the American worker had been "bought off" by the capitalist class. Amusingly, Sombart's work had begun to be serialized in the *International Socialist Review,* the theoretical journal of the Socialist Party, but when Section Two—on the success of American capitalism—appeared, the translation ceased. In the next issue, in a slashing review of the work, the editor remarked: "When we came to the nonsense on the conditions of the American worker, we stopped further publication."

But the *International Socialist Review* (like so many American sociologists who know the work only from its title) had stopped too soon. In the end, Sombart could not accept his own evidence. Like a true academic, he refused to allow mere immediate reality to triumph over theory. He concluded in the penultimate paragraph of his book:

> However, my present opinion is as follows; all the factors that till now have prevented the development of socialism in the United States are about to disappear or to be converted into their opposite with the result that in the next generation socialism in America will very probably experience the greatest possible expansion of its appeal.

The weakness of that expectation is obvious. Just as Marx stated in his introduction to Capital that he had found (using Newton's terminology) "the laws of motion" of capitalism, which would apply not only to England but to all capitalist societies, so Sombart, following Marx, believed that economic relations shape political and all other relations in capitalist society, and that the inevitable class divisions would lead to a polarization of society. And with his own rhetorical flourish, Sombart proclaimed in his broader work that we are in the midst of "one of those great historical processes" whose trajectory cannot be denied, much as "a mountain torrent rushes down from the highest peaks into the valley below in accordance with nature's unchangeable laws."

Yet if one reads Sombart's American book—putting aside the introduction and the conclusion and concentrating on the evidence—the obvious title would be: *Why Should There Be Socialism in the United States?* There is no exception, perhaps, because there is no rule.

## WEBER AND SECULARIZATION

A different kind of issue involving "exceptionalism" is raised by Max Weber's comments on the relation of religion to economic development. In *The Protestant Ethic and the Spirit of Capitalism,* Weber made the argument that the Calvinist strand of Protestantism was a necessary condition for the development of modern capitalism because of the rational principles common to both; their "elective affinity" caused them to reinforce each other. Calvinism spurred methodical work and habits of diligence, sobriety, and parsimony; it provided legitimacy to the profit motive; it gave dignity to achievements in work rather than in war, politics, or other-worldly piety.

But Weber also argued that the further rationalization of society would culminate in the *Entzauberung der Welt*—the spread of a secular, "disenchanted" worldview. Now it is true that many European societies—in particular the United Kingdom and Sweden—have become largely "secularized," so that church attendance is low and theological questions have little appeal in intellectual or cultural life. Yet what can one say of the United States, the land where, more than any other nation, industrialization has raged unchecked, where pragmatism (in the vulgar sense of the word, not that of John Dewey or William James) is the ready and easy way in business and politics? Here fundamentalist and evangelical movements have surged forth time and again, and religious questions are still of serious interest to intellectuals, often in the guise of communitarian and other nonutilitarian values.

Is this another instance of American exceptionalism, a deviation from the "sociological law" of secularization? I think not. The term secularization is deceptive in that it conflates two very different processes—institutional changes (including the decline of religious authority in secular matters) and the more variable nature of *beliefs*—and the two are not isomorphic or even strongly coupled. Religious beliefs are not an epiphenomenal reflection of social structures. Nor are they creeds that are erased by the unfolding of a "rational" consciousness. It is quite striking that every Enlightenment thinker, from Voltaire to Marx, thought that religion would disappear by the twentieth century. They conceived of religion as fetishism, animism, superstition, and the like, an aspect of the "childhood" of the human race, which would be replaced by reason. They believed that science, with its unveiling of exact laws, and practical activities (such as economics or engineering) would discover the objective relations between persons or things, thus eliminating the bases of "magical beliefs." But they completely misunderstood the nature of religious beliefs, since these have always served to give an "answer" to the paradoxes and absurdities of life; or to provide significant meanings in symbolic form to life situations; or to provide some coherent responses to the existential predicaments—such as death and tragedy—that confront every single individual. Religious beliefs fall and rise variously in different cultures, and at different times; there is no one-way track to "secularization" so far as the varieties of religious experience are concerned. Even in Europe, a keen interest in religion among writers and intellectuals has survived the decline of the traditional churches. This same tendency is also apparent in the Soviet Union today.

A third persistent and more manifest aspect of the doctrine of "American exceptionalism" derives from the conviction, inherited from the Founding Fathers, that ours is *the* providential nation, the one whose dedication to liberty and to the dignity of the individual lays the foundation for a new and better world. The Founders believed that we would avoid the decadence and degeneration of previous republics, since the new nation would be morally superior to any that had gone before, and since morality grounded its political order. This was Madison's reading of Montesquieu, especially on the fate of Rome. It was John Adam's reading of Davila on the outcomes of revolution.

This belief in exceptionalism was not wholly unqualified. Deists like Jefferson saw America as God's design worked out in a virgin, paradisaic land.

Others, such as the more worldly and skeptical Franklin, nonetheless saw the possibility that the United States was exemplary, and thus a hope for the future. But has it all foundered? In the international sphere Wilsonian idealism has proven itself feckless in the face of Old World realism and Third World tyrannies. In the political realm, morality seems to have given way to mere moralism and political opportunism. Nevertheless, though our future may be more uncertain than at any time in the past two hundred years, some enduring values of character and even a powerful thread of idealism persist. One senses, in reflecting on American history, that there *was* something exceptional about our nation's history and the national character it created—exceptional not necessarily in the sense of being exempt from whatever "laws" of social evolution may exist, but in the sense of offering a "saving grace" (the theological term is appropriate) that may still make us exemplary for other nations.

In reflection on our two-hundred-year history, one is drawn inevitably to the comparison with France, which is now celebrating (though not unanimously) the bicentennial of its revolution. The conventional wisdom, as in Hannah Arendt's *On Revolution,* is that the French, or at least the Jacobins, attempted a *social* revolution that would inaugurate a blissful new order and incarnate "the religion of humanity"—and that, given the nature of man, the attempt was bound to fail. The United States, in contrast, attempted a *political* revolution that, because it was more limited in its aims, could succeed—presumably by leaving the social order alone and thus allowing people an outlet for their passions while the political order mediated their interests.

There is much truth in this contrast. But the easy division between the political and the social masks the fact that a new kind of social order *was* attempted on this continent. Indeed, this order may be at the root of American society's "success," by which I mean the establishment of an *institutional* foundation that has protected individual liberties and provided a degree of continuity and consensus, and thus a social stability, unmatched in history.

## ANGLO-AMERICAN STABILITY

In the twenties and thirties a large number of European parliamentary regimes—Italy, Portugal, Austrian, Germany, Spain—collapsed and went fascist or authoritarian. In the last century, almost all of Latin America has had intermittent military or authoritarian dictatorships. One-party states abound in most of the "stable societies" of the world. Only the United Kingdom, since the end of its civil war in the seventeenth century, and the United States (with the exception of its civil war), plus a handful of smaller nations (Switzerland and the Scandinavian countries), have achieved political stability. How was this accomplished?

Let me focus on the United Kingdom and the United States. There are some obvious common factors, particularly geographical insulation. The U.K. has not been invaded since 1066. The United States has not been invaded since 1814, and its foreign wars (including the Mexican, Spanish-American, and World Wars) were fought outside its borders. As both countries developed, moreover, there were various outlets—geographical and social—for potentially discontented people, as well as increasing wealth. In Great Britain, there were administrative or military positions in the Empire for "second sons," and Australia for the convicts; in the United States, there were the free farms of the Homestead Acts, free public education, new and expanding industries, and the undiminished promise of opportunity for generations to come.

Another factor common to the U.K. and the United States has been less noticed: the legal system. In contrast to the Continental legal system, with its powerful inquiring magistrates, Anglo-American legal procedure is adversarial, with an emphasis on rights. The Continental legal system seeks to uncover truth; the Anglo-American system seeks to establish guilt. The power of the State is restricted by the rights created by the common law and the Constitution.

But what of the United States itself? Is there a distinctive element in its history and sociological make-up that has contributed to its stability? I think there is, and the answer begins, oddly enough, with that extraordinary German metaphysician, Georg Wilhelm Friedrich Hegel.

## HEGELIAN CIVIL SOCIETY

For Hegel, the United States was always the embodiment of modernity, "the land of the future, . . . the land of desire for all those who are weary of the historical lumber- room of old Europe." Yet Hegel also said, in the introduction to his lectures on the philosophy of history, that America was still only a dream, and in tracing the vicissitudes of historical evolution, in which the rational continually sought to become the real, he retreated to "the Old World—the scene of World history." Today, if we are mindful of what *is*—even if it is not rational—we have to be concerned with the United States, which is the central actor in world history. The twentieth remains the American century. The United States is the foremost military and technological power, and the dollar the uneasy foundation of the world economy. The United States is the media center as well as the cultural marketplace (if not the cultural center) of the world. More important, it remains, with the United Kingdom, one of the few nations of the world to maintain its institutional stability, so that investors, here and abroad, still regard it as a safe haven.

What is the distinguishing feature, then, of the United States, one that has been its strength throughout its history? It is simply that the United States has been the complete *civil society* (to use a Hegelian term), perhaps the only one in political history. Hegel thought that England, as a bourgeois nation, exemplified his idea of civil society (*burgerliche Gesellschaft*) in its emphasis on individual self-interest and the utilitarian mode of thought. But Hegel (and Marx, who lived in England for almost all of his adult life) never understood the *thick* character of England; the symbolism of the Crown, the strength of the landed classes, the centrality of an established church, the desire of the bourgeoisie (or its sons) to join the gentry, the weight of the Establishment, and the lure of titles and honors—the basic fact that England was a society in which a hereditary social order dominated the political and economic orders. Thus the Manchester liberals, such as Cobden and Bright, did *not* wish to rule; not only (as they admitted) did they not know how to govern, but they also sought the economic order's independence from the State, the freedom to pursue trade, industry, and wealth unhampered by restrictions. As Joseph Schumpeter cogently argued, British imperialism of the late nineteenth century, as distinct from the colonialism of the eighteenth, was not a necessity of capitalism, but an extension of the status order allied with finance. The army and overseas administration provided places for the "second sons" disinherited by primogeniture, and—by emphasizing the primacy of the Empire, with its pomp and glory—a means of cowing the bourgeoisie.

The United States never had such a social order. It was built, rather, by a motley assortment of *novi homines,* vagabonds, adventurers, convicts, dispossessed cavaliers, and dissident Protestants from Quakers to Puritans, reinforced in the next century by a flood of immigrants from all the countries of Europe. It was an open society. Each man was free to "make himself" and to make his fortune. Marx was constantly warning the German radicals not to go to the United States, for he saw—as happened with Hermann Kriege and August Willich, and dozens of others—that the democratic and egalitarian atmosphere of the United States would supplant the old European-bred socialist beliefs. For these immigrants the attraction of the future was not some cosmic, universal idea, but the yearning to be treated as a person and the desire for opportunity and advancement—a feature Marx himself recognized, but only in the footnotes to *Capital,* where he wrote with amazement of the number of people who could move about freely and change their occupations "much as a man could change his shirt, egad."

## THE ABSENCE OF THE STATE

In Hegel's sense, there was no "State" in the United States, no unified, rational will expressed in a political order, but only individual self-interest and a passion for liberty. In every European nation (with the partial exception of Britain), the State ruled *over* society, exercising a unitary or quasi-unitary power enforced by an army and a bureaucracy. Paradoxically, even aside from the Civil War the United States probably experienced more internal violence, more class struggle than most countries of Europe: the agrarian struggles against the moneyed interests and, more focused, the conflicts of labor with the capitalists. By any set of rough indicators—numbers of strikes, length of strikes, amount of dynamiting, number of times that troops were called out, number of lives lost in the period from the railroad strikes of the 1870s to the auto and steel strikes of the 1950s—American labor struggles were more prolonged and more violent than any in Europe. But these were not attempts to seize "State power." They were primarily economic conflicts against particular corporations and—in the great union actions of the 1930s in coal, steel, auto making, and rubber—against entire industries; they were not contests for State power. In fact, the tremendous organizing actions against corporate economic power in the 1930s were undertaken with the support of the Roosevelt administration. The AFL-CIO could not have maintained its power without the support of the Democratic administration and the power of bargaining extended by the Supreme Court.

If there was no State,[2] what was there? To make a semantic yet substantive distinction, there was a *government.* This government was a political marketplace, an arena in which interests contended (not always equally) and in which deals could be made. Almost by chance, the Supreme Court became the final arbiter of disputes and the interpreter of the rules that allowed the political marketplace to function, subject only to the amendment of the Constitution—which then was again interpreted by the Court. The Constitution and the Court provided the bedrock of civil society.

The underlying political theme of the Declaration of Independence is one of unalienable rights endowed in all men by their Creator. These rights were vested in individuals, not in groups, and institutions were designed to embody and protect them.[3] The Constitution was a *social contract* agreed to by the sovereign people. It has been the most successful social contract in history, largely due to the weakness or even the absence of the State.

Behind the Constitution stood a distinctive political culture. In the early years of the country's formation, Americans were self-conscious about being citizens of "the first new nation"—not a new quasi-religious utopia as proclaimed in the French Revolution, but a new, free republic founded by recurring to the first principles of government. Along with the strong republican emphasis went a civic (not statist) concern for a kind of republican virtue, derived from reflection upon the history of the Roman Republic and the desire to avoid the degenerative diseases—civil strife spawned by faction, the use of mercenaries rather than a citizens' army, and the arbitrary concentration of power—that had crippled earlier republics. One sees this double-barreled concern—to avoid both the centrifugal dangers of faction and the centripetal hazards of centralized power—in the *Federalist,* with its echoes of Montesquieu, and in the writings of John Adams.[4]

## POPULISM AND PLUTOCRACY

There was, by design, an intellectual foundation for this "new order." But as the nation expanded and political parties developed—an eventuality neither desired nor even foreseen by the Founders—political competition spurred the egalitarianism and populism that have been the distinguishing features of American politics since the 1830s. There was a shift from intellectualism and thought (the Lockean emphasis, in a sense) to sentiment and emotion (a strange Rousseauian twist), for while intellectualism implies a claim to rule based on wisdom or learning, sentiment affirms egalitarianism through its appeal to a common feeling among all men. This shift was reflected as well in a turn away from the past and from Europe, to the land and the moving western frontier. All this was symbolized in the election of General Andrew Jackson, the first "Western" president, in 1828 (and the throwing open of the White House to the people); it was ratified, so to speak, in the "cider barrel" election of 1840, when the high-toned Whig opposition, realizing the necessity of a populist appeal, nominated a second military hero, General William Henry Harrison (nicknamed "Tippecanoe" for his battles against the Indians), and dispensed free cider from the barrel to the great unwashed.

The other transforming element of American politics was the rule of money. With the rise of the plutocracy, money was easily used to gain influence and induce outright corruption—a feature that reached its apogee in the administration of another war hero, General Ulysses S. Grant, and disgusted the fastidious Henry Adams—as is evident in a scene portrayed in his novel entitled, significantly, *Democracy.*[5]

The outcome of these changes is the strange structure of domestic American politics today, which few foreigners, and not even many Americans, understand. The American political order is two-tiered: the President is chosen in a plebiscitarian referendum, in which the person, not the party, is the cynosure of identification and judgment, the focus of mass *passions;* the Congress, however, is elected to respond to group *interests,* though today not necessarily the moneyed interests.

It is no accident that so many presidents have been war heroes, so many of them generals (from Washington to Eisenhower), usually elected soon after a war, in a country that until recently never had a large standing army. Heroes were considered to be "above" party, while during periods of normalcy the presidents have been colorless neuters such as McKinley, Harding, or Coolidge. (The one certified intellectual, Woodrow Wilson, a political-science professor and former president of Princeton University, was elected in 1912 because of the only significant three-way split in American history, and he was re-elected during the war in Europe on the ground that he would keep America out of the war.) Such presidents of the post–World War II years as Truman, Nixon, Carter, and Reagan have been unabashed populists, running against what is called "the Establishment."

Yet congressional elections show a very different pattern. This two-tiered structure was made startlingly clear in 1984. Ronald Reagan, one of the most popular presidents in history, carried all the states in the nation except one—Walter Mondale's home state of Minnesota. Reagan won by one million votes in New Jersey, yet the Democrat Bill Bradley won a Senate seat in that state by the same number of votes. Reagan carried Massachusetts by half a million votes, yet John Kerry, a left-wing Democrat, won by half a million votes too. The same pattern repeated itself in 1988. George Bush carried Ohio handily, but Howard Metzenbaum, one of the Senate's leading liberals, was also reelected. Since World War II, though the presidents have come largely from the Republican side, the Congress has been more often Democratic, and the House of Representatives consistently so.

The populist mentality also characterized small-town culture (not the modern mass-media culture), which was largely religious—Protestant, moralizing, and fundamentalist. It was also, given its emphasis on the literal truth of the Word, anti-intellectual and anti-institutional. There was, of course, no aristocratic tradition or strong artistic heritage; the arts were crafts—plain, simple, and utilitarian. And the Catholic tradition—which in Europe provided a firm intellectual foundation in theology and dogmatics, beauty in litany and liturgy, and distinctive styles in architecture and sculpture, all of which became fused with a historic high culture—was in the United States embodied in the Irish church, made up largely of immigrants or rude self-made men, so that (with the exception of a John Courtney Murray, say) until recently it has lacked intellectual weight and made little contribution to American thought and culture.

Thus we find a society very individualistic and populist, its fluid modernity shaped by the open expanse of geography and by the rule of money, the riches going to rugged individuals bent on pursuing their own ends. Both environment and economy were unencumbered by the polity. Indeed, from the 1870s to the 1930s, the Supreme Court struck down numerous efforts at social legislation and regulation, other than antitrust laws. Freedom was defined principally in individualistic economic terms. That was the consensus. That was the framework of the American civil society.

## THE RISE OF THE STATE

In the last half century, the lineaments of a State—institutions to shape and enforce a unitary will over and above particular interests—have emerged in the United States, beginning with the New Deal of Franklin D. Roosevelt.

The New Deal has usually been interpreted ideologically (from the left) as saving capitalism or (from the right) as instituting "creeping socialism." While there is truth in both arguments, neither is very satisfactory. The rise of the State in America was unplanned and not at all consistently ideological. It was a response, framed during crisis, to three things: increases in the scale of the society, shifting political alignments, and the logic of mobilization for total war.

The problem of scale was fundamental. By 1930 the United States had become a national society: from 1900 to 1930 corporations had begun to operate in nationwide markets. But the countervailing political power was ineffectively distributed among the states. When the economy broke down during the Great Depression, the Roosevelt administration responded first with the National Industrial Recovery Administration, establishing nationwide codes and setting prices for the major industries. It adopted, in fact, the principles of the corporatist state as urged by many capitalists such as Gerard Swope of General Electric and the Du Ponts. When the Supreme Court declared this unconstitutional, the New Deal began to move away from corporatist planning and to rely more on regulatory mechanisms to control markets. Out of this "second New Deal" came the Securities and Exchange Commission to oversee financial markets and the National Labor Relations Board to promote labor stability through collective bargaining. The New Deal thus became a "matching of scales," creating national political institutions and national political rules to match national economic power.

The logic of stabilization and control led to increasing reliance on the tax code to guide private investment, and the emerging State took on the responsibility of promoting economic growth and influencing the allocation of resources. In addition, the domestic political realignment, in which labor, farmers, and minorities swung into the Democratic column, led to national farm subsidies and the protection of disadvantaged groups. More broadly, it led to the idea of entitlements and a welfare state designed to protect people from economic and social hazards.

The third great impetus to statism was war and foreign policy. War has always and everywhere been a decisive motive for creating a State. It focuses emotions against a dangerous foe and requires energy and unity; it forces the State to mobilize the human and material resources of society. A mobilizing society—often, though not always, driven by war—becomes the forcing house of a State.

Significantly, the external foreign-policy pressures and the internal domestic factors were *not* intertwined. The great-power politics of American foreign policy was not a reflexive response to domestic pressures (despite talk of a "military-industrial complex"), though some regions and firms inevitably benefited. The spread of subsidies and entitlements during the Johnson administration was not dependent on defense mobilization. In fact, as budgetary pressures intensified, the two types of spending came more and more into competition with each other, which made it much easier for the Reagan administration to reduce regulation, subsidies, and entitlements in the domestic arena while substantially increasing the defense budget. Thus there was never really a unitary national State.

All these activities are reflected in the growth of government, of public-sector employment, of taxation, of the proportion of the gross national product initiated in the public sector (including defense), and—especially in the last decade—of the federal budget deficit and the national debt. The new statism is also reflected in rising discontents. In many societies, taxes are seen as purchasing public services that individuals cannot buy for themselves; in the United States, however, many people resent taxes, seeing them as "our" money that is taken by "them." The growing regulation of all areas of economic and social life has fed resentment against government intrusion.

It is evident that the problem of "the State" has become central for American political theory and practice. The question of State-society relationships, of the public interest and the private appetite, is clearly *the* salient problem for the polity in coming decades. And with the expansion of the scale of economic and political activities, the national state has become too small for the "big" problems of life (e.g., the tidal waves of the capital and currency markets) and too big for the "small" problems (e.g., the problems of neighborhood and community). Foreign policy, which once forged unity, now prompts disagreements as the idea of a consistent national interest has lost its force, while ideological passions continue to rise and fall. The idea of a managed economy has lost credibility in the face of the difficulties of "fine tuning," and there has been a return to market mechanisms. Bureaucracies have become too centralized and burdensome in most societies. Individuals increasingly wish to deal with social welfare, the environment, and the quality of life at a level at which they can control the decisions. It is striking, in fact, that in country after country—particularly in Poland and Italy—the idea that "civil society" rather than "the State" should be the primary arena of political activities has become a major theme of exploration and debate, now that the old ideologies have faded.

## THE RETURN OF CIVIL SOCIETY

We see then, the return in recent years of the idea of civil society. But of what kind? For Hegel, civil society was characterized by anarchic self-interest—economic individualism that has destroyed the traditional institutions of family and village, but could not replace them with *Moralitat,* the abstract rational beliefs of a unified and universal will. Hegel was wrong in his romantic, overdrawn contrast between unmediated traditionalism and self-centered, appetitive utilitarianism—a contrast that could be mastered only by a State. Yet this romanticism has run like a scarlet thread through German thought. In the social sciences it has given us the simplicities of the *Gemeinschaft/ Gesellschaft* (community/society) dichotomy. In philosophy and politics it has given us the view, embodied in Martin Heidegger's allegiance to the Nazis, of a heroic *Volkstum* and *Staatstum* arrayed against the hated commercialism of bourgeois society. (In German, the terms for "civil society" and "bourgeois society" are the same—*burgerliche Gesellschaft.*) Yet these exaggerated contrasts, and the denigration of civil society as "anomic," disastrously misread the complexities of modern society and the difficulties of establishing the limits of freedom and civility.

The demand for a return to "civil society" is the demand for a return to a manageable scale of social life, particularly where the national economy has become embedded in an international frame and the national polity has lost some degree of its independence. It emphasizes voluntary associations, churches, and communities, arguing that decisions should be made locally and should not be controlled by the State and its bureaucracies. Utopian? Perhaps. But more possible now, given the new technologies, with their promise of decentralized industry and smaller firms.

This idea of civil society does not signify a return to the traditional European idea of civic humanism or republican virtue. Classical republican virtue (which is *not* the republicanism of Adams or Jefferson) rested on the notion that the community was always prior to the individual. The common good was a unitary good. But a modern civil society—one that is heterogeneous and often multiracial—has to establish different rules: the principle of toleration and the need for plural communities to agree on rules governing procedure within the frame of constitutionalism.

All of these issues are engaging political philosophy. The actual existence of civil society, however, has been distinctively American, shaped initially by the varied impulses of rugged individualism and radical populism. Yet to the extent that a renewed appreciation for the virtues of civil society is again required in order to define a new kind of social order that limits the State and enhances individual and group purposes (thereby achieving the goals of liberalism), it is also one more twist to the long tale of American exceptionalism.

## NOTES

1. John Bates Clark was a leader in the fashioning of neoclassical economics and a pioneer in the theory of marginal productivity that was later attacked by socialists for justifying the unequal distribution of income.

2. In a recent paper, Quentin Skinner has argued that the word *State* came to be recognized when political philosophers (he singled out Hobbes) sought a term that would identify an emerging realm of power distinct from *ves publica* or *civitas* (since

those terms designated popular sovereignty) and from the literal power holders, such as the monarch, who insisted that fealty be sworn to them as persons, rather than to an institution. The *State,* thus, was an entity that doubly abstracted sovereignty from the rulers and the ruled and combined the rights alienated from both into the *persona ficta* of "the State." (This theme of alienation of rights is found in Hobbes, who holds that the individual surrenders his natural rights to the commonwealth, and later in Rousseau, who holds that in the "social contract" each person submerges himself and his rights into the general will.)

If one defines the *State* this way then there certainly was no *State* in the United States, for the very character of the founding documents denied the idea of alienated rights and placed sovereignty in "We, the People."

3. This is why there is so much litigation in American society, and such an expansive role for the courts; if the foundation of society is one's individual rights, then one must sue in order to defend and protect them.

4. "It has been the will of heaven," John Adams wrote in 1776, "that we should be thrown into existence at a period when the greatest philosophers and lawgivers of antiquity would have wished to live. A period when we have an opportunity of beginning government new from the foundation. . . . How few of the human race have ever had any opportunity of choosing a system of government for themselves and their children!"

5. Though the end of the century saw the rise of corporate power and huge concentrations of wealth, there was no national "ruling class." Mark Hanna sought to create one through the National Civic Federation, with the goal of welding the plutocracy together as a political force, but his effort foundered. In the economic realm, the anti-trust movement, populist at its source, broke up many of the trusts, as later the Glass-Steagall Act, in the early years of the New Deal, sundered the unified financial power of investment and banking. One can say that in the United States there have always been economic and political elites, but never a unified ruling class.

# 19

# Politics, Morality, and Civility

*Vaclav Havel*

As ridiculous or quixotic as it may sound these days, one thing seems certain to me: that it is my responsibility to emphasize, again and again, the moral origin of all genuine politics, to stress the significance of moral values and standards in all spheres of social life, including economics, and to explain that if we don't try, within ourselves, to discover or rediscover or cultivate what I call "higher responsibility," things will turn out very badly indeed for our country.

The return of freedom to a society that was morally unhinged has produced something it clearly had to produce, and something we therefore might have expected, but which has turned out to be far more serious than anyone could have predicted: an enormous and dazzling explosion of every imaginable human vice. A wide range of questionable or at least morally ambiguous human tendencies, subtly encouraged over the years and, at the same time, subtly pressed to serve the daily operation of the totalitarian system, have suddenly been liberated, as it were, from their straitjacket and given freedom at last. The authoritarian regime imposed a certain order—if that is the right expression for it—on these vices (and in doing so "legitimized" them, in a sense). This order has now been shattered, but a new order that would limit rather than exploit these vices, an order based on freely accepted responsibility to and for the whole of society, has not yet been built—nor could it have been, for such an order takes years to develop and cultivate.

Thus we are witnesses to a bizarre state of affairs: society has freed itself, true, but in some ways it behaves worse than when it was in chains. Criminality has grown rapidly, and the familiar sewage that in times of historical reversal always wells up from the nether regions of the collective psyche has overflowed into the mass media, especially the gutter press. But there are other, more serious and dangerous symptoms: hatred among nationalities, suspicion, racism, even signs of Fascism; politicking, an unrestrained unheeding struggle for purely particular interests, unadulterated ambition, fanaticism of every conceivable kind, new and unprecedented varieties of robbery, the rise of different mafias; and a prevailing lack of tolerance, understanding, taste, moderation, and reason. There is a new attraction to ideologies, too—as if Marxism had left behind it a great, disturbing void that had to be filled at any cost.

It is enough to look around our political scene (whose lack of civility is merely a reflection of the more general crisis of civility). In the months leading up to the June 1992 election, almost every political activity, including debates over extremely important legislation in Parliament, has taken place in the shadow of a preelection campaign, of an extravagant hunger for power and a willingness to gain the favor of a confused electorate by offering a colorful range of attractive nonsense. Mutual accusations, denunciations, and slander among political opponents know no bounds. One politician will undermine another's work only because they belong to different political parties. Partisan considerations still visibly take precedence over pragmatic attempts to arrive at reasonable and useful solutions to problems. Analysis is pushed out of the press by scandal-mongering. Supporting the government in a good cause is practically shameful; kicking it in the shins, on the other hand, is praiseworthy. Sniping at politicians who declare their support for another political group is a matter of course. Anyone can accuse anyone else of intrigue or incompetence, or of having a shady past and shady intentions.

Demagogy is rife, and even something as important as the natural longing of a people for autonomy is exploited in power plays, as rivals compete in lying to the public. Many members of the party elite, the so-called *nomenklatura* who, until very recently, were faking concern about social justice and the working class, have cast aside their masks and, almost overnight, openly become speculators and thieves. Many a once-feared Communist is now an unscrupulous capitalist, shamelessly and unequivocally laughing in the face of the same worker whose interests he once allegedly defended.

Citizens are becoming more and more disgusted with all this, and their disgust is understandably directed against the democratic government they themselves elected. Making the most of this situation, some characters with suspicious backgrounds have been gaining popular favor with ideas such as, for instance, the need to throw the entire government into the Vltava River.

And yet, if a handful of friends and I were able to bang our heads against the wall for years by speaking the truth about the Communist totalitarianism while surrounded by an ocean of apathy, there is no reason why I shouldn't go on banging my head against the wall by speaking *ad nauseam,* despite the condescending smiles, about responsibility and morality in the face of our present social marasmus. There is no reason to think that this struggle is a lost cause. The only lost cause is one we give up on before we enter the struggle.

Time and time again I have been persuaded that a huge potential of goodwill is slumbering within our society. It's just that it's incoherent, suppressed, confused, crippled and perplexed—as though it does not know what to rely on, where to begin, where or how to find meaningful outlets.

In such a state of affairs, politicians have a duty to awaken this slumbering potential, to offer it direction and ease its passage, to encourage it and give it room, or simply hope. They say a nation gets the politicians it deserves. In some senses this is true: politicians are indeed a mirror of their society, and a kind of embodiment of its potential. At the same time—paradoxically—the opposite is also true: society is a mirror of its politicians. It is largely up to the politicians which social forces they choose to liberate and which they choose to suppress, whether they rely on the good in each citizen or on the bad. The former regime systematically mobilized the worst human qualities, like selfishness, envy, and hatred. That regime was far more than just something we deserved; it was also responsible for what we became. Those who find themselves in politics therefore bear a heightened responsibility for the moral state of society, and it is their responsibility to seek out the best in that society, and to develop and strengthen it.

By the way, even the politicians who often anger me with their shortsightedness and their malice are not, for the most part, evil-minded. They are, rather, inexperienced, easily infected with the particularisms of the time, easily manipulated by suggested trends and prevailing customs; often they are simply caught up, unwillingly, in the swirl of bad politics, and find themselves unable to extricate themselves because they are afraid of the risks this would entail.

Some say I'm a naive dreamer who is always trying to combine the incompatible: politics and morality. I know this song well; I've heard it sung all my life. In the 1980s, a certain Czech philosopher who lived in California published a series of articles in which he subjected the "anti-political politics" of Charter 77—and, in particular, the way I explained that notion in my essays—to crushing criticism. Trapped in his own Marxist fallacies, he believed that as a scholar he had scientifically comprehended the entire history of the world. He saw it as a history of violent revolutions and vicious power struggles. The idea that the world might actually be changed by the force of truth, the power of a truthful word, the strength of a free spirit, conscience, and responsibility—with no guns, no lust for power, no political wheeling and dealing—was quite beyond the horizon of his understanding. Naturally, if you understand decency as a mere "superstructure" of the forces of production, then you can never understand political power in terms of decency.

Because his doctrine had taught him that the bourgeoisie would never voluntarily surrender its leading role, and that it must be swept into the dustbin of history through armed revolution, this philosopher assumed that there was no other way to sweep away the Communist government either. Yet it turned out to be possible. Moreover, it turned out to be the only way to do it. Not only that, but it was the only way that made sense, since violence, as we know, breeds more violence. This is why most revolutions degenerate into dictatorships that devour their young, giving rise to new revolutionaries who prepare for new violence, unaware that they are digging their own graves and pushing society back onto the deadly merry-go-round of revolution and counterrevolution.

Communism was overthrown by life, by thought, by human dignity. Our recent history has confirmed that the Czech-Californian professor was wrong. Likewise, those who still claim that politics is chiefly the manipulation of power and public opinion, and that morality has no place in it, are just as wrong. Political intrigue is not really politics, and, although you can get away with superficial politics for a time, it does not bring much hope of lasting success. Through intrigue one may easily become prime minister, but that will be the extent of one's success; one can hardly improve the world that way.

I am happy to leave political intrigue to others; I will not compete with them, certainly not by using their weapons.

Genuine politics—politics worthy of the name, and the only politics I am willing to devote myself to—is simply a matter of serving those around us: serving the community, and serving those who will come after us. Its deepest roots are moral because it is a responsibility, expressed through action, to and for the whole, a responsibility that is what it is—a "higher" responsibility—only because it has a metaphysical grounding: that is, it grows out of a conscious or subconscious certainty that our death ends nothing, because everything is forever being recorded and evaluated somewhere else, somewhere "above us," in what I have called "the memory of Being"—an integral aspect of the secret order of the cosmos, of nature, and of life, which believers call God and to whose judgment everything is subject. Genuine conscience and genuine responsibility are always, in the end, explicable only as an expression of the silent assumption that we are observed "from above," that everything is visible, nothing is forgotten, and so earthly time has no power to wipe away the sharp disappointments of earthly failure: our spirit knows that it is not the only entity aware of these failures.

What can I do, as president, not only to remain faithful to that notion of politics, but also to bring it to at least partial fruition? (After all, the former is unthinkable without the latter. Not to put at least some of my ideas into practice could have only two consequences: either I would eventually be swept from office or I would become a tolerated eccentric, sounding off to an unheeding audience—not only a less dignified alternative, but a highly dishonest one as well, because it would mean another form of resignation, both of myself and of my ideals.)

As in everything else, I must start with myself. That is: in all circumstances try to be decent, just, tolerant, and understanding, and at the same time try to resist corruption and deception. In other words, I must do my utmost to act in harmony with my conscience and my better self. For instance, I am frequently advised to be more "tactical," not to say everything right away, to dissimulate gently, not to fear wooing someone more than my nature commands, or to distance myself from someone against my real will in the matter. In the interests of strengthening my hand, I am advised at times to assent to someone's ambition for power, to flatter someone merely because it pleases him, or to reject someone even though it goes against my convictions, because he does not enjoy favor with others.

I constantly hear another kind of advice, as well: I should be tougher, more decisive, more authoritative. For a good cause, I shouldn't be afraid to pound the table occasionally, to shout at people, to try to rouse a little fear and trembling. Yet, if I wish to remain faithful to myself and my notion of politics, I mustn't listen to advice like this—not just in the interests of my personal mental health (which could be seen as a private, selfish desire), but chiefly in the interests of what most concerns me: the simple fact that directness can never be established by indirection, or truth through lies, or the democratic spirit through authoritarian directives. Of course, I don't know whether directness, truth, and the democratic spirit will succeed. But I do know how *not* to succeed, which is by choosing means that contradict the ends. As we know from history, that is the best way to eliminate the very ends we set out to achieve.

In other words, if there is to be any chance at all of success, there is only one way to strive for decency, reason, responsibility, sincerity, civility, and tolerance, and that is decently, reasonably, responsibly, sincerely, civilly, and tolerantly. I'm aware that, in everyday politics, this is not seen as the most practical way of going about it. But I have one advantage: among my many bad qualities there is one that happens to be missing—a longing or a love for power. Not being bound by that, I am essentially freer than those who cling to their power or position, and this allows me to indulge in the luxury of behaving untactically.

I see the only way forward in that old, familiar injunction: "live in truth."

But how is this to be done, practically speaking, when one is president? I see three basic possibilities.

*The first possibility:* I must repeat certain things aloud over and over again. I don't like repeating myself, but in this case it's unavoidable. In my many public utterances, I feel I must emphasize and explain repeatedly the moral dimensions of all social life, and point out that morality is, in fact, hidden in everything. And this is true: whenever I encounter a problem in my work and try to get to the bottom of it, I always discover some moral aspect, be it apathy, unwillingness to recognize personal error or guilt, reluctance to give up certain positions and the advantages flowing from them, envy, an excess of self-assurance, or whatever.

I feel that the dormant goodwill in people needs to be stirred. People need to hear that it makes sense to behave decently or to help others, to place common interests above their own, to respect the elementary rules of human coexistence. They want to be told about this publicly. They want to know that those "at the top" are on their side. They feel strengthened, confirmed, hopeful. Goodwill longs to be recognized and cultivated. For it to develop and have an impact it must hear that the world does not ridicule it.

Frequently, regular listeners to my radio talks to the nation, "Conversations from Lany," ask to hear what might be called "philosophical" or "ethical" reflections. I occasionally omit them for fear of repeating myself too often, but people always ask for them again. I try never to give people practical advice about how to deal with the evil around them, nor could I even if I wanted to—and yet people want to hear that decency and courage make sense, that something must be risked in the struggle against dirty tricks. They want to know they are not alone, forgotten, written off.

*The second possibility:* I can try to create around me, in the world of so-called high politics, a positive climate, a climate of generosity, tolerance, openness, broadmindedness, and a kind of elementary companionship and mutual trust. In this sphere I am far from being the decisive factor. But I can have a psychological influence.

*The third possibility:* There is a significant area in which I do have direct political influence in my position as president. I am required to make certain political decisions. In this, I can and must bring my concept of politics to bear, and inject into it my political ideals, my longing for justice, decency, and civility, my notion of what, for present purposes, I will call "the moral state." Whether I am successful or not is for others to judge, of course, but the results will always be uneven, since, like everyone else, I am a fallible human being.

Journalists, and in particular foreign correspondents, often ask me how the idea of "living in truth," the idea of "anti-political politics," or the idea of politics subordinate to conscience can, in practice, be carried out. They are curious to know whether, finding myself in high office, I have not had to revise much of what I once wrote as an independent critic of politics and politicians. Have I not been compelled to lower my former "dissident" expectations of politics, by which they mean the standards I derived from the "dissident experience," which are therefore scarcely applicable outside that sphere?

There may be some who won't believe me, but in my second term as president in a land full of problems that presidents in stable countries never even dream of, I can safely say that I have not been compelled to recant anything of what I wrote earlier, or to change my mind about anything. It may seem incredible, but it is so: not only have I not had to change my mind, but my opinions have been confirmed.

Despite the political distress I face every day, I am still deeply convinced that politics is not essentially a disreputable business; and to the extent that it is, it is only disreputable people who make it so. I would concede that it can, more than other spheres of human activity, tempt one to disreputable practices, and that it therefore places higher demands on people. But it is simply not true that a politician must lie or intrigue. That is utter nonsense, spread about by people who—for whatever reasons—wish to discourage others from taking an interest in public affairs.

Of course, in politics, as elsewhere in life, it is impossible and pointless to say everything, all at once, to just anyone. But that does not mean having to lie. All you need is tact, the proper instincts, and good taste. One surprising experience from "high politics" is this: I have discovered that good taste is more useful here than a postgraduate degree in political science. It is largely a matter of form: knowing how long to speak, when to begin and when to finish; how to say something politely that your opposite number may not want to hear; how to say, always, what is most significant at a given moment, and not to speak of what is not important or relevant; how to insist on your own position without offending; how to create the kind of friendly atmosphere that makes complex negotiations easier; how to keep a conversation going without prying or being aloof; how to balance serious political themes with lighter, more relaxing topics; how to plan your official journeys judiciously and to know when it is more appropriate not to go somewhere, when to be open and when reticent and to what degree.

But more than that, it means having a certain instinct for the time, the atmosphere of the time, the mood of people, the nature of their worries, their frame of mind—that too can perhaps be more useful than sociological surveys. An education in political science, law, economics, history, and culture is an invaluable asset to any politician, but I have been persuaded, again and again, that it is not the most essential asset. Qualities like fellow-feeling, the ability to talk to others, insight, the capacity to grasp quickly not only problems but also human character, the ability to make contact, a sense of moderation: all these are immensely more important in politics. I am not saying, heaven forbid, that I myself am endowed with these qualities; not at all! These are merely my observations.

To sum up: if your heart is in the right place and you have good taste, not only will you pass muster in politics, you are destined for it. If you are modest and do not lust after power, not only are you suited to politics, you absolutely belong there. The *sine qua non* of a politician is not the ability to lie; he need only be sensitive and know when, what, to whom, and how to say what he has to say. It is not true that a person of principle does not belong in politics; it is enough for his principles to be leavened with patience, deliberation, a sense of proportion, and an understanding of others. It is not true that only the unfeeling cynic, the vain, the brash, and the vulgar can succeed in politics; such people, it is true, are drawn to politics, but, in the end, decorum and good taste will always count for more.

My experience and observations confirm that politics as the practice of morality is possible. I do not deny, however, that it is not always easy to go that route, nor have I ever claimed that it was.

From my political ideals, it should be clear enough that what I would like to accentuate in every possible way in my practice of politics is culture. Culture in the widest possible sense of the word, including everything from what might be called the culture of everyday life—of "civility"—to what we know as high culture, including the arts and sciences.

I don't mean that the state should heavily subsidize culture as a particular area of human endeavor, nor do I at all share the indignant fear of many artists that the period we are going through now is ruining culture and will eventually destroy it. Most of our artists have, unwittingly, grown accustomed to the unending generosity of the socialist state. It subsidized a number of cultural institutions and offices, heedless of whether a film cost one million or ten million crowns, or whether anyone ever went to see it. It didn't matter how many idle actors the theatres had on their payrolls; the main thing was that everyone was on one, and thus on the take. The Communist state knew, better than the Czech-Californian philosopher, where the greatest danger to it lay: in the realm of the intellect and the spirit. It knew who first had to be pacified through irrational largesse. That the state was less and less successful at doing so is another matter, which merely confirms how right it was to be afraid; for, despite all the bribes and prizes and titles thrown their way, the artists were among the first to rebel.

This nostalgic complaint by artists who fondly remember their "social security" under socialism therefore leaves me unmoved. Culture must, in part at least, learn how to make its own way. It should be partially funded through tax write-offs, and through foundations, development funds, and the like—which, by the way, are the forms that best suit its plurality and its freedom. The more varied the sources of funding for the arts and sciences, the greater variety and competition there will be in the arts and scholarly research. The state should—in ways that are rational, open to scrutiny, and well though out—support only those aspects of culture that are fundamental to our national identity and the civilized traditions of our land, and that can't be conserved through market mechanisms alone. I am thinking of heritage sites (there can't be a hotel in every castle or chateau to pay for its upkeep, nor can the old aristocracy be expected to return and provide for their upkeep merely to preserve family honor), libraries, museums, public archives, and such institutions, which today are in an appalling state of disrepair (as though the previous "regime of forgetting" deliberately set out to destroy these important witnesses to our past). Likewise, it is hard to imagine that the Church, or the churches, in the foreseeable future, will have the means to restore all the chapels, cathedrals, monasteries, and ecclesiastical buildings that have fallen into ruin over the forty years of Communion. They are part of the cultural wealth of the entire country, not just the pride of the Church.

I mention all this only by way of introduction, for the sake of exactness. My main point is something else. I consider it immensely important that we concern ourselves with culture not just as one among many human activities, but in the broadest sense—the "culture of everything," the general level of public manners. By that I mean chiefly the kind of relations that exist among people, between the powerful and the weak, the healthy and the sick, the young and the elderly, adults and children, businesspeople and customers, men and women, teachers and students, officers and soldiers, policemen and citizens, and so on.

More than that, I am also thinking of the quality of people's relationships to nature, to animals, to the atmosphere, to the landscape, to towns, to gardens, to their homes—the culture of housing and architecture, of public catering, of big business and small shops; the culture of work and advertising; the culture of fashion, behaviour, and entertainment.

And there is even more: all this would be hard to imagine without a legal, political, and administrative culture, without the culture of relationships between the state and the citizen. Before the war, in all these areas, we were on the same level as the prosperous western democracies of the day, if not higher. To assess our present condition, it's enough to cross into Western Europe. I know that this catastrophic decline in the general cultural level, the level of public manners, is related to the decline in our economy, and is even, to a large degree, a direct consequence of it. Still, it frightens me more than economic decline does. It is move visible; it impinges on one more "physically," as it were. I can well imagine that, as a citizen, it would bother me more if the pub I went to were a place where the customers spat on the floor and the staff behaved boorishly toward me than it would if I could no longer afford to go there every day and order the most expensive meal on the menu. Likewise, it would bother me less not to be able to afford a family house than it would not to see nice houses anywhere.

Perhaps what I'm trying to say is clear: however important it may be to get our economy back on its feet, it is far from being the only task facing us. It is no less important to do everything possible to improve the general cultural level of everyday life. As the economy develops, this will happen anyway. But we cannot depend on that alone. We must initiate a large-scale program for raising general cultural standards. And it is not true that we have to wait until we are rich to do this; we can begin at once, without a crown in our pockets. No one can persuade me that it takes a better-paid nurse to behave more considerately to a patient, that only an expensive house can be pleasing, that only a wealthy merchant can be courteous to his customers and display a handsome sign outside, that only a prosperous farmer can treat his livestock well. I would go even farther, and say that, in many respects, improving the civility of everyday life can accelerate economic development—from the culture of supply and demand, of trading and enterprise, right down to the culture of values and lifestyle.

I want to do everything I can to contribute, in a specific way to a program for raising the general level of civility, or at least do everything I can to express my personal interest in such an improvement, whether I do so as president or not. I feel this is both an integral part and a logical consequence of my notion of politics as the practice of morality and the application of a "higher responsibility." After all, is there anything that citizens—and this is doubly true of politicians—should be more concerned about, ultimately, than trying to make life more pleasant, more interesting, more varied, and more bearable?

If I talk here about my political—or, more precisely, my civil—program, about my notion of the kind of politics and values and ideals I wish to struggle for, this is not to say that I am entertaining the naive hope that this struggle may one day be over. A heaven on earth in which people all love each other and everyone is hard-working, well-mannered, and virtuous, in which the land flourishes and everything is sweetness and light, working harmoniously to the satisfaction of God: this will never be. On the contrary, the world has had the worst experiences with utopian thinkers who promised all that. Evil will remain with us, no one will ever eliminate human suffering, the political arena will always attract irresponsible and ambitious adventurers and charlatans. And man will not stop destroying the world. In this regard, I have no illusions.

Neither I nor anyone else will ever win this war once and for all. At the very most, we can win a battle or two—and not even that is certain. Yet I still think it makes sense to wage this war persistently. It has been waged for centuries, and it will continue to be waged—we hope—for centuries to come. This must be done on principle, because it is the right thing to do. Or, if you like, because God wants it that way. It is an eternal, never-ending struggle waged not just by good people (among whom I count myself, more or less) against evil people, by honorable people against dishonorable people, by people who think only of themselves and the moment. It takes place inside everyone. It is what makes a person a person, and life, life.

So anyone who claims that I am a dreamer who expects to transform hell into heaven is wrong. I have few illusions. But I feel a responsibility to work toward the things I consider good and right. I don't know whether I'll be able to change certain things for the better, or not at all. Both outcomes are possible. There is only one thing I will not concede: that it might be meaningless to strive in a good cause.

We are building our country anew. Fate has thrust me into a position in which I have a somewhat greater influence on that process than most of my fellow citizens do. It is appropriate, therefore, that I admit to my notions about what kind of country it should be, and articulate the vision that guides me—or rather, the vision that flows naturally from politics as I understand it.

Perhaps we can all agree we want a state based on rule of law, one that is democratic (that is, with a pluralistic political system), peaceful, and with a prospering market economy. Some insist that this state should also be socially just. Others sense in the phrase a hangover from socialism and argue against it. They object to the notion of "social justice" as vague, claiming that it can mean anything at all, and that a functioning market economy can never guarantee any genuine social justice. They point out that people have, and always will have, different degrees of industriousness, talent, and, last but not least, luck. Obviously, social justice in the sense of social equality is something the market system cannot, by its very nature, deliver. Moreover, to compel the marketplace to do so would be deeply immoral. (Our experience of socialism has provided us with more than enough examples of why this is so.)

I do not see, however, why a democratic state, armed with a legislature and the power to draw up a budget, cannot strive for a certain fairness in, for example, pension policies or tax policies, or support to the unemployed, or salaries to public employees, or assistance to the elderly living alone, people who have health problems, or those who, for various reasons, find themselves at the bottom of society. Every civilized state attempts, in different ways and with different degrees of success, to come up with reasonable policies in these areas, and not even the most ardent supporters of the market economy have anything against it in principle. In the end, then, it is a conflict not of beliefs, but rather of terminology.

I am repeating these basic, self-evident, and rather general facts for the sake of completeness and order. But I would like to say more about other aspects of the state that may be somewhat less obvious and are certainly much less talked about, but are no less important—because they qualify and make possible everything that is considered self-evident.

I am convinced that we will never build a democratic state based on rule of law if we do not at the same time build a state that is—regardless of how unscientific this may sound to the ears of a political scientist—humane, moral, intellectual and spiritual, and cultural. The best laws and the best-conceived democratic mechanisms will not in themselves guarantee legality or freedom or human rights—anything, in short, for which they were intended—if they are not underpinned by certain human and social values. What good, for instance, would a law be if no one respected it, no one defended it, and no one tried responsibly to follow it? It would be nothing but a scrap of paper. What use would elections be in which the voter's only choice was between a greater and a lesser scoundrel? What use would a wide variety of political parties be if not one of them had the general interest of society at heart?

No state—that is, no constitutional, legal, and political system—is anything in and of itself, outside historical time and social space. It is not the clever technical invention of a team of experts, like a computer or a telephone. Every state, on the contrary, grows out of specific intellectual, spiritual, and cultural traditions that breathe substance into it and give it meaning.

So we are back to the same point: without commonly shared and widely entrenched moral values and obligations, neither the law, nor the democratic government, nor even the market economy will function properly. They are all marvellous products of the human spirit, mechanisms that can, in turn, serve the spirit magnificently—assuming that the human spirit wants these mechanisms to serve it, respects them, believes in them, guarantees them, understands their meaning, and is willing, if necessary, to fight for them or make sacrifices for them.

Again I would use law as an illustration. The law is undoubtedly an instrument of justice, but it would be an utterly meaningless instrument if no one used it responsibly. From our own recent experience we all know too well what can happen to even a decent law in the hands of an unscrupulous judge, and how easily unscrupulous people can use democratic institutions to introduce dictatorship and terror. The law and other democratic institutions ensure little if they are not backed up by the willingness and courage of decent people to guard against their abuse. That these institutions can help us become more human is obvious; that is why they were created, and why we are building them now. But if they are to guarantee anything to us, it is we, first of all, who must guarantee them.

In the somewhat chaotic provisional activity around the technical aspects of building the state, it will do us no harm occasionally to remind ourselves of the meaning of the state, which is, and must remain, truly human—which means it must be intellectual, spiritual, and moral.

How are we to go about building such a state? What does such an ambition bind us to or offer us, in practical terms?

There is no simple set of instructions on how to proceed. A moral and intellectual state cannot be established through a constitution, or through law, or through directives, but only through complex, long-term, and never-ending work involving education and self-education. What is needed is lively and responsible consideration of every political step, every decision; a constant stress on moral deliberation and moral judgment; continued self-examination and self-analysis; an endless rethinking of our priorities. It is not, in short, something we can simply declare or introduce. It is a way of going about things, and it demands the courage to breathe moral and spiritual motivation into everything, to seek the human dimension in all things. Science, technology, expertise, and so-called professionalism are not enough. Something more is necessary. For the sake of simplicity, it might be called spirit. Or feeling. Or conscience.

# Index

# About the Contributors

**Daniel Bell** is the author of numerous books, including *The End of Ideology* and *The Cultural Contradictions of Capitalism,* both of which are identified on the Times Literary Supplement's list as one of the 100 most important books of the second half of the twentieth century. Bell is professor emeritus of social science at Harvard University and a resident scholar at the American Academy of Arts and Sciences. He is a cofounder of *The Public Interest* magazine and former editor of *The New Leader.*

**Robert N. Bellah** is professor of sociology at the University of California, Berkeley, and coauthor of *Habits of the Heart* and *The Good Society,* from which the essay in this book was drawn.

**Peter L. Berger** is director of the Institute for the Study of Economic Culture and professor of economics at Boston University. He authored or coauthored several books, including *Sociology Reinterpreted; The War Over the Family; The Capitalist Revolution;* and (along with Richard John Neuhaus) *To Empower People,* from which the essay in this book was taken.

**John J. DiIulio Jr.** is a professor at the University of Pennsylvania, a nonresident senior fellow in governmental studies at the Brookings Institution, and director of the Partnership for Research on Religion and At-Risk Youth (PRRAY) in Philadelphia, which provides technical assistance and financial support to inner-city youth. He is widely regarded as a leading expert on the role of religion in family and neighborhood revitalization. He has authored numerous scholarly essays in journals and contributed widely to the public debate about civil society.

**Don E. Eberly** is the author or editor of numerous books on American society and culture, including *Building a Community of Citizens: Civil Society in* *the 21st Century; The Content of America's Character: The Recovery of Civic Virtue;* and most recently *America's Promise: Civil Society and the Renewal of American Culture.* Eberly contributes widely to the debate on civil society in regular submissions to journals and magazines. He has also founded several national civic initiatives, including the Civil Society Project, which he directs, and the National Fatherhood Initiative, for which he serves as chairman and CEO.

**Alan Ehrenhalt** is executive editor of *Governing Magazine.* He is the author of *The Lost City: Discovering the Forgotten Virtues,* a book focusing on life in Chicago in the 1950s, from which the essay in this book was adapted. He is a former reporter for the Associated Press, a former Nieman Fellow at Harvard University, and a former visiting professor at the University of California at Berkeley.

**Jean Bethke Elshtain** is the Laura Spellman Rockefeller Professor of Social and Political Ethics at the Divinity School of the University of Chicago and the author of numerous books and essays on women, politics, and the family. Her books include *Public Man, Private Woman; Women and War;* and *Democracy on Trial,* from which the essay in this book was adapted.

**Amitai Etzioni** is a professor at George Washington University and a leading contributor to communitarian thought. Among his best-known books are *The Active Society, Modern Organization; The Moral Dimension; Public Policy in a New Key; The Spirit of Community; The New Golden Rule;* and *The Essential Communitarian Reader.* He is regarded as a founder of the communitarian movement and directs the Institute for Communitarian Studies at George Washington University.

**Francis Fukuyama** is a former senior social scientist with the Rand Corporation and presently teaches at George Mason University. He is widely regarded as one of the leading social thinkers of our time. He is the author of numerous critical essays on topics of society and economics, the author of *Trust: The Social Virtues and the Creation of Prosperity,* from which the essay in this book was drawn, and more recently the author of *The Great Disruption: Human Nature and the Reconstitution of the Social Order.*

**William A. Galston** is a professor in the School of Public Affairs at the University of Maryland at College Park and director of the university's Institute for Philosophy and Public Policy. In addition to numerous articles on American politics, public policy, political theory, and family issues in the United States, he has written six books, most recently *Liberal Purposes: Goods,*

*Virtues, and Diversity in the Liberal State.* Galston also directed the National Commission on Civic Renewal.

**Mary Ann Glendon** is professor of law at Harvard University. She is the author of *Rights Talk,* from which the essay in this book was partially drawn. She writes extensively on issues of law and society, and is widely recognized as a leading expert on family law.

**Vaclav Havel** is an internationally renowned playwright and the author of many influential essays. He was imprisoned in 1979 for his involvement in the Czech human rights movement, and after his release in 1989, he became his country's president. The essay in this book appeared originally in *Summer Meditations,* trans. Paul Wilson, and is reprinted here with permission.

**Gertrude Himmelfarb** taught for twenty-three years at Brooklyn College and the Graduate School of the City University of New York. She has written extensively on Victorian history. Her books include *The Demoralization of Society; On Looking into the Abyss; Poverty and Compassion; The Idea of Poverty; On Liberty and Liberalism;* and most recently, *One Nation, Two Cultures.*

**John L. McKnight** is director of the Community Studies Program at the Center for Urban Affairs and Policy Research at Northwestern University, where he is a professor in the School of Education and Social Policy. He has worked with communities across the United States and Canada and is the co-author of a popular workbook for community organizers entitled *Community Building from the Inside Out.* He is the author of *The Careless Society: Community and Its Counterfeits,* from which his essay in this book was adapted.

**Richard John Neuhaus** is a leading voice on issues of religion and society in America. He is the author of the *Naked Public Square* and the coauthor or editor of numerous other books. He is president of the Institute on Religion and Public Life and editor in chief of its monthly journal, *First Things.* He is the coauthor, along with Peter Berger, of *To Empower People,* from which the essay in this book was taken.

**Robert Nisbet** was formerly a professor of sociology at Columbia University and authored numerous critical books during his lifetime, including *The Present Age; Twilight of Authority; The History of the Idea of Progress;* and most notably *The Quest for Community: A Study in the Ethics of Order and Freedom,* from which the essay in this book was adapted.

**Michael J. Sandel** is a leading political theorist and professor of government at Harvard University. He has written widely on topics of politics and society and is the author of several books, including *Liberalism and the Limits of Justice* and *Democracy's Discontents: America in Search of a Public Philosophy,* from which the essay in this book was adapted.

**William A. Schambra** is director of general programs for the Lynde and Harry Bradley Foundation in Milwaukee, Wisconsin. He has written widely on topics of civil society and served on the National Commission for Civic Renewal. His previous experience includes appointments in the Bush administration in Washington and a research post at the American Enterprise Institute.

**James Q. Wilson** was professor of government for twenty-six years at Harvard and has taught management and public policy at UCLA. He has advised presidents and is the past president of the American Political Science Association. Among his most notable books are *On Character* and *The Moral Sense.*

**Alan Wolfe** is professor of sociology and political science at Boston University. He is the author of *Whose Keeper? Social Science and Moral Obligation,* from which the essay in this book was drawn, and *One Nation, After All.*